Nahuas and Spaniards
Postconquest Central Mexican History and Philology

Nahuatl Studies Series
Number 3

Series Editor
James Lockhart
Associate Series Editor
Rebecca Horn

UCLA Latin American Studies
Volume 76

Nahuas and Spaniards

Postconquest Central Mexican History and Philology

James Lockhart

Stanford University Press

UCLA Latin American Center Publications
University of California, Los Angeles

Stanford University Press
Stanford, California
© 1991 by the Board of Trustees of the
Leland Stanford Junior University
Printed in the United States of America

CIP data appear at the end of the book

Contents

IV. Spaniards

Tables and Texts

Tables

Texts

Two signatures from the late sixteenth century

Don Juan de Guzman (Item 5)

Diego de Santa Cruz Orduña (Item 13)

Preface

During the now considerable stretch of time I have spent inquiring into early Mexican history, I have published a certain number of essays, research articles, and other pieces relevant to the topic. They have, I must admit, appeared in widely scattered, often obscure or inaccessible places. The present collection consists of such items, plus a few others that remained unpublished until now.[1] My purpose, of course, is to render the material more useful by assembling it in a single readily available volume. Beyond that, however, I am employing this means to bring together types of things more often left apart, assigned to separate disciplines or subdisciplines, and published in different kinds of journals or anthologies for different sets of readers. And I am not referring to the somewhat anthropological leanings of some of my work; fortunately, rapprochement between "historical" and "anthropological" ethnohistorians has by now become a standard, expected feature of the scholarly scene.

I began my Mexican studies practicing a type of career-pattern social history, mainly of Spaniards and the Hispanized, which I helped develop in the field of early Latin American history. I subsequently turned to the history of Indians as a complement, using some of the same methodology but of necessity becoming involved in Indian-language study. This in turn led to philological work, editing and commenting on Nahuatl documents, and that led further to a type of historical linguistics, on the one hand, and on the other to cultural/intellectual/literary analysis. During the whole time, I have remained very conscious of method and operating concepts and have been concerned with the development of a field of Mexican ethnohistory and its place within Spanish American history more generally. The pieces here touch on all these matters. It is my opinion that all the topics and approaches go together in a natural, almost inevitable way, complementing and illuminating each other to produce something on the order of a whole, and it is my hope that having all the facets represented inside the covers of a single book can help readers understand the overall congruity, accustoming them to perceive this particular range of interests as normal for early Mexican history. At the same time, it is with considerable trepidation that I offer to a broader public pieces mainly intended, in the first instance, for an inner circle, and I ask for readers' understanding.

In the evolution of European music, there was a time when the same artist-craftsman might go to the forest to select wood and other raw materials, prepare them, fashion them into a musical instrument, arrange or compose music appropriate for the instrument he had made, and play it himself, with results that in some ways have not been matched in more recent times. I think that a breadth of interrelated interests and skills within a well delimited arena can serve scholarship as well as it can artistic endeavor (in my perception, the two are not so very different).

Over and above its general rationale, a given publication often responds to a particular occasion or a special impetus. In this case the occasion was given by the recent completion of my book *The Nahuas After the Conquest*,[2] representing the provisional culmination of fifteen years or more of work on the general social and cultural history of central Mexican Indians in the first three post-contact centuries. As the book project grew ever larger, I incorporated into it rather abbreviated sketches of some topics I had already dealt with in print, relying on the previously published items to provide the serious reader with further documentation or a more thorough treatment. In the case of some collaborative work which has appeared in book form,[3] this way of doing things should cause readers little inconvenience, but I cannot in good conscience refer them to pieces published in the occasional papers series of universities in remote lands, or to pieces in out-of-print linguistic anthologies, or to items available only in bad Spanish translations. Hence collection became an urgent matter, and the present book is as much as anything a companion volume to the larger opus.

The relation of the items included here to *The Nahuas* varies. Most of the pieces comprise primary research and analysis on which the latter publication partly rests. One essay, however, included here as Item 1, is an accessible summary of the content and thrust of the large book, representing in my view possibly a better first introduction to it than anything inside its covers.[4] A different relationship obtains in the case of the pieces devoted primarily to the history of Spaniards. These may seem highly tangential to *The Nahuas*, and in a sense they are. Yet in the end a very large part of the story of that book is the interaction of Nahua and Spanish societies and cultures. There the Spanish side is seen only indirectly; the "Spanish" pieces in the present volume thus serve as a partial complement and corrective. Above all they are meant as a reminder that eventually both sides of the process must be studied with equal intensity, each on its own terms, yet jointly. It is for that reason that I gave the present volume its title.

I have arranged the pieces into four sections or parts. The distinction between Part I, "Nahuas," and Part II, "Nahuatl Philology," is perhaps somewhat arbitrary. All of this material is ethnohistory based on close study of Nahuatl-language texts; all of it contains both general substantive discourse and specific references to the texts. In Part I, however, the emphasis is on thematic, substantive analysis, whereas in Part II the texts themselves come to the fore.[5] Mainline historians will likely find some of the pieces in Part II rather hard going, especially when it comes to those of a more linguistic nature, but I assure them that linguists would smile at the notion that these items are very technical, or even very linguistic.

Part III, "Historiography," contains two essays on the development of the field of postconquest central Mexican ethnohistory. The first of them attempts to elucidate and put in perspective the work of a giant in the field, Charles Gibson, and the second describes some research in the emerging school of ethnohistory based (in large part, at least) on Nahuatl language study. Together the two go far toward showing the background against which my book *The Nahuas* was written.

Part IV, "Spaniards," contains two pieces on the kind of provincial Spanish societies which maintained themselves in the Nahua heartland and thus were central to the history of social and cultural interaction. Since these items are full of fleshed-out life portraits and elements of human interest, and at the same time are relatively devoid of exotic terms, some may find that they make easier reading than most of the rest of the volume.

Some regional threads run through the collection and perhaps can help unify it for the reader. I conceived a special interest in the Valley of Toluca in 1969 when I was allowed to spend an absorbing two weeks in Toluca's Notaría Número 1, reading and taking notes on the earliest of the volumes then shelved around the walls of the reception room. Item 12 here is the result of that period. Zacualpan, the subject of Item 13, was chosen in relation to Toluca as a nearby area devoted to mining in contrast to Toluca's agriculture, stockraising, and heavy indigenous population. Later it turned out that the Toluca region is rich in extant Nahuatl documents, especially for the eighteenth century, and the philological pieces Items 7 and 8 use Toluca Valley texts.

A second well represented region is Tulancingo. Its intellectual attraction is that it is located off the beaten track, on the far northeastern edge of the Nahua culture area, yet it follows mainline trends very closely, thereby demonstrating their generality and the unity of the Nahua macroregion. The more specific reason for Tulancingo's presence here is the existence of a fine documentary collection from that district in the Research Library of UCLA, my home institution. Items 2 and 6 both deal with Tulancingo, and the pieces throw considerable light on each other.

Finally, let me remind the reader that Spaniards and things Spanish are not to be found mentioned in Part IV alone; they figure in some capacity in nearly all the pieces, perhaps especially in Items 1, 5, 6, and 7.

I do not wish to prolong these prefatory remarks with further detail on the individual items, but since the circumstances and timing of their genesis are of some potential interest, I have prepared a roster providing the relevant information; it appears as an appendix to the volume. A great many people have aided me, either personally or through their work, in producing the pieces assembled here. I invite the reader to peruse the acknowledgments I have made in the introduction to *The Nahuas*, for the list of benefactors is the same and my gratitude is identical.

J. L.
Frazier Park, California
August, 1990

Map: Central Mexican places mentioned

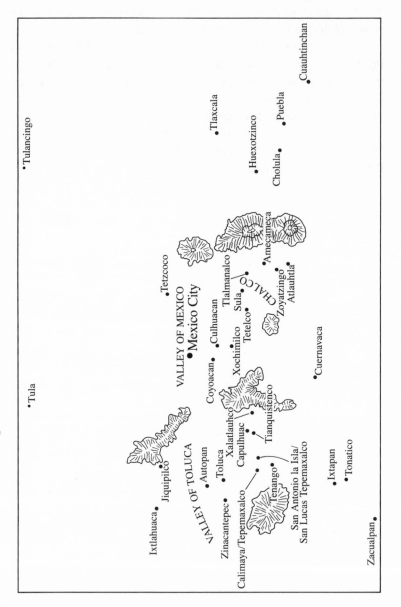

I. Nahuas

1. Postconquest Nahua Society and Culture Seen Through Nahuatl Sources

The Nahuas of central Mexico (often misleadingly called Aztecs after the quite ephemeral imperial confederation that existed among them in late pre-Hispanic times) were the most populous of Mesoamerica's cultural-linguistic groups at the time of the Spanish conquest, and they remained at the center of developments for centuries thereafter, since the bulk of the Hispanic population settled among them and they bore the brunt of cultural contact. For these reasons, more was written about them in the colonial period than about any other group, and they have been equally favored by modern scholars. Yet until the last few years hardly anyone took advantage of the mass of documents the Nahuas produced in their own language, Nahuatl, in the time from about 1550 to about 1800, using the European alphabetical script which took hold among them almost immediately. It was as though Roman history were being done without Latin. Let us look at one of the documents the Nahuas have left us:[1]

On an unspecified day in the year of 1584, more than two generations after the conquest, an indigenous clerk or legal representative appeared before one of the two Indian municipal councils in the important town of Tulancingo, located on the northeastern edge of central Mexico, and presented a written petition on behalf of one Simón de Santiago, an Indian commoner. Beautifully penned and perfectly spelled, the petition was set down by the clerk, not by the doubtless illiterate Simón, a person so humble that he took his surname from his district of Santiago and probably went through life with no other appellation, on ordinary occasions, than Simón. But the writer maintained the convention of a first-person presentation by Simón, and he seems to have followed Simón's actual spoken words very closely.

After briefly calling out "my lords, my rulers" in the preconquest style of public oratory, Simón got right down to business. His complaint concerned a certain Cristóbal, a commoner of the same district, as humble as himself if not more so, who was presently lodged in the municipal jail. In the night of Tuesday preceding, Cristóbal had entered Simón's property by stealth, meaning to steal a turkey. But when he got among them, the turkeys gave the alarm, causing Simón's wife to awake and run to the turkey pen to investigate. By then Cristóbal had wrung a turkey's neck and was on his way out with it, but Simón's wife got a good look at him as he sped past the grainbin, whereupon she woke her husband, shouting to him what had happened. Simón forthwith ran to Cristóbal's house, finding him and his wife warming themselves by the fire, and demanded his turkey back. Cristóbal denied all and threatened to kill Simón; taking an iron-tipped digging stick, he knocked him down with a blow to the head, and Simón, while lying there in a pool of blood from the cut, heard Cristóbal tell his wife to fetch him the knife lying on the chest in order to spill Simón's guts. Simón managed to push Cristóbal's hand aside, and in their struggle Cristóbal's clothes, which were old and worn out, began to rip off: first his cloak, then his shirt, and finally his loincloth, leaving him naked. Even so, Cristóbal, imagining himself the victor, ran off to Simón's house, told his wife to come recover his body, and proceeded to beat her up. She was the one left in the worst shape; by now Simón had spent 2 pesos on her treatment, had borrowed more from some merchants, and owed yet more to a Spaniard. He therefore petitioned that Cristóbal's wife be required to help take care of his own wife during convalescence and that Cristóbal cover all costs.

Here is postconquest indigenous life seen through a new prism and in new dimensions. More than twenty years ago Charles Gibson, using Spanish documents, brought about a great advance in our understanding of indigenous corporate development, showing that numerous local indigenous states or kingdoms—some petty, some not so petty—survived the conquest intact, becoming the basis of encomiendas, parishes, and Hispanic-style municipalities organized under Spanish auspices, and out of these most of the larger structures of the Mexican rural scene gradually evolved.[2] What went on inside this corporate framework continued to be a relative mystery. One had to rely on generalizing, partisan statements of Spaniards who in any case knew and cared very little about Indian-to-Indian relationships. Prominent in this corpus were the *Relaciones geográficas*, surveys of localities compiled by provincial Spanish administrators, who when it came to Indian customs were likely to say simply that they were "bad," in line with the Indians' notorious idleness and inconstancy, and that they dressed "poorly."

It was a revelation, then, to discover the existence of documents in which ordinary Indians spoke to each other about everyday things in their own language. We are delivered from hearsay, we see actual individual cases and the original categories of thought. The immediate message, as in the story of the stolen turkey, is often a double and apparently contradictory one. On the one hand, the Indian world appears to be maintaining its balance, concerned at least as much with internal affairs as with Spanish-

Indian relations, while many preconquest patterns retain their vitality. On the other hand, evidence of contact with Spaniards and Spanish culture is everywhere, even in surroundings as humble as those of Simón and Cristóbal.

Simón begins his address, as we have seen, with a string of vocatives taken directly from preconquest practice; his complaint to the municipal judges and the remedy he seeks from them put us in mind of descriptions of preconquest adjudication in the Florentine Codex of Sahagún.[3] All the personnel directly involved—accused, accuser, and judges—are indigenous. Simón's establishment, with its grainbin and fowl, appears unchanged in the basics from a modest household of preconquest times. Cristóbal (presumably Simón as well) wears the man's traditional cloak and loincloth.

But Cristóbal also has a shirt, called a *camixatli* (from Spanish *camisa*), the fitted and buttoned garment type brought by the Spaniards. Looking further, we see much more evidence of Spanish material culture incorporated into the life of this indigenous commoner, so near the bottom of the scale that he is reduced to stealing turkeys. He hits Simón over the head with an indigenous digging stick, but this traditional instrument is tipped with the new material iron and does corresponding damage. He tries to stab Simón with a knife, not of the traditional obsidian-bladed type, but one of steel, a *cochillo* (from Spanish *cuchillo*). And the knife happens to be lying on a chest, not a traditional container made of mats or reeds, but a Spanish-style *caxa* (*caja*) of wood, lockable, with iron hinges and latch. To this extent, by the late sixteenth century, has the life of even the poorest members of indigenous society been affected. Simón is paying money to have his wife treated; he mentions not only the Spanish denomination *peso* but the generic term *tomines* (originally referring to a specific coin, but extended by the Nahuas to signify cash or money). Indigenous merchants (*pochteca*) are still active in Tulancingo, but among other things they are lending out Spanish money. A Spaniard (*español* in the Nahuatl text) is also somehow involved in the treatment of Simón's wife; probably he is an apothecary who has provided Spanish medicines on credit.

The "Spanish" things are treated no differently from the indigenous things; all seem to be unselfconsciously accepted for what they are and incorporated into life as lived. Once chests, knives, shirts, and money had been built into indigenous culture, there was no longer any awareness of them as something foreign. Indeed, elements of Spanish origin were soon capable of becoming a badge of local pride and self-identity. The ostensibly Spanish-style council (*cabildo*) of each Indian municipality was its primary vehicle of corporate representation, and the ostensibly Spanish patron saint its primary symbol of corporate identity.

Both council and saint, however, were identified in the indigenous mind with preconquest antecedents. Not many years from the time of the Tulancingo turkey theft, in the small settlement of San Miguel Tocuillan in the Valley of Mexico, a woman named Ana petitioned the local council, of which her brother was a member, for a piece of land where she and her husband could build a house. The notary chose to tell the whole story in dialogue form rather than restrict himself to Spanish legalities, thus showing us for once what really went on on such occasions.[4] No sooner had Ana told her brother Juan Miguel (whose second name was taken from the town saint) of her intention than he went out to collect the other members of the council while Ana prepared tortillas and pulque (pulque being, as the reader no doubt already knows, the indigenous staple alcoholic drink from maguey juice). On their return, eating, drinking, and polite conversation were the first order of business, followed by Ana's request, couched in words of elaborate humility, and a quick acceptance of the petition by the guests. Thereupon she took them to the site she had chosen; they measured it out, declared it hers, and politely declined her pro forma invitation to come back and have a bit more pulque. Ana promised "I will burn candles and always provide incense for my precious father the saint San Miguel, because it is on his land that I am building my house." The town fathers expressed their approval, each giving a little speech, after which all embraced and the function was adjourned. Thus the annually elected town officials with Spanish titles were really in operation, and the Spanish patron saint received real allegiance, but they had become so closely identified with the indigenous tradition that, as in preconquest times, a feast for the officials and parties involved was an indispensable part of the legitimation of land transfers, and the entity's land was thought of as ultimately belonging to a supernatural being symbolizing the corporation, now a patron saint rather than an ethnic deity as before the conquest.

Most Nahuatl writing had the purpose of communication among indigenous people, and that is its strength. But at times texts produced for Spaniards can be instructive too. Around 1570 or 1580 in one of the old imperial capitals, Tetzcoco, a Nahua who must have been serving as an aide to the Franciscan friars there composed for them a set of language lessons in the form of speeches and dialogues on all sorts of everyday occasions: greetings, small talk, addresses apropos of marriage, birth, and death. Though the transactions are ordinary, the discourse is in the grand manner, for the speakers come from the circle of the town council, and some are descendants of preconquest kings. Within the framework of Spanish-style municipal government and enthusiastic Christianity, an exquisite protocol for daily interaction continued, closely defining the nature of a given occasion and the relative position of each actor in it. In a dialogue, the arriving party always spoke first, remaining standing, and going to extremes in apologies for intrusion of his (or her) worthless self into such an august presence, whereas the stationary party, adopting the attitude of a superior, remained seated, responding with the formula "you have wearied yourself," i.e., "welcome." Inferiors never called superiors or elders by name and rarely even referred openly to any relationship that might exist between them, whereas superiors could do both (though sparingly). A system of inversion of kinship terms had rulers calling their aides "uncles," while to subjects the ruler could be "our grandchild." Children were not exempted from the formalities. Consider how two boys of the nobility greet their mother in the morning:[5]

> The elder: Oh our mistress, oh lady, I kiss your hands and feet, I bow down to your dignity. How did our Lord cause you to feel on rising? Do you enjoy a bit of His health?
> The younger: Oh my noble person, oh personage, oh lady, we do not wish to distract you; we bow down to you, we salute your ladyship and rulership. How did you enjoy your sleep, and now how are you enjoying the day? Are you enjoying a bit of the good health of the All-pervasive, the Giver of Life?

It was not only certain fundamental patterns of the indigenous world, then, that persisted into Spanish times. A rich and flowery language of polite social intercourse also long survived, bearing within it a multitude of subtle concepts which were thus given time to enter in one way or another into the evolving ideational systems of the postconquest period.

A great many of the most spectacularly informative Nahuatl documents stem, like the three just drawn upon, from the second half of the sixteenth century, when the new techniques of writing had been mastered but were so fresh that one seems to detect a positive joy in using the medium, and furthermore many preconquest survivals were then still starkly evident. Documents from later times also sometimes open up to the reader, however, particularly those of the genre often called "titles," though they could be more accurately described as attempts to make up for the lack of proper title. In the first half of the colonial period, because of a massive and long continuing decrease in indigenous population, combined with slow growth in the numbers of Spaniards from a small base, there was relatively little pressure on the land and correspondingly little concern with authenticating title to it. By the second half of the seventeenth century things had changed. The Hispanic sector had expanded, land had risen in value and was becoming scarce, and Indian towns were being pressed to document their land rights in the Spanish fashion. Often they could not; instead a town would resort to writing down its oral tradition of how it came by its rights, going far beyond a recital of boundaries and Spanish official acts to tell as much of the entity's history as legend had preserved. The self-view that emerges from these documents emphasizes the autonomy of the local entity in both pre- and postconquest periods and its solidarity against all outsiders, be they indigenous or Spanish. More distant outsiders, however, such as the Spanish king, viceroy, and archbishop, are seen as potentially benevolent allies against external threats coming from the immediately surrounding Indian towns and Spanish estates.

As in the first postconquest century, Hispanic cultural elements are inter-mingled in the "titles" with those of indigenous origin, but now the process has gone even further. Christianity is sometimes projected upon figures from the remote preconquest past, stone images of that time may be referred to as saints, and the postconquest organization of Hispanic-style munici-palities may be taken for the original foundation of the entity centuries earlier. Such identifications are no doubt related to the indigenous cyclical view of events in general, but simple merging and loss of historical awareness are also involved. Nahuatl writers of the first colonial century, though they saw postconquest entities as retaining an identity and history carried over from before the arrival of the Spaniards, nevertheless were able to distinguish clearly between the two periods, and many of them still possessed a large amount of objectively correct historical information about their own groups before the conquest. The writers of the later titles, despite preserving much lore of preconquest origin, were often unaware which elements belonged to which tradition (presenting Spanish officials, for example, with a tale of an ethnic leader being converted into a feathered serpent by way of supporting their claims). Indeed, some writers seem not to have been able to imagine two sharply differentiated succeeding periods at all; some of those who were able to do so and attempted partial portrayals of the preconquest world proved to have woefully little information, resorting instead at times to Spanish-influenced reinvention, with results bearing little resemblance to the original phenomena.[6]

Much the same trends are seen in another form of Nahuatl ethnic-historical writing, the annals genre, in which discrete bits of information are organized by the year of their occurrence, marching chronologically forward so mechanically that if no noteworthy event is known for a given year, the year designation is often included anyway, with next to it a blank space or an apologetic note. In preconquest times such annals consisted of a glyphic-pictorial document plus a memorized oral recital; postconquest annals quickly went over to an alphabetical text as the primary vehicle, though the pictorial element long remained strong and never disappeared entirely. The pre-Hispanic annals covered events such as the foundation of the local state, the succession of its kings, its wars, its internal strife, and also natural phenomena, including earthquakes, plagues, and the appearance of comets. Sixteenth-century annals often devoted a large amount of space to preconquest material, adapted to the new medium but otherwise unchanged, before continuing in the same vein for the postconquest years, though now reporting changes in the governorship and town council of the local entity rather than successors to the dynastic rulership.[7] Annals continued to be written in the late seventeenth and early eighteenth centuries, still primarily concerned with the affairs of a single town, still retaining the same type of organization and subject matter. But in the late annals the preconquest era hardly figures, and even events of the sixteenth century are reported skeletally, often unreliably. The full specification of years by the indigenous calendrical scheme is sometimes simplified. The appointments of new viceroys and archbishops, often reported from the beginning, are now such standard annals fare that they rival the changes in local indigenous government.[8]

To convey in a small space a notion of how communicative Nahuatl documents can be, as well as something of their thrust, I have been concentrating on some of the more colorful, juicy types and examples. The bulk of Nahuatl documentation preserved today was produced by municipal notaries as a function of routine activities of indigenous local government. It includes sales and grants of land, litigation, town council minutes, and above all thousands of testaments.[9] Most of the material sticks much closer to Spanish legal formulas and procedures than the writings we have been sampling. Testaments, the staple item, normally follow the Spanish model closely, proceeding from an abbreviated credo to dispositions concerning the burial and masses, then apportioning houses and land to relatives and liquidating debts. But even here there are reminiscences of the Nahua declamatory style, with a great many admonitions and spontaneous outbursts one would not expect in a Spanish will.

Aside from massive evidence on the nature of Spanish influence and the elucidation of a multitude of general indigenous concepts, the special contribution of Nahuatl testaments is to teach us about the Nahua household.

When first seen in sixteenth-century documents, the household unit is of variable size, periodically moving toward a complex containing two or more related nuclear families, then splitting into its constituent parts and repeating the process. The household's lands were scattered and divided into relatively small plots even when the aggregate amount was large, and the different adult household members were responsible for their respective portions. Inside the home complex were separate buildings arranged around a patio, each containing and in a sense belonging to an adult family member or nuclear family. And for all the changes and additions that over the centuries the introduction of Spanish techniques, varieties, and artifacts brought about, the essential structure of a complex of clustered separate dwellings and scattered landholdings remained the same in the indigenous sector across the whole colonial period, and labor-intensive cultivation of indigenous crops remained the core of indigenous agriculture. In the earliest sources there is great variation in the amount of land held by different individuals and family groups, not only, as expected, between the nobles and the commoners, but among the commoners themselves, indicating a great deal of flexibility and low-level autonomy in the land regime, and this attribute too is maintained over the centuries, even while the indigenous sector as a whole lost land to the expanding Hispanic sector.[10]

Some important insights coming out of Nahuatl documentation are not to be gleaned from any one genre but pervade the whole corpus. We become privy to unfamiliar concepts and procedures and aware of the absence of familiar ones. Among the most striking absences is that of the category "Indian." Nahuatl contained no word covering this semantic range, and later, when it began to borrow Spanish words, including much ethnic terminology, Spanish *indio* did not become a standard part of the language. Indeed, no large-group category for indigenous people had much currency. The term "Nahua" in the sense I am using it here was understood but rare.

Self-definition and differentiation between indigenous groups was primarily in terms of the *altepetl*, the type of local kingdom mentioned above as having survived the conquest all over central Mexico; this the Spaniards usually called a *pueblo*. The entity was partially defined by its tradition of ethnic distinctness, partially by its possession of a certain territory, and partially by its dynastic ruler, the *tlatoani*, whom the Spaniards immediately and correctly recognized as such, terming him the *cacique*. As to the internal structure of the altepetl/pueblo, the Spaniards, in line with their own traditions, perceived it to consist of a *cabecera* or capital ruling a set of *sujetos* or subject hamlets. And in fact, one could often find the semblance of a central settlement in an altepetl. The residence of the tlatoani, the site of the kingdom's main temple, and its central marketplace often coincided, leading to a settlement cluster in that vicinity. The cluster, however, had no separate name and no juridical identity or organizational unity. Different segments of it belonged to different constituent parts of the entity. These named parts, called *calpolli* or *tlaxilacalli*, comprised an ideally symmetrical whole (often but not always in groups of 2, 4, and 8); each part was separate, equal in principle, and self-contained, with its own territory, subethnic identity, and subrulership. The parts were arranged in a fixed order of rotation according to which all mechanisms of the altepetl operated. This order of the parts, indeed, defined the whole at a level even more basic than the rulership. Where the Spanish view included three types of entities— pueblo, cabecera, and sujeto—, Nahuatl documents recognize only two: the altepetl, being the whole, and the calpolli or parts. The Spanish view emphasizes urban nucleation and a stepped hierarchy; the Nahua view emphasizes a symmetrical arrangement and rotational order. Through indigenous-language sources it becomes clear that the Spaniards operated under a partial delusion, and modern scholars have followed them in it. Over the course of the colonial period the altepetl underwent many modifications, but, half undetected by Spanish authorities, it retained its basic principles of organization.

The office of tlatoani was gradually transformed into the Spanish-influenced governorship, in principle a removable, elective post, as was already well understood from Spanish documents alone. Subsequently much of the machinery of Spanish municipal government was introduced into the altepetl. A Spanish city council had two *alcaldes* or first-instance judges and a larger number of *regidores* or councilmen. Nahuatl documents show us how these offices were fitted to the indigenous mold. In the Spanish tradition, each official in a sense represented his extended family and clientele, a kin-based faction, but functioned at large. Among the Nahuas, office continued to be tied closely to the constituent parts of the (now municipal) entity. Thus an alcalde above all represented his calpolli; soon either the alcaldes were being rotated systematically among the calpolli following the fixed order or—in the long run the dominant trend—the number of alcaldes increased until there was one for each major constituent part. Regidores followed the same pattern, to the point that there was no general distinction between the two offices than that of rank, alcalde being higher, whereas in the Spanish system the often longer-lasting office of regidor had greater prestige. Indeed, whereas a Spanish town council (*cabildo*) was a well defined corporate entity, clearly set off from the commonwealth in general, an indigenous town council, though equally meaningful, was in a sense an ad hoc group of representatives of the constituent parts, and as such it merged imperceptibly into the generality of prominent citizens and former office holders.

The altepetl scheme is but the best and most central example of a type of cellular or modular organization that appears in several forms in indigenous life. The Nahuatl songs preserved from the second half of the sixteenth century consist of self-contained verses, often eight of them, arranged in pairs. The pairs relate similarly to a central theme but never refer directly to each other, and therefore in variant versions the pairs are often found differently arranged, although the overall numerical scheme remains the same, and the integrity of each pair is maintained. A similar organization of decorative motifs has been noted in preconquest indigenous art and again in survivals associated with postconquest religious architecture.[11] Although not involving such marked symmetry, the annals genre, reporting events in discrete segments under individual years, operates on the same principle. So do the home complex, divided into separate subhouseholds in separate buildings, and the land regime, dividing holdings into many independent subunits.[12]

After absorbing the fresh humanity and color of Nahuatl documents in a direct, philological fashion, exploring the topical content of various documentary genres, and tracing certain central concepts through the entire corpus, the natural next step in building a history based on indigenous-language sources is a linguistic approach, trying to win meaningful patterns about society and culture from the language of the texts itself. Like other languages of the world, Nahuatl has been neither static over time nor uniform over space. The Nahuatl-speaking world functioned as a cultural unit in many ways, with similar trends in all its parts, and new elements often affected the whole within a very short period of time. Yet each altepetl had its own specific way of speaking and writing. Paying close attention to such differentiation, we can tell something of which areas retained the most elaborate development of preconquest culture and which were losing the refinements; which were at the forefront of new trends and which lagged behind. For example, it becomes apparent that many of the larger altepetl, which felt the full force of Spanish intrusion into the countryside and consequently underwent the greatest change, nevertheless at the same time had and retained the greatest corporate strength; far into the colonial period they kept more of the social and other distinctions embodied in preconquest Nahuatl polite discourse than did smaller and less centrally located entities. Amecameca in the southeastern part of the Valley of Mexico is a good example of such a center.[13]

It is hard, however, to achieve more than impressionistic results through cultural-linguistic research unless the potentially vast and amorphous field of investigation is somehow restricted. A naturally restricted field is available in the form of the Spanish loan words that leap to the eye in Nahuatl texts, and the choice of this topic is further justified by the fact that it is at the very core of the question of cultural change and continuity. Frances Karttunen and I thus set out some time ago to discover the patterns in Spanish-Nahuatl language-contact phenomena (on the Nahuatl side, that is), primarily by collecting all the loan words in all Nahuatl texts then known to us, with attention to the date of each example, and subjecting the resulting lists to several kinds of simple linguistic analysis. A dynamic picture emerged, characterized by three successive well defined stages.[14] Since the process went on over generations and centuries, doubtless beneath the level of awareness for the most part, we have no contemporary comments on what motivated it, but considering the general movement of early Mexican history and what is known about two-language situations in other parts of the world in modern times, it is clear enough that the stages correspond to increasing amounts of everyday contact between Nahuatl-speaking and Spanish-speaking populations.

Stage 1, extending from the arrival of the Spaniards in 1519 until about 1540-50, involved minimal contact between Spaniards and Indians; hence hardly any change in the Nahuatl language took place at all. Since during most of this time the Nahuas were not yet producing alphabetical texts in any number, Stage 1 remains shadowy and little documented, but it is embodied in a few texts written probably in the time period 1535-45, and we can reconstruct aspects of it from relics left in dictionaries and texts of the succeeding period. Rather than borrow Spanish words for the new things which they were after all seeing more than hearing about, the Nahuas described them with the tools of their own language, using various kinds of extensions, circumlocutions, and neologisms. The new material wool, for example, as a usually whitish fiber for textile use, was called *ichcatl*, "cotton," and the word was then extended further to the animal that bore it, coming to mean "sheep." *Tepoztli*, "copper," as a designation for a workable metal, soon took on the additional meaning "iron." The Christian sacraments were called *teoyotl*, "holy things," and *quaatequia*, "to pour water on the head," became the term for speaking of baptism.

The only loans taking place in Stage 1 appear to have involved names. Many of the Nahuas began to receive Spanish baptismal names, and Hernando Cortés' title-name of Marqués (often *Malquex* in Nahuatl texts) became widely familiar, as did the name of his indigenous interpreter, doña

Marina (*Malintzin*). Full of implications was the place name *Castilla*, "Castile," taken into Nahuatl in the naturalized form *Caxtillan*. Using it as a modifier, the Nahuas could now express simultaneously their perception that introduced items shared defining characteristics with items already known and their awareness of the Spanish items' newness; thus wheat was *Caxtillan centli*, "Castile maize." *Caxtillan* also gave rise in some fashion to *caxtil*, one of the words the Nahuas were to use for the European chicken. It is tempting, if perhaps too whimsical, to think that since the Nahuas took the final -*lan* to be their own suffix "place characterized by," and since they saw the Castilians always accompanied by chickens, they deduced that "Castilla" meant "place with chickens," then proceeded to retrieve and use the presumed root in that meaning.

In Stage 2, beginning 1540-50 and extending over about a hundred years to approximately 1640-50, the Nahuas borrowed Spanish words readily and copiously. In this time period Spanish cities grew in size, economic and institutional networks brought Spaniards into steady contact with Indians, and a long slow process of formation of Hispanic residential nuclei in the countryside got under way. The words now pouring into Nahuatl belonged to several semantic domains, representing different aspects of a massive cultural impact. All the loans were alike in naming an element introduced by the Spaniards that in one way or another had become a part of indigenous life. Words for new plant and animal varieties head the list. Spanish *trigo* now replaced *Caxtillan centli* for "wheat" and *caballo* the earlier extension *maçatl* ("deer") for "horse"; *vaca*, "cow," pushed *quaquahue* ("one with horns") into the specialized meaning "ox." Some of the Stage 1 forms lived on. *Ichcatl*, mentioned above, remains a common Nahuatl word for "sheep" to this day. New tools (often metal), materials, and artifact types form a second important category. Our turkey theft story, written in the first half of Stage 2, offers good examples in Cristóbal's knife (*cochillo*), chest (*caxa*), and shirt (*camixatli*). A third category consists of new role definitions: the names of the ubiquitous local officers, *gobernador, alcalde, regidor*, and others; of Spanish officers, from *virrey*, "viceroy," and *obispo*, "bishop," on down; group designations, such as *cristiano*, "Christian," and *español*, "Spaniard" (which also appears in the turkey story). More abstract loans were by no means lacking. They included specific Spanish-style concepts and procedures, whether economic (such as *prenda*, "pledge, pawn, security"), legal (such as *pleito*, "lawsuit, litigation"), or religious (such as *misa*, "mass"). Especially pervasive in the indigenous world and important in enabling Nahuas to act in a Spanish context were the loans involving words for the measurement of time, extension, weight, and value. The turkey story again offers examples: *martes*, "Tuesday," and the denomination *peso*.

The Spanish words that during Stage 2 became an integral part of Nahuatl vocabulary by the hundreds (probably thousands, if the record were more complete) represent a vast cultural input and a considerable addition to the lexicon. Lest anyone should imagine that the loans are an artificial, minority phenomenon restricted to the written expression of a few well educated notaries, consider whether we have any earthly reason to doubt that humble Cristóbal really did have a knife, chest, and shirt, and that he called them by the Spanish loans used in Simón's account. What else, indeed, *could* he have called them? No alternative expressions are found.[15] Consider too that although postconquest Nahuatl writing was highly developed in its own way, it did not constitute an independent canon. What we call "words" lacked any universal spelling; rather the individual letters followed the writer's actual pronunciation, whatever form that happened to take. The purpose of writing was simply to reproduce speech. Consider further that every altepetl of the hundreds across central Mexico, including very small and humble entities where it would be an exaggeration to separate an educated upper group from the rest (as in Tocuillan in the story of Ana and her house site), had its notary or notaries; yet the same kinds of loans are found in the texts of all of them, in all the types of documents they produced. And this despite the fact that writing was handed down directly from generation to generation within each altepetl, leading to pronounced local peculiarities.

Yet the impact of Spanish on Nahuatl was in another sense severely limited during Stage 2. The grammar of the language hardly changed. Essentially all the loans were grammatically nouns, leaving everything else unaffected. The loan nouns were treated no differently than Nahuatl nouns, not only acting as subjects and objects but being compounded with native elements including nouns, verbs, subject prefixes, and relational suffixes. It is true that after a brief period in which some loan words received the absolutive suffix (*-tli* and variants) found on most native nouns, as in *camixa-tli*, "shirt," new loans were left without the absolutive, but this was not an innovation in principle, since Nahuatl did already have a class of absolutiveless nouns.

Nor was pronunciation affected at this time. Nahuatl had no voiced obstruents (that is, it had *p, t,* and hard *c* but not the corresponding *b, d,* and *g*); among the liquids it had *l* but lacked *r*; among the vowels it had only *o* where Spanish had both *o* and *u*; it did not tolerate initial or final consonant clusters. None of these things changed during the bulk of Stage 2. No new sounds were added to the repertoire. Rather each loan was pronounced in a way conforming to the existing Nahuatl phonetic system, with substitution of the closest Nahuatl sound for missing Spanish sounds and insertion of an extra vowel or omission of a consonant to break up impossible consonant clusters. We know this because of the Nahuas' propensity to write as they pronounced, often making exactly the adjustments we would expect. Thus for Spanish *trigo* ("wheat") we can find *tilico*, for *sábado* ("Saturday") *xapato*, for *vacas* ("cows") *huacax*, for *cruz* ("cross") *coloz*, for *cristiano* ("Christian") *quixtiano*, and so on. And since the Nahuas heard no difference between *p* and *b* or *l* and *r*, they were prone to hypercorrection, writing such things as *breito* for Spanish *pleito* ("lawsuit"), and even sometimes using *b*, *d*, *g*, and *r* in native vocabulary.

Spanish words in Nahuatl did not always mean exactly the same thing as in the original language. We have already seen how the Nahuas, having borrowed the word *tomín*, "an eighth of a peso," extended it to serve as their primary term for money or cash, a meaning which Spaniards probably would not have understood immediately, especially as they increasingly abandoned *tomín* in favor of *real*. *Cristiano* or *quixtiano* often meant not "believer in Christianity" but "person of European extraction," and *señora* or *xinola* ("lady") usually referred specifically to a Spanish woman. The names of the municipal officers, though they had the same referents in Nahuatl as in Spanish, connoted different functions and characteristics. Spanish words in Nahuatl, naturalized as they were in both external form and inner meaning, were as much a part of the general linguistic and conceptual equipment as vocabulary that had been in the language for centuries.

Coming to Stage 3, it can be considered to have begun around 1640-50, continuing for the rest of the colonial period and indeed until today, wherever Nahuatl is still spoken. Now Nahuatl opened up to take (though still selectively) whatever Spanish had to offer. The language remained very much itself, but it was now permeated with elements of Spanish origin which affected grammar and pronunciation as well as lexicon. This type of penetration can only mean that a large number of Nahuas were by now bilingual; not nearly a majority, no doubt, but a critical mass. Speaking Spanish in the marketplace or where they worked, they needed easy ways to report the events of the day to the monolingual Nahuatl speakers at home. Thus Nahuatl began to go beyond borrowing primarily to name new things for which no other word was readily available to reproducing common Spanish expressions even when nearly equivalent indigenous expressions existed, sometimes with the result of displacing the latter. By Stage 3, Spaniards were firmly ensconced in every part of the central Mexican countryside. They lived cheek by jowl with Nahuas in what once were purely Indian settlements, owning large amounts of rural land. Here they had created a network of haciendas, ranchos, and other enterprises connected with the urban market, which permanently employed an ever increasing number of Nahuas, in addition to continuing seasonal employment of yet larger numbers. For their part the Nahuas were now more inclined than ever to move back and forth between the countryside and the large Spanish cities, Mexico City and Puebla.

The discovery of Stage 3 and its timing represents an especially large contribution to the periodization of Mexican history. Scholars had already known of the just mentioned characteristics of the seventeenth century, but the trends began in the sixteenth and continued full force in the eighteenth and later. Whereas a series of large reorganizations were taking place around the time of the transition from Stage 1 to Stage 2, so that we are not surprised to find that they coincide with a major social and cultural shift, nothing so dramatic occurs in the seventeenth century; there was little reason to think of any one stretch of time as more crucial than another. Nor are bilingual Indians distinguished in contemporary censuses and population estimates from any other Indians. Once discovered, however, the onset of Stage 3 proves to coincide approximately with a whole set of changes in the indigenous world, as we will see in more detail below.

As to the linguistic content of Stage 3, Nahuatl now developed a convention for borrowing Spanish verbs, adopted some Spanish particles (prepositions and conjunctions), found equivalents for many Spanish idioms, and added new sounds to its phonetic repertoire in loan vocabulary. Although these things happened more or less simultaneously over a few decades, the change did not come overnight; some signs appeared in the early seventeenth century, then the movement gathered strength as mid-century approached, and by 1650 late colonial Nahuatl was essentially in place as far as its mechanisms are concerned (though individual accretions along the same lines continued and still continue). To borrow verbs, Nahuatl developed the strategy of adding the native verbalizing element -oa to the Spanish infinitive; the construction then conjugated like any other Nahuatl verb. Loan verbs were not very numerous—a drop in the bucket compared to nouns—but they became a standard feature, found sprinkled here and there in texts of all kinds. They tended to be technical legal, religious, or economic terms, such as confirmaroa, "to confirm (an appointment or administrative action)," or prendaroa, "to hock," but perhaps the most widespread of them, pasearoa, "to take a stroll, parade about," referred to a general social practice, and simple everyday vocabulary could also be affected, as in *cruzaroa,* "to cross (a street, etc.)." The first presently attested true loan verb is an isolated example from the 1590's; another is known apparently from the second decade of the seventeenth century, and momentum gathers in the following decades, but it is not until around 1650 that loan verbs become a normal, expectable feature of Nahuatl texts.

Loan particles are as striking a symptom of Stage 3 as are verbs. Nahuatl made little distinction in native vocabulary between conjunctions and adverbs, and it had no construction remotely like a preposition, expressing similar notions instead through suffix-like relational words. Yet it now began to accept from Spanish both conjunctions and prepositions, at first primarily the latter. They were few, even fewer than the verbs, but they were pervasive, especially *para,* "(destined) for, in order to," and above all *hasta* "until, as far as, even," which became an indispensable part of the language. Introductions of this type went beyond expanding the lexicon to bring about substantial changes in Nahuatl syntax.

Another important characteristic of Stage 3 is the frequent use of calques, that is, expressions in which native vocabulary is employed to express foreign idiom. This tendency had been developing for a long time, but it reaches full flower only in Stage 3. Though Nahuatl was rich in ways to signify possession, inclusion, and connection, it originally lacked a close equivalent of the ubiquitous Spanish verb *tener,* "to have." As early as the second half of the sixteenth century the Nahuatl verb *pia,* "to guard, take care of, have charge of, hold," seems to have been veering in the direction of "to have (possess)." By the early seventeenth century we can find *pia* used in expressions which would have made no sense in preconquest Nahuatl, deriving their meaning instead from a Spanish idiom involving *tener.* Thus *quipia chicuey xihuitl,* which once would have been a meaningless "he guards eight years," meant "he is eight years old," following the Spanish *tiene ocho años,* literally "he has eight years." By Stage 3, a full-scale equivalency relationship had come into existence, that is, *pia* could automatically be used to replicate in Nahuatl any Spanish idiom involving *tener.* The same was true of some other common verbs, including *pano,* originally "to traverse (a body of water, field, or the like)," which became the equivalent of the much-used Spanish verb *pasar,* "to pass." One of the most subtle, hard to detect, and hard to date aspects of Stage 3 was a change in the pronunciation of loan vocabulary as the Nahuas learned how to reproduce the sounds of Spanish. This development took place over a good stretch of time, often by intermediary steps; thus Nahuatl speakers first acquired a single new pronunciation for Spanish *d* and *r,* then later learned to distinguish one from the other. Exact pronunciations cannot always be deduced through the inconsistent spellings and ambiguous orthography. Yet it is clear that a large change occurred across the middle of the seventeenth century, and before 1700 Nahuatl speakers in general were able to pronounce new loans as in Spanish (older loans, however retained their original form).

The stages of the linguistic adaptation of Nahuatl to Spanish have close parallels in almost every facet of indigenous life.[16] Since the whole field of Nahuatl-based historical studies is so new, much remains to be learned, but something can already be said. Perhaps the most striking example of parallelism concerns the mechanisms of procurement of short-term Indian laborers by Spaniards. Given the lavish use of temporary labor characteristic of the colonial period as of the preconquest era before it, bulk labor mechanisms were a major department of indigenous organization as well as one of the most important ties between the Indian and Spanish populations.

During Stage 1, Spaniards acquired temporary Indian labor through the encomienda, a device which, essentially, gave a single Spaniard for his lifetime the tributes, in kind and in labor, which one altepetl would otherwise have rendered to the Spanish government. This system involved as little contact as it did change. An unaltered local indigenous state, through the prerogatives of its ruler and the operation of its internal rotational order, delivered work parties to a single Spaniard (and, to be sure, often to his employees); the parties usually remained intact, under corporate indigenous supervision, and did things in or close to the indigenous tradition.

At the end of the time period I have assigned to Stage 1, the central Mexican encomienda lost its labor power. During Stage 2, temporary labor was procured through a system that the Spaniards called *repartimiento*. The constituent parts of the altepetl continued to provide contingents through rotation as before, but the operative indigenous authority was now usually the governor and town council rather than the dynastic ruler per se, and above all the assembled contingents were now divided ad hoc into more numerous smaller parties which worked for a short period for whatever Spanish estate owners and entrepreneurs happened to need them. The new framework involved more Spanish-Indian contact; smaller groups worked at tasks more Hispanic in nature under closer Spanish supervision.

By Stage 3, the repartimiento had given way to informal arrangements in which individual Indians made agreements to hire on for seasonal labor with individual Spaniards at a negotiated wage (usually simply the going rate for less skilled work). Ordinary Indians now had absorbed enough Hispanic lore to be able to deal with Spaniards one to one, without need of a corporate prop; on the other side of the coin but for the same reasons, the indigenous corporations were less and less able to deliver laborers when so required.

The legal abolition of the central Mexican agricultural repartimiento came in the 1630's, a few years before the time I have set for the beginning of Stage 3, but the coincidence is still quite close, and as I indicated above, advance signs of the developing linguistic shift did show themselves earlier in the seventeenth century.[17]

Indigenous government is another area in which the stages can be detected. During Stage 1 the organization of the altepetl remained basically untouched, with the tlatoani retaining his full traditional powers. At the onset of Stage 2 the governorship and town council took shape. Although no later transformation is of quite the same magnitude, as well defined in content, or as sharply etched as to dating, several traits prominent after about 1650 make it appropriate to speak of a Stage 3 form of town government. In most places the regidores (councilmen) either faded from the scene altogether or were relegated to sharply subordinate rank. The governor and alcaldes were joined on many occasions by the *fiscal* (church steward), and they, together with previous holders of those offices, who ostentatiously bore the title *pasado* "past (officer)," and often returned to active status after an interval, constituted a consortium which made the most important internal decisions or appeals to the outside and was indispensable in all sorts of ceremonial legitimation. Stage 3 also saw a widespread fragmentation of large altepetl into their constituent parts (or confederations thereof), the new smaller independent units operating on the same principles and with the same type of officials, though often lacking a governor. These independence movements took place through energetic campaigns carried on by the seceding parts; although especially characteristic of the late colonial period, they at the same time represent a realization of one of the tendencies inherent in cellular altepetl structure from preconquest times.[18]

Altepetl office and the system of social distinctions had always been closely intertwined among the Nahuas. The tlatoani or king was at the apex of the social pyramid; *teteuctin*, "lords," held the same position in each constituent part, and it was from among the *pipiltin*, "nobles," that all officeholders were recruited. Unchanged in Stage 1, the terminology of noble rank not only largely continued in use in Stage 2, it became associated with the introduced Hispanic-style offices. Thus the governor was often called "tlatoani" even if he was not the dynastic ruler, and the council in general would be referred to as teteuctin and pipiltin. By Stage 3, the indigenous terminology of social rank effectively disappeared; only rare, frozen remnants can be found. In its place, a subtle system of differential naming patterns had grown up, making many of the same distinctions in a more flexible fashion.

At the level of the household, the nature and pace of change is hard to detect. Simple continuity seems the dominant note, but kinship terms do provide some interesting evidence of patterned change. As late as Stage 2 the system was altered only by the concept of monogamous Christian marriage and some loan words associated with it, such as *viuda* and *viudo*, "widow" and "widower," and *soltera* and *soltero*, "spinster" and "bachelor." (The Nahuatl word *-namic*, "spouse," may or may not have been a new formation during Stage 1.) In any case, all these terms had quite close equivalents in preconquest times. In Stage 3, the Nahuas moved nearer to the Spanish system, largely abandoning the indigenous categorization of siblings, cousins, and in-laws, which had been the most obvious points of difference in the two systems, and adopting the Spanish categories instead.

In the field of historical writing, we have already seen the distinction between Stage 2 annals, reporting many authentic preconquest events, and those of Stage 3, devoted entirely to the postconquest period. Stage 2 was the time when a mixed Hispanic-indigenous style of expression flourished, executed by individuals still cognizant of preconquest skills and lore, buttressed by a still strong solidarity of the altepetl. Stage 2 has left us the annals of Chimalpahin, the Florentine Codex, the collections of Nahuatl song,[19] and other such monuments, and in the realm of art the great monastery complexes, complete with stone carvings and frescoes still close to indigenous traditions.[20] Nothing comparable exists from later times. The syncretizing, synchronizing "titles," on the other hand, are entirely a phenomenon of Stage 3. Only Stage 3 writings make prominent mention of the Virgin of Guadalupe, and this is no chance occurrence. In Stage 2 many local cults arose around the patron saints of individual altepetl (with a preconquest substratum). A few saints won reputations in the surrounding area beyond the limits of the altepetl, and Guadalupe was one of these; but only in Stage 3 did the devotion to Guadalupe spread beyond the vicinity of Mexico City to become a symbol of the nascent sense of identification of indigenous (and Spanish) people with a general Spanish-Indian Mexican framework over and above the home altepetl and the immediate locality.

The marvelous and many-dimensioned new world of Nahuatl sources, then, is showing us that indigenous structures and patterns survived the conquest on a much more massive scale and for a longer period of time than had seemed the case when we had to judge by the reports of Spaniards alone. The indigenous world retained much social and cultural as well as jurisdictional autonomy, maintaining its center of balance to a surprising extent, concerned above all with its own affairs. Yet viewed in their totality, Nahuatl writings show us movement and intermingling, not stasis and isolation. Change went on constantly, and it occurred precisely because of contact with Spaniards. Increasing degrees of contact with the numerically growing and territorially expanding Hispanic population caused successive general waves of indigenous structural adjustment. The Spaniards represented, however, more the fuel than the motor of the development. They did not by themselves, either individually or en masse, determine the nature of change; change was a transaction between two groups and two cultures. Indian numbers were as important as Spanish numbers. The long demographic slide of the indigenous population, lasting well into the seventeenth century, meant that the Spanish impact was divided among fewer and fewer recipients, so that a given number of hours of contact represented an ever larger proportion of the Nahua world's total experience.

Above all, though, it was the nature of Nahua culture in relation to Spanish culture that determined the shape (as opposed to the tempo) of change. Mere Spanish decisions to implant certain elements, either through forcible imposition or through benevolent teaching, did not suffice to bring about the desired results. Nahua culture had to have structures and values close enough to the new Spanish elements to make them viable in the indigenous context. When this was the case, there was often no need for imposition or teaching. Everyday contact between Spaniards and Indians in the course of routine, often economic activities emerges as the primary vehicle of cultural transfer, with governmental and ecclesiastical influence merely one congruent subset within that framework. Major policy decisions of Spanish authorities, including the establishment of encomiendas and ancillary parishes, were made in awareness of the nature of indigenous structures; there was no other choice. When Spanish officials tried to replicate such institutions in areas lacking a close equivalent of the altepetl, they failed. And even as time went on into the later periods, Spanish administrative decisions, including the basic ones concerning labor mechanisms, were made in response to the social and cultural constitution of the indigenous population at that point in its evolution, doing little more than ratifying what the two populations had gradually, spontaneously brought about. To give another example, official urging from about 1770 forward that the Nahuas do more of their recordkeeping in Spanish and allow Spaniards more direct intervention in community affairs had a good deal of effect because as a result of long-standing trends these things were already happening and the Nahuas were ready; similar Spanish concern in the sixteenth century had had no impact. In areas where less contact occurred and the indigenous sector remained in the earlier stages, the institutional forms corresponding to Stages 1 and 2 persisted longer, sometimes by centuries, than in the Nahua sphere, despite occasional metropolitan urging of reform.[21] Whereas in the earlier stages it was largely Nahua-Spanish similarities that allowed adoptions to succeed, later, as rapprochement proceeded, it might be those things that were different which were adopted, as was seen in the case of the kinship system.

Nahuatl writings illustrate for us the common perception that continuity and change are often to a large extent the same thing. As we have observed, the Spanish elements which the Nahuas were able to take over because of a perceived affinity with things already current in indigenous culture then immediately veered from the Spanish model, or rather never fully embodied that model in the beginning. A partially unwitting truce existed in which each side of the cultural exchange seemed satisfied that its own interpretation of a given cultural phenomenon was the prevailing, if not exclusive one. Elsewhere I have called this the process of Double Mistaken Identity.[22] The Nahuas accepted the new in order to remain the same; the Spaniards for their part were generally willing to accept a new title as evidence of a new role definition. Under the cover of this truce or mutual incomprehension, Nahua patterns could survive at the same time that adaptations worked themselves out over generations. Nothing could illustrate the evolution better than Nahuatl alphabetical writing itself. Readily adopted because the Nahuas already had paper, documentary records, and professional record keepers, alphabetical writing in Nahua hands nevertheless at first retained a large pictorial element and a declamatory text corresponding to the preconquest style of recital. The illustrations gradually faded away, and the texts assimilated more to Spanish models, but they never lost their idiosyncrasy entirely, and new specifically indigenous genres, such as the titles, continued to evolve. A large task still facing historical scholarship is to determine how and to what extent patterns like these, of ultimately indigenous origin, entered the general Mexican cultural stream in the nineteenth century, when upper groups in small Mexican towns had gone over to speaking Spanish, and Nahuatl writing, having flourished in central Mexico for two and a half centuries, was already a thing of the past.

---

2. Complex Municipalities: Tlaxcala and Tulancingo in the Sixteenth Century

Since the appearance of Charles Gibson's *Aztecs* in 1964, it has been known that indigenous states at the subimperial level were the essential carriers of continuity past the sharp break created in central Mexico by the Spanish conquest. Persisting in recognizable form through the sixteenth century and in many cases to the end of the colonial period or beyond, they provided both the shape and the organizational core for the basic institutions of the postconquest countryside. They were like city-states in size, and also in their degree of independence and strong ethnic awareness. But though the Spaniards were to see each state as a *cabecera* surrounded by *sujetos* (and Gibson too makes much use of this terminology), nucleation and urban domination were not central to their manner of organization. Rather each *altepetl* (the indigenous term) consisted of a set of quite equal, distinct, independent units, often called *calpolli* or *tlaxilacalli*, which divided the entire territory of the altepetl among them. No common indigenous term differentiated a core settlement (to the Spaniards, cabecera) from outlying settlements (to the Spaniards, sujetos), nor was there any special role for such a settlement in the scheme.

As a confederation of equal constituent parts, the altepetl stood in need of principles of unity, of which the strongest was the common allegiance of the parts to the same *tlatoani* or dynastic ruler. Each part separately paid its allotted share of the general tax to the tlatoani and rotated in services to him; sharing and rotation in relation to the tlatoani were thus the basic mechanisms of the altepetl. Hence the tlatoani was to be crucial for the Spaniards as well, not only in channeling benefits but in defining units. Gibson saw the essence of the process when he wrote that "despite exceptions, a one-to-one relation between tlatoani community and encomienda was surely regarded as a norm."[1] The general sense, then, of what happened in central Mexico after the conquest is that each altepetl under its tlatoani became an encomienda, following that a parish, and following that a Spanish-style municipality with a cabildo. The basic truth and explanatory power of this insight are such that it should by no means be abandoned. Yet as we learn ever more about central Mexico before and after the conquest, we realize that the process in all its purity may have taken place in only a minority of cases.

Sometimes a new entity was created where no recognized tlatoani had existed; often the borders of the three new units (encomienda, parish, and town) coincided less than perfectly; but the greatest and most common exceptions to the norm were cases in which the entity contained more than one ruler. By the time the Spaniards came, no independent altepetl was without its tlatoani, and the office remained crucial to operations and structure, but many of the most important states were composite altepetl with two or more sets of calpolli and a tlatoani for each, and quite a few of these complex states survived as viable units after the conquest.[2] Xochimilco, Tlalmanalco, Amecameca, Coyoacan, Huejotzingo, and Tlaxcala are among the examples. Clearly entities such as these must be integrated into our view of regular postconquest processes. In fact, as we proceed to delve deeper into documents in Nahuatl throwing light on the creation of Spanish-style Indian municipal corporations and their manner of operation, we find that an inordinate amount of the best evidence concerns precisely those prominent complex altepetl and, indeed, that it was apparently in such situations that the new system first took root and reached full development. Often we must use evidence from complex situations to make deductions about basic processes that must have been in operation in simple altepetl as well but remain undocumented.

In all central Mexico the largest complex altepetl to survive was the quadripartite kingdom of Tlaxcala (Tlaxcallan), and it has also left the largest legacy of documents, Nahuatl or otherwise, on the manner of operation of its municipal corporation in the sixteenth century. Over thirty years ago Gibson used much of this documentation to produce, among other things, the fullest large-scale portrait of the structure and operation of an Indian town government that we have to this day.[3] Now a unique resource only partially utilized by Gibson has become available, the Nahuatl minutes of the Tlaxcalan cabildo (primarily for the years 1547 to 1567).[4] Close work with the minutes, the only such series known to exist, has made me more aware of several patterns, some perhaps specific to conglomerate towns, others more general, which I will briefly present in the following.

More especially I wish to discuss another, less well known complex situation, that of Tulancingo (Tollantzinco), for which some fresh (if highly fragmentary) evidence is also available.[5] The Tulancingo data at times reinforce, at times complement or throw a different light on what can be learned from the Tlaxcalan records. It is the reinforcing that interests me in the present context, for Tlaxcala is so prominent and has played such a peculiar role in the myth-making of the twentieth century that it is all too often looked upon as an altogether exceptional phenomenon rather than as the in many ways typical Indian corporation that it was. Tlaxcala was perhaps the first and probably the greatest ally the Spaniards had in the conquest of Mexico, but it found early and expert imitators. In the sixteenth century other Indian towns resented Tlaxcala not because, as the twentieth century has tended to feel, they were traitors for turning on the "Aztecs," but because they seemed to get all the credit and reward for doing the same thing everyone else was doing all over the country.

Representation of subunits. It now appears that one of the deepest-reaching differences between municipal governments as they existed among Spaniards of early modern times and as they took shape among indigenous central Mexicans lay in the nature of representation. In a Spanish cabildo each member, although joining the others in dealing with general concerns, represented primarily the interests of his own family; the strongest family complexes of the entire municipal unit, based essentially in the unit's urban core, somehow found representation, with minimal attention to distribution of seats among geographical districts or subjurisdictions. In indigenous cabildos, on the other hand, each member was chosen as a function of belonging to a certain constituent part, so that through rotation and proportional representation each part would get its due.

In simpler municipalities, where the parts (calpolli/tlaxilacalli) were closely interlocked in a traditional, well-defined scheme, subunit representation functioned so automatically that specific connections between cabildo member and subunit hardly ever get mentioned. It is in a situation where the actors are larger, weightier, and more independent that the process is more likely to become visible, especially in the Tlaxcalan cabildo minutes, which give us a documentary dimension unmatched for any other indigenous corporation of any size. The first organization of the Tlaxcalan municipality, apparently conceived by the Spaniards in unawareness of the complexity of the entity, led to internal strife, followed by a definitive reorganization in 1545. As Gibson has shown, the result was a cabildo chosen rigidly on the basis of equal representation of the four constituent altepetl. Each contributed one alcalde, three regidores, and a tlatoani sitting as perpetual regidor, while the governorship rotated among the four altepetl in an eight-year cycle.

Close examination of the Tlaxcalan cabildo minutes reveals how far this principle went, affecting every known sphere of the municipal government's activity. An elaborate scheme was devised to have notaries rotate equally by altepetl, with two always present at sessions (though in fact two of the corps were so much more expert than the others that they did most of the writing). The city majordomos (treasurer/stewards) at first rotated by twos among the four altepetl, then it was found necessary to have four majordomos, one from each, but this proving unwieldy, the earlier scheme returned. Each altepetl took its turn providing tribute labor to the City of Tlaxcala, with cabildo members from that particular altepetl providing supervision. Deputies supervising the market rotated by altepetl. A delegation sent to Spain in 1562 consisted of four members, one from each altepetl. A single chest contained Tlaxcala's city treasury, but inside that chest were four separately managed funds into which all payments were made and from which all disbursements came. Although fully unambiguous evidence is lacking, apparently the officials at the clearing house for city tribute (*tequicalco*) and at the inns the city ran were also appointed proportionately or in rotation, and where applicable they performed duties relevant to their home altepetl. And needless to say, provincial peace officers named by the cabildo operated in their own home regions. Indeed, officials at all levels were doubtless chosen not merely from a certain altepetl but from a specific subentity which would figure in a scheme of rotation or proportional representation in that framework in turn. Unfortunately (but typically) the Tlaxcalan records hardly descend to this level. The subentities which are most likely to have been relevant to the choice of officials are *teccalli* (lordly houses), *tequitl* (tax-paying jurisdictions into which each altepetl was divided), and a large number of named settlements within each tequitl. At present these entities and their relationship to each other are little understood, and the municipal records tell practically nothing about the cabildo members' more specific bases.

Tulancingo, my secondary example, had been a double altepetl in preconquest times, containing two named parts or halves, each with its own supreme dynastic tlatoani. Tlatocan in the south hailed back to conquering and immigrating Nahuas, Tlaixpan in the north to the Otomi,[6] though by postconquest times both parts appear to be dominated by Nahuatl speakers. The kingdom of Tulancingo underwent a more radical division than Tlaxcala. Although the area remained a single jurisdiction under one Spanish corregidor, based in the settlement called Tulancingo which served as capital for the entire region and contained a Franciscan church shared by the two parts, each part became a separate encomienda, and above all each acquired its own separate governor and cabildo. Here, then, the principle of representation of constituent parts is carried to the extreme of creating two entirely separate governing bodies. The only hint in the formal structure that the two might in some sense belong together is the apparent existence in each of a single alcalde rather than a cabildo's normal complement of two.

About the constituent parts of the two halves and their manner of representation, as little is known as in the case of the inner workings of the four
Tlaxcalan altepetl. From miscellaneous partial glimpses of the membership
of the two cabildos (see Tables 2 and 3), I surmise that each had four
regidores, who probably represented an equal number of subentities. By the
late seventeenth century the monastery of Tulancingo had seven dependent
visita churches, three belonging to Tlatocan and four to Tlaixpan (possibly
Tulancingo proper represented a fourth subentity of Tlatocan).[7] Some
unlabeled papers from the Tlaixpan half, dated 1567 to 1571 and apparently
constituting records of extraordinary tax levies and expenditures for miscellaneous purposes, speak of separate collection made by the officials in
four calpolli which seem to be the constituent parts of Tlaixpan.[8] The
number of collectors named, however, does not correspond exactly to the
number of parts (see Table 1); in only one year are there the expected four;
one year there are three, one year six, and two years five. Nevertheless, my
impression is that the normal complement was one collector for each
calpolli plus a general coordinator or supervisor (Pedro Colhuateuctli).

In Tlaxcala, where four entirely parallel, distinct, and complete entities
were brought within a single institutional framework, unity was achieved
only through a kaleidoscopic turn-taking and sharing; in any one function at
any one time, in truth only one of the four parts was generally at work.
This manner of operation satisfied each of the four constituents and made it
possible to get something done because officials were always dealing with
people from their own unit, who would obey them and identify with them,
and they were primarily concerned with carrying on that unit's affairs. The
main problem was coordination of the four parts. Over the twenty years of
the mid-sixteenth century which are closely covered by the cabildo records,
council members again and again expressed concern over how to combine
unified management with operation by fours. With the majordomos, with
collection of the maize tax, with supervision of rotary labor on city
projects, the same pattern is observed; fluctuation between fewer officials, in
the name of unity, and more, in the name of satisfying the four parts and
making things work. No definitive solution emerged; rather one sees a periodic return from one pole to its opposite. Nevertheless, the complex unit
held together into the seventeenth century and beyond. Eventually many
smaller settlements all across Tlaxcala's territory gained a great deal of
autonomy, but the municipal corporation never split at the center.[9]

Having been decentralized into its two main constituents, Tulancingo
would seem to have found a permanent solution to Tlaxcala's dilemma, but

Table 1.

Tribute collectors (tlapachoani) *in the Tlaixpan half of Tulancingo, 1567-71*

1567	1570
Pedro Colhuateuctli	Pedro Colhuateuctli
Andrés Tlapaltecatl	Juan Tlacochteuctli
Pedro Xochicalcatl teuctli	Andrés Huecamecatl teuctli
Andrés Huecamecatl teuctli	Baltasar Tlapaltecatl teuctli
Juan de la Cruz	
Juan Tezcacoacatl teuctli	1571
	Pedro Xochicalcatl teuctli
1568	Pedro Colhuateuctli
Pedro Colhuateuctli	Andrés Huecamecatl teuctli
Andrés Huecamecatl teuctli	Martín Macuexhua
Juan Tlacochteuctli	Martín Coçotecatl

1569
Pedro Colhuateuctli
Juan de la Cruz
Andrés Huecamecatl teuctli
Pedro Xochicalcatl teuctli
Baltasar Tlapaltecatl teuctli

Source: Tulancingo collection, Folder 1. The names are in their original order. Spanish is written according to modern conventions and Nahuatl according to the conventions of Horacio Carochi (with omission of diacritics).

not so. The nobles of the two halves were probably closely intertwined through marriage, descent, and economic interests. Both governors maintained residences in Tulancingo proper, and so, in all likelihood, did many of the other members of both cabildos. In the monastery atrium, on Sundays after mass, one could find the two governors surrounded by a large number of present, former, and future cabildo members, not noticeably segregated according to the two halves, to judge from the Spanish-made list of those present on one such occasion that has come down to us. Although each cabildo paid tribute to a different encomendero and dealt separately with the corregidor, there were still things they needed to do together, and such common action could run into serious difficulties.

In 1582 the Franciscan monastery church needed a bell, and a bellmaker was in town. Tlatocan and Tlaixpan agreed to share the cost equally, but the delegation going to borrow 100 pesos from a local Spanish resident and minor corregimiento official consisted only of the governor, alcalde, and regidores of Tlatocan. The Tlatocan governor then took the money to the monastery and in the presence of the father guardian paid it to the bellmaker. In due time Tlatocan repaid its share, 50 pesos, but Tlaixpan did not. After two and a half years the Spaniard sued not Tlaixpan but Tlatocan for the remaining 50 pesos, and the alcalde mayor jailed several Tlatocan officials for the debt. The latter naturally asked that the Tlaixpan people acknowledge responsibility, which they immediately did, but instead of releasing the Tlatocan cabildo members already in jail, the alcalde mayor imprisoned some Tlaixpan officials in addition. They remained in jail as the alcalde mayor tried unsuccessfully to auction off a house in town belonging to Tlaixpan to cover the debt. How the issue was resolved remains unknown.

Similar problems may have arisen with the joint municipal sheepraising operation, often leased out to Spanish entrepreneurs. Aside from the lack of coordination on the Indian side, a persistent problem was Spanish failure to recognize the existence of two entities in the same town. Clerks speak of one or the other of the governors simply as "the governor of Tulancingo." Surely the alcalde mayor grasped the dual organization, to which after all Spanish officials must have assented, if they did not indeed foment it. In keeping Tlatocan leaders in jail even after Tlaixpan responsibility was established, the alcalde mayor may have been making Tlatocan as the senior entity ultimately responsible,[10] or he may have felt that despite the formal division the two halves were really one and must answer together. At any rate, by mid-seventeenth century (and probably before) the Tulancingo municipal corporation had been reorganized as a single set of officials with one governor, though the rest seem still to have been divided between Tlatocan and Tlaixpan in the expected way.

Order of rotation and preference. We have already observed the importance of rotation among constituents in altepetl structure. Rotation cannot proceed smoothly without a fixed order; such an order was therefore the most basic part of what one might call the specific constitution of an altepetl in either preconquest or postconquest times. For Tlaxcala, the historical writings of the sixteenth and seventeenth centuries often use an order based on the supposed chronological sequence of foundation of the four altepetl: Tepeticpac, Ocotelolco, Tiçatla, and Quiahuiztlan. In the Tlaxcalan cabildo records this sequence is in a sense confirmed; ongoing rotations operate as follows:

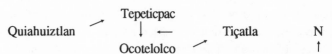

Whenever something begins anew, however, one starts with Ocotelolco, which by mid-sixteenth century seems to have been the strongest of the four altepetl, with Tepeticpac weakest. The simple device of beginning with number two, leaving year-round rotations untouched, accomplished a major adjustment in matters of precedence. In the cabildo minutes, lists of cabildo members or other officials almost always begin with Ocotelolco and end with Tepeticpac.

The Tulancingo papers deliver no particulars on rotation order. It is to the Nahua historian Chimalpahin and his home region of Chalco that we must look for well depicted ranking systems. Chimalpahin's constant concern with who is first, second, or third underlines the importance of sequence in his view of political structure. Primarily referring to the preconquest period, he establishes a consistent order for the four parts making up greater Chalco (each of the four itself a composite altepetl) and for the subkingdoms of one of the parts, Amaquemecan (Amecameca). In both cases, as originally in Tlaxcala, the sequence of foundation dictates the order, though again as in Tlaxcala, certain posterior adjustments took place.[11] Despite the importance of chronological sequence, however, the possible relevance of the four cardinal directions to ordering schemes cannot be dismissed. The four parts of Chalco and Tlaxcala have the same relative orientation, and both orders originally began in the north (though from that point on they vary). It now also appears that a fixed order of rotation characterizes the internal parts of Mexico Tenochtitlan.[12]

The role of tlatoque. The Tlaxcalan cabildo minutes confirm what was already known: in the post-1545 scheme, the tlatoque or dynastic rulers of the four constituent altepetl sat on the cabildo as permanent regidores but were excluded from the governorship or any other office. The time of more open tlatoani dominance had been the early, poorly documented period of the 1520's and 30's. After 1547, when complete records begin, the tlatoque were in fact rigorously restricted to their prescribed positions as perpetual regidores (except that one of them once held office as annually elected regidor before becoming the Quiahuiztlan tlatoani, which after all does not represent a violation). A more covert dominance may have persisted for some time; the tlatoque are once referred to obliquely as the wealthiest of the Tlaxcalans, while the four tlatoque plus the governor held the keys to the municipal treasure chests, and the same group, rather than the entire cabildo, made the decision to defy the corregidor's wishes on a matter of tribute collection. The governor, however, seems to have been rising in power and protocol above the tlatoque, and the body of governor, alcaldes, and tlatoque in some ways acted as a unit with formal precedence over the regidores. The overall impression is one of the tlatoque gradually merging into an upper group of noble cabildo members from whom they were hardly distinguishable. Yet the formal distinction (and restriction) continued to obtain.

That Tlaxcala had four high tlatoque rather than one doubtless served to shorten the long transitional period typical of altepetl with a single clearly supreme tlatoani, in which the dynastic ruler would also serve as governor, in many cases for a lifetime. Tulancingo had two tlatoque, but the existence of two corporations with separate governorships created a situation potentially favorable to continued tlatoani dominance. In fact, a document published by Pedro Carrasco shows very much the picture one would expect.[13] In 1579 witnesses say that a don Julián de San Francisco, the tlatoani of Tlatocan for over thirty years in the middle part of the century, was "cacique y gobernador," giving the impression that he monopolized the governorship. The same double title is given to don Julián's son don Miguel Alejandrino, who inherited the rulership from his father; don Miguel is in fact found as governor of Tlatocan in 1570, in the first direct documentary attestation of the occupation of Tlatocan's governorship. By 1579 don Miguel has died and his son don Diego Alejandrino, having inherited the rulership and its perquisites, is bidding for official approval of the succession. Don Diego did not, however, immediately become governor; the post changed hands frequently among non-tlatoque in the 1580's (see Table 2). Yet don Diego was not permanently out of the picture. In 1587 he appears as alcalde, and by 1590 he seems to have acceded to the governorship.

For Tlaixpan the situation is even more sketchily documented. From the 1560's into the 1580's several governors held office for short periods. Whether or not any of them was also tlatoani is not known at present, but the fact that a don Juan Maldonado was governor of all Tulancingo as late as 1720 inclines one to suspect that the don Pedro Maldonado who was governor of Tlaixpan in 1570-71 was, if not tlatoani, at least a member of the Tlaixpan dynasty. Apparently a situation was growing up by the late sixteenth century in which, in both halves of Tulancingo, members of the tlatoani family were highly eligible, indeed almost predestined for the governorship, but did not monopolize it. This is indeed the picture quite generally, whereas the situation in Tlaxcala, with no tlatoque-governors, would seem to be exceptional (though it remains to be seen if the same did

Table 2. *Known officers of the Tlatocan cabildo, sixteenth century*

1570

governor	Don Miguel Alejandrino
alcalde	Don Antonio de Padua
regidor	Antonio de Santiago
regidores?	Martín Cortés Tlacochteuctli
	Cristóbal Sánchez

1579

alcalde	Don Cristóbal Sánchez
regidores	Martín de Tapia
	Domingo de Santiago
	Pedro Juárez
	Domingo de Valencia

1582

governor	Don Cristóbal Sánchez
alcalde	Don Martín de Tapia
regidores	Calisto de Santa Ana
	Pedro Bazán
regidores?	Juan de San Francisco
	Martín de Santa Cruz

1585

governor	Don Gabriel Vásquez
alcalde	Don Domingo de Valencia
regidores	Don Bernardino de San Juan
	Antonio Hernández

1587

governor	Don Cristóbal Sánchez
alcalde	Don Diego Alejandrino
regidores	Juan de San Francisco
	Martín de Santiago
	Joaquín Hilario
	Gabriel Vásquez
majordomo	Juan de San Pedro

1590

| governor? | Don Diego Alejandrino |

1600

| alcalde | Don Gabriel Vásquez |
| regidor | Don Juan Lorenzo de San Francisco |

Source: Tulancingo collection; Pedro Carrasco, "Los caciques chichimecas de Tulancingo," *Estudios de Cultura Náhuatl*, 4 (1963), 87. All the office titles appear as loan words in the Nahuatl texts.

not happen in altepetl like Huejotzingo and Xochimilco, where, as in Tlaxcala, multiple tlatoque corresponded to only one cabildo).

Other offices and career patterns. In the Tlaxcalan records, it becomes apparent that there was a career ladder in which certain individuals advanced from regidor to alcalde and finally governor, after which they might return to occupy some of the lower posts. At the same time, other cabildo members never reached higher than regidor. Unlike Spanish cabildos, where regidores in many ways outranked alcaldes, in Tlaxcala the alcalde post was treated as the higher of the two. Frequent repetition in cabildo office kept the total number of officeholders very small. Individuals holding higher posts had more prestigious names; generally speaking, indigenous surnames ranked lowest, saints' names and other religious surnames next up the scale, and Spanish surnames highest, with some but not much distinction being made between plebeian patronymics (Hernández, etc.) and high-sounding last names taken from encomenderos, corregidores, and ecclesiastics. The title "don" was the ultimate symbol of having attained the highest level. Although more highly valued names correspond quite closely with those individuals holding higher office, or who had at least held such office earlier, the system was not rigid, since as a cabildo member gained in experience, influence, and rank, his name would change accordingly. One Tlaxcalan abandoned an indigenous name for a religious surname, then a Spanish one, and finally, at the time of being made governor, he acquired the "don" too.

Tulancingo confirms the wider existence of all these phenomena. As can be seen even in the fragmentary data of Tables 2 and 3, returning to office after a short interval was a common pattern. Few indigenous names are seen on the cabildo, and their possessors are lower-ranking persons not going above regidor and often associated with the sub-cabildo post of majordomo. Individuals may rise from regidor to alcalde to governor. In Tlaixpan, Martín de Valencia (named after a famous Franciscan friar, hence probably an especially high-ranking nobleman) was apparently regidor in 1567, alcalde in 1568 and 1570, possibly regidor again in 1571, again in 1582 (and very likely in office in the intervening unrecorded years as well), by now having acquired the "don," and then governor in 1585. By 1580 it had become the practice that anyone holding the office of governor or alcalde in either cabildo was automatically "don," whereas most regidores remained without the title. The "don" could actually be lost when one went back to being regidor (in Tlatocan see don Gabriel Vásquez, governor in 1585, who becomes plain Gabriel Vásquez as regidor in 1587, and don Gabriel again as alcalde in 1600). The same happened in Tlaxcala too, but rarely. Once the "don" was acquired, it generally stuck regardless of what office one might hold subsequently, as in the just cited case of don Martín de Valencia of Tlaixpan. Within the context of close similarity, Tulancingo does manifest one significant difference: relatively fewer of the name attributes associated with highest rank appear. By the 1570's and 80's, most Tlaxcalan cabildo members bore the "don," and the proportion of surnames in the full Spanish style was much higher than in Tulancingo. The general meaning of the divergence appears to be that Tulancingo was following the same path as Tlaxcala but had probably got a later start, and being more distant from the centers of Mexican life and having a smaller base, was moving more slowly.

Looking at municipal officeholding beneath the level of the cabildo, the Tlaxcalan records provide a considerable amount of data. The cabildo directly appointed a large number of peace officers in the province and in the city of Tlaxcala, as well as tribute supervisors, market constables, and persons in charge of special enterprises, notably the city-run inns for travelers. As mentioned earlier, all seem to have been chosen on the basis of membership in one of the four altepetl and to have acted primarily on behalf of and in relation to their home unit. Incumbents usually held any one post for only one year, but as at the higher level, they might return to office quickly. Individuals tended to circulate among all the positions at this level without much regard to specific expertise; clearly the general managerial and judicial/supervisory aspects took precedence.

In a Spanish municipality, a sharp distinction was made between the cabildo members, who were well connected and presumed noble, and the sub-cabildo employees of the city, who were plebeians with no claim to high status and would never expect to serve on a cabildo at any time in their lives. In Tlaxcala, on the other hand, it appears that even the lower municipal posts were associated with nobility and that all the occupants were nobles or accepted as such. Many were so prominent as to be members of the corps of 220 electors who chose the governor and cabildo. Nor did any absolute barrier stand in the way of lower officials' advancement to the cabildo. Sometimes passing first through the positions of cabildo notary, city majordomo, or provincial lieutenant, which stood highest in rank, over the years persons who had occupied the lower posts repeatedly became cabildo members. A couple got as far as alcalde. Despite all this, a distinction existed between the cabildo members and the others. Only a small

Table 3. *Known officers of the Tlaixpan cabildo, sixteenth century*

	1567	
governor?		Don Pedro de San Cristóbal
regidor?		Martín de Valencia
majordomo		Pedro Mexicatl
	1568	
governor?		Don Pedro de San Cristóbal
alcalde		Martín de Valencia
majordomo		Luis de León
	1569	
alcalde		Francisco de San Juan
regidor		Pedro Jiménez Tepanecatl teuctli
majordomo		Pedro Huecamecatl
	1570	
governor		Don Pedro Maldonado
alcalde		Martín de Valencia
regidores?		Martín de Santiago
		Francisco de San Juan
majordomo		Pedro Tlacochcalcatl
	1571	
governor		Don Pedro Maldonado
alcalde		Don Pedro de San Cristóbal
regidor		Francisco de San Juan
regidor?		Martín de Valencia
majordomo		Pedro Tlacochcalcatl
	1582	
governor		Don Francisco de San Juan
alcalde		Don Bernardo de San Juan[a]
regidores		Don Martín de Valencia
		Martín de Santa Cruz
		Martín de Santiago
majordomo		Pedro Jiménez
	1585	
governor		Don Martín de Valencia
alcalde		Don Andrés de Soto

[a]Doubtless not the same person as the regidor of Tlatocan in 1585.
Source: Tulancingo collection.

proportion of the lower officials ever rose to cabildo membership. Their names were of the less prestigious sort, with mainly indigenous surnames, some saints' names, and no "don" at all. Cabildo members with the highest lineage or best education, those who frequently served as alcalde and governor, had rarely done duty in lower posts.

For Tulancingo, the information on sub-cabildo posts is presently very sparse, and it appears unlikely that the staff of lower municipal officials with direct connections to the cabildo was as elaborate as in Tlaxcala (which was perhaps New Spain's most highly developed indigenous municipal corporation), but some similarities do emerge. As in Tlaxcala, so in Tulancingo the post of majordomo was just at the edge of cabildo membership. Some majordomos have indigenous surnames, some religious, and some fully Spanish; one of them, Pedro Jiménez (Tepanecatl teuctli), had previously served as regidor. For the most part they hold office for only one year at a time, as in Tlaxcala.

All the rest of the data on lower officials come from the fragmentary records of extraordinary collections and expenses of Tlaixpan which form the basis of Table 1. The documents show some officials collecting tribute items from the populace and making disbursements of both items and money, with the permission of the majordomo, so we are justified in considering these persons to be collectors and managers of tribute. They refer to themselves once as *tlapachoani*, "governors," although the term seems to have had the specific sense, according to the dictionary of fray Andrés de Molina, of manager of someone's property and family. In an accompanying document the term *tequitlayacanque*, literally "tribute leaders or guides," is found, apparently with reference to the same group. No Spanish word for them appears (nor does it for their approximate counterparts in Tlaxcala).

Of the group of ten persons serving in this capacity over five years (1567-71 inclusive), all but one have indigenous surnames, and that one bears a religious name.[14] The indigenous names, however, indicate high status, since the great majority of them end in *teuctli*, "lord." It is indeed apparent that all the surnames are actually high titles, either for traditional altepetl officers or for leaders of subunits. None of the group is known to have risen to the cabildo or even to the majordomo position, but in a sample this small, with an equally small sample of cabildo membership for comparison, one would expect much the same thing in Tlaxcala as well. Two of the ten are present all five years, two more in three of the five years, another in two years, and the remaining five in one year only. This is a higher repetition rate in the same post than typical of sub-cabildo office in

Tlaxcala, but in fact there are relatively few data on rotation among Tlaxcala's tribute officials. The officers appear to vary in number from year to year, but this may be a result of chance appearance in the fragments preserved, or of the inclusion of the names of aides as well as principals. Pedro Colhuateuctli, present every year and named first every time but one, seems to have a special position. As mentioned above, I suspect that he is a superior and that normally there would be four others, one for each of the calpolli which the records mention. The overall situation implied by these documents is entirely compatible with the role and nature of sub-cabildo officeholding in Tlaxcala, except that we have no reason to imagine that officials in Tulancingo were equally numerous.

Miscellaneous parallel phenomena in Tlaxcala and Tulancingo. With both Spanish and preconquest indigenous precedent, Mexican Indian town corporations from the first gave strong support, including financial contributions, to ecclesiastical organizations and observances. The Tlaxcalan cabildo is known to have paid for vestments, ornaments, musical instruments, and other items for church use, as well as providing direct subsidies for the maintenance of the local Franciscan friars. We have already seen the largest example of such activity in Tulancingo, the two cabildos jointly paying for the bell at the monastery church. The Tlaixpan tribute collectors' records also contain yearly disbursements of three or four pesos as the pay of the church singers (*Tullantzinco cuicanime yntlaxtlahuil*); presumably Tlatocan contributed an equal amount (or each cabildo may have supplied half the singers and then paid its own people). Expenses in 1569 to buy nails and pay masons and plasterers (the latter from Tetzcoco) probably had to do with church maintenance.

A great deal of the support muncipal governments gave to ecclesiastical causes was not monetary but consisted in channeling tribute goods and services to church purposes. In Tlaxcala the records make it clear that such was the primary mechanism for organizing religious festivities and carrying out church construction projects. Little specific evidence is forthcoming for Tulancingo, but similar efforts can be deduced from a petition (see Item 6 in the present book) by a group of eleven indigenous painters who had done work in 1570 on church buildings at the behest of the municipal officials (whether of one or of both cabildos is not specified). The painters complain to the alcalde mayor that the officials have withheld their pay, as has often happened before; the town officials, on the other hand, seem to have taken the attitude that what the painters did was simply their duty to the altepetl and not something meriting monetary pay. Tlaxcala had similar problems with artisans; in 1550 the people making an altarpiece in the monastery church wanted their work to be considered as performed in fulfillment of private vows and redounding to the credit of their own subunit, whereas the cabildo and the friars wanted it to be considered tribute duty for the city.

In Tlaxcala, the cabildo engaged in Spanish-style agrarian enterprise, including the ownership of a flock of sheep and the operation of a farm using European implements, animals, and techniques. These properties were managed by Spaniards, with whom the Tlaxcalan cabildo made partnerships (*compañías*), putting up the money for capital investment and either paying the Spaniards set salaries or sharing profits with them. Much the same is found in Tulancingo. By 1570 there were municipal sheep estancias, one for each of the cabildos, although leased to the same Spaniard; 600 pesos was being offered for a new lease. Over time the leasing out of municipal ranches and farms became a popular option for Mexican Indian towns, and Tlaxcala too probably adopted the practice later (evidence in the Tlaxcalan cabildo minutes is from the 1550's). By the 1580's the Tlatocan cabildo was selling maize futures to Spaniards (17 fanegas of *iztac tlaolli* or "white maize" for 25 pesos, 4 reales in 1587), presumably supplies acquired as tribute. In the single documented instance, however, the cabildo did not come through with the promised maize.

Tlaxcala's cabildo members frequently went on missions for which they received a per diem allowance from the city treasury; many of these trips took them to Mexico City to make special pleas to the viceroy, be confirmed in office, or carry on litigation before the Royal Audiencia. The Tlaixpan tribute collectors' records show the same trends; though no sophisticated per diem arrangement is seen, money, food, and other supplies were collected for cabildo members going to Mexico City for confirmation in office or to carry on lawsuits.

*   *   *

In brief, then, significant parallels to the structure and manner of operation of the complex and in some respects unique government of Tlaxcala in the sixteenth century can be seen in the more fragmentary documentation concerning another complex jurisdiction, Tulancingo, at around the same time. It appears that, gaining perspective from various only partially recorded situations in this way, we can make use of the unusual Tlaxcalan documentation to draw broader conclusions, and that more generally we can use the relatively well documented complex municipalities to throw light on processes affecting Indian towns of all sizes and configurations.

3. Views of Corporate Self and History in Some Valley of Mexico Towns, Late Seventeenth and Eighteenth Centuries

Studies of indigenous Mesoamerican culture and society have concentrated heavily on two widely separated points in time: the contact period, or the fifteenth-sixteenth centuries, and our own epoch, the twentieth century. This has been so not only in the less temporally oriented disciplines of anthropology and linguistics, but in certain kinds of historical investigation as well. It is true that students of some aspects of indigenous matters— social, political, and even linguistic—have by now found sources which enable them to trace patterns of continuity as far as the end of the colonial period. But work on indigenous views of the conquest, for example, leaps from texts like Sahagún to twentieth-century folklore. In the general area of materials for the study of indigenous thought and expression—and hence for study of expressed views of self and events—the rich codices of the immediate postconquest epoch have seemed to lead only to a select few individual native historical writers such as Chimalpahin and Tezozomoc in the later sixteenth and early seventeenth centuries, followed by a void until the recent time of collection of tales, dramas, and dances from living informants.

As the investigation of native-language sources of the colonial period proceeds, however, materials begin to come to light which are potentially revealing of indigenous historical thinking at points far into the later centuries. In the present essay I discuss some samples of one genre with this kind of potential: the type of document often referred to as *títulos primordiales,* "primordial titles."

Levels of indigenous awareness

Let it be clear from the outset that I do not present certain documents and their implications as the sole indigenous view, even where they prove consistent internally and across samples. Within a corporate entity existing in a sedentary, differentiated society, there will always be more than one view of that entity's nature and its relation to the overall social environment. Some members of the corporation will have the specific function of dealing with external relations; as a result, they will have a quite broad, realistic conception of the outside world, as well as of their own corporation's perhaps minor role in it. For others, often the majority, the corporation tends to loom larger. Among them, a more nearly hermetic, internally centered tradition may prevail and perpetuate itself.

In central Mexican Indian towns of the middle and later colonial period, there existed an upper group who shared the Nahuatl language and ethnicity of the rest of the local population, but stood out from it in various ways. Heirs of the preconquest nobility, they had more properties and more dependents than the average; they dominated the semiautonomous town governments, they married across town boundaries in quasi-dynastic matches, creating regional familial networks which transcended the individual towns; many of them carried on enterprises not unlike those of the Spaniards and sold their products in the region's broader Spanish economy; some began to intermarry with Hispanics, who were growing in number in the main Indian towns. After about 1700 it is increasingly common to find that Indians of the upper level are described as fluent in Spanish. People like these had a very adequate grasp of the overall configuration of Spanish colonial society and government. Their own personal and official dealings took them frequently to their subprovincial capital, seat of the Spanish alcalde mayor, and on occasion to Mexico City itself. The many Nahuatl documents left by this group bespeak a full comprehension of Spanish legal and religious concepts and procedures, as well as an easy familiarity with the workings of the European calendar.

Although these members of the higher stratum may not have been quite as conversant with the details of Spanish royal succession as was their predecessor, the previously mentioned Amecameca historian Chimalpahin,[1] they must have understood and even, to a large extent, have shared general Spanish notions of New Spain's organization and historical process, especially in their own larger subregion and during times close to their own period, on a year-to-year, decade-to-decade basis. Since they were the dominant group, one can assert that central Mexican Indian communities as a whole had such an understanding. In fact, a relatively sophisticated grasp of supramunicipality structures and procedures may have been common at the lower levels, too, since precisely the poorest and most marginal community members spent much of their time working short stints in haciendas and other Spanish enterprises outside community borders; the same people also quite frequently changed residence from one community to another.

Nevertheless, the cross-regional view of things was not the prevalent one among the general populace of central Mexican Indian towns. From various indications it appears that the dominant group-internal lore, disseminated by the elders and only occasionally written down, took the local town or provincial unit as an autonomous, autochthonous people radically separate from all that surrounded them. Certain constituents of Spanish and Christian culture were deeply integrated into this local lore, but there was little concern with or expertise about any outside elements, be they indigenous or European, except as they directly affected the local entity. In this perspective the king and the viceroy were much the same thing; except for the supposed dates of grants or surveys of local territory, the march of Spanish calendrical years passed unnoticed.

It is probably too simple to identify the dichotomy of overall views with two separate sets of people inside the Indian community. More likely, the upper group also shared in the more localized tradition but understood that it was not an appropriate mode for conducting legal business or something to be brought before the eyes of Spanish officials. The distinction would be, then, one of levels within the individual, or of different idioms for different purposes, rather than of discrete groups with divergent beliefs. A corporation-centered view, which had large components of legend, stereotype, and ignorance of the outside, thus seems to have maintained itself as a group phenomenon, despite the fact that many individual corporation members had conflicting information or thought differently part of the time.

The written sources

The best means presently available of obtaining access to this corporate consciousness in its late colonial form are some documents composed in Nahuatl inside the communities by people who were in some fashion literate, although not fully trained as notaries, and who wrote outside the usual Spanish-influenced documentary genres of will, sale, grant, petition, or investigation. The latter sort of documents, written by experts, make up the bulk of the postconquest Nahuatl written legacy. There is also much diverse court testimony from the lips of uninstructed Indians, but most of it is in Spanish, having passed through the filter of an interpreter; even where the testimony is in Nahuatl, court procedures demanded direct responses to prepared questions, restricting spontaneous expansiveness.

Several kinds of nonprofessional Nahuatl writing have so far come to my attention. Annals kept on a more or less private basis constitute one such genre (although the authors were usually well educated and shared the broader upper-level perspectives). Also relevant are legal documents from minor or peripheral centers, where even the notaries were somewhat outside the Spanish and Nahuatl mainstream. Though based on Spanish genres, their documents varied widely from Spanish equivalents, partaking of local popular lore and modes of expression. Both types of writing bear on historical consciousness, but the genre most squarely confronting this issue is that already referred to as "primordial titles"—an appellation apparently not given to such documents until a very late time, possibly the nineteenth century.

It is understandable that not much advantage has been taken of the primordial titles until now. Even for those of us who rejoice in the rich local peculiarities of Nahuatl documentation, the orthography of the Nahuatl originals of the titles tends to appear abominable, inept, and aberrant, a cause for puzzlement and hilarity. The language itself, once the intention of the orthography has been recognized, is often extremely obscure, whether one approaches it from "classical" or from "colonial" Nahuatl, that is, from the rarified language of the high-cultural codices with a preconquest flavor or from the quotidian language of mundane postconquest documentation. Even the generally expert court translators had trouble with these texts, producing Spanish versions which sometimes yield no surface meaning and are frequently in grave error even when they do make sense.

Nor are these the only deterrents. The "titles" appear to deal with events of the conquest and early postconquest years; only on fairly close examination does one see that the examples which have come down to us were uniformly set on paper in the later colonial period. Though there must have been earlier oral versions, and doubtless at least some written ones too, I know of no text of this type which in its present form dates from earlier than the latter seventeenth century. This fact leads us to another reason why primordial titles have not received much attention. As reports of certain events or justification of certain territorial claims, they are (all known to me, in any case) patently inaccurate, poorly informed, false, and even in some sense deliberately falsified, often in the most transparent fashion. (For instance, in the Tetelco title which I will discuss later, a Franciscan friar was imagined to have been present at the original occasion as a witness; not knowing his name, the writer made a signature at the end, complete with rubrics, reading *deopixqui fratzicano*, "Franciscan friar.") Spanish officials to whom such documents were presented at the time usually labeled them false or ignored them entirely.

What is, then, the exact nature of these documents called titles? The notion of "title" in the colonial Spanish world went beyond the concept of a simple deed. Full title—whether to land, territory, or jurisdiction—involved not only an original grant or sale, but also an investigation on the spot to consult third parties and see if the situation was as described, and finally formal acts of giving and taking possession. Only then did the grant or sale, until that point merely virtual or hypothetical, enter into force. A Spanish notary would keep a running record of the whole proceeding, repeatedly signed by officials and witnesses; this record, appended to the original grant, order, or the like, constituted the title.

During the first postconquest generation, the viceregal government sent representatives into the countryside to establish the precise territories of the various Indian towns. This involved investigations like those just described and included stepping out the boundaries, setting markers, obtaining the acquiescence of people of neighboring towns, and so on. Rarely was the result fully unambiguous in a juridical sense, but the proceedings did give the community involved some legal basis for the possession of its territory. If the "primordial titles" were what many of them purport to be, they would be either the original record made by the notary present or an authorized contemporary copy. But they are not. Such originals exist in the central archives in Mexico City and probably also in the provincial centers where local administrators had their headquarters; they look like other Spanish acts of possession and bear little resemblance to our primordial titles. Apparently the originals did not stay in the towns concerned; if they did, they were lost (they may have been neglected because at that early time hardly anyone knew enough Spanish to understand them). It might seem that the records could have been given a competent translation into Nahuatl. The capability existed. But in colonial Mexico translation was mainly a one-way street; with the exception of standard religious texts and a few proclamations and ordinances, the general direction was out of indigenous languages into Spanish in order to support indigenous claims before Spanish authority. The ultimately original form of the indigenous "titles" would appear to have been not the Spanish record but a parallel record, whether in oral or written form, made by the Nahuatl speakers as interested observers of the proceedings. This version would never have had any legal standing with the Spaniards. On the other hand, the independent redaction allowed the Indians to make note of things of importance to them which Spaniards would have omitted.

As time went on, through the sixteenth century and on into the early seventeenth, other occasions presented themselves on which Spanish officials would carry out investigations of people and land, in one way or another confirming local rights. Many towns at some point underwent "congregation," or rationalization and concentration. Investigations took place periodically to review the tributary population and local resources, and others occurred at the instance of aggrieved parties. The "primordial titles" frequently add accounts of some of these subsequent occasions to the report of the original survey, or at least give a date for them. These sections seem to be in the nature of parenthetical remarks, but often the effect is to make it nearly impossible to say which occasion is being discussed (actually, we cannot presume that the later rewriters of the titles imagined different occasions located sequentially on a time continuum).

At the core of a "primordial title," then, is an account of an early local border survey, which is often overlaid with mention of subsequent surveys. The document has been prepared by local figures primarily for a local audience and has been redrafted as often as felt necessary. The style is declamatory, the tone that of advice by elders to present and future generations; much general historical material is often given, including versions of the first foundation of the town, the coming of the Spaniards, and the establishment of Christianity. Quite a few "titles" of this type are known to exist for towns widely scattered through Mesoamerica, and a great many other examples doubtless await discovery in the archives or in their places of origin. As noted by Charles Gibson, who has already provided a succinct description of the genre, a close approximation of the entire content of the documents appears to this day in speeches given in public meetings in certain indigenous communities,[2] so that the "title" is widely diffused temporally as well as spatially.

The specific corpus under examination here consists of four texts from the Chalco region, in the southeastern arm of the Valley of Mexico. All four documents are presently preserved in the section Tierras of the Archivo General de la Nación in Mexico City. It would be possible to choose examples with a wider geographical spread, but taking several from the same subarea allows us to see some direct connections and cross-references and thus to get some sense of the degree of diffusion or common tradition involved.

The items are as follows:

1. The first document is from San Nicolás Tetelco (also called Teteltzingo), in the far northwest of the Chalco region, subject to Mixquic yet a town in its own right, with several subdivisions. The Nahuatl text is in Tierras 1671, exp. 10, ff. 13-15, written on six very small pages made from a piece of already partially used paper, accompanied by a large map of Mixquic and Tetelco with their dependencies; the written place names and remarks seem to be in the same hand as the document. The content relates to a Tetelco border survey, or perhaps two, dated variously at 1534, 1536, 1539, and 1556. There is no definite indication of the date of composition, except that the hand appears later than the sixteenth century. The document was presented in litigation which began in the year 1699; it was said to have been recently "found."

2. The second item is a set of documents from San Antonio Zoyatzingo (just south of Amecameca), which was subject to Tenango Tepopula despite being a fullfledged *altepetl* or city. Tierras 1665, exp. 5, ff. 166r-182v, contains a series of substantial, carefully written Nahuatl texts, partially duplicating each other, telling of Zoyatzingo border surveys; one section purports to be a grant and act of possession. The largest text contains a full complement of added historical material, including conversations taking place among local leaders at the time of the Spanish foundation of the town. Elements of the language used, especially some Spanish loan verbs, indicate a time of composition not earlier than the second half of the seventeenth century; the documents were presented in litigation in 1699. A schematic picture-map of Zoyatzingo at the time of acknowledgment of its rights shows the territory, the church in the center, and declaiming figures at the four corners. Another diagram (called a *maban*, or "map") portrays a great hand enclosing the church of Zoyatzingo in its palm. Also included is a set of portraits of early leaders with preconquest accoutrements, apparently involved in territorial defense.

3. The third document is from San Miguel Atlauhtla (southeast of Amecameca), which not only was an altepetl but apparently had its own "governor" at times, even though it was in some sense subject to Amecameca. Tierras 2674, exp. 1, consists entirely of the ten-page Nahuatl títulos primordiales of Atlauhtla, with a nineteenth-century Spanish translation. As with the Zoyatzingo documents, there is much historical matter in addition to reports on border surveys and investigations variously dated, from 1521 forward. The document is introduced by a drawing in which an early ruler of Atlauhtla and the various barrio chiefs—dressed in European style and sporting Renaissance hats, haircuts, and beards—kneel before Charles V. The language of the text, especially the inclusion of the Spanish particle *como*, tends to indicate a later redaction date than for the other samples; apparently the people of Atlauhtla presented the document to the authorities in Mexico City as late as the mid-nineteenth century (the translation is dated 1861), though there can be little doubt that it was written down before Mexican independence.

4. The fourth document is from Santiago Sula, on the south side of the road from Chalco to Tlalmanalco and by the latter eighteenth century considered a *formal y rigoroso pueblo*, though without a governor and in some way subject to Tlalmanalco. This is the only one of the four documents not preserved in Nahuatl. All that is left is a Spanish version made by the translator of the Royal Audiencia around 1700-1703, if one judges by the dates of the seals on the paper; for some reason this version

went back to the people of Sula, who presented it again in 1778, having apparently in the meantime lost the Nahuatl original. The loss must be judged a great one, for the Sula document has by far the richest historical-legendary overlay of all the samples considered here, causing one almost to lose sight of the border measurement aspect. Still, the translator has actually reproduced the original Nahuatl of several special terms, and at times has stayed so close to the phrasing of the original that, on the basis of parallel sections in other Nahuatl documents, we could reconstruct some passages almost word for word.

I will now proceed to a more detailed thematic discussion of the kinds of material contained in these four samples. My purpose is twofold, to establish the characteristics of the genre as well as to explore the historical consciousness of people such as those who composed the documents.

Retention of preconquest elements

The first question that comes to mind concerns the extent and nature of preconquest elements preserved in the texts. The spread is great, ranging from the lack of anything overtly pre-Columbian in the small Tetelco title to the magical transformation of the ruler into a serpent in the Sula papers. Yet certain facets of the documents repeat themselves enough to indicate trends.

Memory of local personages and events. All four titles have as their central personages figures thought to have presided over the local entity during the generation immediately following the conquest. These first-generation notables, or ones like them, must in fact have taken a prominent part in the various ceremonies related to the establishment of Spanish rule and religion in the Indian towns. On close inspection, however, the conquest-period leaders are sometimes seen to incorporate autochthonous figures, originators and symbols of the ethnic group. And whereas the ostensible emphasis is on relations between the local town and the outside, especially the Spanish government, the local figures sometimes embody internal subdivisions such as moiety-like halves, or relate to important preconquest historical events such as invasions.

Among our samples, those from Tetelco and Atlauhtla do not go beyond simply naming the current ruler and some other notables. A trace of the autochthonous does appear in the latter document, where it is said that the story is being told by Miguel Quauhcapoltecatl and Juana Acachiquiuhtecatl, the grandfather and grandmother of the local citizens. The Zoyatzingo and Sula documents, on the other hand, are well populated with ethnic representatives.

In the case of Zoyatzingo, there are three figures of major proportions: Huehue Xohueyacatzin, (Josef Yaotepotzo) Quauhcececuitzin, and Juan Ahuacatzin. After presentation of the basic postconquest border survey, the principal document becomes a dialogue among these three leaders. Quauhcececuitzin, an outsider, requests land of Xohueyacatzin; Ahuacatzin variously objects, but the objections are surmounted. Clearly such transactions could not have been a postlude to a Spanish land investigation. The reference must be, in part at least, to indigenous interrelationships that date back to preconquest times.

Who are the three figures? Huehue Xohueyacatzin (Old Long-foot) not only is generally referred to without a Christian name, but shares the name of a mountain which is said in these texts to be a prominent feature of the Zoyatzingo area. In an introductory passage, Xohueyacatzin is said to have been involved in winning Zoyatzingo's territory for later generations. He is surely, then, the primary symbol of Zoyatzingo as a people and place from its first inception.

As to Juan Ahuacatzin (Avocado), he appears rather late and secondarily in the dialogue; yet he has the character of a local person. Apparently he is the representative of the lower moiety; the function of this figure in legend is often to express qualifications and minority opinions, as is also exemplified in the Sula document. From colonial times to the present day the town in question has been known as Zoyatzingo. However, while some of the four sections of the town's titles refer to it as Zoyatzingo, Soyatzinco, etc. (apparently for standard Çoyatzinco, or "place of the palms, diminutive"), others call it Sihuatzinco (Cihuatzinco, or "place of the woman, dim."), and in yet other sections it is called Soyasihuatzinco and Sihuasoyatzinco (i.e., a combination of the two).[3] One section, purporting to report on the situation at the time of a congregation of 1532, 1555, or 1559, pictures two individuals in a form of preconquest dress, though with postconquest names. Here don Juan Ahuacatzin represents Cihuatzinco, whereas a don Felipe, who has a surname hard to decipher and who is holding a device which might be a palm frond, represents Zoyatzingo. Apparently, for the upper moiety (Zoyatzingo), legend has bypassed the ruler of the postconquest generation and has fastened directly on the mythic autochthonous figure, while the lower moiety (Cihuatzinco) is content to use the historical figure as representative.

Our third person may well be two. The dialogue presents him first as Josef Yaotepotzo Quauhcececuitzin, and this form is once repeated; mainly, however, he appears simply as Quauhcececuitzin (Shivering Eagle). In the diagrammatic representation of Zoyatzingo at the time of acquiring its postconquest rights, Josef Yaotepotzo stands in one corner and Quauh-cececuitzin in another. A person of the latter name was an actual historical figure of the Chalco region. Indeed, he was a major ruler, and Chimal-pahin's writings repeatedly mention him as king of Panoayan, one of the five kingdoms of Amecameca, in the late preconquest years. He lived to meet Cortés but died not long after and may never have been baptized, since Chimalpahin gives no Christian name for him. The Quauhcececuitzin of the Zoyatzingo account is said to be from Atzaqualco, in the same part of the region as the domain of the famous king (if, that is, present-day Panohuayan can be associated with the kingdom), so we may suspect that the two are the same. Josef Yaotepotzo, on the other hand, may have been a separate person, more local and less renowned.

The dialogue of the Zoyatzingo titles runs approximately as follows: Old Xohueyacatzin of Zoyatzingo makes friends with Quauhcececuitzin, who then comes to him as a supplicant. He offers him some boys and girls to serve him and asks him for a bit of land in reward for his unspecified services, land where he and his followers can settle, rest from their exertions, and be buried, land which they can leave to their descendants. Xohueyacatzin responds enthusiastically, exhorts Quauhcececuitzin to stay, and hastens to begin preparations for distributing plots to Quauhcece-cuitzin's people. At this point Ahuacatzin intervenes, not once but twice. His first objections are set in the framework of the Spanish organization of the town. Ahuacatzin says that the distribution must not be formless and irregular; there must be four town subdivisions (*tlaxilacalli*), and each must have its constables (*merinos*). Ahuacatzin's second set of objections are even easier to place in a preconquest context. He warns that Quauh-cececuitzin and his successors must never claim that they got their land by conquest. In both cases Ahuacatzin's advice is heeded, though Quauh-cececuitzin still gets the land. Further comments in the text assert that Quauhcececuitzin came to Zoyatzingo for no special purpose, merely being tired after much moving about and founding of towns. Rumors about conquest, it is maintained, are not true. Xohueyacatzin had full rights to the territory, and the people of Zoyatzingo had nothing to fear; Quauhce-cecuitzin only helped out (presumably in the defense of the land). One passage seems to imply that Quauhcececuitzin was returning to his home to finish out his life.

It is impossible to know for sure what facts occasioned this account. One can speculate, however, that in late preconquest times Zoyatzingo may have been forced into a rather disadvantageous confederacy with more pow-erful outsiders, giving up some part of its territory to them. From that moment forward, the Zoyatzingo people probably told a version of the arrangement which made them the dominant partners and preserved their full autonomy. This body of material then became amalgamated with postconquest happenings, and we cannot know to what extent the late colonial writers were conscious of the preconquest dimension. Clearly, though, they were still smarting under the implication that any other indigenous group had ever conquered them.

In the Sula document the protagonists are much more openly and unambiguously autochthonous, yet they too are presented as being alive in the early postconquest period and receiving possession from the Spanish authorities. The figures are two brothers, the older one Martín Molcatzin (Sauce-bowl) and the younger Martín Huitzcol (Bent-thorn). It is tempting to think of them as a timeless, entirely mythic pair, who are assigned the same Christian name in order to show their underlying unity (and perhaps also because it was rather hard for the late writers to imagine anyone who was entirely without a Christian name). Yet the Zoyatzingo titles give added support to their partial historicity, twice mentioning a border shared with "Martín de Molcax of Sula." Thus we must conclude that one, if not both, of the Martíns actually flourished in Sula in the conquest generation. Nevertheless, the two also deal with a threat from the Mexica before the establishment of Tenochtitlan. As the text says, "They came from nowhere else, they are from here and were the first dwellers of this town" (despite which their parents and grandparents were also from Sula). Martín Molcatzin bears the title of Çolteuctli, or "Quail-lord"; the original Nahuatl of "Sula" is "Çollan," or "place of the quail."

The tale of the encounter with the Mexica, inserted between the acts of possession and the full border recital, is the Sula document's outstanding feature and the most remarkable piece of later colonial legend I have yet seen. I present here a version of the principal passages, complete with their liberal admixture of postconquest elements:

> Here will be seen and declared how the Mexica, before they settled the site of Mexico City, came to Sula, and they did not permit these Tenochca or Mexica, who are called Tenochtitlan people, to settle. They were walking along and came to Sula, and [the Sula people] came out to meet them, and they could not halt there. The Mexica came along the highway with trumpet and banner, and the people of Sula came there to meet them so that they would not take away their rule; those of Sula came to the defense of their town.

Then one called Aza Persia came shouting, saying, "My lords, you here of Sula, let us make a halt here, for we are very tired and have come walking a very long way."

And then Martín Molcatzin, the Çolteuctli, answered and said, and they said to Martín Huitzcol (sic), "I and all those who are here are the dwellers of this town, and so you can go ahead, for you cannot halt here."

These two Martíns who are named here are two brothers, one called Martín Molcatzin and the other Martín Huitzcol, and they said, "Lady Ana García, we are from here and we are sons of the ancients; we were born in this valley and our grandfathers and grandmothers are from here; they came from nowhere else, and they are those of the ancient time (for their ancestors were pagans). And you, where do you come from? Perhaps you have been exiled from somewhere. Go on with you, we have our questionnaires. Just go ahead and take the highway which begins at our border...[here a short recital of borders and measurements]...And know and understand that it is not far to where you are to go; you come from a lake, and now you are very close to another lake there ahead. It could be that there would be a place for you there and you would find what you desire. You are already close to the place and they might admit you there. And so have a good trip, you are very close to a town where they might admit you and give you some place."

And when they heard what they told them, they all went away, and Ana María (sic) and her daughter called Juana García began to shout, saying "Señor, señor, you have these lands; señor Çolteuctli, we have heard what you said."

Well, my very beloved sons, I will now tell you and declare that God our lord saw fit to create him whom they call Çolteuctli, who is Martín Molcatzin, who turned himself into a serpent in the manner of a quail. The Mexica, whom they call the people of inside the water, were leaving, and got to the borders of Sula, and just where the border of the people of Sula is, they found a very large and frightful serpent in the fashion of a quail, as to its feathers, and for this reason they called it *Çolcoatl* [Quail-serpent], and it was all spread out there and frightful. And the Mexica were greatly taken aback, for never had they seen a serpent like that, so they were very frightened, and they went away and the people of Sula were left very content. Because if the Mexica had stayed, they would have ruled the land which the people of Sula possessed, which their ancestors and grandparents left them and which they are still possessing now.

My beloved sons, what we say here occurred this way, and understand it very well. This Martín Huitzcol wanted to feed them, and they were going to give them what they call in their language *maçatl ynenepiltzin* [deer tongue], which are a kind of small nopal

cactus, and they were going to give them what they call
tlanquaxoloch [wrinkled knee], which are beans, and as a third food
they were going to give them what they call *cuentla ococolmic*
[what has died off in the field], which are squash, and also what
they call *cempolihuini centlamini* [what entirely disappears and
ends], which is amaranth seed, and what is to be sprinkled on top
of the food, what they say is pointing toward the ground, which is
green chile; and they were going to give them *quahuitl yxpillotl*
[what looks down from the tree], which are avocados—this is what
they were going to give them last of all. But the older brother,
who is Martín Molcatzin, did not want it to be; if they had fed
them there, they would have stayed there and not gone away. God
our lord orders everything, and so all the food was left behind.

The startling passage in which Ana García heads the Mexica is no
simple error, since she and her daughter Juana are mentioned a second time
as having brought along so many lords and vassals to no avail. Two other
details in the document are directly relevant to the preceding section. At one
point it is said that the whole population of Sula turned into quail and
frightened the Mexica away. And at the beginning of the border recital
proper it appears (though the condition of the document and the vagueness
of the language make it uncertain) that the people of Sula have a border with
Martín Huitzcol, as though his group were more a foreign ethnicity than a
lower moiety. This is congruent with the apparently confused passage just
quoted in which it is not clear whether Molcatzin is addressing himself to
Huitzcol or speaking jointly with him.

Sula's version of its relation with the outside in preconquest times lacks
the plausibility and possible historicity of the Zoyatzingo materials. Since
no incident remotely like that narrated can have taken place, we face here
legend or reshaping in a quite straightforward form. We can ask directly,
therefore, what the received version shows about consciousness. Also,
some sixteenth-century documents of sale which the Sula people preserved
demonstrate that in preconquest times and through most of the sixteenth
century Tlalmanalco, or some nobleman from there, held lands inside Sula's
territory. As with Zoyatzingo, Sula has inverted the situation, making
itself the entirely autonomous victor, threatened only by treachery from the
inside, that is, the half-foreign subsidiary group of Huitzcol. Sula at least
acknowledges the existence of the Mexica, as none of the other towns do.

No chronological dimension can be assigned to the Mexica episode,
although it does occur after the Sula people have become a fixed entity with
a distinct territory. The story is symbolic of outside threats successfully
warded off. These threats are amalgamated; the preconquest imperial power

is associated with the postconquest Garcías, who were likely early proprietors of one of the Spanish estates ringing Sula's territory by 1700. (A conflict with a neighboring hacienda brought on the litigation in which the Sula document was presented.) The means to ward off the threats are equally the postconquest questionnaire and border survey, and the preconquest powers of the totemic quail. There can be little doubt that the quail legends go back to preconquest times in Sula; the quail-serpent is a naturalization of the general Mesoamerican feathered serpent. Even the notion of the cry of the quail as a frightening sound has precedent in preconquest myth; when the Lord of the Dead wanted to prevent Quetzalcoatl from stealing the jade bones to create man, he sent the quail to frighten him.[4]

Thus two of our samples show evidence of preconquest historical and legendary matter circulating openly in the indigenous communities of the Chalco area in the time around 1700. There was little feeling that such matter was different in kind from postconquest beliefs and events, or that the two were in conflict; rather they were so thoroughly integrated with each other that there was an entire merging and loss of sight of the preconquest-vs.-postconquest perspective. Both kinds of elements were placed in the service of the autonomous territoriality of the local ethnic group.

In this context there is an aspect of the Zoyatzingo and Sula papers which I hardly know whether to view as a survival or as a new reaction to the colonial situation. In the Zoyatzingo titles—at the end of the conversation of Quauhcececuitzin, Xohueyacatzin, and Juan Ahuacatzin—the latter disappears, having been enclosed by God inside the local mountain Xoxocoyoltepetl. From here he will watch after the people until he reemerges at the end of the world. This would seem to be a messianism in response to Spanish domination. But note that it is the minority representative, the objector to Quauhcececuitzin, who goes into the mountain, and not Old Xohueyacatzin. Conceivably, then, we have here in part a reflection of the resentment of one indigenous group displaced by another. The dominant note, however, seems to be the one struck at the end of the passage—that eventually the old pagans will revive. The same is true in the Sula document, where although no messianic incident occurs, a prominent sentence asserts that "our ancient fathers," though they died, did not die, and will resuscitate on judgment day (Christian orthodoxy, of course, but surely with another dimension here).

The Chichimecs and the sweep of cultural evolution. Before the conquest, many Mesoamerican groups preserved the tradition that at a remote time they had not been sedentary people with houses and fields but had wandered about the countryside; they were also aware of repeated invasions of the settled areas by other wanderers. The general symbol of the nonsedentary was the Chichimec. How much of all this had the writers of our samples retained? In the three larger documents there are definite traces of retention of such matter, but, as we have come to expect, it is amalgamated in various ways. The three notions of an original general nonsedentary stage of existence, of Chichimec invasions of the sedentary area, and of a time of troubles and flight immediately after the conquest all tend to come together.

The first portion of the Zoyatzingo documents asserts that the town received confirmation of its rights to the land shortly after the conquest because the inhabitants of Zoyatzingo had not, like the people of all the other towns around, fled in fear of the Chichimecs who were everywhere entering and destroying. It is in this light that we must see the passage in the principal section of the Zoyatzingo papers to the effect that after the arrival of the Spaniards there were many people (this time from Zoyatzingo too) who did not want to accept the faith and went to hide. For seven years they dwelt in the woods, ravines, and caves, until the archbishop ordered that the recalcitrant ones be brought down forcibly from the mountains and collected, leading to a general congregation in 1555. Atlauhtla gives a version so close to Zoyatzingo's (specifying that the order came from Archbishop Zumárraga) that this must be a single tradition common to the area. The hiding place of the refugees is given in almost the same words in the two versions.[5]

Something similar appears in the Sula document. We can hardly doubt that the following passage is related to the same tradition observed for Zoyatzingo and Atlauhtla: "In the old days they did not yet know God, but worshiped whatever they felt like . . . and they went about in the wilds, hiding among the crags and in the grasslands, before they were baptized in the year of 1532." And again: "Before the faith came, they all went scattered about, hiding among the wilds and crags." But here this behavior is no mere temporary flight from Chichimecs or Spaniards, nor is it something attributed primarily to others. Rather it is an integral part of Sula's own evolution. The document begins with the creation of the world by the Christian God, proceeds to the stage of the existence of the Sula people as wild wanderers or nonsedentaries, and then tells of the coming of the Spaniards and the foundation of the town. All these happenings are seen as one related series of events. The categorization—one can hardly speak of the chronology—equates paganism with the stage of nonsedentariness, and Christianity and the Spanish king with the sedentary stage. The threat by

the Mexica falls into the latter grouping, and hence it is natural that the
Mexica should speak of God's will and that the Sula people should wave
their Spanish titles at them.

Hints of a broader ethnicity. In what we have seen so far, almost all indigenous cultural inheritance is referred directly to the local entity. Insofar
as there is recognition of nonlocal indigenous groups such as the Mexica,
they are classed with the Spaniards as outside threats. Is there any evidence
in the texts of Indian solidarity, referring either to past times or to the times
in which the texts were written? In general, the coming of the Spaniards is
a transaction between the intruders and the local group, other indigenous
groups being mentioned only for their bad behavior in fleeing, resisting
Christianity, and the like. Once, indeed, in the Atlauhtla document, there is
mention of the exact time of the surrender of Tenochtitlan-Tlatelolco to the
Spaniards in 1521. But this passage, which is without introductory context,
gives every appearance of having been lifted (as something interesting about
distant times) from some other text that came into the hands of the writer or
a predecessor. Once again a reference to the local situation is made
immediately thereafter. The writer remarks that locally too there was war, at
the end of which the town acquired its rights.

Nowhere in the texts is any derivative of the Spanish word *indio* used,
nor is anyone called by any other term that could be translated as "Indian."
As in other colonial-period Nahuatl texts, each indigenous person or group
is referred to by the name of the local ethnic-political entity: Atlauhtecatl,
"person of Atlauhtla"; Çoyatzincatl, "person of Zoyatzingo," etc. Only two
brief and very similar passages have any implication of recognition of an
overall indigenous ethnicity. In the Nahuatl of the twentieth century,
macehualli, earlier "commoner" or "vassal," has come to be the approximate
referential equivalent of "Indian." Some texts of the middle and late colonial
period show it already beginning to move in that direction. In the Atlauhtla
document too, after a warning that Spaniards are not to take the
townspeople's land, there comes the statement "yaxca masehuali y tlali,"
"the land belongs to the commoner [or *masehual,* as the Spaniards said]";
the effect of the passage is very close to "this is Indian land." One section
of the Zoyatzingo documents is nearly identical; the Spaniards are warned
off, "ca masechualtlalpan yn ticate," "for where we are is commoner land."
But let me repeat that these words are the only hint of any arising general
Indian ethnic consciousness to be found in the whole set of texts.[6]

On the other hand, there is an awareness of the larger language group.
Three of the documents make some reference to Nahuatl. In the two of
these which are preserved in that language, it is called *mexicacopa,* "in the

fashion of the Mexica," a back translation from the Spanish *mexicano*. In these cases Nahuatl is seen as a defense against the prying eyes of Spaniards, though the local people are also aware that the documents will need translation in order to be brought to the attention of the authorities. Ironically, it is the Sula document, preserved only in translation, which makes the most of the language and of the language group: "God gave me these words, which are not the word (language) of Michoacán nor of the Matlatzincas nor the Otomis, but that which we set forth and state here in our Mexican language." Here we have not the possibly Spanish-induced awareness of "Mexican," but an older Nahuatl-speaker patriotism in contradistinction to other major indigenous language groups of central Mexico. Implied here, though not fully expressed, is a view in which civilized sedentary life in the Mesoamerican sphere is restricted to a Nahuatl-speaking world of autonomous towns with their territories, surrounded by barbarians of various kinds.

Style, social concepts, and ritual. Apart from the framework of corporation and wider world, what other indigenous cultural elements do our texts demonstrate to have been retained? The vehicle of preconquest public life was a rich oratory which embodied both a manner and a highly specific set of concepts. There are strong traces of this in all the texts. For the preconquest Nahuatl-speaking sphere, higher public discourse in general is often associated with the term *huehuetlatolli*, "speech of the elders" or "ancient speech." All of our texts, even the shortest one from Tetelco, purport to be spoken by elders for the benefit of the young and those yet to be born. All retain the characteristic forms of address: "oh my children," "oh my younger brothers," etc. Formulas designating the young and future generations are preserved in full uniformity in all the titles: "those who crawl, those who drag themselves"; "those who are not yet born, [those who will come] after five or ten [years], in the time to which we look." The declamatory and metaphorical presentation typical of preconquest lore is still very much in evidence in our texts. The Zoyatzingo and Atlauhtla documents agree in calling the boundary settlement the town's "measure, seal, shield, and battle rampart." The Sula document compares its words of advice to precious stones set in gold, a standard metaphor of the old rhetoric.

Deeply embedded in that rhetoric were notions of social organization, especially of the roles of noble and commoner. In all the texts one will find standard preconquest phrases denoting the dignity of rulership, here applied to the holders of municipal office in the postconquest Hispanic-style polities. All also contain standard formulas for the common people, especially the phrase "the wings and the tails," which appears in the three in Nahuatl (probably also in the Sula original, if we had it). A final section of the Sula document is directed to "you who are present, whether you are sons of lords or sons of commoners." Those who are lords and exercise the staff of office well will be fortunate, thanked by God and given bouquets of flowers by the townspeople, but if they should not heed the advice now given, they will be treated as commoners; they will go about with the carrying frame and the tumpline, and have to perform tribute labor. The preconquest stereotypes of social differentiation are thus still familiar.

The titles also betray a considerable carryover of preconquest ritual, at least that pertaining to boundary verification. Gibson speculates that the "title" may be at least partially a preconquest genre. In view of the deviance of such documents from Spanish documentary forms and their wide range, from central Mexico to Guatemala, the suggestion is an attractive one. A preconquest original would presumably have consisted of a map with pictures and glyphs giving the date as well as the names of the places and ethnicities involved. The visual record would have been accompanied by an extensive oral recital much like the prose of the postconquest written titles. However boundary settlements were recorded, the presence in the titles of some items which would be extraneous in parallel Spanish documents indicates the existence and partial persistence of an indigenous ritual or set behavior relating to the finalization of such matters.

The most striking ritual element is that of the feast. This was given by the ruler of the town for all parties, including the elders of bordering ethnicities. Even the short Tetelco document mentions that all came to the house of don Nicolás Tlacamaçatzin for turkey and *atole*, and afterward went to their homes in peace. The ceremonies of Atlauhtla and Zoyatzingo also end with the general feast. We have here not only a deeply ingrained custom but an act with juridical force, much like making a signature. In the Sula document, had Molcatzin fed the Mexica, he would have had to acknowledge their claims.

In the Atlauhtla and Zoyatzingo titles, wind instruments are played at every turn; the Atlauhtla document even preserves the name of the principal player, Pedro Macxochitzin. Although the Spaniards surely made use of music for important ceremonies, trumpets were not to my knowledge part of the general baggage of Spanish land investigations. In at least some cases, the instrument being played is apparently the indigenous conch shell trumpet, pictured in the mouth of one figure in the Zoyatzingo documents; ones looking much like it can be seen in maps and pictures of the Historia Tolteca Chichimeca.[7]

Several passages in the documents say that the local people acquired the land with effort and trouble, and for Zoyatzingo there is the specific claim that the ancestors gained their right to the town's territory "through war and dying." It appears indeed that having fought successfully for the land was a main source of legal right to it. Hence a show of war may have been part of boundary settlement ritual. In the two pictures in the Zoyatzingo materials showing the principals of founding ceremonies, most of the dignitaries hold preconquest weapons in their hands, either the obsidian-edged sword or the bow and arrow. In the Atlauhtla document the representatives of the bordering ethnicities bring their swords to the ceremonies, and the survey is punctuated by incidents in which the neighbors temporarily threaten to make objections and want war. These sections could be an oblique reference to historical border wars, but I am more inclined to think that they refer to mock battle gestures taking place as part of border verification ritual, here reported by successors who may or may not have grasped the nature of the transaction.

Here, as elsewhere, there is more retention than awareness of retention. The people of each town know that once their ancestors were pagan, while their towns lacked saints' names, the people Christian names, and the leaders the title of "don." They know, too, that all this changed with the coming of the Spaniards and Christianity. But they view the bulk of their cultural inheritance simply as theirs, attaching little importance to whether its origin is indigenous or European; rather, elements from the two spheres are freely projected upon each other.

Incorporation of postconquest elements

The preceding discussion anticipates much of what I have to say about the indigenous view of the postconquest period and the new phenomena characteristic of it. The amalgamation of the two epochs and the two kinds of cultural elements has already been demonstrated. Certain aspects of the new era were seen as so basic or taken so much for granted that the preconquest period could no longer be imagined without them. Despite divergent beliefs such as the quail-serpent or the sojourn of Ahuacatzin in the mountain, nowhere in the titles is there any hint of disbelief in Christianity or of continuing resistance to it. Moreover, despite the intense striving for local autonomy, there is no hint of any disloyalty to the Spanish king (though knowledge about the latter personage is extraordinarily weak). Rather, God and king are seen as the ultimate support for the legitimacy of the town's claims.

How fully integrated Spanish-Christian material could be appears from the legend of the choosing of Sula's patron saint. The two oldest of all the Sula people, Miguel Omacatzin and Pedro Capolicano, decide that the choice of a saint should come from within the town. They convoke all the inhabitants and ask them to choose, but the people, saying that the two are their fathers, turn the choice back to them. That night Santiago appears in a vision to each of the two separately; when they tell each other the next day, they are fully convinced and the choice is made. The two elders are clearly the autochthonous pair in a different guise, so that the choice of the Spanish saint is an act on a level with the original foundation of the town, carried out by its deepest symbols of ethnic identity.

Postconquest historical references. Against this background let us examine the salient aspects of what the titles say about postconquest phenomena. As previously asserted, a title is built around a report on an early postconquest border survey of the local area. Certain other matter is standardly presented as more or less simultaneous with the survey: laying out the town in Spanish-style lots,[8] naming the various barrios, establishing local Spanish-style officials (such as the governor or alcaldes), baptizing the people, building the church, and (sometimes though not always) congregation. The whole cycle of acts has such a strong aura of a legendary first foundation and source of legitimation that, as we have seen, the Sula document quite rigorously takes it as equivalent to the origin of the town as an organized territorial entity.

In view of this, are we to imagine that the survey reports refer to any actual historical occasion or occasions at all? Apparently they do. There are several indications of authenticity in the naming of the indigenous notables said to be present at the ceremonies. First of all, they have names typical of the first postconquest generation: a Christian name plus an indigenous name, with a still quite loosely attached "don" for only a few of the most prominent. This was not at all the mode of the later colonial period. Further, in the Atlauhtla and Tetelco documents the main local figure has the same Christian name as the town's patron saint (a common congruence, which would, however, not be hard to counterfeit at a later time). Then there is some independent evidence of the existence of two of the figures mentioned. As we saw, the Martín Molcatzin so central to the Sula document receives passing mention in the Zoyatzingo titles too. More conclusively, the Atlauhtla document gives a don Tomás Quetzalmaçatzin as the representative of Amecameca at Atlauhtla's border survey, and Chimalpahin repeatedly mentions just this personage as ruling Amecameca in the early postconquest years (yet it is abundantly clear that the Atlauhtla title writers of the eighteenth century had no copy of Chimalpahin at their disposal).

As to the Spanish officials involved, only two of our samples mention an actual individual who came to the local scene, but these two do agree on a name: in Tetelco, "Do Petro de Omada"; in Zoyatzingo, "Do P⁰ te Omemadad." One of the Spanish translators may be right in equating this appellation with "Ahumada"; a Pedro de Ahumada (not "don") came to Mexico in 1550, in what capacity I do not presently know.[9] Although the dates supplied in the documents for postconquest events vary so widely and heap upon each other so thickly that one could reach almost any conclusion, there is a certain clustering in the 1530's for the primary border surveys and in the 1550's for congregation. I rather expect that future research on the Chalco region will show this to correspond to the facts.

The conquest proper hardly figures in the titles. It is merely signaled as "the coming of Cortés" or "the coming of the faith," something taken as a cosmic event. Only the repercussions for the immediate area are seen as something needing telling.[10] No regret is expressed about the conquest as the end of an epoch; rather, as seen earlier, there is disapproval of those who fled in the first years. The emphasis is on the first coming of outside representatives to set up the town in the new style; in the Zoyatzingo and Atlauhtla versions, a high dignitary—whether king, viceroy, or archbishop—becomes concerned in a God-like fashion about the people and sends someone out, leading to the border survey and foundation. Only the Sula document gives us a rounded picture (purely legendary, or at least composite) of the coming of the Spaniards to the town:

> When the señor Marqués brought the Catholic faith, the fathers of the order of our father St. Francis came carrying a Holy Christ in front, and the Spaniards, those with the white hides and with tubs on their heads, carrying their swords under their armpits, said they were called Spaniards and that they had been given license to establish all the towns formally, and they [the Sula people] should think what saint they wanted to be their patron, because the Catholic faith was in Mexico City already.

Spanish officials and legal concepts. At the level of the high dignitaries who send out representatives, it is apparent that the writers of the titles had no clear conception either of the individuals or of the offices. Cortés is frequently used as symbol of the Spanish advent and as source of legitimacy. However, some writers are not sure whether or not he is the same person as the Marqués (del Valle), and occasionally Viceroy Velasco is seen as having arrived jointly with him. Viceroy don Luis de Velasco is in fact a favorite figure, and after him Viceroy don Antonio de Mendoza and Archbishop Zumárraga. In Atlauhtla, Emperor Charles V enjoys great fame. But the writers so frequently mix all these figures and their titles together that the names seem to be functioning as alternate designations or different aspects of the same thing (just as gods, towns, and rulers often had multiple names and titles in preconquest times). A viceroy may be called king, or a king viceroy; there is an outside seat of Spanish power, but whether it is in Spain or in Mexico City hardly matters and is hardly grasped. Consider the following examples:

[Zoyatzingo:]
    the Marqués and [the] Cortés . . .
    Cortés and don Luis de Velasco, the Marqués . . .
    the archbishop don Pedro de Ahumada . . .
    don Luis de Velasco, the Marqués del Valle . . .
    the king our lord in Mexico City, his majesty . . .
    The Viceroy de Salinas...[with no awareness that this is Velasco]
[Atlauhtla:]
    our great lord the viceroy emperor Charles V . . .
    the king our lord inside the water in Mexico City . . .
    The king came from Castile to Mexico City . . .
    the king don Antonio de Mendoza entered Mexico City . . .
    the king don Luis de Velasco . . .
[Tetelco:]
    don Luis de Velasco de Salinas, general

The Spanish titles *juez* ("judge"), *visitador* ("inspector"), and *registrador* ("registrar") are also sprinkled through the texts almost haphazardly.[11]

Essentially there is concern with these outside personae and offices only as something to appeal to in the defense of one's territory. The same is seen with certain procedural concepts of Spanish governance. A full grasp of the procedures from the inside is not sought. The local people are concerned only with the end result, confirmation of their rights, so that *merced* ("grant"), *posesión* (formal act of taking unchallenged possession), and *interrogatorio* ("questionnaire") come down to the same thing. One sheet of the Zoyatzingo papers attempts to approximate a record of the town's grant and act of possession; but while the "posesión" part does somewhat appropriately report assent by the neighboring groups, the "merced" portion bears no resemblance at all to a Spanish grant, nor does it involve anyone's giving anything to anyone.[12] Perhaps the term acquiring the most independent existence was the Nahuatl version of the Spanish word "interrogatorio." Since *in* is the Nahuatl article "the," the local Nahuatl speakers took the word proper to begin thereafter, resulting in written forms such as *teloca-*

dorio, *derocadorio*, and *delogadorio*. Even the Spanish version of the Sula document has *terrogatorio*, for the translator was demonstrably a native speaker of Nahuatl. This word then became the most basic and general one used in the area for "true title." We have seen the Sula people employing the term to the Mexica, and of Xohueyacatzin of Zoyatzingo it is said that he had nothing to fear of other local groups "because the questionnaire truly belonged to him." The map of Tetelco is prominently labeled *dodelogadorio potzesio*, which makes little sense as literally "this is our questionnaire and act of possession"; rather the utterance is like one of the old preconquest double metaphorical phrases, with the intention "this is our title."

Christian chronology. As regards chronology, too, the years according to the European calendar are important only as they are thought to confirm a given town's claims. Two or even three mutually contradictory or individually implausible dates may be given for the same event. In one part of the Zoyatzingo papers, the Spaniards are said to have come in 945. Perhaps the most egregious example involves the previously quoted passage picturing the arrival of the Spaniards and the faith in Sula, which is dated 1607 at the beginning and 1609 at the end (despite a statement earlier that the Sula people were baptized in 1532). The events of the titles appear to take place in the timelessness of legend or dream, in which progression is short-term and any two related events may fall together. This cannot explain, however, the utter caprice and apparent incompetence in dating or even the presence of dates at all. All Mesoamerican peoples understood well the principle of an indefinite unidirectional progression of time with the events of each consecutive year assigned a separate space. The composers of the titles doubtless also knew the principle, but they appear not to have been full masters of the European numerical system of counting the years, nor even, in many cases, to have grasped fully that one set of numbers was exclusive of any other. The years are there not because the writers themselves had counted them and understood them, but because they knew the authorities gave importance to them. Here even more than with Spanish personae, offices, and procedural concepts, it seems as if the local people are using the Spanish paraphernalia as magic, as something efficacious rather than understood. They appear to have believed that if one only shouted out the right abracadabra of years, names, and titles, the genie would deliver eternally unchallenged possession of one's territory. The more dates the better, apparently, and they were not inclined to abandon any they found in their various sources (and indeed, Spanish preoccupation with voluminous, precise documentation and dating of past legal acts gave them ample justification for their belief).

Christianity. As regards religious concepts, we have already noted the unorthodox legends of Sula and Zoyatzingo, as well as some vagueness about the identity and powers of the archbishop, but the writers display a grasp of some of the central tenets of Christianity and of the working of the sacraments, which are standardly detailed as the rationale for building the local church. Community identification with the church as a building is strong; the church is felt to have been erected entirely by the people themselves and is an important symbol of the town's existence and relative status, as indicated in the various pictures and maps included in the titles. Although the local Spanish friars or priests are not much mentioned, we see their influence in various ways. Most of the documents begin with an invocation, the sermon style of the cleric, with its rhetorical questions, is reflected in certain passages, and they are surely responsible for some biblical references scattered here and there. Like material of whatever origin, the biblical enters into the general stream of local tradition. The "Aza Persia" among the Mexica in the Sula document seems to take his name from a biblical king. Persia has apparently become a symbol of the exotic. Santiago is also from Persia, "which they say is toward the east."

The lack of general history. The titles contain very little that could be considered under the heading of a simple account of newsworthy events of the past, such as the eclipses and storms so often mentioned in Nahuatl annals. The Zoyatzingo and Atlauhtla documents do make mention of the great epidemics of the sixteenth century (the Atlauhtla title by mistake puts the epidemic of 1576 a century later). Even this is reported in reference to the local group and in close relation to the main subject matter. Thus in the Atlauhtla document the loss of life is seen as an additional reason for the viceroy to favor the town, while in the Zoyatzingo document an epidemic of 1556 comes, very plausibly, on the heels of a congregation in 1555.

Attitudes toward individual Spaniards. If an affirmative attitude is shown in these texts toward an overall Spanish-Christian framework, the same is not true when it comes to Spaniards as individuals. Prominent sections of each of the three lengthier documents are given over to admonishing the local inhabitants not to show the papers to anyone, most especially to Spaniards, and not to let Spaniards get the land, as will surely happen if they get at the papers. (The notion of a secret text as a source of group power may be partially carried over from the preconquest era.) The Zoyatzingo title warns the people to watch lest Spaniards coming in the future should make friends with their descendants, eat with them and become their *compadres*, then force them to sell them land or give it to them for friendship. The Sula document specifically denounces the Spaniards as tricky and deceitful ("es muy gente satírica," says the Nahuatl-speaker translator, probably rendering something like "huel teca mocacayahua," "they greatly deceive people"). This concern over individual Spaniards coming into the local indigenous community is not new, but in sixteenth-century Nahuatl documentation no such ready stereotype appears, and the source of concern was at least as likely to be other indigenous groups. With the change in the situation, particularly as Hispanic people poured out of the city into the countryside in the middle and later colonial period, the emphasis in indigenous attitudes has switched. The corporation has properly recognized the Spanish influx as the primary threat to its existence and offers resolute, blanket opposition. (Indians as individuals often felt quite differently about it, as follows in fact from the nature of the warnings alone.)

Area-wide traditions. That the town-province is the universal arena and reference point in the titles does not preclude the existence of a common tradition across the broader area, in this case the Chalco region. Each town has a similar view of itself and its surroundings. A concept such as the "terrogatorio" is area-wide (and also, so far as I have seen to date, area-specific). The similarly deviant forms of postconquest names and offices betray that the title writers consulted with one another across town boundaries. On occasion the writers incorporated whole passages from other texts; the Atlauhtla document inserts, as an afterthought and between sections, a paragraph identical to one in the Zoyatzingo title, telling in flowery langue how the borders extend in the four cardinal directions and giving a date. The Tetelco people may have gone further than this; they were accused of copying their entire document from an original in Mixquic. Reciprocal influence on various points was somehow possible in the face of the fact that official Nahuatl documents and more professional writers in the same towns could have supplied conflicting and more objectively correct information. The dichotomy is seen even in the orthography. The three titles preserved in Nahuatl have deviant spellings in common which I have not seen elsewhere in texts from the Valley of Mexico and which also fail to appear in eighteenth-century Nahuatl documents written by municipal officials of these very towns, included in the same dossiers as the titles (Zoyatzingo and Tetelco).[13]

If one presumes, as I do, that even in preconquest times the popular view made each city-state an entirely autonomous territorial entity, the protagonist of cultural and political movements which were really of broader scope, then little had changed by the later colonial period. God and king now supported legitimacy, but surely the towns had come to similar terms with earlier partially understood outside religious and political powers. The town-centered, atemporal view of our documents is no simple deterioration from the broad view and long chronology of preconquest imperial rulers or of Chimalpahin; rather the approximate equivalent to these existed in the outlook of the town officials and other notables who in the later colonial period still had supramunicipal connections, an education geared to their time, and a grasp of its complex Hispanic-Indian society.

II. Nahuatl Philology

4. And Ana Wept: Grant of a site for a house, San Miguel Tocuillan, 1583

One of the first impressions arising from the growing body of published Nahuatl documents of the postconquest centuries is that of a strong Spanish influence upon their form. Indeed, the impression is not incorrect. Nahuatl wills and land sales, the most frequent types, generally follow Spanish models very closely. The Spanish imprint on certain kinds of legal investigations is almost as strong. Even the freer forms such as letters and petitions are clearly affected by Spanish conventions. But as one becomes more accustomed to the body of material, one grows more aware of its idiosyncrasy. Not only is the language Nahuatl and the content embedded in the local world of Nahuatl speakers, but the very forms and conventions vary from the Spanish, sometimes subtly, sometimes obviously.

For one thing, Nahuatl written texts, not unexpectedly in view of the pre-Hispanic tradition, are more oratorical or declamatory. Even in the testaments there is some evidence of this tendency. Clause for clause they may run like their Spanish counterparts, but each clause commonly ends in an exhortation that the testator's will be respected, that the bequests be carried out, that what is left to an heir not be taken away. Such statements are rare in Spanish documents; in the Spanish tradition a simple assertion, especially by an interested party, had no legal value. In some Nahuatl documents having to do with verification of land boundaries, in addition to reports of the action of officials, much attention is given to the statements of the parties that certain land in fact is theirs and they intend to keep and work it. It seems that in the Nahua tradition a strong statement or admonition, if given in public on a solemn occasion, had something approaching legal force.

Sometimes Nahuatl texts, in describing the circumstances of legal proceedings, mention apparently petty details that would be omitted in Spanish equivalents. In speaking of a land boundary settlement, a document may say, for example, that after having surveyed the entire area and set markers, everyone went to the house of the alcalde to have turkey and atole, and after having eaten and rested they went in peace to their various homes. One of the principal reasons for this phenomenon is that, though both Nahuatl speakers and Spanish speakers were concerned to validate certain acts by reporting the proper performance of ritual, the content of ritual varied somewhat between the two cultures. In Spanish culture, pulling up grass and throwing stones was a ritual act of taking possession, and was always reported; in Mesoamerican culture to eat together was an important ritual signifying assent and agreement, and as such plays a role in the present document. In a sense, almost everything that is reported here is ritual: surely the questioning as to who is to measure the plot, when everyone must know from the beginning who it is to be; the embraces at the end; even, though it is human and real, the weeping of those who received the land.

Ordinarily one might expect to see the grant of a house site in a post-conquest Indian town reported briefly (if at all), in a paragraph or so, which would say more or less that on a certain date so and so appeared before the honored lords the governor and alcaldes of the town of such and such and requested the grant of a site for a house on land not held by others, and that after reviewing the situation they made the grant, warning all and sundry to heed their command, and appending their signatures.

In the present document, however, all the circumstances surrounding the grant are told in detail, and almost entirely in dialogue form. This procedure gives us far more color, humanity, and basic information, as the reader will see. On the other hand, the text may at first seem ingenuous and rather hard to understand; it starts out with the presumption that the reader already knows who a certain Ana is, as well as other characters who are gradually introduced. Actually this is no more ingenuous than saying "Sahagún" or "Motolinia," without further identification, when one writes for *Tlalocan* or *Estudios de Cultura Náhuatl*, on the presumption that the readers of those journals will recognize the names; the text is intended for local eyes. One soon gathers that Ana is the sister of a town councilman, and that the people he goes to call are the other members of the local council. It is true perhaps that the writer of our document as a provincial person was not apprised of the practices of his colleagues in larger centers whose texts might approach much more closely to Spanish models. His ignorance in this respect is our gain, for in lieu of a Spanish-style presentation he has relied on an indigenous tradition.

A few important background items which do not emerge from the document itself can be supplied from the remainder of the dossier (Archivo General de la Nación, Tierras 2338, exp. 1) in which it is contained. The town is San Miguel Tocuillan; hence the phrase "land of our dear father San Miguel" to denote town land, and offerings of thanks to the same saint. Tocuillan was in the jurisdiction of Tetzcoco, located on the east bank of the lake of the same name. The church and the best residences were located on

high ground, which is why Ana's brother says "let your things be brought
up." Other land, including that being given to Ana, was at the lakeside and
often flooded. It is not entirely clear whether Tocuillan at this time had a
formal cabildo, to which all those called in for the ceremony belonged, or
whether perhaps the only official regidor was Juan Miguel, who might have
represented Tocuillan on the council of some larger entity, while the others
were only ward heads or the like, constituting an informal local council.

The names of the characters are typical of those used by Indians throughout most of the colonial period; some have two Christian names, one
serving as a surname, while others bear one name only, as is patently the
case with Ana herself. A few common names were used again and again.
Here half the characters are named Juan. Ana's husband and child are both
simply Juan, while her brother is Juan Miguel (adding the name of the
patron saint), distinguished from another council member only by the fact
that the latter lives in and represents the district of Pelaxtitlan ("where the
pear trees are"). Yet another council member is Juan Francisco. Popular as
a second appellation is the name of the town saint, Miguel, which hardly
serves to distinguish one person from another. Note that in the signatures
at the end the notary gives himself and the council members the title "don,"
but it does not appear in the actual speech reported. This is in sharp distinction to Spanish usage of that time, in which "don" was a basic, invar-
iable part of the name.

The notary is an interesting figure whose role in the proceedings here is
not quite clear. All the conversation is so realistic that one would think
surely he was present at everything. Yet he does not mention himself
among the four men invited to eat at Juan Miguel's house, or on any other
occasion. And surely he was not there for the private talk of Ana and Juan
Miguel at the beginning. It was often observed in the sixteenth century that
Nahuatl speakers had the ability to remember and reproduce long conversations and speeches with great precision. The present document is to
some extent an example of this art. Yet despite the appearance of an entire,
natural conversation, there has been a great deal of selection and omission.
Indeed, it seems that at paragraph 5 we are to imagine the passage of a
month.

A document such as this one (and it has few peers) requires a wide
framework for its proper analysis, and I have looked at it repeatedly from
various angles in *The Nahuas.*[1] Here I will mention only one special
aspect, the light thrown on the role of women. In both Spanish and
indigenous cultures during the postconquest centuries, women were sub-
ordinated in some ways, able to assert themselves in others. The overall

picture in the two spheres was quite similar, but the details varied considerably. Spanish women, for example, rarely appeared as witnesses to legal documents. But in Nahuatl documentation of the time nothing is commoner than that—after the male witnesses, it is true—there should appear the heading *cihuatzitzintin*, "the women," followed by a listing of all the women in attendance.

In the present document a woman has the primary role as spokesperson for the family and recipient of the land grant. Judging by this instance alone, we might be inclined to think her preeminence was owing not to her gender but to the fact of her being related to a town official. But Ana's case is not without parallel. Consider what Gonzalo Gómez de Cervantes, who had been a provincial magistrate in various parts of the central Mexican countryside around the time of our document, has to say:[2]

> When an Indian has some lawsuit, though the Indian should be very important, able, and knowledgable, he will not appear before the judge without taking his wife along with him, and they report and say what is needed to be said in respect to the suit, and the husbands remain very silent and retired in themselves; and if the judge asks something he wants to know, the husband replies: "here is my wife, she knows"; and this to the point that I have had occasion to ask an Indian, and many of them, "What is your name?", and before the husband would answer, the wife would tell it; and so it is in other things, so that these people are submissive to the will of the woman.

Nevertheless, surely we see here a social convention rather than a pure predominance. Perhaps it would have offended the man's dignity to condescend to ask for something. In other aspects, though Ana is treated with great respect throughout, there is also some evidence of sexual subordination. Ana promises obedience to her older brother as long as she is under his roof, and when the elders come, Ana leaves the room while they eat the meal she has prepared for them. The grammatical forms of respectful speech are largely the same for both sexes, but note that as Molina prescribes in his vocabulary, only the men use the true vocative.

The Nahuatl original, on ff. 8r-9r, is accompanied by an eighteenth-century Spanish translation, f. 10 r-v, which was useful to me, but which I do not reproduce because of its many obvious errors. The original text lacks paragraphs or consistent division into words, both of which I have supplied, though leaving the original orthography unchanged and adding no punctuation. The paragraphs suggested rest on more than arbitrary judgment, since they follow the sections indicated in the original through the words *niman*, "then," and *auh*, marker of a new independent utterance. Here "niman" usually marks everything one person says until the beginning of the speech of the next, or a brief narrative transition in the spoken dialogue. "Auh" seems to signal important junctures or the end of substantial episodes. The one exception to the use of these two division markers is a section introduced by the all-purpose particle *ca*; the passage (paragraph 5) is also exceptional in its function, for unlike all the others it, as seen above, indicates the passage of a longer period of time, breaking the dialogue into two parts. Despite the colloquial nature of the text and its apparent artlessness, it is quite a sophisticated product.

As almost always happens when one deals with highly individual local documents, there are some problems of transcription and translation, of which I will mention a few that are not self-explanatory.

A strip of paper glued over the left margin of the document obscures its first letter; three horizontal lines at the very beginning seem to imply a capital "E." Possibly there was also a "Y," yielding *ye*, "already," and *e* itself could be a form of that word.

In paragraph 7, I am unsure how to divide the string "moquemecamo"; immediately before the string, one or more letters may or may not be missing. I have provisionally taken the last part to be *camo*, "not," with the rest still a puzzle.

In paragraph 15, "nochito" might be a variant of *mochi*, "all," plus the diminutive ending *ton*. Or it might be a synonym of "noxihuato," "my little Juan" (this use of "my" with the first name of a relative, by the way, is something characteristic of the Tetzcoco region). The *no-* would then be the possessive, the *-to* the diminutive, leaving the element *-chi-*, which I cannot identify. Conceivably it could be a form of *ixhuiuh-*, "grandchild," but that sense does not seem appropriate.

In paragraph 17, I am unsure how to divide "canoticacayanoxti," or what it means. The final "noxti" may be equivalent to *nochtin*, "all."

In paragraphs 22 and 23, the term *tlaocole*, literally apparently "one who is compassionate," is new to me in the present context, but it seems to be a term of affection or respect.

In paragraph 32, though "otlatlatoli" clearly has to do with speaking, its exact form is puzzling.

---

1. (E?) onquimitalhui yn anatzin quimolhuili yn iatzin jua migeltzin notlaçoatzin ma quezquilhuitl mopaltzinco toyeca ca ça quilhuitzintli (sic) camo miactin niquipian no-	Ana spoke and said to her older brother Juan Miguel, "My dear older brother, let us be under your roof for a few days—only a few days. I don't have many children, only my

pilhua ca ça yehuatl y noxihuato ca
çan icelto ca çan i teyxtin y mote-
tzin y xihuatzin,

2. niman oquimitalhui y teatzin ma
yuhqui mochihua [no]tecauhtzinne
ma xiqualmoquanilica y tlen aquip-
p[ia] ma hualeco y tlen amotlatnqui,

3. niman otlananquili y çihuatl quito hotinechmocnelili notlaçoatzin
nictlaçocamati y motetlaçotlalitzin y
manel nicnomaçehuia y mixitl tla-
patl auh ca niquitohua ca niman ayc
nitlamahuizpoloz yn ipa quihuatl
(sic) ythuali ca nitlamahuiztiliz Auh
nica metztica y nonamictzin y xihuatzin ytla quemania ytla yc tla-
mahuizpoloz ca tel ocan ametzticate
ca ahmomactzinco nicahua yn oquic
aquimopialia yn ibaratzin y Rein

4. ninman oquimitalhui y jua migeltzin quimolhuili yn ite[n?]catzin
yn anatzin notecauhtzinne Cuix
niquixnepehualtiz y notetzin ytla
quali yc mehuititaz

5. ca huel ipa hotobre yc çepohuali
tlapohua metztli yn iquac y nican
ometzticatca ça huel çe metztli yn
oquimochihuilique

6. niman oquimitalhui yn anatzin
macamo huel çenca miac netequipa-
choli timitztomaquilica ma noço tepitzin tictehuica ytlaçotlaltzin y to-
tlaçotatzin y santo sa migel ca hoca
ticquetzazque çetetl caltzintli ytla
ontemoc yn atzintli ytla ohuac ca
titemotazque

7. niman oquimitalhui ytextzin
mac niquinolhuili y jua francizco-
tzin nima yehuatz[in] juan migeltzin
y pelaxtitla nima yehuatzin y fra-

little Juan, the only child. There are
only three of us with your brother-
in-law Juan."

Then her older brother said,
"Very well, my younger sister.
Move what you have, let all your
things be brought up."

Then the woman answered and
said, "Thank you very much, my
dear older brother, I appreciate your
generosity. Even if I should get in-
toxicated, I declare that I will never
act badly in your house, but behave
respectfully, and as to my husband
Juan here, if he should ever lose
respect, well, you are all there, I
leave it in your hands as long as
you hold the king's staff (are members of the town government)."

Then Juan Miguel spoke and
said to his younger sister Ana, "My
younger sister, am I going to pick
arguments with my brother-in-law,
if he goes along behaving himself?"

Now it is far into October, the
20th of the month, and they have
spent a whole month here now.

Then Ana said, "Don't let us
give you so much trouble; let us
take a bit of the precious land of our
precious father the saint San Miguel, and there we will build a little
house. When the water has gone
down and things have dried out,
we'll move down."

Then her older brother said, "Let
me tell Juan Francisco, and Juan
Miguel of Pelaxtitlan, and also
Francisco Baltasar, and also Antón

çizco bartesaltzin nima yehuatzin
Ato migeltzin teopaquiahuac amo
ximotequipachotzino notecauhtzinne
[. . .]moqueme camo quimonequil-
tizque ma nima niquihualnanili ma
çe tlaxcaltzintli xicmomanili tihua-
tzin amo mitzmotequipachilhuiz ca
oca y tlachictzintli comitiquihue
8. niman ic omohuicac quimanilito
9. niman oquimolhuili yn itecatzin
ca ye hualhuilohuac tecatzinne xi-
hualmonochili
10. niman oquimitalhuique y nahui-
ti tlaca ma dios amechmopialitzinno
quen ohuamoçemilhuitiltique ca ye
ontihualaque
11. niman oquito yn anatzin ma xi-
mocalaquica
12. niman ic ocalacolacohuac (sic)
onetlaliloc
13. niman oquimitalhui yn anatzin
quimolhuili yn iatzin ma xiquima-
quili y tlaxcaltzintli ma quimoma-
çehuitzinnoca
14. niman otlananquilique y hue-
huetque ma tictomaçehuica yn amotetlaçotlalitzin cuix [ytla a]monete-
quipacholtzin çihuapille
15. niman oquito yn anatzin ca axca
aquimocaquitizque y tonetequipachol

16. auh in otlaqualoc niman ic ocal-
ac yn anatzi quitlauhtia quimilhui
camo tlen ic onamechnonochili ca
yz catqui y titocnoytohua ma noço
tepitzin tictotlanica ytlaltzin y totla-
çotatzin sato sa Migel ca oca ticnequi tictlalizque çetetl xacaltzintli ca
tellamo miac nicpia noconeuh ca ça
niquixcahuia y noxihuato nochito

Miguel of Teopanquiahuac. Don't
worry, younger sister, they will not
want. . . Let me go get them right
away, and you be making a tortilla
or two. There's nothing for you to
worry about; there's pulque for them
to drink when they come."

Then he went to get them.

Then he said to his younger sister, "We're already back, younger
sister; come greet us."

Then the four men said, "May
God keep you, and how have you
been today? Here we are."

Then Ana said, "Do come in."

Then they all came in and sat
down.

Then Ana spoke and said to her
older brother, "Give them some tortillas, let them enjoy them."

Then the elders answered, "Let
us enjoy your hospitality. And is
there something that concerns you,
lady?"

Then Ana said, "In a moment
you will hear what it is that concerns us."

And when they had eaten, Ana
came in and addressed herself to
them, saying to them, "I have sum-
moned you for a negligible matter.
Here is what we beg, that we might
apply for a bit of the land of our
precious father the saint San Miguel, for we want to put up a hut
there. I don't have many children;

cuix tihuelitizque

17. niman oquimitalhui y jua franç iz^{co}tzin ma tel momaca tlen aquimitalhuia ma ticmacaca xihualmohuica jua migeltzin xocomanili y mocaRochatzin ca no ticacaya noxti yc motamachihuaz ma tihuia çihuapille ma tiquitati cani ticmelehuilia
18. niman omohuicaque cani [tic]-monequiltia cuix nica cuix noço nepa capa ticmonequiltia ma xicmitalhui
19. niman oquito çihuatl ma nica

20. niman oquitoque y teteuhti ma tel oca
21. niman oquimitalhui y jua françizcotzin aqui quihualtamachihuaz
22. niman oquitoque y teteuhti aquinel amo yepa yehuatl y tlaocole y juatze quitamachihuaz
23. niman oquilhuique y tlaocole xihualauh juatze xocona (sic) y caRocha momatica xictamachihua nauhcap[a] chiquase caRocha xictamachihua
24. Auh n oquitamachiuh nima quilhuique ca [ç]a ixquichtzin y timitzmaca y tlaltzi[ntli]
25. niman oquito yn anatzin ca ohuatechmocnelili (sic) ca tictla[ço]-camati yn amotetlaçotlalitzin
26. niman oquitoque y tla[to]que ma niman opeuhtihuetzin macamo amechmotequipachilhuiz y tetzintli ma ochitotihuetzin ynic opehua[z çi]mieto
27. niman oquito yn anatzin mac ti-

the only one I have is little Juan alone. May we?"

Then Juan Francisco said, "Let it be given them. What do you say? Let's give it to them! Juan Miguel, take your cattle prod ... to measure it with. Let's go, lady, and see where you wish it to be."

Then they went. "Where do you wish it to be? Here, or maybe over there? Say where you wish it to be."

Then the woman said, "Let it be here."

Then the lords said, "Then let it be there."

Then Juan Francisco said, "Who is going to measure it out?"

Then the lords said, "Who indeed? Other times, wasn't it good old Juan? He'll measure it out."

Then they said to him, "Come, good Juan, take the cattle prod in your hands and measure it out. Measure out six lengths on all four sides."

And when he had measured it, then they said, "That's how much land we're giving you."

Then Ana said, "Thank you very much; we appreciate your generosity."

Then the rulers said, "Let it begin right away; don't let the stone concern you, but let it quickly be prepared to begin the foundation."

Then Ana said, "Let's go back

huia ca oc tepitzin atzintli aquimo-
maçehuitzinnozque

28. niman oquitoque y tlatoque tlen
oque ticnequi ca ye otictomaçehui-
qu[e]

29. Auh yn anatzin mochoquili y-
hua yn inamic mochoquili yn iquac
macoque y tlalli

30. niman oquimitalhui yn a[na]-
tzin ca ye polihuiz cadelatzin yhua
popotzintli nicnomaquilitaz y notla-
çotatzin y santo sa Migel ypanpa ca
ytlalpatzinco y ninocaltia

31. niman oquimitalhui y jua Migeltzin ca oticmocnelili y motlaço-
tatzin ma mochipa yuhqui yez camo

32. tenahuatecoc yn iquac yn
otlatlatoli (sic) mochiti y macuilti
tetecuhti —

33. axcan ipa ce[. . .]ilhui viernes
tlapohua metztli de otobre yhuan ipa
xih[uitl] de 1583 anos nehuatl honi-
tlacuilo nixpan omochiuh Do jua
bautista escr⁰ amaxocotitla nica
motecpana y tlatoque

　Do jua Migel Regidor　Do
Bartesal françiz^co　Do juan françiz^co
Do juan migel pelaxtitla　Do Ant⁰
Migel teopaquiahuac

and you must enjoy a bit more
pulque."

　Then the rulers said, "What more
do we wish? We've already had
(enough)."

　And Ana wept, and her husband
wept, when they were given the
land.

　Then Ana said, "Candles will be
burnt, and I will go along providing
incense for my precious father the
saint San Miguel, because it is on
his land that I am building my
house."

　Then Juan Miguel said, "We
thank you on behalf of your
precious father; let it always be so,
not . . .

　When all five lords had spoken,
everyone embraced.

　Today, Friday, the (20th?) day of
the month of October of the year
1583. I did the writing and it was
done before me, don Juan Bautista,
notary. The rulers convened here in
Amaxocotitlan.

　Don Juan Miguel, regidor. Don
Baltasar Francisco. Don Juan Francisco. Don Juan Miguel of Pelaxtitlan. Don Antonio Miguel of
Teopanquiahuac.

5. The Testimony of don Juan

Conversation was the lifeblood of Nahua society, and traces of orality run through the whole corpus of Nahua documents. The normal Nahua way of presenting a detailed narration of anything whatever was to dramatize it, repeating the statements of each speaker in turn, in the first person and the present tense, with all the niceties of a real speech situation. Yet very few extended records of actual conversations in Nahuatl seem to exist. The original testimony given by Nahuas in litigation in postconquest times must have contained vast amounts of fully repeated dialogue, but in the indigenous world oral testimony was very rarely written down. And though we have multitudinous written records of testimony given by indigenous people in Spanish courts, the material has been translated from Nahuatl into Spanish, with further mutilation through paraphrase and use of Spanish narrative conventions.

Most extant written Nahuatl of a conversational nature belongs to the genre of formal texts generated under Spanish ecclesiastical auspices for broadly educational purposes.[1] Of these the best known are set speeches, for occasions from the inauguration of a ruler to the haranguing of a child by a parent, and the strictly conversational aspect is at most secondary. One text of this general type does exist precisely to illustrate conversation, the "Bancroft Dialogues," recently published in two separate full-scale, up-to-date editions.[2] Probably put together originally in Tetzcoco around 1570 or 80, and known to us in a version done in the circle of the seventeenth-century Jesuit grammarian Horacio Carochi, the Dialogues present not only formal speeches but models of everyday conversations with the air of having been taken directly from life. From these texts one can extract rules of polite behavior, a lexicon of polite idiom, and principles of language use such as the systematic inversion of kinship terms in extended meanings.[3]

The lore about polite speech derived from the Dialogues is found partially confirmed in the more formal texts such as those contained in Book 6 of Sahagún's Florentine Codex. One is left, however, with many uncertainties. Was the type of speech illustrated in the Dialogues really used by anyone in everyday life? If so, was it perhaps confined to Tetzcoco, alleged by some (primarily Tetzcocan apologists, it is true) to have been home to refinements unknown elsewhere?[4]

Such questions can be at least partially answered by the Nahuatl testimony here presented, given in Xochimilco in 1586 by don Juan de Guzmán, a member of the ruling lineage of Coyoacan.[5] Two of the sixteenth-century

rulers (*tlatoque*) and governors of Coyoacan bore the same name as our protagonist, "don Juan de Guzmán,"[6] but he is neither of them, nor has his
exact connection with them been established, though it must have been
close. Don Juan was at this time serving as governor of Xalatlauhco (to the
west of the Valley of Mexico), where Coyoacan may have had interests going back to the preconquest period, and where a close relative of don Juan's,
possibly his sister, had previously married the local ruler.[7] Don Juan's older
sister (or conceivably cousin), doña Juana de Guzmán (the same name again,
in the feminine gender) had married the ruler of one of the three divisions of
Xochimilco, don Pedro de Sotomayor, now deceased, and had lived in
Xochimilco since her marriage. The two prinicipal interlocutors here, then,
although both located elsewhere at the moment, are from Coyoacan. The
notary who wrote it all down, however, and who may have had some
influence on the language of the final version, was a born inhabitant of
Xochimilco.

Whether what we have here is shaped more by Coyoacan speech habits
or by those of Xochimilco, both were large, important, complex altepetl
with their own strong traditions, both in the southern part of the Valley of
Mexico and somewhat removed from the orbit of Tetzcoco. Yet the language and conventions used are, allowing for the nature of the occasion,
very much those of the Tetzcoco Dialogues. Doña Juana expresses her
thanks to the women who have visited her with two formulas well worn in
the Dialogues: "oannechmocnelique otlacauhqui yn amoiollotzin," literally
"you have befriended me, your heart has granted things."[8] Equally familiar
is her manner of expressing her presence among the others: "aço çayyoppa
yn onamechnotlanehuitzino," "perhaps this is the last time I have tarried
among you (literally, lent myself to you transitorily).[9] Another staple of
the Dialogues is echoed in don Juan's phrase "yntla oc çemilhuitzintli
nechmochicahuiliz ttote⁰ dios," "if God grants me health for a while longer"
(literally "if our lord God strengthens me for yet another day"). As in the
Dialogues, the particle combination *auh inin*, literally "and this," or in
effect "well then," or "in brief," is employed to indicate the impending conclusion of a speech.[10] Don Juan uses it before topping off his complaints
that doña Juana has mistreated him and his family.

Being august personages at the highest level of indigenous society, don
Juan and doña Juana avoid calling each other by name or specifying their
relationship to each other. He as the visitor and the younger treats her as
the superior, twice addressing her with a phrase on the order of "Totecuioe
Cihuapille," which might be translated "oh mistress, oh lady."[11] As one
would expect from the Dialogues, she is not reported as reciprocating in

kind, though she does several times address him as "tehuatzin," the reverential form of the independent second-person pronoun. On the other hand, doña Juana does not hesitate to call her employee (probably majordomo) Martín de Rojas or Rosas by his first name, using the form "Martintzin," with the Nahuatl reverential suffix -*tzin* appended to the name despite its Spanish origin. Precisely the same thing happens in the Dialogues.[12]

Overall, one seems justified, on the basis of the present example, in concluding that in the late sixteenth century the type of conversational usage seen in the Bancroft Dialogues was indeed characteristic of polite speech in upper circles of the Nahua world in the Valley of Mexico generally (and possibly farther afield; from the present example alone it is clear that one would expect the same vocabulary and etiquette in western Xalatlauhco). Such a conclusion is further strengthened by the existence of some letters of this time written by high nobles of Mexico Tenochtitlan.[13] Though not quite conversation, they are in a conversational mode; they use much of the same vocabulary and obey some if not all of the conventions of address. Both the present text and the letters contain good indications of how a broader uniformity had come into being and was maintained. The individuality and proudly proclaimed autonomy of each altepetl were no mere façade (in this case, one senses that doña Juana's birth outside Xochimilco is making her position more precarious and her testament easier to challenge). But even so, the dynastic lineages of the region had come to constitute a single network in some respects.

Here, the high nobility of Coyoacan has made matches in both Xochimilco and Xalatlauhco, resulting not only in the permanent migration of Coyoacan noblewomen, but in constant visiting back and forth. Even with the death of doña Juana, don Juan apparently does not foresee a halt to the weekly visits that he, his wife, and his son have been making to Xochimilco. Having come directly from Xalatlauhco, don Juan is accompanied by relatives from there and from Coyoacan. The letters just mentioned strengthen the impression of interconnectedness. In one of them, a Mexica noble is addressing relatives in Itztapalapan; in another, the writer (himself in Spain) expects his Mexica nieces to be in touch with the various altepetl all around.[14]

Another question raised by the Bancroft Dialogues relates to the compatibility of Spanish loan words with a high conversational tone. In the Dialogues only the barest minimum of loan words is present, a grand total of two in the entire wordy text, and both of these occur in a single phrase repeated six times.[15] Now we already know that loan words occur quite profusely in other highflown forms of Nahuatl expression, including annals, oratorical letters of petition, and the testaments of the high and mighty.[16] One is led to suspect that the near absence of loan words in the Dialogues is the artificial result of the peculiar nature of the text, intended to instruct Spaniards in polite Nahuatl speech, but there remains the hypothetical possibility that loan words were felt to jar against the traditional language of polished conversation.

The words of don Juan and doña Juana settle this matter for us handily. Spanish loan words abound in don Juan's account, not only in his third-person narration, but in direct quotes from himself and doña Juana. "Money" (*tomines*), "bill of payment" (*carta de pago*), "God" (*Dios*), "soul" (*a-niman*), "mass" (*missa*), "memorandum of testament" (*memoria testamento*)[17] "fathers" (i.e., priests, *padreme*), "Saturday" (*sabado*), and "horse" (*cahuallo*) appear as the occasion demands. These occur in rather neutral contexts, but once don Juan includes a loan word at the very climax of a grand rhetorical flourish. Talking vividly of the dire consequences for the ruling house of Tepetenchi if doña Juana's testament is carried out, at the very height of his speech don Juan utters the phrase "Cuix amo huey pleito mochihuaz," "will there not be a great lawsuit (*pleito*)?" Don Juan's testimony thus constitutes convincing evidence that Spanish loan words were quite fully integrated into the register of polite conversation, far more than one could infer from the Dialogues.[18] (Much the same conclusion arises from the above-mentioned letters from Mexica nobles, which are likewise free in their use of loan words.)

The conversation reported here supplements the Bancroft Dialogues in another detail or two. In the Dialogues, kinship terms are repeatedly extended to non-kin, especially using a principle of inversion by which terms for older kin refer to subordinates and terms for younger kin to superiors.[19] Such indeed is, together with other kinds of extension, the principal use of kin terms in the Dialogues. Here, inversion fails to occur, because the main people involved are actual relatives, and inversion applies primarily (perhaps exclusively) to extended meanings. In fact, our two interlocutors repeatedly use kinship terms for each other in their literal meanings (-*iuc*, "younger sibling/cousin of a female," and -*hueltiuh*, "older sister/female cousin of a male"). They always do so, however, in the third person, never making a specific reference to their kin relationship when addressing each other directly.

Note as a detail the way that third-person references are frozen in an often elaborate form to be repeated in its entirety every time the person is referred to. The main example is don Pedro de Sotomayor, ruler of Xochimilco's subrealm of Tepetenchi and doña Juana's late husband, who is repeatedly called something like "señor don Pedro de Sotomayor, your late husband, whom God took."

Given its testamentary focus, the conversation also throws some light on wills. It has been noticed that Nahuatl wills tend to be more declamatory or conversational than their Spanish counterparts. At the same time, it is clear that the notaries doing the writing abstracted from what was actually said to use their own versions of formulaic statements.[20] At times, we may wonder if there is much connection with the speech of the testators after all. Yet here we have in doña Juana's reported speech whole sentences indistinguishable from those one can find in many testaments, as when she speaks of selling things for masses for herself and her husband. Doña Juana also utters the much-written exhortations of Nahuatl testaments, "neltiz, mochihuaz, ayac aca quitlacoz," "it is to be fulfilled and done, no one is to stand in the way."

Don Juan's account contains some unexpected information on interethnic relations. Notice that he uses the loan word *señora* to mean "Spanish woman," a sense the clerk feels no need to explain, even though the parallel title *señor* is applied to high indigenous authorities, don Juan himself and don Pedro de Sotomayor. In provincial situations, the highest-ranking Nahuas and the relatively humble Spaniards who took local roots often gravitated to each other. When the position of the indigenous person involved was extraordinarily preeminent, as with doña Juana, the Spanish partners in such relationships might actually be the clients and supplicants, seeking to gain prestige from the connection. Such may be the case here. Two of the three Spanish women bear surnames smacking of a certain position in the Spanish world, but none of them merits the title "doña," the sure sign of a Spanish woman of any rank by the late sixteenth century. The fact that they have come to pay their respects to doña Juana says a great deal; notice also that she feels free to dismiss them, though graciously, when she needs to do so.

One would dearly like to know for sure what the language of discourse was between these women. The account ignores the question, giving the impression that it was Nahuatl. If the Spanish women were born in Mexico, as by this time they probably were, it may have been Nahuatl in fact, despite the great general predominance of Spanish in conversation between Spaniards and Nahuas. It is hard to imagine an interpreter being used in such a situation. Possibly each side spoke the maternal tongue, relying on the other side's passive understanding.

To finish setting the scene for the reader, the section of text that follows is extracted from longer proceedings in which the municipal council of Xochimilco opposes and acts to nullify doña Juana's will. A notary has come to the ruler's palace, where don Juan is still to be found after doña Juana's expected death, and the testimony included here is then taken. Afterward don Juan makes new dispositions favoring doña Juana's noble relatives in Xochimilco and, in a minor way, her employees, at the same time relinquishing some of her extravagant gifts to him "in order not to upset them" (*ynic amo niquinnahmaniliz*). Don Juan de Guzmán went on to live a long if rather obscure life. He did not forget doña Juana. His will of 1622 mentions his older sister doña Juana de Guzmán, married in Xochimilco to don Pedro de Sotomayor, saying "she died a long time ago."[21] He ordered no less than three high masses for her soul (as touching as this sounds, we must not forget the possibility that he did so now because he had neglected to honor her request at the time of her death).

Don Juan's testimony is one more example of the Nahua ability to reconstruct long conversations after they had taken place. It is not that we are to believe don Juan implicitly. Doubtless he has twisted things to achieve the desired result—the modification of the testament of a childless widow who had forgotten her duties as holder of a ruler's estate in a foreign realm. Yet he had to stay within the limits of verisimilitude. Most of what he tells probably really happened, most of the words he repeats probably really were said, and the manner of saying them, which is what matters to us most, is entirely trustworthy. Don Juan's version contains a certain kind of truth and a large quotient of humanity. May the reader enjoy it for those qualities.

Auh çan niman yquac yn ipan omitto ylhuitl yn metztli yhuan yn xihuitl Niman hualmohuicac yn omoteneuh s^or Ju^o Valeriano muñoz alldde yn nican xallan yn itecpanchan catca señor don pedro de sotomayor yhuan yn inamictzin catca cihuapilli doña juana de guzman oncan moyetzticatqui yn omoteneuhtzino señor don ju^o de guzman gouer^or juez yn ompa xallatlauhco yn icatzinco su mag^d Niman conmocaquitili yn testimonio, ynic ytlacauh-

And thereupon on the aforesaid day, month, and year the aforesaid señor Juan Valeriano Muñoz, alcalde, came here to Xallan to the former palace of señor don Pedro de Sotomayor and his late wife doña Juana de Guzmán, where the aforesaid señor don Juan de Guzmán, judge-governor at Xalatlauhco in the name of his majesty, was staying. Then they informed him of the testimony of how the testament that the afore-

tica memoria testamento, yn quimo-
tlalitia omoteneuhtzino doña juana
de guzmā. Auh niman motlananqui-
lili yn señor don ju⁰ de guzman
quimitalhui. Ca yn nican naçico
ypan domingo ynman nahui oras
motzilinia yn ipantzinco naçico çihuapilli nohueltihuatzin doña juana
de guzman. ca oc monoltitoc, mo-
chicahualtitoc motlatoltitoc: amo
ma motlapololtitzinoa. yhuan oncan cate Eyntin señoratin yn ce
ytoca juana mendez yhuā Isabel de
Vargas, yhuan Antonia dauila; nimā
noconnotlatlauhtili, noconnotlapal-
hui: yhuan omentin pipiltin niquinhualhuicac, ce tlacatl ytoca Grabriel
de santiago, çanno ycuhtzin yn
çihuapilli, coyohuacā chane ynic
ome ytoca don diego de velasco
chane xallatlauhco ypilotzin yn cihuapilli ypiltzin catca yn don nicolas de aguilar gouernador catca yn
xallatlauhco, mochintin conmotla-
palhuique conmoçiauhquechilique:
auh yn ie iuhqui yn oconmotlatlauh-
tilique, niman ye ic quimotlaqualti-
lia yn señoratin oncan timochintin
tiquiztzticate: auh yn iquac ye ocon-
motlaqualtilique yn iehuantin señoratin, ye oaçic chicome oras motzilinia ye yohua. Niman ye quinmolhuilia yn iehuantin señoratin yn
iehuatzin çihuapilli doña juana de
guzman oannechmocnelilique otlacauhqui yn amoiollotzin aço çayyoppa yn onamechnotlanehuitzino
yn ascan / aço moztla ninotocaz: ca
tel ohualmohuicac yn nicuhtzin don
ju⁰ de guzman ynic onicnotemo-

said doña Juana de Guzman made
was spoiled. And then señor don
Juan de Guzmán answered and said:
I arrived here on Sunday when the
bells were ringing four o'clock, and
when I arrived the lady my older sister doña Juana de Guzmán was still
alive, strong, and talking, and in her
senses, and there were three Spanish
women there, one named Juana
Méndez, and Isabel de Vargas, and
Antonia de Avila. Then I addressed
her and greeted her. And I brought
along two noblemen, one named
Gabriel de Santiago, also the lady's
younger brother (or cousin), who is
from Coyoacan, and the second
named don Diego de Velasco, from
Xalatlauhco, the lady's nephew, son
of the late governor of Xalatlauhco
don Nicolás de Aguilar; all greeted
and saluted her. And when they had
addressed her, then the Spanish women fed her with all of us there
watching. And when those Spanish
women had finished feeding her,
seven o'clock was already ringing
and it was dark. Then the lady doña
Juana de Guzmán said to the Spanish women: "Thank you for your
generosity; perhaps this was the last
time I will tarry with you, perhaps
tomorrow I will be buried; but my
younger brother don Juan de Guzmán has come, whom I was looking

litoya ynic oninentlamatoya ca
cenca yn oninoyollalli, auh ma oc
xinechtlalcahuilicā ca oc oncan nic-
nōnochiliz çentlamantli ypampa:
auh nimā moquixtique yn señoratin
conmonahuatiliq̄ yn cihuapilli, niman ye yaque Ynon ye cuel açitiuh
chicuhnahui oras, Niman yc nech-
hualmonochili yspan yn itoca Mīn
de rosas yhuan yn icuhtzin ytoca
grabriel de sᵗtiago yhuan ypilotzin
don diego de velasco yn omoteneuh
tlacpac chane xallatlauhco Niman
oquimolhuili yn itoca Mīn de Rosas. Martintzin tla oc xitechmo-
tlalcahuili, tla oc ximoquixti. Auh
yn nehuatl ni don juᵒ de guzman
niman yn nonniquani, tlapechtenco,
nōnotlali, auh in iehuatzin çihuapilli yn nohueltihuatzin doña juana
de guzmā mohuetzititoc. Niman ye
ic nicnolhuilia Totecuioe Cihuapille, nimitznotlatlauhtilia aço nelli
yn ie oticmotlalili yn motestamen-
totzin ma achiton çan motlatolti-
catzinco niccaqui yn quenin oticmotlalili yn ipampa yn itecpancaltzin
catca sᵒʳ don pedro de sotomayor yn
ttoteᵒ dios oquimohuiquili yn mo-
tlaçonamictzin catca, quen oticmi-
talhui quen otimotlanahuatili yn
ipan motestamētotzin. Auh nimā
nechmonanquilili quimitalhui. tle
ypampa yn timotlatlania. Niman
nicnolhuili ca çan ypampa yn nic-
matiznequi, aço ytla yc otimotla-
tlacalhui yn ipan in tlatocacalli,
yhuan yn ipan ysquich tlatocatlalli,
milli, chinamitl, ma achitzin niccaqui, quenin catqui. Niman oqui-

for and languishing after, and my
mind has been put to rest. So do
please leave me now, for I must talk
to him about something." And then
the Spanish women went out; they
took their leave of the lady, then
departed. That was already at nine
o'clock. Then a person named Martín de Rojas came to call me to her,
along with her younger brother
named Gabriel de Santiago and her
nephew don Diego de Velasco who
was mentioned above, from Xalatlauhco. Then she said to the person named Martín de Rojas, "Dear
Martín, do please leave us, do go
out." And I, don Juan de Guzmán,
changed my place and sat down at
the edge of the bed where the lady
my older sister was lying. Then I
said to her, "Oh my mistress, oh
lady, I ask you, is it true that you
have already made your testament?
Let me hear a bit just in your words
how you have disposed concerning
the former palace of señor don Pedro
de Sotomayor whom our lord God
took, your dear late husband, what
you have said and ordered in your
testament." And then she answered
me and said, "Why do you ask?"
Then I said to her, "Just because I
want to know if you have done
something wrong about the ruler's
house and all the ruler's lands,
fields, and chinampas; let me hear a
bit how it is." Then she said, "This

matalhui ynin calli yn mochi yma-
nian ca mochi monamacaz: auh yn
quexquich neçiz tomines yn ipatiuh
mochihuaz ca mochi teupan calla-
quiz, yc missa topan mittoz yn tonehuan notlaçonamictzin moyetzti-
catca dios oquimohuiquili señor don
pedro de sotom^{or} canel ayac çe to-
conetzin monemiltia / ca yntla onca
çe momahtzî canel mochi ytech pohuiz ytech niccauhtiaz ypampa yn,
canel ayac, ypampa yn yn mochi
monamacaz yhuā yn isquich yn
tlatocatlalli, yhuā yn quexquich o-
nicnotzinquixtili niscoyan ynic oni-
tlatlaxtlauh yn in isquich yn quimi-
tlacalhuitiuh yn notlaçonamictzin ca
çenca miec ynic onitlaxtlauh yhuā
tel mochi oncatqui amatl cartas de
pago yn onechmacaque yn tlatqui-
huaque. Auh yn iquac yn oniccac
yn isquich yn oquimitalhui cihuapilli. Nimā onicnonanquilili, Onicnolhuili. Ca çenca otimotlatlacal-
hui ca amo qualli yn oticmochi-
huili Cuix amo oncate tepilhuā,
temachhuā, teyshuihuā, Cuix amo
cenca mitzonmahuilizque yntla dios
omitzmohuiquili, mitzonmotlatel-
chihuililizque Cuix amo huey pleito
mochihuaz ȳ micampatzinco cuix
amo tlatzatzatziz ycahuacazque yn i-
machtzitzinhuā catca yn ttote^o dios
oquimohuiquili s^{or} dō pe^o de soto-
m^{or} yn mopilotzitzinhuā ȳ nemi
ascā, yhuā cuix yca huel mopampa-
tzinco quimotlatlauhtilizque yn tto-
te^o dios Yhuan onicnolhuili: auh
yn nehuatl yntla oc çemilhuitzintli
nechmochicahuiliz ttote^o dios yhuan

house and everything that goes with
it is all to be sold, and however
much money is raised from what
turns out to be its price will all be
delivered to the church and masses
will be said with it for both of us,
my dear late husband señor don
Pedro de Sotomayor, whom God
took, and me, since no child of ours
is alive, for if there were a nephew
or niece of yours, certainly it would
all belong to him or her and I would
leave it to that person, but since
there isn't anyone, because of that
everything is to be sold, with all the
ruler's lands, (aside from) however
much I have reduced it myself, with
which I have paid at various times
all the debts my dear husband left,
for I have paid a great deal, and there
are all the papers, the bills of payment the creditors gave me." And
when I heard everything the lady
said, then I replied and told her,
"You have done very wrong; it is a
bad thing you have done. Aren't
there children, nephews, grandchildren, and won't they complain greatly of you when God has taken you,
and curse you for it? Won't there be
a great lawsuit after you are gone?
Won't there be shouting, and discord
among the nephews of the late señor
don Pedro de Sotomayor, whom
God took, your nephews as well,
who are now alive? And because of
this will they be able to pray to our
lord God on your behalf?" And I
said to her, "And what about me? If
God gives life a while longer to me

yn mopilotzin ca oquichtzintli yn
onechmotlau[c?]tili ttote⁰ dios yhuā
yn nonamic ȳ mopilotzin ca mochipa nican hualmohuicatiuh yn chichi-
cohometica yn ipā sabado, auh intla
quenmanian nican topan oyohuac
campa tontohuicazque campa tonto-
callaquizque cuix tepan ticacallaquiz-
que, ca o no çenca titechmotolinili,
ca yuhquin ma titechmotelchihuili-
tehuac ynic nican ayocmo ceppa
tihuallazq̄, tihualcallaquizque yn nicā ytic tecpancalli auh ynin ca çenca
otitechmotolinili. Auh yn iquac
oquimocaquilti yn çihuapilli nimā
nechmonanquilili, nimā quimitalhui: Ca ça nelli ca çenca onitlatlaco
onamechnotepohuili onamechno-
tolinili, canel ayac onechnanamic
ynic nictlali notestamēto yhuā
tehuatzin amo mispantzinco yhuā
amo no çeme ymispan mochiuh yn
tlatoque yn pipiltin ca yehuātin
çeme nechnanamiquizquia, nechpale-
huizquia yn ipan notestamento,
yhuā nechmolhuili xicmonochili yn
Martin quicacticate yn omentin yn
pipiltin yn niquinhualhuicac yn
omoteneuh tlacpac yntoca gabriel
de S.tiago don diego de velasco
xallatlauhco chane yhuā Mīn de
rosas Niman oquinmolhuili Xicmocaquilticā yn tlein niquitoz ynic
nicnonahuatiliz yn nicuhtzin don
ju⁰ de guzmā yn nican mehuiltitica
caye hehuatl ynic onicnochielitoca
yn ie izquilhuitl nonitztica Niman
oquimitalhui onechmolhuili Xicmo-
caquilti yn tehuatzin nimitznonahua-
tilia yn ascan yn quexquich ynic

and the boy your nephew, whom
our lord God has granted me, and
my wife, your niece, why she always comes here every week on
Saturday, and if nightfall catches us
here sometime, where are we to go,
where are we to take shelter? Are
we supposed to go to other people's
houses? You have greatly mistreated us too, it is as though you
had scorned us, so that we are not to
come here ever again, to enter inside
the palace here. In a word, you have
greatly mistreated us." When the
lady heard this she answered me and
said, "It is true, I have done very
wrong, I have afflicted and mistreated you, since no one helped me
make my testament, and you weren't
there, nor was it done in the presence of any of the rulers and nobles, for one of them would have
helped and aided me with my testament." And she said to me, "Call
Martín." (Then when he came,) the
two noblemen that I brought with
me whose names were mentioned
above, named Gabriel de Santiago
and don Diego de Velasco of Xalatlauhco, and Martín de Rojas were
listening to her. Then she said to
them, "Listen to what I am going to
say and how I am going to instruct
my younger brother don Juan de
Guzmán who is sitting here, for it
is he whom I have been awaiting
and looking forward to these past
days." Then she said and told me,
"Listen; I order you now that you

oniquitlaco yn nomemoria testamento tehuatzin mochi ticmopatiliz
yn aquin amo niquelnamic yn amo
ipā catqui memoria testamento ti-
quinmomaquiliz quexquichtzin tlal-
tzintli yhuā tiquinmispantiliz yn
teupisque yhuan yn tlatoque tepetenchi ynic huel tehuatzin ticmopahtiliz. Yhuan çatepan nechmolhuili yn çihuapilli xinechmotlapo-
polhuili ca nelli onimitznoteopo-
huili ca yn iehuatl yn iancuic caltzintli yn quin onicnoquechili yn
icallaquianhuic tonatiuh ytzticac
nimitznomaquilia yhuan yn temi-
milchayahuac yn quimoquechilitia
motextzin yn dios oquimohuiquili
don pedro de sotom⁰ʳ yhuā yn
cuezcomatl ompa ycac çan tocōmo-
tlamellahualtiliz yhuan yn callotli
yhuā yn cuezcomatl ompa ycac xa-
calli ycpac mani tepancalco, mochi
ticmocuiliz, aço oncan mocauallo-
tzin ticmoquechiliz yn iquac nicā
timaxitiquiuh yhuan yn caltepotzco
mani tlalcahualli ynic açitica yn
tepantli aço ompa tihualmocallaquiz
yn ompa mizquitl mani, Niman ye
quinmolhuilia yn oncan catca, O
cuix anquimocaquiltia yn tlein oni-
quito, no yuh anquimononochiliz-
nequi yn teupixqui yhuā yn tlatoque
ye isquich yn notlatol ma huel no-
pan ximotlatoltiz yn ipampa, nani-
mā yntla moztla nechmohuiquiliz
yn ttote⁰ dios yhuā yn isquich yn
calli tlatquitl ma mochi mispantzinco yn monanamacaz ynic amo
tle ahuilquiçaz yhuan yn ompa
coyohuacā yn manic calli yhuā yn

are to fix whatever I have done
wrong in my testament; you are to
give a little land to whomever I
have not remembered and who is not
in my testament, and you are to report to the friars and to the rulers of
Tepetenchi how you will be the one
to remedy it." And afterward the
lady told me, "Pardon me, for I have
truly mistreated you. I give you the
new house I just built, facing west,
and the [courtyard with stone pillars
arranged around it] that your brother-
in-law whom God took, don Pedro
de Sotomayor, built, and the grainbin as one goes straight in, with the
alley, and a grainbin where a hut
stands above an enclosure (corral);
you are to take it all. Perhaps you
can put up your horse there when
you come here. And behind the
house is some empty land that
reaches as far as the fence, perhaps
you will come in that way, where
the mesquites are." Then she said to
those who were there, "So do you
hear what I have said? Please also
be so good as to tell the friar and the
rulers. This is all my statement.
(She turns to don Juan again.) And
do see well to my soul if our lord
God takes me tomorrow, and all the
things in the house are to be sold in
your presence, so that nothing will
be dissipated. And as to the house
and fields that are in Coyoacan, I

milli, ca tehuatzin mochi motechtzinco onictlali, ticmottiliz yn testamento yhuā ticmottiliz yn quenin
onictlali ayocac aca oc çe çan mochi
tehuatzin mochi, motechtzinco nic-
çencauhtiuh ye isquich ynic ynic
(sic) nimitznonahuatilitiuh maca⁰
xitechmoxiccahuili huel ypā timotlatoltiz yn taniman yn nican yhuā
yn ompa coyohuacā yhuā nechmolhuili yn iehuatl yn Mīn de rrosas
onicteopouh onicnotolinili ca çan
oniquelcauh amo niquelnamic ma
ypan timotlatoltiz ca çenca huecauh
yn otechmotlayecultili Ma yehuatl
ytech pohuiz yn xalli yn ompa mani
xant lucas amo çenca huey notlalco-
hualtzin niscoyā. Xicmocaquilticā
ye isquich ynic nicnonahuatilitiuh
nicuhtzin don ju⁰ de guzmā yehuatl
neltiz, mochihuaz, ayac aca quitlacoz. Auh yn iquac ye iuhqui onech-
monahuatili, nimā çatepā nicnolhuili Totecue çihuapille ca yn isquich
ynic otinechmonahuatili ca yntla
dios quimoneq̨ltiz, ca yuh muchi-
huaz, ca niquinnononochiliz yn teu-
pixque yhuā yn tlatoq̄, yhuan
nimitznotlalnamictilia aço cana ytla
ticmoteitlacalhuililitica, anoçe aca
ytla, mascatzin ynic mitlaniliz.
Niman nechmolhuili ca amo: ca yn
isquich quimoteitlacalhuililitia tlacatl s⁰ʳ don pe⁰ de sotom⁰ʳ ca
mochi oniquistlauh yhuā mochi
nechmacaq̄ carta de pago: auh ca
nonqua mani yn Españoles yn
incarta de pago ma huel mochi
mopie ynic amo çatepan aca ni-
campa ytla quitoz, Auh ca nican

have left it all in your hands. You
are to look at the testament and you
will see what I have disposed. I
leave it all in the hands of no one
else but you. This is all I instruct
you. Don't abandon us, see well to
our souls, here and in Coyoacan."
And she told me, "I have afflicted
and mistreated Martín de Rojas, I
have just forgotten him and not remembered him; intercede for him,
for he has served us for a very long
time; let the sandy land in San Lucas, not very large, that I bought
myself, belong to him. (She speaks
to the others.) Hear, this is all that
I am instructing my younger brother
don Juan de Guzmán; it is to be fulfilled and done, and no one is to
stand in the way." And when she
had thus instructed me, then after
that I said to her, "Oh my mistress,
oh lady, if God so wills everything
will be done as you have instructed
me, and I will tell the friars and the
rulers, and I remind you that you
may be owing something to someone, or someone may make some
demand on your property. Then she
said to me, "Why no; I have paid
everything that señor don Pedro de
Sotomayor owed, and they gave me
all the bills of payment, and the
bills of payment of the Spaniards
are in a separate place. Let it all be
well preserved so that later when I
am gone no one will make any

notzontlan mani yn iyōteistime m^a testamento. ma xicmopohuili yn ompa coyohuacā ticmotquiliz huel ticmoneltililiz auh nican ca yn onictlali yn testamento nicā ticmoteititiliz tehuatzin yn imispantz^{co} yn padreme yhuā yn tlatoque tepetenchi chaneque: yehica yn oniquitlaco ynic oncā mochi ticmopahtiliz Ysquich in ynic nechmonahuatili çihuapilli nohueltihuatzin doña Juana de guzmā, yn iuh nechmolhuili ynin tlatolli ymispan testigos Martin de Rosas Grabiel de stiago coyohuacā chane yhuā don diego de velasco xallatlauhco chane çanno ypilotzin yn cihuapilli doña Joana de guzman auh ynic quineltilia yntlatol ypampa nicā quiquetza çeçen cruz ytech yn intoca ypāpa ca amo huel tlacuiloa yn omentin. auh yn don diego de velasco ynic quineltilia huel ymatica quitlalia yn ifirma y- huā ytoca—

+ Martin de Rosas + Gabiel de s.tiagon + Dō d̄iē de vs^o

objections. And here under my head are both testaments; read them, and take (the one concerning there) to Coyoacan and carry it out fully, and the testament I have made for here you are to show to people here in the presence of the fathers and the rulers who are citizens of Tepetenchi, because you are to remedy everything I have done wrong in it." All this the lady my older sister doña Juana de Guzmán instructed me; she made this statement to me before the witnesses Martín de Rojas; Gabriel de Santiago, from Coyoacan; and don Diego de Velasco, from Xalatlauhco, likewise the nephew of the lady doña Juana de Guzmán. And to verify their words they each place a cross here by their names, because two of them cannot write. But to verify it don Diego de Velasco with his very own hand places here his signature and name.

+ Martín de Rojas. + Gabriel de Santiago + Don Diego de Velasco.

6. The Tulancingo Perspective: Some Documents from the UCLA Tulancingo Collection

As the process of collecting, transcribing, translating, and publishing a corpus of mundane Nahuatl documentation continues, we see the importance not only of a chronological spread and a wide variety of document types but also of a wide representation of regions across central Mexico. To date, the Valleys of Mexico and Toluca are somewhat overrepresented. Concentrations of documents from Tlaxcala, Cuauhtinchan, and Cuernavaca go far toward correcting the imbalance, but whenever a cache of Nahuatl texts from an additional region reaches the eyes of scholars in the field, a wider perspective is gained, and our sense of the universality or peculiarity of a whole range of social-cultural developments is strengthened.

The Tulancingo Collection of UCLA is a potentially valuable resource in this respect, concerning as it does a large province on the northeastern periphery of the Nahuatl-speaking peoples (east of Pachuca and north of Tlaxcala) about whose internal development until now little has been known. The collection is in two parts, of which the one relevant here is numbered 2073 in the Research Library's Special Collections.[1] It consists of diverse documents dated from the 1560's to the 1820's, apparently taken at some time from the archive of the chief magistrate or alcalde mayor of the Tulancingo district. Most of the papers are in Spanish, but perhaps a fourth or fifth are in Nahuatl, dated variously from 1567 into the 1760's. Many were written in Tulancingo proper, others in surrounding settlements such as Acatlan, Tototepec, Xaltepec, and Acaxochitlan. The material is distributed in 34 folders, none containing more than fifty to seventy pages, and most far less.

Fragmentary as it is, containing only a small fraction of the larger archive of the alcalde mayor reputed to be in private hands, the collection is the only one presently known to me which originates in a single Mexican provincial center, is distributed chronologically across all three postconquest centuries, and contains Nahuatl documents of diverse types integrated with Spanish documents (as opposed to some invaluable collections that are largely from one period—usually an early one—, are entirely internal to the Indian community, or consist entirely of one kind of document, such as testaments).

From the collection quickly emerges the fact that, despite its relatively peripheral position, Tulancingo shared the general characteristics of post-conquest central Mexico in several basic ways: internal organization of the indigenous community, the latter's cultural, social, and economic practices, its manner of expression, its relation to the Spanish community growing up alongside it. The overall chronology of change was also similar, with perhaps a retardation of some years in certain respects, compared to centers such as Tlaxcala and areas close to Mexico City. Item 2 in the present volume points these things out in the realm of sixteenth-century local governmental practice, comparing Tulancingo with the better known Tlaxcala.

It is a bit surprising to find out how much in the mainstream Tulancingo was as to language and writing. The style of writing and orthographic conventions in the Nahuatl texts of Tulancingo are very much like those seen in the larger centers of the Valley of Mexico, more polished and standard than what is typically found, for example, in the Valley of Toluca or in smaller or more remote centers generally. The same is true of the language itself, which turns out not to share any of the special characteristics of the Tlaxcala-Puebla region to the south.[2] By the late seventeenth and eighteenth centuries, it is true, some of the texts do show greater idiosyncrasy, but that fact itself places them within the broader trend of the time.

Two outstanding subsections of the collection are 1) a liberal selection of documents from the 1570's and 1580's, in which individuals both Spanish and Indian recur frequently enough to throw some light on the overall articulation of the community, and (2) a sheaf of documents, mainly in Nahuatl, showing how a Gómez family gradually bought up bits of land over two generations (middle and later seventeenth century) from individual Indians, usually commoners. In the first section especially, and to a lesser extent throughout the collection, one will find scattered details concerning the organization of indigenous Tulancingo into two halves, Tlatocan and Tlaixpan (see Item 2).

The Spanish-language materials are also instructive, especially for the late sixteenth century. For that time they reveal dominant encomendero families, based in Mexico City, with employees and lesser relatives taking care of family interests on the local scene. Mainly humble Spaniards, with some foreigners among them, were beginning to raise stock, especially sheep, and in some cases to grow wheat and maize for sale. Some mulattoes and mestizos held intermediate positions, while a certain number of Indians had learned enough Spanish skills to enter Spanish employ as craftsmen and keepers of stock. The center of the town of Tulancingo was beginning to become Spanish. At the main church, a mass was said for Spaniards after the one for Indians. A Spanish merchant rented a store on the square, and a black owned a house there. Also to be found on the square was Antonio Genovés, an Italian *tratante* (petty trader) and tavern keeper. In a word, the picture is strikingly similar to that seen in the Toluca region at the same time (see Item 12 in this volume). Indeed, one of the stockmen in Toluca, Francisco Gómez Maya, came there directly from Tulancingo, where he had leased the sheep ranches (*estancias*) belonging to the two halves of the indigenous corporation.[3]

Here follow, then, some sample Nahuatl documents from the collection, in transcription and translation, with comment. Texts 1 and 2 belong to the materials of the 1570's and 80's. Document 3, from the mid-seventeenth century, belongs to the Gómez papers, and Document 4, dated 1720, shows the municipal council of Tulancingo in its late-colonial unified form, in contrast to the two separate cabildos of the earlier period.

Text 1. *Petition of a group of painters to the Spanish alcalde mayor for pay from the altepetl.* Tulancingo, 1570. Folder 1.

Conflicts over whether indigenous artisans should be paid by the altepetl for services performed for the municipality or its church are a recurring theme in Nahuatl documents of the sixteenth century. An example is found in the cabildo minutes of Tlaxcala.[4] Here the altepetl officials have refused to pay a group of painters for some work done in connection with the church (not on the church building proper, apparently); nor is this the first time they have done so. The reason for their reluctance is doubtless not any feeling that the matter was outside their purview, for Nahua municipal organizations in general shouldered a large financial responsibility for church construction and other functions, but a belief that by preconquest standards craftsmen should work on palaces and temples as part of their altepetl duty. (It is not clear whether this matter affects Tlatocan or Tlaixpan, or both.)

The eleven artisans requesting pay are an interesting set about whom the document contains some suggestive hints. They refer to themselves as *tlapallacuiloque*, "painters with color," apparently to distinguish themselves from writers on paper, who shared the generic term *tlacuiloque*. None of them is able to sign his name. On the other hand, the names themselves tell us something of the group's status, for even though rank and name type do not always correspond in a single case, a whole set of names can be very indicative.

Not one of the painters bears an indigenous surname, which, given the time period, tends to place them above the lowest ranking members of society, nor do any show the double first name that was the next step up. Five, however, have saints' names as surnames, a name type that at a moment's notice could become a double first name. That is, it is possible that the Juan de San Francisco on the list was known ordinarily as just Juan Francisco and appears here somewhat dressed up for the occasion. Two painters have a higher-sounding religious surname, de los Angeles. Four have surnames of the same type as Spaniards, the most prestigious kind borne by Indians, but some distinctions must be observed. Three of the four are patronymics, the lowest-ranking among Spanish names, and two of these are Juárez, which for whatever reason was often used as a name for Indians and was per se not especially prestigious. Only one person bears the kind of non-patronymic surname, Delgado, that was characteristic for the highest-ranking nobles. Not a single one of them has the "don" which preceded first names at the highest level. Thus the overall naming pattern is consonant with a group status intermediary between ordinary commoners and noblemen.

The following listing can perhaps render the above clearer:

non-patronymic Spanish surname	1	Leonardo Delgado
ordinary Spanish patronymic	1	Marcos Alvarez
Spanish patronymic much used as an Indian surname	2	Francisco Juárez
		Pedro Juárez
religious surname	2	Gabriel de los Angeles
		Pedro de los Angeles
saint's name as surname	5	Juan de San Francisco
		Antonio de San Juan
		Francisco de San Juan
		Baltasar de San Miguel
		Pedro de San Gabriel
	11	

Linguistically and orthographically, the most unusual feature of the document is its attempt to notate the glottal stop. Full consistency is not achieved (for example, in "toveytlátocatzin" no glottal stop is indicated after *o*, and in "huallaqh" none is indicated after the second *a*), but even so it would be hard to find another text done outside Spanish auspices with such a full notation. The notational devices employed are equally unusual. The use of *h* is in itself not uncommon, though the notation of a word-final glottal stop in any fashion is virtually unseen elsewhere (as in "tlátoqh," "otihuallaqh"). The most unique aspect of all is in the diacritics employed.

Spanish-inspired texts of the seventeenth and eighteenth centuries often use
a grave accent to indicate glottal stop, but here an acute accent is put to that
use. In all likelihood, some Franciscan friar with his own notions about
how to write Nahuatl was stationed at Tulancingo at some point, and the
writer of the present document had been his pupil.

al muy magnifico señur
Ca nican catqui yquixpatzinco oti-
huallaque y tlacatl totlahtocauh yn
téhuantin titlapallácuilóque nican
tochan tollantzinco ca tictlatlauhtia
yn itlátocayotzin yn toveytlátocatzin
son majesdad yhua yn yehuatzin yn
señur toalcalde mayor ca nican catqui ynic yxpatzinco titlacaquiztilia
yn ipampa yn totlatequipanoliz yn
ipa axca xihuitl yn otictequipanóque
yn itechcopa sancta yclesia otitlah-
cuilóque yey metztli yn ixquich o-
ticchiuhque nauhtetl calli yn otiqui-
cuilóque yoa chiquaçentetl tilmahtli
huéhuey tlayxtlapachiuhcayotl yn
ipampa yn ca hamo tle techtlaocolia
yn altepetl yn totlaxtlavil ca oti-
quintolhuilique yn tlátoq̄h ca hamo
techtlaocoliznequi auh ca ypampa yn
ixpantzinco otihuallaq̄h yn totlátocatzin ca çecá miyecpa yn techtza-
cuilia y totlaxtlavil yn ipampa y
totlatequipanoliz ca yxquich in yni-
quixpatzinco otihuallaq̄h y tlacatl
totlahtocatzin ynic tictennamiqui yn
itlátocamatzin yn itlátocaycxitzin
ma yxpatzinco titlaxtlavilocan ynic
ahmo ça tlapic tleyn totech tlamiz
ca ye yxquich ynic tictotlatlauhtilia
yn tlacatl totlátocatzin
/Ca nica titotocayotia yn tehuantin
otitlatequipanóque yn ipa xivitl año
de mill y quinientos y setenta añus

To the very magnificent lord:
Here is that with which we have
come before the lord our ruler, we
painters whose home is here in Tulancingo; we address ourselves to
the rulership of our great ruler the
king, His Majesty, and to the lord
our alcalde mayor. Here is what we
announce about our work; in the
present year we worked three
months for the holy church; the
total of what we did is that we
painted four houses and six large
cloths for covering (i.e., awnings?),
for which the altepetl has not granted us any of our pay. We have told
the rulers (the cabildo members),
but they do not want to grant us
anything. Therefore we have come
before our ruler, for very often they
withhold our pay for our work.
This is all with which we have
come before the lord our ruler and
with which we kiss his rulerly
hands and feet. Let us be paid in his
presence, so that we will not be
falsely accused of something. This
is all with which we implore the
lord our ruler.

/Here we who have worked in the
year of 1570 give our names:

- gabriel de lus ageles   - marcos
aluarez   - pe⁰ de lus angeles
- ju⁰ de sanc fran^co   - balthasar d.
s. miguel   - ant⁰ d. s. ju⁰
- fran^co juarez   - leonardo dergado
fran^co d. s. ju⁰   - pe⁰ d. s. gabriel
- pe⁰ juarez
(all in the same hand)

Gabriel de los Angeles. Marcos
Alvarez. Pedro de los Angeles.
Juan de San Francisco. Baltasar de
San Miguel. Antonio de San Juan.
Francisco Juárez. Leonardo Del-
gado. Francisco de San Juan. Pedro
de San Gabriel. Pedro Juárez.

Texts 2A and 2B. *Petition and counterpetition concerning the activities of (don) Martín Jacobo in Xaltepec.* Tulancingo, ca. 1570. Folder 1.

Xaltepec was a major constituent part or subkingdom of the complex altepetl of Tulancingo, and the person accused here, who then makes petitions in return, must have been Xaltepec's dynastic ruler, or at least the head of one of its lordly houses. He styles himself don Martín Jacobo, though his enemies deny him the "don." The brunt of the accusation, made in the court of the Spanish alcalde mayor, is that don Martín has been taking calpolli land as his own and alienating it to Spaniards; one of these Spaniards has married don Martín's daughter. In his own statement don Martín reveals that he has also been accused of excess in exercising the traditional prerogatives of a lord. Both of these complaints were common all over sixteenth-century central Mexico. It is not entirely clear what body the accusers represent, but some if not all of them are persons of rank rather than the directly affected commoners. Pedro Jiménez, who heads the list of petitioners, was regidor on the Tlaixpan cabildo in 1569 and majordomo in 1582. He is the same person as the Pedro Tepanecatl teuctli at the head of don Martín's list (as regidor he appeared as Pedro Jiménez Tepanecatl teuctli). *Teuctli* means "lord," and in don Martín's list two of the accusers bear this title. The Andrés de Soto who is second among the petitioners must be the same person as the don Andrés de Soto who was alcalde on the Tlaixpan cabildo in 1585. (For the cabildo positions see Item 2 in this volume, Table 3.) Xaltepec, then, clearly belonged to the Tlaixpan half of Tulancingo.[5]

Each side in the controversy has Spanish allies, and each accuses the other of aiding them or being instigated by them. In Spanish-language documents in Folder 1, it turns out that don Martín's Spanish son-in-law, Francisco de Morillones, had occupied the rather lowly post of constable in Tulancingo and had worked for an encomendero. The friend of the other side, Pedro Giraldo, was a farming entrepreneur (*labrador*) residing in Xaltepec. Although he was somehow related to an earlier encomendero of the area, his enterprises were not very high flying; he had been accused of selling beef to local Indians without precise weight. As usual, Spaniards who are directly involved in Indians' affairs prove to be relatively marginal in Spanish society.

Text 2A contains some noteworthy Nahuatl terminology. The document makes one of the clearest explicit statements known concerning the basic structure of Nahua land holdings, which consisted of two types, first a central plot where the household was located and second, optionally but characteristically, one or more often smaller plots at some distance. The statement runs "atley yn ijolal yvā anotley yn ivecāmil y q̓chivā," "they have no lot, nor do they have any distant field to work." The usual term for the central plot was *callalli*, "house-land." Here it is *jolal*, taken from Spanish *solar*, "lot." In Spanish the word usually means an assigned residential lot of uniform size and rectangular shape in an urban setting, but it is clear that to the writer of the present text it signifies the same thing as "house-land." House-land is mentioned quite frequently in Nahuatl documentation generally. But though scattered additional plots are frequently seen in wills and other sources, a well defined general term for this kind of holding is mainly lacking. Here we have such a term, *huecamilli*, literally "far field."[6]

Equally interesting, but more obscure, is the term *nauhcoco*. Since it contains the element *nauh-*, "four," and since Nahua sociopolitical units at all levels often had four subdivisions, I take it to refer to four parts of Xaltepec, but the *-coco* element remains mysterious to me at present.[7]

Text 2A. *Complaint against Martín Jacobo by a delegation from Xaltepec.*

muy mag^{co} señor	May our precious redeemer Jesus
Ma evatzin y dotlahçomaquixticatzin	Christ be with you, our dear hon-
jesu x̄p̄o [m]otlahcincō ye dotlah-	ored ruler; it is with only a small
çonmaviztlahtōcahçinne çan achiçin	matter that we bow down to your
yc dicnepechteq̄lia y mojosticiatzin	justice. Recognize us, for we make
ma xintechmiximachilin ca tevanti	complaint before our great ruler the
y ditoteylviyā yn ixpācinco yn do-	king.
veitlahtocauh Rey	We, Pedro Jiménez, Andrés de Soto,
Ca tevatin p^o xinmenez yvā ātres de	Agustín Huitznahuatl, Pablo Tepan-
suto yvā augustin viznavatl yvā	ecatl, Nicolás, and Francisco de San
pablo tepanecatl yvā nicolas fra^{co} de	Marcos, our home being Xaltepec,
sā marcos tochan xaltepec nauhcoco	mixpāçinco tineçin y titotlatocatzin
Very magnificent lord:	cah ticteylvia y m̄ı̄n sacobo ma xic-

momachitin ca y yehuatl y m̄īn sacobo chicotetl y veveȳ yn ixtlāvactl
y tocalpolal y tomil ōq̇nanamaq̇iltin
espanoles vel tocolhua totava ynmil
tovevemil yvā cenquitin doxvivā do-
pilvā ymil y q̇ncuilia yn oq̇maxcatin
y castilā tlācah av ivā yn maceval-
tzitzinti cenca ye motoliniayā aoctle
ȳ quimochivilia y miltzintli av ivā
y cenq̇ndi y macenvaltin atley yn
ijolal ça moch q̇mocuilitiuh çan
moch ēvatl q̇tlacova y m̄īn sacobo y
moch q̇maxcadia y q̇motlatq̇tia yn i-
tlatq̇ n altepetl auh cenq̇ntin macenvaltin çā q̇nemānā yn tlahcalāq̇lli
atley yn ijolal yvā anotley yn ivecāmil y q̇chivā ca ō moch caxcahtin
yn imo fra^co morilonis ypapā cenca
e motolinniā y macevaltin oca yx-
q̇ch in yn ixpāçino odiq̇toque in señor diego de surio deniete av ascan
ōtivalmovicac in tintotlātocantzin
ma xintechmomāq̇lli y tojosticia y
tley dictitlaniliyā ytlatocauh Rey
canel ic ça cenjostiçia yn amomac-
tzincō cā

p^o xinmenez / atres de joto /
augustin viznavatl / pablo tepānecatl
/ nicolas / fra^co de sa marcos /
alonsu tlilvatecuhtl (signatures all
in same hand)

the four [parts], appear before you,
our ruler, and accuse Martín Jacobo.

Be informed that this Martín Jacobo
has sold seven large meadows, our
calpolli land and our fields, to various Spaniards, which were very
much our fathers' and our grandfathers' fields, our patrimonial fields,
and from some of our children and
grandchildren (i.e., constituents) he
takes their fields and has made them
the property of Castilians. And the
poor commoners are suffering greatly and no longer plant fields. Some
of the commoners have no lot; this
Martín Jacobo takes it all and spoils
everything and appropriates the property of the altepetl. Some commoners wrongly pay tribute who
have no lot nor any distant field to
plant, for he gave it all to his son-
in-law Francisco Morillones, for
which reason the commoners are
suffering greatly. All this above is
what we have said before señor
Diego de Soria, lieutenant (of the
alcalde mayor), and now you have
come, our ruler. Give us our justice
and what we are demanding of our
ruler the king, since entire justice is
in your hands (or since that would
be entire justice and it is in your
hands?).

Pedro Jiménez. Andrés de Soto.
Agustín Huitznahuatl. Pablo
Tepanecatl. Nicolás. Francisco de
San Marcos. Alonso Tlilhua
teuctli.

Text 2B. *Rejoinder of don Martín Jacobo to the complaint against him.*

Al moy mag^{fco} señor
Nehuatl don m̄īn̄ jacobo yhua juā de
la Cruz mixpantzinco tineçi yn ti-
xiptlatzin yn tohueytlatocauh por so
magestad ma xicmocaquititzinno
tlatohuanie ca niz cate y nechteixpa-
huia yn ixpatzinco justicia ytoca p^o
tepanecatl tecvhtli yua antres de jodo
yhua aloso tlilhua tecvhtli yhua juā
çacancatl yhuā pablo tepanecatl yhua
fran^{co} de s. margus yhuā fabia yc-
notl yhua juā ycnoquauh ca yehuā-
tini yn ixpatzinco moquetza justicia
/ auh ca niz catqui y notech quitla-
mia ynic niquitolinia yn totoli yn
ca[ca]huatl yn quahuitl yn ocotl
yhua aquin atlacuih aquique yn teci
y nocha yhua y nechmiltia y nech-
caltia ma mixpatzinco quimelahuaca
ceceyaca xiquimotlatemolili y mo-
chinti tlayacanque auh ma tlachia-
loqui y nocha yn quenami ca yhua y
nomilpa ca yn axca momactzinco
ninocahua nicnitlania nojusticia ma
huel melahuac yn xicmocaquiti auh
yniȳ can za yehuatl oquicuihtlahuilti
yn itoca p^o giralto auh yniy can ça
tecocoliztica quineltilia yn ixpatzinco justicia auh yn axca ca onicno-
maquili yn senor deniēte centetl no-
petiçio yhua nosentecia auh quenin
oquimochihuili y nosenteçia yhua ȳ
nopeticio Cuix oquimotzōquixtili ca
hamo nicmati ma xicmitlanilili ynic
ticmotzōquixtiliz ca ye ixquich ynic
mixpatzinco ninopechteca

To the very magnificent lord:
I don Martín Jacobo and Juan de la
Cruz appear before you who are the
representative of our great ruler His
Majesty. Listen, O lord, here are
the names of those who are accusing
me before the law: Pedro Tepanecatl teuctli, Andrés de Soto, Alonso Tlilhua teuctli, Juan Çacancatl,
Pablo Tepanecatl, Francisco de San
Marcos, Fabián Icnotl, and Juan
Icnoquauh. These are the ones who
are presenting themselves before the
law. And here is what they are accusing me of: that I mistreat them
(by demanding from them) turkeys,
cacao, wood, pine torches, and people to fetch water, grind maize at
my home, plant my fields, and build
my house. Let each one of them
verify it before you; interrogate all
the (subdistrict) leaders, and let
someone come to see how my home
and fields are. Now I leave myself
in your hands and demand my justice; hear it truly. And further, a
person named Pedro Giraldo pres-
sured them (into complaining), and
they are verifying it before the law
only through malice. Now I have
given the lord lieutenant (of the alcalde mayor) a petition of mine and
a judgment (in my favor). What has
he done with my judgment and
petition? I don't know whether he
has concluded with them or not.

Demand them from him so that you
will conclude the matter. This is all
with which I bow before you.
dõ mīn jacobo   Don Martín Jacobo.

Text 3. *Sale of house and land by Agustín de Santiago to Juan Gómez Monteagudo, Spaniard, and wife.* Tulancingo, 1645. Folder 14.

The present document is one of several Nahuatl land sales in the Tulancingo collection concerning the Gómez family; in each, the Gómezes acquire a small piece of land from an indigenous individual. Some of the persons selling land in one document appear as witnesses in other transactions. One gets the impression that the Gómez family was gradually accumulating plots around the borders of their property from Indian neighbors who possibly also worked for them. The documents probably came into the archive of the alcalde mayor of Tulancingo as evidence in one of the campaigns of title verification (*composición*) which took place in central Mexico in the seventeenth century. Without confirmation by higher Spanish authority, sales by individual Indians to individual Spaniards were of dubious legality, and all the more so if the local indigenous municipal council did not sanction the transaction. Such is the case here, for no mention is made of the cabildo of Tulancingo or any of its officers. The document is prepared by a Juan Hernández who calls himself a notary, but he does not say that he is presently employed by the cabildo.

As far as one can tell, the process of land accumulation by the Gómez family was not very swift, aggressive, or methodical. The main strategy seems to have been simply to await likely opportunities. In the present case, opportunity came in the form of the death of one Agustín de Santiago, leaving an aged wife, Cristina Cecilia, and no son or daughter. The proceeds from the sale could pay for Agustín's burial and provide some support for Cristina, who would doubtless not have been able to work the land. Thus the transaction seems to have been in the interest of the sellers as well as the buyers. Similar sales frequently took place in which all the parties were indigenous. The unknown quantity here is a grandchild Baltasar Juan who might have expected to inherit the place; the buyers are concerned enough about him to give him a pittance and have him specifically renounce further claims. Possibly Baltasar Juan was too young to care for the property; possibly he had other assets, perhaps inherited from Agustín's now dead son or daughter; or possibly his interests suffered in the sale. Without more information, we have no way of knowing.

A notable feature of the original document is a diagram of the house and land in question, reproduced on p. 101. Its style contains nothing reminiscent of preconquest pictorial conventions, but its very existence and its placement on the page put it within a certain indigenous tradition. In Tetzcoco in the sixteenth and early seventeenth centuries, land documents were often written around a preconquest-style pictorial representation of the land in question, placed in the center of the page. The pictorial part must have been done first; the alphabetical document would then comment upon it, in part duplicating it. As it happens, Tulancingo was in the cultural and political orbit of Tetzcoco in preconquest times, and some hints exist of ties continuing after the conquest. It is entirely possible that the land diagram here goes back in some sense to the Tetzcoco tradition even though there is nothing in the drawing itself that a local Spaniard might not have done.

Note that while the witnesses for the Spaniard are male, those for Agustín de Santiago are female. The Nahuas long remained more willing than the Spaniards to call upon women to attest to the authenticity of legal proceedings.

- Y nican ypan alltepetl tollantzinco propicia Sant juᵒn pabtista axca ypan mardez yc 8 ylhuitl mani metztli Agosto yn ipan niquinnomaquillia notlatol yn yehuantzitzin señor juᵒn gomez modeacodo yhuan yn ynamictzin señora franᶜᵃ diaz ca noçeyollocacopa y niquinnonamaquiltilia y notlal yhua nocal yhuan mochi cacahuatl quahuitl yn ipan mani notlal yhuā yhua (sic) yn omac mani notlal ypan icac dorazno yhuan nochtli mochi niquinnonamaquiltilia yca caxtolli pesus tominez yztac teocuitlatl onicçelli 11 pesus nomatica auh yn oc çequi ca yc ninotocaz nechmotoquiliz yn señor juᵒn comez ca nima ayac tlen quitos yn huecauhtica ytla oninomiquili ca notlatqui ca naxca y nicnamaca hayac ytlatqui ypanpa nican ninotocayotia y nehuatl agustin de

Here in the altepetl of Tulancingo, province of San Juan Bautista, today Tuesday the 8th day of the month of August, I give my word to señor Juan Gómez Monteagudo and his wife señora Francisca Díaz; with my entire will I sell them my land and my house with all the walnut trees which are on my land, and a piece of my land on the other side of the road on which there are peaches and fruit cactus. I sell it all to them for 15 pesos in silver reales; I have received 11 pesos in my hands, and with the rest señor Juan Gómez will bury me. When I have died, no one whosoever is to make any objections for a long time to come, for it is my property I am selling, not anyone else's property, wherefore here I give my name, Agustín de Santiago, and so that my statement

s.tiago ypanpa yc neltitiaz y notlatol nica nicmachiotia y nocal y-
hua notlal yn queni ca nican neztiez
—

will be verified I manifest here my
house and land; how it is will
appear here:

(Here the picture)

- auh y nehuatl xpina çecilia yhuan
noxhuiuh ytoca paltaçar juᵒn ca
nican tiquitohua ymixpantzinco y
señores diego de gastro yhuan luyz
lopez ytezticotzitzihua yehuatzin
juᵒn gomez yhuā tehuanti totezticohua ysabel clara yhuan melchiora
de s.ta maᵃ tleynel tiquitosque yc
oquimonamaquillitehuac y nonamictzin agostin de s.tiago yn ical y-
huan y noxhuiuh ca ayocmo cepa
tlen quitoz y huecauhtica yc oqui-
cauh y tlalli auh ca çano yuhqui y
nehuatl ca ça nomiquiz nicchixtica
ca hayocmo ytech nitlatohua yn tlalli yhua calli ca tonehuan otiquaque y
nonamictzin oticoncahuique yn otic-
popoloque ca huel ymaticatzinco yn
otechmomaquilique yn tomi oqui-
mocuiliz (sic) nonamic yztac teocuitlatl ca nima ayac tlen quitoz y huecauhtica auh y nehuatl juᵒn pathacar
ca nican nechmomaquilia ome pesus
y yehuatzin señor juᵒn gomez ca
çaniuh motlaocolia ca çenca nictlaçocamati onechmotlaçoycnelilitzino
ca nima ayac aquin tlatoz y huecauhtica ca ye ixquich ca ye oticcauhque
yn tocal ca ye yc çe. . . ytlatquitzin
yn señor juᵒn gomez yhua ynamictzin señiora franᶜᵃ dias ca nima ayac
aquin quinmocuililiz y huecauhtica
auh yn aquin tlatoz y quenmania ca
quixtlahuaz huaz (sic) matlactli pe-

And I Cristina Cecilia and my
grandchild named Baltasar Juan say
here, in the presence of the gentlemen Diego de Castro and Luis López, witnesses for Juan Gómez, and
our witnesses, Isabel Clara and Melchora de Santa María, that what we
will say is that my husband Agustín
de Santiago sold his house at dying,
and my grandchild will never make
any objection in the future about
how he gave up the land, and likewise I am awaiting my death and I
no longer have any say about the
land and house which sustained us
both, my husband and me, and we
shared (our expenses? that which
we have now given up?), for with
their very hands they gave us the
money and my husband took it in
silver, and no one whosoever is to
make any objections for a long time
to come. And I Juan Baltasar am
being given 2 pesos by señor Juan
Gómez, which he is just giving me
as a favor, and I am very beholden
and grateful to him, so no one whosoever is to make any objections far
into the future. This is all, for we
have left our house and it is once
and for all the property of señor
Juan Gómez and his wife señora
Francisca Díaz, and no one whosoever is to take it from them in the

sus tominez ytech monequiz yn
ijusticiacaltzin tohueytlatocatzin
Rey ns̄t̄ro senor yn techmopielia yn
oquimotequimaquilli yn dios yn tohueytlatocatzin totemaquixticatzin -
tt⁰ jesu christo ca amo tahahuiltzin
ca toteoyocoxcatzin ma çemicac tic-
toyectenehuillica yn timochinti nican ticate ma yuh mochihua amen
jesus

auh nican tiquintocayotia yn teztigo
yn tehuanti totezticohua nican tiquintocayotia ynic neltities yn totlatol ynic ce ytoca ysabel clara yc
ome melchiora de s.ta maᵃ
auh yn yehuatl yn señor juᵒn gomez
mondeacodo ca nican cate yn itesti-
cohua
　diego de gastro luys lupez de ribera
　ysabel clara　melchiora de s.ta mᵃ
　(all signatures by notary)
- nehuatl juᵒn hn̄dz ezcrivano nica
nictlallia y nofirma yc neltitiez ynin
tlatolli ca melahuac yn oniquicuilo
amo tle onicpollo axca ypan mardes
yc 8 tonalli mopohua metztli agosto
años 1645 yn ipan quimoçelilia yn
tlallamatl y yehuatzi señor juᵒn
gomez mondeacodo yhua ynamictzin
seniora franᶜᵃ diaz ypanpa nican
nictlallia nofirma　　juᵒn hrnz
escrivan⁰
- yhua ynic omotocac y nocoltzin
yn tomi 4 pᵒs yhua 4 tᵒs yc onaci
yn ipatiuh y calli caxtolli pesus nel
yc oquipanahui nahui tomi nican
neztica ayac aqui tlatoz

future. Whoever should sometime
make objections is to pay 10 pesos
in cash to be used for the courthouse
of our ruler the king our lord who
guards us, who was given office by
God our great ruler and our redeemer
Jesus Christ, who is not our play-
thing but our divine creator; let all
of us who are here always praise
him. May it be so done, Amen,
Jesus.
And here we name the witnesses:
we name here our witnesses to how
our words are true: the first is
named Isabel Clara and the second
Melchora de Santa María.
And here are the witnesses of Juan
Gómez Monteagudo:

Diego de Castro. Luis López de Ribera. Isabel Clara. Melchora de
Santa María.
- I Juan Hernández, notary, place
here my signature verifying this
statement, and I wrote it truly and
left nothing out. Today, Tuesday
the 8th day of the month of August
of the year 1645, señor Juan Gómez
Monteagudo and his wife señora
Francisca Díaz receive the land document, wherefore I set down here my
signature.　　Juan Hernández, notary.
- And the money with which my
grandfather was buried was 4 pesos
and 4 tomines, with which it attains
the price of the house, 15 pesos, and
in truth exceeded it by 4 tomines.
Here it appears, and no one is to
make objections.

The diagram from the center of the page:

(Nahuatl)

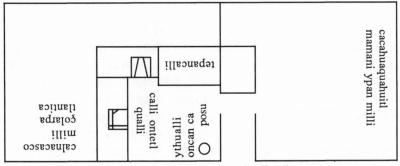

çolar yc toncalaqui calitec

milli ypan icac
torasno

(English)

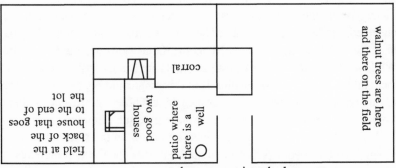

where you go into the lot

field on which stand
peaches

Text 4. *Confirmation of the status of fields belonging to Santa Elena.*
Tulancingo, 1720. Folder 19.

In a common convention of postconquest Nahua inheritance, a dying person bequeathed a piece of land not to a relative but to a saint (or saint's image); the relative was then put in charge of the land, "to serve the saint with it," i.e., to support the saint's cult. What are we to make of such arrangements? It is hard to achieve certainty, for the Nahuas themselves could not; ambiguity and contention pursued the lands of saints. In most cases, the actual intention seems to have been to leave the land to the relative, with some expectation that a saint to which the family was devoted (often housed in the family residence) would receive some candles, flowers, and incense. Yet by an underlying Nahua rationale, saints were conceived to be the residual owners of land, perhaps indeed of all lands. In some cases, and particularly when the whole community was involved, the holder of the land really was a custodian only, a steward for the saint. Yet such a holder might still aspire to full ownership.[8]

The present document, at whose instigation we cannot be sure, attempts to clear up the picture for one saint's lands case, but with dubious success. The text speaks at times of the land being left to María Agustina, the holder, but it also says in no uncertain terms that the land belongs to Santa Elena. Where the document says "her grandfather Francisco de la Cruz bequeathed it to her," or "left it all to her," the English is no more ambiguous than the Nahuatl. Either Santa Elena or María Agustina could be meant. While it appears that María Agustina's rights are being confirmed, the mere fact that the municipal corporation is intervening could be ominous. Cases of this type, often eventuating in prolonged and bitter controversy, abound from central Mexico in the seventeenth and eighteenth centuries.

Notice the form of the cabildo illustrated here. In the sixteenth century Tulancingo had two separate municipal councils for the two moieties of Tlatocan and Tlaixpan, each with its own governor, alcaldes, and regidores (see Item 2 in this volume). At some point in the seventeenth century the two were consolidated, with one governor, one "regidor mayor" (with no simple regidores as far as one can see), and four alcaldes, apparently two each for Tlatocan and Tlaixpan.[9]

yn nican ypan Altepetl S[n] Ju[o]
Bap[ta] tollantz[co] axcan yc cempo-
hualli yhuan matlactli mani metztli

Here in the altepetl of San Juan
Bautista Tulancingo, today the 30th
of the month of July of the year

julio mill setezientos y Veinte años
Nenhuatl D^n Ju^o maldonado go-
u^{or} - D^n Antt^o de galizia Rexidor
m^{or} - D^n P^o de la cruz - D^n Bartholome de la cruz - D^n Ju^o rramos - D^n Joseph de S^n Ju^o alcaldes Antt^o rrodrigues escriu^o de
Republica - nenhuatl D^n Ju^o
maldonado gou^{or} yn timochintin ȳ
titlatequipanohua yn it[ec] yn altepetl omoteneuh auh ca nican tixpan
omonexiti yehuatzin maria aug^{na}
temascaltitlan ytechcacopa yn tlali
onpa mani motenehua atenpa mil-
yahualtontli meyotoc ocan pehua yn
itech yn itlaltzin D^n Aug^n omoetzticatca onaçi yn itech yn otli ynic
huilohua tianquizco oquimonemacti-
litiaque yn inantzin maria Augustina
omoetzticatca oquimomaquilita yn
itlaçotatzin omoetzticatca ytocatzin
fran^{co} de la cruz yhuan oc çe calte-
tzontli onpa mani caltitla ce xololpa
ycaltitla antt^o de S^n Ju^o omoetzticatca auh ynin tlali omoteneuh ca
ytlatquitzin Sta Elena yc quimotequipanilhuis y maria Aug^{na} oqui-
monemactilita yn icoltzin omoetzticatca fran^{co} de la cruz yhuan oc çe
tlalli meyotoc onpa mani tetela ocan
pehua yn itenco yn apamitl ynic
yauh yn atl teopan timocuaxoch-
namiqui yn tlatohuani D^n Diego de
galizia niman yauh tlamelahua onaçi
atenco niman yauh huitecoya tlamelahua atentitech niman tlacolohua oc
çepa tlamelahua onaçi oc çepa yn
itech yn apamitl ynic yauh yn atl

1720, before me don Juan Maldonado, governor, don Antonio de
Galicia, regidor mayor, don Pedro de
la Cruz, don Bartolomé de la Cruz,
don Juan Ramos, and don Josef de
San Juan, alcaldes, and Antonio
Rodríguez, notary of the commonwealth—before me don Juan Maldonado and all of us who serve within the aforesaid altepetl, appeared
María Agustina of Temazcaltitlan
about the land at the place called
Atempan, a small round field planted in maguey; it begins next to the
land of the late don Agustín and
reaches as far as the road going to
the marketplace. María Agustina's
mother (and her grandfather?) bequeathed it to her; her (the mother's)
late father named Francisco de la
Cruz had given it to her, with another house foundation beside a
house on a lot, next to the house of
the late Antonio de San Juan. This
aforesaid land belongs to Santa Elena, with which María Agustina is to
serve her, since her late grandfather
Francisco de la Cruz bequeathed it to
her, along with another piece of land
planted in maguey at Tetela, beginning at the edge of the irrigation
ditch by which water goes to the
church, where we border on the lord
don Diego de Galicia, and then it
goes straight as far as the edge of
the water; then it goes to the
threshing place, straight along the
edge of the water, and then it turns
and goes straight again until it again
reaches the irrigation ditch by which

teopan niman ontlami y canin
opeuh ca mochi ytlatquitzin y Sta
elena yc quimotequipanilhuisque yn
santa Elena mochi oquimocahuililita
yn icoltzin omoetzticatca y maria
Aug^{na} auh tiquitohua timochintin
Gou^{or} Rexidor m^{or} yhuan alcaldes
timochintin ofiçiales de rrepublica
ca neltiliztli melahuac ca tixpan
opanoc yn iamayo ӯ tlali omoteneuh y quenin yaxca ocatca yn tlali y
fran^{co} de la cruz auh yn axcan ca
oquimocahuililitiaque y maria augustina yc quimotequipanilhuis ӯ
Sta Elena auh ypanpa yn axcan tic-
tomaquilia ynin amatl yn yehuatzin
maria Aug^{na} ypampa ca tixpan
opanoc yn iamayo yn tlali omoteneuh tlacuitlapa auh ynic nelli melahuac ca nican tictlalia yn tofirma
auh yn xihuitl yn tonalli ca ye
tlacuitlapan omoteneuh

    D^{n} juan maldonado Gou^{or} D^{n}
Antt^{o} de Galizia Rexidor m^{or} D^{n}
p^{o} de la cruz alcalde   D^{n} Juan
rramos Alcalde   D^{n} Bartholome de
la Cruz alcalde   D^{n} Antt^{o} mexia
ynterino alcalde tlayxpan

    Antt^{o} rrodriguez escriu^{o} Repu-
blica   (signatures all in same
hand)

water goes to the church, and then it
ends where it began. All of it is
Santa Elena's property; with it they
are to serve Santa Elena, and María
Agustina's late grandfather left it all
to her. And all of us, governor, regidor mayor, and alcaldes, all of us
officials of the commonwealth say
that verily and truly we were shown
the documents for the aforemen-
tioned land, (proving) how the land
belonged to Francisco de la Cruz,
and now they have left it to María
Agustina to serve Santa Elena.
Therefore now we issue this document to María Agustina, because we
were shown the documents for the
land mentioned on the other side (of
the sheet). Here we set down our
signatures; the year and day were
already given on the other side.

    Don Juan Maldonado, governor.
Don Antonio de Galicia, regidor ma-
yor. Don Pedro de la Cruz, alcalde.
Don Juan Ramos, alcalde. Don Bar-
tolomé de la Cruz, alcalde. Don
Antonio Mejía, interim alcalde for
Tlaixpan.
    Antonio Rodríguez, notary of
the commonwealth.

7. A Language Transition in Eighteenth-Century Mexico: The Change from Nahuatl to Spanish Recordkeeping in the Valley of Toluca

By the mid-eighteenth century central Mexico's dominant indigenous language, Nahuatl, had been in contact with Spanish for over two hundred years. As a result, it contained numerous Hispanisms, and many Nahuatl speakers habitually used Spanish in certain contexts.[1] At what point in time, among what groups, and for what reasons did Spanish replace Nahuatl as a vehicle of communication? In general, one must still answer such questions rather schematically and speculatively, but for one aspect of the matter—the language used in conducting corporate community business— texts are beginning to come to light which give us a closer view of how certain towns, in the course of the eighteenth century, made the transition from Nahuatl to Spanish in their internal recordkeeping. The particular texts to be used here come from the southern part of the Toluca Valley (the western neighbor of the Valley of Mexico), supplemented by a glimpse at some parallel texts from a segment of the indigenous community of Mexico City.[2]

The countryside of central Mexico during the colonial period, the area lying in between the dominant but widely interspersed "Spanish" towns such as Mexico City and Puebla, was organized into a large number of Indian municipalities, based on local preconquest states, which despite numerous obligations to the outside were, on a day-to-day basis, locally autonomous under their own town councils. From the mid-sixteenth century forward these Indian towns maintained records of council meetings, trials, land grants, wills, property sales, and the like, in essentially Spanish genres, but written (using the Roman alphabet) in Nahuatl. In some towns, at some periods, a large portion of the local upper group was literate in Nahuatl; in other situations Nahuatl literacy was confined to two or three local specialists who rotated as notaries attached to the town council or church. While almost universal over a wide area, the tradition of Nahuatl writing and recordkeeping was handed down locally in each case, and the numerous texts still preserved are a rich source for the study of Nahuatl speech in a time dimension one might have thought lost to direct observation.

Since the bulk of the Spaniards in colonial Mexico were long based in a few large cities, somewhat removed from the bulk of the Indians, it was possible for the Indian towns to retain indigenous speech and many indigenous practices for centuries—in some cases on into our own times. But the two components of the population could not be kept apart forever; in the seventeenth and eighteenth centuries there came to be increasingly important nuclei of Spanish speakers resident in the Indian countryside, creating new Spanish-style settlements, until the whole area was honeycombed with them. Spanish enterprises hired a large number of the Indians at least part of the year; in the larger regional markets Spanish speakers with connections to the cities were dominant; Spanish-speaking administrative officials grew in numbers until there were some of them located in relative proximity to almost any Indian town.

One of the many results of this spilling out of Spanish speakers into the country was that the leaders of the Indian communities—the more or less noble, more or less wealthy figures who manned the town councils—began to become at least partially bilingual. (Not that indigenous speech was actually being lost; even by the time of Mexican independence in the early nineteenth century, the majority of the rural population of central Mexico still spoke various Indian languages, with Nahuatl the most widespread.) We can follow the process of acquisition of Spanish through observing the legal testimony of Indians which is so abundantly preserved in the archives. In order to be understood by the Spanish officials who reviewed appeals and disputes at the supracommunity level, testimony had to be rendered in Spanish either directly or through an interpreter. With very few exceptions, local Indian notables of the sixteenth century, and far into the seventeenth, in fact needed and used a court interpreter. In the latter years of the seventeenth century, for areas all over central Mexico, one begins to see rather frequently the notation that an interpreter was used for a given witness, in the name of juridical unimpeachability, "sin embargo de ser ladino en nuestra lengua castellana," or some such phrase. By the middle of the eighteenth century such statements are almost the expected thing; it was also not uncommon for a Spanish official to interrogate an entire Indian town council as a body, noting the use of an interpreter despite the fact that *all* of them were fluent in Spanish. Over the century it was also becoming more common for original testimony in Spanish to be accepted from Indian council members. By about 1800 one begins to see whole sets of testimony in which there is no mention either of an interpreter or of what language was used; apparently there was coming to be a presumption that Indian notables could and would use Spanish in their depositions.

Another way of seeing the level of Spanish competence which was building up among the Indian leaders is to examine the Nahuatl texts they were producing. Generally speaking, over time these texts came ever closer to Spanish models—without ever literally duplicating them, because locally-grown formulas and turns of phrase always retained some currency. Late colonial Nahuatl had developed a set of standard mechanisms for adopting almost any needed Spanish word or phrase. Special Spanish legal terminology, in loan words new and old, and also in entire borrowed frozen expressions, came to dominate some texts to such an extent that superficially they almost seem to be in Spanish.

For illustration let us look at Text 1, a land grant issued in Nahuatl in 1750 by the council of the important Toluca Valley town of Calimaya.[3] Although nothing in it, as to type of phenomenon, goes beyond parallel texts from the Valley of Mexico at the same time, it is the most extreme example I have yet seen, presented here for that very reason and because we know from later evidence that Calimaya was on the verge of going over to Spanish recordkeeping.[4] If one somewhat arbitrarily divides Text 1 into 284 "words," the result is that aside from 28 elements of proper names (all Spanish), 154 of the constructs are indigenous Nahuatl, and 102 (underlined in the transcription)[5] are derived from Spanish, so that the lexical content is, depending on what one counts, some 40 to 46 percent overtly Spanish in origin. The material includes whole set phrases as well as nouns, verbs, and particles (especially *de* and the much-used *para*, *y* being only part of set loan phrases). Most of the loan vocabulary is legal in nature, or at least has to do with normal Spanish ways of referring to land (*pedazo, esquinas*), but some is more general, as with the particles in their various uses, or a *grano* of maize, or *mantener* (with the indigenous reflexive) for supporting oneself. Spanish influence in the text goes even beyond what is seen in overt loan words. Some indigenous words are used as equivalents of Spanish ones rather than in their original application. *Quenami*, originally "how, in what manner," is used here as a substitute for Spanish *como* in two senses: "as, in the capacity of" (*nehual quenami jues*, "I as judge"), and as an introducer of dependent clauses, in effect "that" (*quenami mitlania se pedaso tlali*, "how—or that—a piece of land is requested"). Similarly, *yca* (*i-ca*) represents Spanish *con*, *pie* (*pia*) Spanish *tener*, and *pano* Spanish *pasar*.[6]

On the other hand, the text is by no means incompetent or incongruous as Nahuatl. All the Spanish phenomena are handled according to the then current conventions. The indigenous Nahuatl vocabulary is standard, varied, correctly inflected, and arranged by the usual principles of Nahuatl syntax. What may appear to be some simple errors are general characteristics of the

---

Text 1. *Land grant, Calimaya, 1750*

Nican ypan yaltepetzin *sannto*
Sⁿ Pedro Calimaya niquitua nehual
juez y *gᵒʳ por Su Magᵈ* yca nu *sʳᵉˢ*
alcaldes yhuan *oficiales de Reppᶜᵃ*
quenami tuchpa oqui*presentar*o se
petision Marselino Anntᵒ yhuan y-
sihuahuatzin Maria Madalena yhuan
nehual quenami *juez* y *gᵒʳ* oniquin-
mosentlalili muchtintzitzi altepe-
huacatzitzinti *señores gʳᵉˢ pasados*
yhuan *señores alcaldes pasados* yca
muchi *comun* yhuan oniquinmoca-
quistilili ynon amatzintli yhuan
ytech onesi ytlaytlanilis ynin *Dˢ*
yconetzi quenami mopechtecatihuis
yca ychoquis yhuan yyelsisihuilis
quenami mitlania se *pedaso* tlali
para campa quitucas ome yey *grano*
tloli yhuan *para* quipies campa qui-
quichtis *para* mu*mantener*os quesqui
tonali *Dˢ* quimochicahuilis yhuan
para quichtlahuas ytlatocatlacalaquil-
tzi tohueytlatocatzin *el Rey nuestro*
sʳ yhuan oc sequi *obensiones* mi-
tlani ypan toaltepe campa sa nima
otlananquililique muchtintzitzi *sʳᵉˢ*
gʳᵉˢ pasados yca *comun* que* ma
momaca ynin *Dˢ* ypiltzi tlen qui-
tlani yhuan nehual quenami *jues* y
gʳ sa nima onipano yca nu *Reppᶜᵃ*
otictemulique se *pedaso* sacatitla
mani cuactenco mocuaxuxhuia yca
ymiltzi *Sⁿta* Rosa *para* ycalaquian
tonali yhuan *para* yquisayan tonali
mocuaxuxhuia yca Calistro Joseph
onicmaca *posesion* ynin *Dˢ* yconetzi
en nombre de Su Magᵈ onicasi yca

Here in the town of holy San
Pedro of Calimaya, I, the judge/gov-
ernor through His Majesty, with my
honorable alcaldes and officials of
the municipality, declare that before
us Marcelino Antonio and his wife
María Magdalena presented a petition, and I as judge/governor assembled all the town citizens, the
honorable past governors and past
alcaldes, with all the ordinary people, and I had that document read to
them, and in it appears the request
of this child of God, that he bows
down with weeping and sighing and
requests a piece of land where he can
plant two or three grains of maize
and to have some place where he can
get the means to maintain himself
for the time that God should give
him health and to pay the tribute of
our great ruler the king our lord, and
other duties which are demanded in
our town. Then immediately all the
honorable past governors and ordinary people replied to him "Let this
child of God be given what he
asks," and I as judge/governor immediately went with my municipal
officials and we sought for him a
piece of land next to the grassland at
the edge of the forest bordering with
the field of Santa Rosa on the west,
and on the east bordering with Calisto José; I gave possession to this
child of God in the name of His
Majesty; I took him by the hand,

yma quitepectiaya tlali yhuan tlasuli yhuan tlen casia ye muchi onicchihua *en nombre de Su Mag^d* ynic onic*paxal*uchti ypan nahui *esquinas* yhuan *para* amo aquin quemania quipies tlen quitos onoso quixitinis totlatol tictemaca ynin amal *de posesion* ypan sempuali yhuan yey tonali *de nobiembre* xihuil *de mil setesientos sincuenta* yhuan niquitua tla aquin tle quitos quemania nicmotlatlactilia sasu aquin *s^r jues de Su Mag^d* quimuquichtililis sempuali yhuan macuili *pesos pena para ycajatzin* tohueytlatocatzin *el Rey nuestro s^r* nehual *jues y g^r por Su Mag^d* D^n Pablo Destrada nu *s^res alcaldes* D^n Asensio de la Cruz yhuan D^n Agustin de la Cruz *Regidor mayor* D^n Fran^co xabiel yhuan muchtintzitzi nu*ofisiales de Repp^ca*

    Es^no de Republica Julian Asensio

and he went about scattering earth and waste and whatever he put his hands on; I did it all in the name of His Majesty, causing him to stroll to the four corners. And so that no one will ever have any objections or abrogate our declaration, we issue this bill of possession on the 23rd day of November, year of 1750, and I declare that if anyone should ever raise objections, I implore any honorable judge of His Majesty to extract from him a penalty of 25 pesos for the treasury of our great ruler the king our lord; I the judge/governor through His Majesty, don Pablo de Estrada, and my honorable alcaldes don Ascencio de la Cruz and don Agustín de la Cruz, and the chief councilman don Francisco Javier, with all of my municipal officials.

    Municipal notary, Julián Ascencio.

Nahuatl of the area of Calimaya and Tianquiztenco in the seventeenth and eighteenth centuries.[7] Moreover, as a statement in a certain genre the text is in touch with the great tradition of Nahuatl public documents. The language moves in formulas and accustomed phrases, some going all the way back to preconquest rhetoric, as in the assertion that the petitioner "bows down with weeping and sighing:"; there is also the authentic archaic wording "where the sun comes out" for "east" and "where the sun enters" for "west" (though it is true that these venerable phrases are here introduced by *para* rather than by the traditional indigenous *inic*). Another traditional phrase is *quesqui tonali Ds quimochicahuilis* "for however many days God should strengthen him (give him health)," i.e., "for the rest of his life."

    All in all, Text 1 shows a writer of Nahuatl who has absorbed a great deal in the way of Spanish vocabulary and concepts, who is writing a type of document which has very close Spanish parallels, and who, conceivably, part of the time, may have been actually thinking in Spanish and translating back. We can see the temptation that might exist in him to go over to Spanish entirely, and the potential for doing so. Yet persons like the writer of the present text were under no compelling necessity to make the switch. They were entirely competent as writers and speakers of Nahuatl, in a context where Nahuatl was widely understood, while still adequate conventions of Nahuatl written expression were at their fingertips. The switch, when it came, was brought on by factors other than simple loss of the ability to produce intelligible Nahuatl texts.

What were the factors motivating a change? Nowhere does direct testimony from a participant appear, so we must look a bit into the logic of the overall context. Central Mexico, having been in the sixteenth century the arena of two almost separate societies, was evolving in the late colonial period toward a situation in which each local territorial subdivision of society consisted of an upper Spanish segment and a lower Indian segment. Consequently everything Spanish, language and all the rest, was acquiring a prestige which was not merely hypothetical or applied to distant spheres, but which was felt tangibly on the local scene. Whereas Indian towns, valuing their autonomy greatly, may once have found it advantageous to conduct their business in a medium Spaniards could not comprehend, now they faced the increasing necessity of having their affairs reviewed by Spanish speakers, with the consequent utility of keeping records in Spanish in the first place, not to speak of the increased urging on the part of the Spaniards that they do so. In such a context, it would not be surprising if the transition in recordkeeping antedated true linguistic necessity or even appropriateness.

Whatever the reasons, for they must remain up to a point in the realm of speculation, it is a fact that the transition sometimes preceded the ability to write reasonable Spanish prose. Consider Text 2, composed in Spanish in 1733 in the little town of Casulco, somewhere in the jurisdiction of Tianquistenco.[8] The transition here is premature, carried out by a writer who is convinced that it is better to use Spanish at all costs. The resulting text is intelligible only by reference to general documentary conventions, common sense, and the Nahuatl substratum. The writer masters neither number nor gender agreement (apparently not even the principle thereof, much less the details, especially with number), nor can he inflect verbs. He tends to prefer the infinitive for all cases and seems to lean to the view that all infinitives are in -ar, as seen in his form *morirar* (though possibly he intends his -ar as the future). In one case he actually uses a loan verb form much as it would be in Nahuatl, *quitaros*.[9] The text shows little knowledge of the idiomatic use of Spanish prepositions (note the frequent lack of a necessary *de, a ,* or

---

Text 2. *Bill of sale, Casulco in the jurisdiction of Tianquiztenco, 1733*

Año de 1733 a^{os}
Escrituran
 El mes de diciembre a 28 pongo este escritura llo me llamo D^n Andres Martin, sobre vn pedason de tierras que le bendin, estos hijos se llaman Andres Ju^o lo que me di su m^e estos hijos lo que balen, las tierras, que son berdan 3 p. 4 r. la uerdan pongo, mis juramentos, delante de Dios, que si D^s pedir juramentos a mi qui si Dios me lo perdonar, me morirar, y para que ningunos se les quitaros esta tierras besino la comonidad, esta tierras ninguno, molestete estos hijo, pongo mi juramento, delante mis hijas Ger^{ma} Angelan, y su hijo, fra^{co} pedro tengo los alguaseal, que jue testigon los ofisiales, de republican el fiscal, y para que ninon se aga perjuision estos hijon si algunus sempiese pleitos pena para justisian, dosesos y dos mes de carse, el gouemador tampie lesi beintequatros asotes pena sinco p^s para go^r no mas que bongo juramentos delante de D^s

D^n Saluador Mathias	D^n matheo fra^{co} fiscal
alcalde ordinario	de la s^{ta} yglesia
alhuasil mayor	
Nicolas de Tolentino	Siendo testigo todo esto
SS^{no} publico	Fer^{do} Belasques

---

en), and there is properly speaking no ability to construct Spanish sentences at all. Texts like these are amusing, but also distinctly ridiculous and close to meaningless, and hence they are apparently few. Not until the latter half of the eighteenth century, and indeed in the main not until its final quarter, does one see Spanish documents prepared by Nahuatl speakers of the Toluca Valley in numbers and as a matter of course. Such productions could still have their laughable side, as witness Text 3, from Santa María de la Asunción near Calimaya and dated 1781.[10] But aside from some expectable *o-u* and *i-e* merging, *n* intrusion, and *r* metathesis, the effect in Text 3 is caused almost entirely by the use of *b* for *g* (*otorbamos* for *otorgamos*) and especially of *d* for *b* and *v* (*denifisios* for *beneficios*, *dedino* for *divino*, *cade* for *cabe*, etc.); perhaps the writer really did merge voiced obstruents in speech, since Nahuatl originally lacked them. In matters of vocabulary, inflection, agreement, and even overall syntax and idiom, the text is quite sophisticated, on a different level entirely from Text 2.
 An intermediate step in the direction of original Spanish texts was the

---

Text 3. *Obligation of the council of Santa María de la Asunción, jurisdiction of Calimaya, 1781*

En este pueblo de S^nta Maria la Assump^on en bentio dias de febrero de 1781 anos estando todos juntos congregados el alcalde autual D^n Andres Florensio Rexidor mayor D^n Julian Faustino y demas ofisiales de Rep^ca en ·conpanian de todos lo señiores alcaldes pasados y demas comun deste dh^o pueblo los que en vuena confromindad le otorbamos esta obligasion a S^ra Josefa Antonia de Albirde en conpania de su ermana Petrona Ygnasia tocante un pedaso de tierra de labor que tiene n^ra s^ntisima madre y s^ra de la Assump^on de la que nos obligamos en todo tienpo trabagarla en sus denefisios para en su cultu dedino poniendo y nonbrando un mayordomo para su santo serdision y es dentender que en la dh^a tierra cade de sendradura una fanega de mais y para que coste ser derdad lo firmamos en dicho dia mes y año los que supimos escridir

el alcalde autual D^n Ander Florensio

Rexidor mayor D^n Julian Faustino

es^on de Rep^ca Juan Bernardo

Luis de Fransia fiscal de la santa yglesia el escribano quando fallesio la difunta

D^na Pasquala Maria

y para que conste en todo tienpo delante de todos s^res pasados y demas comun

D^n Antonio Silberio alcalde pasado

Urbano Jph esno pasado

---

preparation of Spanish translations of Nahuatl originals. Throughout most of the colonial period, whenever it was necessary to present a document to higher authorities, the interested party would appear with the Nahuatl original, which a court translator would then render into Spanish. In the second half of the eighteenth century, some of the local Indian notaries began to make their own Spanish translations of Nahuatl originals which their predecessors or they themselves had written. Finally, apparently around 1775-1780 in the Calimaya region, some of these local clerks began doing Spanish originals which differed in no way from the translations; all of the local conventions, whether concerning the general ordering of the document, the ceremonial mention of certain saints, or the way of describing a piece of land, remain the same. It is quite impossible to distinguish a translation from an original without a specific contemporary notation deciding the question.[11] The known translations and originals, taken as a single corpus, show enough consistent characteristics to allow for some generalization about the nature and source of their deviance from more standard Spanish texts.

Among the first things drawing attention in the Spanish texts by Nahuatl speakers are some Nahuatl loan words; in fact, however, a large number of Nahuatl terms had entered general Mexican Spanish by the eighteenth century (many long before that). They are mainly nouns, with a scattering of verbs, and most of them designate characteristic indigenous objects and activities. Terms such as *milpa*, "field," *tepisque*, "ward head in an Indian town," or *sacamolear*, "to clear a field (especially by weeding and removing turf)" were widely understood and occur in Spanish texts of all kinds.[12]

All in all, despite Text 3, Spanish texts produced by indigenous persons in the Toluca Valley after about 1750 show considerable mastery of orthography (with probable implications for pronunciation), of number and gender agreement, and of verb inflection. The Spanish vocabulary is broad and is mainly used in ways showing inner comprehension. Some residual slips aside, most of the deviance has to do with syntax and use of larger idioms.

As to syntax, one notices a great deal of deviant use of Spanish object pronouns and of the preposition *a*, or to put it another way, an inability or disinclination to mark objects as they are ordinarily marked in Spanish. In effect, the writers tended to retain elements of the Nahuatl system, which is at considerable variance from the Spanish one. In Spanish, as I hardly need say, one marks a personal object of a verb with the preposition *a*, and also, optionally, according to dictates of emphasis and style, adds an object pronoun before the verb: *(lo) veo a Juan*. In Nahuatl the object pronoun, as a prefix incorporated into the verb complex, is the obligatory part; if the object is given in noun form at all, the noun merely specifies the content of the object prefix: *ni-qu-itta Juan* "I-him-see (him being, or i.e.,) Juan." Anything on the order of a preposition would be entirely out of place in the Nahuatl framework; and in any case, Nahuatl had no prepositions before it borrowed some from Spanish. Almost predictably, Nahuatl speakers failed to see the function of the Spanish *a* and often left it out, as in the following examples:

le dio el difunto ocho pesos   He gave eight pesos to the deceased
  (Text 4)
les dejo mis hijitos[13]   I leave it to my children

In Nahuatl there is no formal distinction between direct and indirect object prefixes, and rarely are both present at the same time, the direct object indicator almost always being omitted when the indirect object is marked. Nahuatl speakers were thus ill equipped to handle Spanish's elaborate system of differentiated object pronouns. They often used *lo* direct object and *le* indirect interchangeably, showing a tendency to use *lo* for all cases, as in *quien lo estorbe dho posecion* (Text 4) "whoever should disturb (to him) said possession," where *lo* should be *le*. Nahuatl object prefixes show no gender differentiation, and our writers had corresponding difficulty in keeping *lo* and *la* straight, again often deciding for the former. An especially mystifying element to the Nahuatl speaker was the non-reflexive *se* which Spanish uses to represent the indirect object when the direct object pronoun is also present. Consider *se los encargo a los s^{res} jueses. . . que* (Text 4) "I charge the honorable judges. . . with . . ." The standard form would be *se lo encargo*, *se* representing the plural judges and *lo* the grammatically singular clause which follows; but the writer has made *los* agree with the judges, to whom he presumably takes it to refer, and has put in *se* only because he has observed that Spaniards include that syllable in such sentences. In general, the Nahuatl speakers were extremely unsure about when object pronouns should be used, or which ones, leading to strings like the following:

> mi querido padre *me la* dexo la casa y mi hauelo y mi auela asimismo *le* dejo a mi hijo y asi tambien si se muere *le* dexara a su hijo[14]

In more standard Spanish, with modern orthographic conventions, this would be:

> Mi querido padre *me* dejó la casa, y mi abuelo y abuela [antes de él]; asimismo *(se) la* dejo a mi hijo, y así también si se muere (muera), *(se) la* dejará a su hijo.

Since the Nahuatl speakers did not really understand the object-marking function of Spanish *a*, they seem to have construed it as an ornament conducive to good style, or perhaps as a marker of a personal noun regardless of its role in a sentence. At any rate, they often placed *a* before subjects as well as objects. In Text 4's passage *esta dha se lo fue dexando a Marselino Antonio*, Marcelino Antonio was the one who left the land to the other person named, as can be deduced not only from the thrust of the entire text, but from other relevant documents in the dossier.[15]

In a set of texts written by a Nahuatl-speaking notary of Mexico City at this time (1782-83) there is a feast of hypercorrect *a*, apparently associated with the high tone the writer seems to be aiming for; the following are only some of the examples:[16]

se a seruido de la tierra *a* dho mi compadre D^n Domingo Ramos	my said compadre don Domingo Ramos has made use of the land

es dueño de dho citio *a* Dⁿ Marcos de la Cruz para que *a* V md puede mandarnos *a* la Chepa no tiene que dizir	Don Marcos de la Cruz is the owner of the said site so that your grace can order us... La Chepa (nickname) has nothing to say (about the matter)

In this writer's usage, *a* is also sometimes employed as the general preposition, filling in for others in cases where the writer may not be sure of Spanish idiom. In the following two examples, the preposition would be *de* in standard Spanish:

con consentimiento *a* nuestro hijo lexᵐᵒ todo es sullo *a* mi sobrino	with the consent of our legitimate son . . . it all belongs to my nephew . . .

Just as Nahuatl lets the specified object of a verb stand in a kind of apposition to the object pronoun without further overt marking, so also what appear to be dependent clauses in Nahuatl are often left overtly undifferentiated from main clauses, connected to them only by the implicit cross-reference (despite the existence of much machinery for overt subordination when desired). Something of the same tendency appears in the texts. The chaotic Text 2 contains (apparently) several examples, starting with *pongo este escritura llo me llamo Dⁿ Andres Martin*. The same thing is seen in *ago mi testamento yo me llamo Dⁿ Lazaro de Santiago aqui es mi barrio Nra Señora de la Limpia Concepcion*.[17] Nevertheless, writers like those of Texts 3 and 4 evince considerable competence in distinguishing independent from subordinate clauses and in constructing unified several-clause strings.

Another characteristic of Nahuatl syntax is the absence of verbs in equative statements. Every noun has a subject pronoun affixed (the third person affix being zero) and by itself constitutes a statement that some entity belongs to the class designated by the noun: *ni-tlacatl*, "I (am a) person"; *tlacatl*, "he (is a) person." Residues of this phrase type can be found in the texts. For example, from Text 4:

no tiene nada mas que su cuerpo ni vn pedasito solar onde puede bivir ni vn surco para senbrar y tributario	he has no more than his body, not even a bit of a lot where he can live nor a furrow to sow, and (*he is a*) tribute-payer

A favored larger construction in Nahuatl was to single out one constituent and equate it verblessly to all the rest of the sentence, as opposed to making it serve directly as subject or object. Nahuatl might say the equivalent of "what he saw yesterday (is a) woman" rather than simply "he saw a woman yesterday." An example of this type appears in the Mexico City texts mentioned just above (this one too contains a hypercorrect *a*):[18]

lo que daua cada vez que se benia	what the said doña Feliciana gave
a mexico a dha Dª Felisiana	every time she came to Mexico
quatro rr^s	(*is*) four reales

In Nahuatl, place names and names of settlements are nearly all locatives which already contain within themselves some such notion as "in, at, on," etc. That is, a word like *Tetzcoco* by itself means "in Tetzcoco"; it neither needs nor will suffer any further locative expression. We are not surprised, then, to see some omission of *en* with place names in texts by Nahuatl speakers:

Coaticpac estâ[19]	it is in Coaticpac . . .
vna tierra que esta Santa Maria	a piece of land which is in Santa
Asumpcion[20]	María de la Asunción

In Nahuatl, nearly all indication of the direction of motion is contained within the verb complex; Spanish directional indications attached to nouns had been being misunderstood by Nahuatl speakers since the sixteenth century, when they had borrowed *huerta* as *alahuerta* and taken *la Florida* to be *Alaflorida*.[21] That something of this Nahuatl conception remained alive among the writers of our texts can be seen in such preposition-less phrases as *esta milpa entra dos almudes de mais* "two almudes (grain measure) of maize enter into (can be planted in, a Nahuatl idiom) this field."[22]

The Nahuatl tense system differed from the Spanish very considerably, yet writers like those of Texts 3 and 4 show a good grasp of the Spanish tenses, including the subjunctive. The deviance concerning verbs came not so much from an inability to handle the Spanish system as from a partial dissatisfaction with it, a determination to make certain distinctions which are usually made in Nahuatl but not in Spanish. There are two principal phenomena of this type, both having to do with Nahuatl auxiliary verbs which were suffixed to main verbs to indicate certain modal notions. A form of the verb "to go," used in this way, indicated that the action took place on departure or death. It is in the attempt to duplicate that sense and structure that the writer of Text 4 put *fue dexando*, "went leaving." Other Nahuatl auxiliaries had a progressive sense; various kinds of progressives were much more in use in Nahuatl than in Spanish, with the result that the Nahuatl-speaking writers, like modern English speakers, overused the Spanish progressive of *estar* plus the present participle, this being a partial explanation of Text 4's phrases *todo lo esta pagando* and *mas que se ofrese lo esta dando*.[23]

The Nahuatl speakers' vocabulary in terms of individual words far surpassed their grasp of Spanish idiom, or vocabulary in terms of frozen larger constructs. The texts bristle with thinly disguised Nahuatl idioms in lieu of the corresponding Spanish ones. To take one example, Spanish has several ways of speaking of fields abutting on each other, ways which need little discussion because they are so similar to those seen in English. Nahuatl, however, has a very special phrase type in which not only are the owners of the fields rather than the fields themselves construed as the actors, but as in all Nahuatl "we"-constructions, only the non-speaking member of the we-pair is specified: *titomilnetechana Mateo Juarez*, literally "we-ourselves-field-each-other-abut Mateo Juárez," i.e., "the fields of Mateo Juárez and myself abut on each other." A phrase like *nos lindamos señor San Miguel*[24] (literally "we border the lord San Miguel") conforms to the Nahuatl model quite exactly, although it hardly yields a sense in Spanish unless one knows from the general context what to expect.

But not all such phenomena in the texts we are dealing with can be attributed to entirely naive retention of Nahuatl idioms and ignorance of Spanish equivalents. The texts betray a tenacious hanging on to local conventions over and above the language switch. In each Indian town, small or large, the order and wording of each type of document differed in its details from the equivalent either in other towns or among Spaniards. These idiosyncrasies held true over generations of Nahuatl recordkeeping, and it is clear that the writers of each community placed great value on them, perhaps as the truly right and legal way of doing things, perhaps as a mark of community distinctiveness. The texts originally in Spanish follow the older Nahuatl texts point by point, even when what is said is awkward to express in Spanish or is something not usually said in Spanish documents. Thus a 1779 Spanish will ends each bequest with a phrase like *esto a de ser fuerte mi palabra ninguno lo perjudique ni lo estorua*, which corresponds to a Nahuatl model probably on the order of *chicahuatiez notlatol ayac quitlacoz quixitiniz*, "my statement is to be strong (valid); no one is to spoil it, to abrogate it."[25]

Text 4, from which I have already been taking examples of individual phenomena, can also serve to give us a good overall impression.[26] Cast in a reasonably competent and persuasive Spanish, it nevertheless, as we have seen, has all the hallmarks of its genre, including deviance in object marking and in use of verb tenses. In addition to the facets pointed out before, there are some uncertainties concerning gender (the writer treats *posesión* as masculine) and the use of the article with titles (*por mandado de señor gobernador*, etc.), a few omissions of *s* and *n*, one or two other deviant spellings, and some Nahuatl-related idioms.[27] Above all, Text 4, written

---

Text 4. *Land grant, Calimaya, 1783.*

En el pueblo de Calimaya jurisdiccion de Tenango del Balle oy dia martes beinte y sinco de febrero año de mis setecientos ochenta y tres — digo governador autual juntamente con mis alcaldes D^n Ygnacio Joseph y D^n Julian Antonio y toda la Republica que le fuimos a dar posecion a Joseph Juaqui de vn pedaso de tierra que cita en el camino de Sacango y esta dha se lo fue dexando a Marselino Antonio como consta en el testamento del difunto Marselino y por eso le dimos posecion y como es tributario y obencionero todo lo esta pagando lo que se pide en el pueblo y es vn pobre que no tiene onde puede senbrar vn granito de mais mas que este pedaso que le yso el difunto vn bien y buena obra y por eso le di posecion en nombre de Su Mag^d lo coxi de la mano yba desparramando tierra piedras y lo que coxia todo lo yse en nombre de su Mag^d lo pacie en cuatro esquinas para que no agia quien le diga nada o desbarate nuestra palabra damos este posecion y digo yo jues y g^r si hubiere en algun tiempo quien lo estorbe dho posecion se los encargo a los s^{res} jueses y juticias de Su Mag^d que haga por este pobre guerfano porque no tiene nada mas que su cuerpo ni vn pedasito solar onde puede bivir ni vn surco para senbrar y tributario y mas que se ofrese lo esta dando como lo dira a senores governadores pasados por eso le dimos poxecion yo jues y governador por Su Mag^d D^n Nicolas de Alvarran alcaldes D^n Ygnacio Jph y D^n Julian Antonio Rexidor mayor Baltasar de lo Reyes jues Lionisio Lorenzo tepihque Asencio Basilio y toda la Republica testigo estaba

y mas digo le costo su trabajo de sacamoliarlo y linpiarlo y conponerlo y tanbien le dio el difunto ocho pesos como costara Resibo que tengo o bale

y yo escriui por mandado de s^r g^r y alcaldes como escriuano Pablo Jph

---

in Calimaya in 1783, is based on the same model as Text 1, written in that town in Nahuatl in 1750. The circumstances of the two documents are somewhat distinct, so that they are not absolutely identical in all respects, but note the similarity of the justification of the grant, including the phrase about the recipient needing some place to plant a grain or two of maize, and note especially the portion of Text 4 describing the actual rite of giving possession (from *le di posecion* to *damos este posecion*), which is literally the same in every detail as the relevant part of Text 1 and could pass for a translation of it.

How widespread was a Nahuatl to Spanish transition of the kind studied here, and what was its dating pattern? The same general conditions, including the penetration of Spaniards into country life, the ability of local leaders to speak Spanish, and a strong Nahuatl writing tradition ever closer to Spanish vocabulary and norms, obtained throughout central Mexico. I have the impression, from having surveyed much parallel documentation for other purposes, that what was happening in the southern Toluca Valley was happening in other Indian towns over the whole region at much the same time, but not uniformly, for some towns preserved Nahuatl recordkeeping up to the time of Mexican independence and perhaps longer.

Rather than dwell on my impressions and speculate about the reasons for the spottiness of the timing, I will try to give a certain perspective by discussion of some texts of a similar nature, already alluded to, which chance to be preserved among the Toluca Valley documentation but are from another area, namely the capital itself.[28] Mexico City was the very core of the Spanish-Mexican world, a Spanish city if there ever was one, yet it was established in the midst of what had been the Aztec capital before the conquest. The still strong and populous Indian community of Mexico City/ Tenochtitlan was given recognition as an Indian town and had its own government like any other such entity, with four subdivisions corresponding to the four great sectors of the city. Since the Nahuatl-speaking community of the capital was exposed to an absolute maximum of all kinds of Spanish penetration and influence, one would expect a priori that language transition in its various aspects would have come earlier and perhaps more suddenly or cleanly than in the countryside. Indeed, the Mexico City texts (a land donation and a letter-statement composed by the notary of the San Sebastián district of the Indian municipality in 1782-83) do betray a more advanced situation, but within the same general framework. That is, despite having a much fuller mastery of Spanish legal terms and attempting more ambitious formulations, the writer still shows the deviant use of *a* as seen above, has some deviant spellings, composes some sentences which are ungrammatical or incomplete, especially in longer constructions, and retains some hint of Nahuatl idiom. *Decir* is *dizir*, with the *i* which Nahuatl speakers often put for unstressed Spanish *e*; several *n*'s are omitted (*grade* for *grande*, *quato* for *quanto*, etc.); there are some examples of the Nahuatl speaker's *o* for *u*; *herencia* is hypercorrected to *heriencia*. One repeated phrase is *tierra citio*, in which two synonymous terms are juxtaposed and become a frozen designation of a single thing; this is the famous Nahuatl "diphrasis" and something not at all characteristic of Spanish, which would at least demand *y* between the two nouns.

The writer has a quite impressive familiarity with the more high-flown phraseology of Spanish law and correspondence. He knows for example that a polite greeting calls for the use of vocabulary such as *afecto*, *agrado*, and *fina voluntad*. But when he tries to compose in these realms, he overreaches himself. Consider the following courtesy preamble, which maintains all the right vocabulary but wanders further and further from grammaticality:

> Mui s^r mio apreciare de muchisimo gusto que â V md se halle gosando de mui cabal salud que nuestro fino afecto le desea a cuia evedicia ofresemos la que el altissimo Dios nos consede para que V md la desfrocte en cosas de su mayor agrado que â V md puede mandarnos que executare-mos con fina boluntad —

These texts show no definite signs of being based on a Nahuatl model in the fashion of Text 4, but they do have their rather idiosyncratic shape and formulas, indicating that to some extent the writer was still following internal community norms instead of general Spanish ones. On the basis of this glimpse, it would appear that the Nahuatl-speaking community of Mexico City had gone over to Spanish records somewhat earlier than the Toluca Valley towns, and by the 1780's was somewhat further advanced toward standard Spanish documentary types and ways of expession, but was, on balance, at the same essentially transitional stage. After all, the two communities were in direct touch with each other, and we owe this sample of Mexico City practice to the attempt of the people in the capital to communicate, in Spanish, with the people in Calimaya. One can even sense the existence of something on the order of a Nahuatl-speaker Spanish, to be used in community-internal communication, not unlike the special brands of English spoken in Hispanic and black communities in the United States today.

Overall, the texts studied show us a case in which the change from Nahuatl to Spanish records in Indian towns was primarily motivated not by the decadence of the older Nahuatl system, but by considerations of prestige and easier communication with an increasingly present Spanish sector. It is true that as the Nahuatl tradition came closer and closer to the Spanish tradition, and at the same time the writers were gaining considerable mastery of Spanish itself, it may have struck them as artificial or frustrating to keep Nahuatl as the vehicle. Yet the transition occurred well before the point at which the writers were able to produce fully grammatical and idiomatic Spanish texts.

In Karttunen and Lockhart, *Nahuatl in the Middle Years,* the progressive adaptation of Nahuatl to Spanish is seen as occurring in three stages: a first brief period of no borrowing; a second lasting a hundred years, until about 1650, of extensive noun borrowing; and a third, until today, associated with large-scale bilingualism, of borrowing also verbs, particles, and idioms. Seen from the perspective not of Nahuatl per se, but of the evolving speech of the people who originally spoke Nahuatl, the phenomena seen in the present paper can be taken to represent a fourth stage, in which Spanish has been adopted, but Spanish vocabulary still obeys many of the rules of Nahuatl syntax, formula, and style.

---

8. Toward Assessing the Phoneticity of Older Nahuatl Texts: Analysis of a Document from the Valley of Toluca, Eighteenth Century

There are various opinions on the question of how closely older Nahuatl texts reflect speech.* In general, it seems to me that the people who know them least tend to discount them in this respect, while those who know them more take them more seriously. Perhaps if the matter receives some direct discussion in a context of closeness to the evidence, a consensus will begin to arise among students of Nahuatl, and a valuable resource for historical linguistics and dialectology will be more fully utilized.

One useful way to attack the problem is to compare deviant written examples with examples well attested in present-day speech. Sullivan and Dakin have shown that a -*qui/quetl*, preterit and agentive, which occurs in the Twenty Hymns of Sahagún, corresponds to a /ki/ still so used in Huasteca Nahuatl today. Karttunen and Lockhart (1976) collected written forms of many Spanish words in Nahuatl texts which agree with existing modern spoken variants, for example *xinola* < *señora*, "lady," today in some places in fact pronounced [šinola]. Comparisons of this type can be systematized, as Karttunen and Lockhart have already done up to a point, and as I hope to do quite rigorously in the future with documents I have collected from the Valley of Toluca, comparing them with the data published by Lastra and Horcasitas on the Nahuatl spoken in the same region today. Anticipating one of the main findings, I can already say that the majority of the texts, nearly all from the eighteenth century, agree with Lastra and Horcasitas in respect to the predominance of -*l* over the -*tl* which is standard in the central region (i.e., today final [l] predominates over [tˡ] in the Toluca Valley). On the other hand, at the eastern side of the valley is a zone where final [tˡ] is predominant today, and in the case of the only town of this subarea for which I have older texts, -*tl* instead of -*l* is in fact in evidence.

But before carrying out large-scale operations, I believe that it is necessary to demonstrate, on the basis of specific documents, two things: first, that older texts were markedly deviant from the norm of Molina and Ca-

---

*Many readers may find the present piece forbiddingly technical. They could nevertheless get something of the gist by reading the first three paragraphs (making allowances for the second), as well as the last three.

rochi; and second, that the deviation is not haphazard, but that it stems from a practice consistent in itself however peculiar, and that the deviances tend to correspond to linguistically plausible phenomena. To this end I will discuss a document from the town of San Lucas Tepemaxalco, written in 1731 by a local person, with much briefer reference to two other texts written in the same place in 1735 and 1736. (The town, in the past sometimes called San Lucas Chiquito, is attached to the larger San Antonio la Isla just to its north; both are on the east side of the main road from Toluca to Tenango, not far from Calimaya.) Two of the texts are among the most idiosyncratic I have seen, while the third appears superficially to approach fairly close to the standard. Yet all three agree in giving *-l* instead of *-tl* and in showing some evidence of omission of *-c*, *-uh*, and *-ch*, substitution of other letters for them (specifically *-x* for *-ch*), and "epenthesis" of *i* after them.

Nothing equals the close examination of individual documents in its power to convince, and I would like to be able to give all three texts the same treatment, but for considerations of time and space, though I reproduce them all here, I will comment in extenso upon only the first, a testament written by Anastasio de Benavides in 1731.

Weakening of final consonants. In this text there is occasion for only two tests of the *-ll-tl* question. Both result in *-l*: *nechual* (eighteenth-century standard *nehuatl*, "I") and *cuscomal* (*cuescomatl*, "grainbin"). But there are two instances, the only ones in the whole larger body of Tolucan texts I have seen, where *-l* for *-tl* extends beyond word-final position: *centlamali* (*sentlamantli*, "one item") and *miltoli* (*miltontli*, "small field"). Lastra and Horcasitas do give examples of [l] for /t^l/ in analogous environments in some modern Toluca Valley speech. The omission of an immediately preceding *n* in both cases makes it hard to say whether the presumed substitution of [l] for [t^l] has occurred intervocalically or postconsonantally, but postconsonantal weakening seems the most natural second step, and it appears to be the second most common type in the Lastra/Horcasitas modern examples. After all, orthographic omission does not necessarily imply zero pronunciation, but is equally compatible with pronunciation as one of the weak segments not usually reproduced in writing. *Centlamali* likely corresponds to [sent^{l}amahli]. At any rate, here is some evidence consonant with the Lastra/Horcasitas suggestion that [l] for [t^l] starts as weakening in final position and extends to other environments only later. For the rest, there is no deviance from the standard in writing prevocalic *tl*, nor any other prevocalic consonant, except for the puzzling matter of *hu-* (see below).

The document contains a great deal of evidence of a more general weakening of syllable-final consonants, including *c* [k], *ch* [č], *x* [š], and *uh*

[w], not only word-finally as with -*tl* (that being the only place syllable-final -*tl* occurs in standard writing, or final [t^l] in standard speech) but also word-internally. There is not a final -*c* in the whole text. In twelve instances where it would standardly appear, the writer has simply omitted it. These cases include a good number of transitive reverential verbs such as *ninotlatlatilia* (*nicnotlatlauhtilia*, "I implore him") where one might suspect that the omission is on morphological rather than phonological grounds. That is, Nahuatl does not mark the direct object if the indirect object prefix is present, and some varieties, like most in present-day Morelos, have extended this principle to omitting the direct object when the oblique reflexive prefix is present, which would cover these cases. But *c* is also missing in simple nonreverential forms such as *nichichua* (*nicchihua*, "I make it") and *nisonquixitia* (*nictzonquixtia*, "I conclude it"). Presumably a glottal stop or [h] (not represented in most older writing conventions, including this one) still marked the object in speech, as occurs with many modern speakers in the area. Standard Nahuatl demands, when sufficient supporting vowels are lacking, that the object prefix take the form [ki] rather than [k], and in such cases the writer gives us the standard *qui*: *niquitochua* (*niquitoa, niquitohua* [niki?toa], "I say it"). Thus the letter representing [k] reappears when a vowel follows. The same pattern occurs with syllable-final *c* generally (these examples are all word-final, but in this text the only word-internal syllable-final *c* called for is the object prefix): *yni* (twice) (*ynic*, "through which," ordinal marker), *ynema* (*ynemac*, "his portion"), but *ylchuicaqui* (*ylhuicac*, "in heaven"), *calitiqui* (*calitic*, "inside the house"), *nonemaqui* (*nonemac*, "my portion"). The nonstandard final -*i* in these cases is associated with the preservation of the letter representing [k]. One is hesitant whether or not to call this epenthesis. All Nahuatl consonants were followed by a vowel in reconstructable times, and any reduced vowel has historically taken the form [i] as its last and weakest manifestation. In the [k]~[ki] alternation of the verbal object prefix, the *i* is definitely not epenthetic, but a reflex of a segment in the original form of the morpheme, [k] being a shortened form occurring only when a vowel is adjacent and there is no unmanageable consonant cluster. Various dialects of Nahuatl have preserved idiosyncratic [i] in certain words and morphemes through the centuries, long past the time of its loss in the speech of the central area. In this case, nevertheless, I tend to think the nonstandard final [i] may have been lost and then reinserted in true epenthesis to avoid loss of the consonant. However that may be, the text seems to portray a speaker who

---

*Insertion of a vowel adjoining a consonant for ease of pronunciation.

customarily either weakens standard syllable-final [k] or pronounces an [i] after it.

The picture is exactly the same with -*ch*, which never occurs finally either, being either omitted, weakened, or replaced by -*chi*. In *cuahutenco* (*cuaxochtenco*, "at the edge of the border") it is omitted. In *nechimotlapo-polchuilisque* (*nechmotlapopolhuilisque*, "they will pardon me"), *ncehimo-palechuilis* (orthographic metathesis of *e* and *c*, *nechmopalehuilis*, "he will aid me"), *ixiquichi* (*ixquich*, "everything"), and *nechimaquilis* (*nechmaquilis*, "he will give it to me"), -*ch* is followed by a nonstandard *i*. Rather complicated are two stabs at the same word: *nu^{x}puchi* (*nochpoch*, "my daughter"), where the first -*ch* was originally omitted, then as an after-thought a weakened substitute was written in above (*x* = [š]), though without following *i*, while the second -*ch* is indeed followed by *i;* and *nohipo* (*nochpoch* again), where the first -*ch* is reduced to *h*, possibly representing some weakening, though I am not sure of its form, yet nonstandard *i* follows anyway, while the second -*ch* is simply omitted this time.

With -*x*, the writer falls just short of the same consistency. In one case -*x* is omitted: *nocococatlatol* (*nococoxcatlatol*, "my sick person's statement"). In several cases nonstandard *i* follows: *nicocoxiqui* (twice) (*nicocoxqui*, "I the sick person"), *noteopixicatzin* (*noteopixcatzin*, "my priest"), *nisonquixitia* (*nictzonquixtia*, "I conclude it"), *ixiquichi* (*ixquich*, "everything"), *yxitlahuateco*, "at the edge of the plain"). In two cases *x* appears syllable-finally, but in both there are extenuating circumstances: in *ax^{c}a* (*axcan*, "now") the word was first written *axa*, then the *c* was written in above as an afterthought (in several places today, including Tepoztlan, the [k] of this word has been dropped and the [š] retained); in *nu^{x}puchi* the *x* is also a posterior addition, as we just saw, aside from representing standard *ch*. In one case *x* is changed even though intervocalic: *cuahutenco* (*cua-xochtenco*, "along the border"); as mentioned above with *nohipo*, I am not sure just what is intended by this *h*.

With -*uh*, the writer omits it in the three cases where it would standardly appear, all in the same word and form: *ninotlatlatilia* (*nicnotlatlauhtilia*, "I implore him"). Nonstandard *i* after *uh* (which would then be *hu*) fails to appear. The same is true in the other texts to be mentioned. Possibly the weakening of final [w] was farther advanced than that of most of the other final consonants.

In the writing of Anastasio de Benavides of San Lucas, then, the following correspondences exist:

18th-century orthographic standard	Benavides
-tl	*-l*
-c	Ø or *-qui*
-ch	Ø, *-chi*, or *-x*
-x	Ø or *-xi*
-uh	Ø

I infer that the orthographic correspondences reflect the following state of things in Benavides' speech:

general standard		Benavides
[tˡ]		[l]
[k]	#	[ʔ]~[h]~Ø ?, or [ki]
[č]	_ C	[h]~Ø ?, or [či] or [š]
[š]		[h]~Ø ?, or [ši]
[w]		[h]~Ø ?

The substitutions [l] for [tˡ] and [h] or Ø for [w] seem stable, while the other substitutions appear to be at a transitional stage, the sporadic nonstandard [i] serving to preserve the standard consonant part of the time. On the other hand, Benavides does consistently write standard *-l* and *-s*, and I presume this corresponds to his pronunciation. He has *-n* something over half of the time where it is "standard," which in fact would be about the normal performance for a writer of the Valley of Mexico in the postconquest centuries.

Syllable-final nasals. Syllable-final *n* (in colonial-period texts in general, final *m* rarely appears even before *m* or *p*) is by far the most volatile orthographic element in older Nahuatl texts, in more or less standard ones as well as more idiosyncratic ones, early ones as well as late ones, ones written near Mexico City and ones written far away; indeed nasals account for the majority of all deviance from the Molina or Carochi norm. Gemination of medial nasals, reduction of geminates, omission, and intrusion all occur frequently. Some of this behavior clearly corresponds to speech; even the early grammarians commented on the frequent omissions. Gemination and reduction are phonetically plausible and often occur as a means of tying an introductory particle to the following nuclear word (*san ixquich* > *sannixquich*, "only," a variant of which is found in this text, or *yn noyolia* > *y noyolia*, "my spirit," as also here). Other phenomena, especially intrusion in the absence of an adjacent nasal, require a great deal of background discussion and long lines of reasoning if one is to explain the nature of their correspondence to speech. In brief, Karttunen and I have felt

(1976, 1977) that since final [n] was apparently the weakest and most unstable segment in the speech of the central area to be represented in the Spanish-based orthography introduced in the sixteenth century, it came to be used to represent (sporadically) all manner of weak and reduced segments in a given writer's speech.

There is nothing out of the ordinary in Anastasio de Benavides' use of -*n*; that is, as opposed to dictionary or grammar usage, it is like most texts whether of the Toluca Valley, the Valley of Mexico, or Morelos, in its frequent omissions, intrusions, and occasional gemination of *n*, with yet other cases done the "standard" way. Several times *n* occurs in the location of a weak syllable-final segment, as in *ytlasonpiltzin* (*ytlasopiltzin*, "his precious child"), where it coincides with an expected glottal stop or perhaps [h] in Benavides' dialect; the standard pronunciation is [īt¹aso?pilt^{S}in].

The problem of chu-. Standard *hu-*, representing prevocalic [w], is replaced by *chu-* with rather alarming consistency throughout this text, 16 times in all. Two exceptions, *ycha* and *yhua* (*yhuan*, "and"), are likely orthographic errors within the writer's convention, since it is the commonest words and phrases which are most frequently misspelled. In *ytlasomausnatzin* (*ytlasomahuisnatzin*, "his precious honored mother") one could imagine that the rounding of the glide had been extended rightward, converting [awi] to [au], but no conclusions can be drawn from a single exceptional occurrence. I have seen this same *chu-* for -*hu* in a very few isolated Valley of Mexico texts of the seventeenth and eighteenth centuries, but I am still very unsure of its intention. Is it simply a more convoluted way of representing [w], somewhat as final [k^W] was often written as -*cuh* rather than Molina's -*cu* or Carochi's -*uc*? On the other hand, in many varieties of Nahuatl [k^W] has weakened to [w] in some environments, with consequent occasional hypercorrection of [w] to [k^W], of which *chu* conceivably could be a representation. In fact, there are some examples of [g^W] for standard [w] among modern Toluca speakers recorded by Lastra and Horcasitas. Older Nahuatl prevocalic [w] may have been fortis under certain conditions. Some of the old grammars say that men pronounced it more forcefully than women; Spaniards usually transcribed it as *gua* in loan words (*macegual*, etc.) or when amateurs tried to write Nahuatl (*ygua* for *yhuan*, etc.); in Tetelcingo today, standard [wi] is [fi] postconsonantally.

If all this tends to lead in somewhat the same direction, in a second San Lucas text, to be considered briefly below, standard *hu-* is replaced with equal consistency by *ahu-*, which points the opposite way in every respect except in strengthening the notion that some speakers of eighteenth-century San Lucas may have had a nonstandard pronunciation of prevocalic /w/.

To me, the *chu* is an example of a deviance that is surely interesting, but so opaque, ambiguous, and lacking explanatory context that no definite conclusion can be drawn from it, except indeed that it illustrates the high degree of autonomy of Nahuatl texts. The writer was perhaps not conversant with any other writing convention than his own; he was totally undeterred by the fact that nearly everyone else in the Toluca Valley, not to speak of the Valley of Mexico, was writing /w/ differently.

Spanish loan words. Special care is demanded in interpreting Spanish loan words in Nahuatl texts as to their phoneticity. From the present text alone one can clearly see the general procedure with indigenous vocabulary: to apply the orthographic canon to each segment as it was pronounced rather than to make any attempt to "spell" "words." There was a lack of concern with making the same word or root uniform orthographically even across a line or two. The system cannot give us fine phonetic detail that the orthography is not equipped to represent, but otherwise it is calculated to deliver a good deal of information on variation in speech. The problem with Spanish as distinct from indigenous vocabulary is that there were two different ways to approach it. One was the normal way, applying the orthography to the writer's pronunciation of the item in context, resulting in many substitutions, omissions, and intrusions which we have good reason to accept as evidence of actual speech patterns. The other way, since some Nahuatl speakers apparently felt very much in the dark about Spanish vocabulary, was to refer to authority. Whether they asked Spaniards, kept lists, or looked in dictionaries (this I doubt), some writers produced "correct," uniform renderings of Spanish loan vocabulary which give every sign of having been created on the "word-spelling" principle and thus no more reflect individual speech than does modern standard writing in Spanish or English. In other words, a deviant form probably reflects speech, while a standard form either may or may not (see NMY).

One must compare all of a writer's examples before reaching even tentative conclusions. The standard *viernes*, "Friday," in itself tells us nothing, nor do the immediately following words. With *año*, "years," however, since Benavides otherwise makes his *s*'s dance to the standard tune, we may suspect that he uses the singular for the plural demanded here, and on the other hand *Resposos*, "response," has a plural where a Spaniard would usually put a singular. These cases seem to represent speech, though they speak to Benavides' nonstandard conception of the Spanish plural rather than to any omission or insertion of [s].

In *Enbangelista*, "Evangelist," we see that the writer is as ready to intrude an *n* in Spanish as in indigenous vocabulary, while in *Marti*

(Martín) he omits one. In *yllesia* (*yglesia*, "church") an awkward consonant cluster has been avoided, and I would consider it likely that the written form corresponds closely to Benavides' speech, particularly in view of the second text's *lesia* and the third's *gelsia* and *gelesia*. *Leonisio* (Dionisio) is an often-seen form (also *Lionisio*) apparently frozen in the earlier time when Nahuatl had not yet acquired [d] and often substituted [l], so that here too the form appears to correspond to speech.

As to *r*, Spanish [r] originally caused Nahuatl speakers considerable trouble; they ordinarily substituted [l] or omitted the [r], especially in consonant clusters. By the time of this document one expects [r] to have been acquired by the writers of central Mexican Nahuatl, but there is no way of being sure in a given text. At least we can say that syllable-final *r* is treated as in Spanish in the several instances of its occurrence here, except for a single omission, *Bernadino* (*Bernardino*); in fact one very often sees exactly this form of the name in Nahuatl texts, or sometimes *Bernandino*—the Spaniards themselves often used the form *Bernaldino*. Prevocalic *r* is also mainly handled according to Spanish convention, with word-initial *R* to indicate trilled [r] (of course we cannot be sure the consonant was pronounced in the standard Spanish way), but there are two instances of an interesting deviance: *Risto* (*Cristo*, "Christ") and *Rus* (*crus*, "cross"). Generally speaking, older texts, supported by some modern pronunciations, reveal that the earliest postconquest speakers often adapted a Spanish consonant cluster by omitting its first segment, while if one of the segments was [r], that one was omitted whether it was first or second. In the present case, the first segment has been omitted orthographically despite the fact that the second is *r*. This is not the usual way of resolving the problem (with *crus* or *cruz*, epenthesis between the two consonants was a frequent solution), but I imagine that Benavides' orthography corresponds to an idiosyncratic local pronunciation, probably carried down from an earlier century.

Gesus (*Jesus*) is decidedly nonstandard for this particular word, but tells nothing about pronunciation, since Spaniards frequently interchanged *g* and *j* in their writing. Benavides' *Retor*, (*Rector*, "rector") omits a syllable-final *c* of the standard Spanish form, which would surely be in line with his general -*c* omission, but the fact is that the great majority of Spaniards of the time wrote V*c*CV as VCV, and presumably pronounced accordingly.

Miscellaneous reflections of speech. At the beginning of the text, the writer puts *Nica* for *Yn ica*, "in the name of." In many dialects of modern Nahuatl the [i] of the article [in] has been dropped and the [n] has been reanalyzed as the beginning of the following earlier vowel-initial word, especially with the second person plural pronouns and subject prefixes.

Surely something of the kind had occurred in Benavides' speech, perhaps as a regular feature, though we cannot be sure because all the other instances of *yn* in the text precede words beginning with consonants.

In some cases (of many more handled the usual way) Benavides puts *u* instead of standard *o*; this itself is so common as to be almost standard in Valley of Toluca or Morelos texts, especially for long [ō] (in today's Tetelcingo Nahuatl, the historical long vowel is transcribed as [u], the short vowel as [o]). Some of the *u*'s here do coincide with long vowels, but in other instances the vowels are short, at least in general Nahuatl. The relatively frequent use of *u* where standard short [o] is expected, especially with the [o] of the possessive prefixes, is a marked characteristic of Toluca Valley texts. In view of these texts' many idiosyncrasies compared with each other, from which we can be sure they were not slavish imitations, I tend to think this *u* corresponds to a different vowel quality of /o/ in Toluca Valley speech than in the speech of the Valley of Mexico.

Toluca Valley texts generally show less vowel elision than Valley of Mexico texts, especially between the possessive prefix and a vowel-initial possessed noun. Standard speech, with Valley of Mexico writing reflecting it, called for [o] + [a] > [a], [o] + [e] > [e], and [o] + [i] > [o] (except that [o] would be the one elided when the [i] was long or followed by a glottal stop) . The present text comes down on both sides of the question. Both versions of standard *nochpoch*, "my daughter," are deviant, but they do embody the normal elision. *Noermanotzin*, "my brother," is not elided, but on the other hand I have seen the form in Valley of Mexico texts written the same way or with an intervening *h*, which may even have been pronounced originally, preventing elision. But unelided *noanimatzin*, "my soul," goes against the overwhelmingly predominant standard elided form *nanimatzin* or *nanimantzin*. I conclude that Benavides shared the Toluca Valley reluctance to elide.

Omitting no relevant detail, for I am concerned to show that there is almost no deviance without its rationale, often a phonetic one, I will mention three more small items. In *nimoyoloytlacalchuili* (*nicnoyolloitlacal-huili*, or *nicnoyolitlacalhuili*, "I have offended him"), not only are there some deviances previously discussed, and an *l* for standard *ll*—an extremely common reduction in Valley of Mexico texts as well—but in place of the *n* of the standard first-person reflexive prefix Benavides has written *m*, making the prefix look like that of the second and third person, *mo*. The latter was in fact historically the universal reflexive prefix, as it still is in many places today; it appears as the first person prefix in many older texts from outside the Valley of Mexico, and specifically with great frequency in Toluca Valley texts, though in many of them not to the exclusion of *no*. Thus despite the fact that Benavides has used *mo* only once and *no* many times, I do believe that this is an instance of the general Toluca Valley tendency and evidence of fluctuation in the writer's speech. In *nisonquixitia* (*nictzonquixtia*, "I conclude it"), standard prevocalic *tz* is replaced by *s*; the same thing happens with this very word in other Toluca Valley texts. Lenition of [t^s] to [s] is widespread in Nahuatl speech and is implied in many older texts from a broad area, primarily syllable-finally but also sometimes prevocalically. With *cuscomal* (*cuescomatl*, "granary, grainbin") we are dealing with an extremely common word which has numerous local variants and a first segment /k^w/ which was relatively unstable in older Nahuatl. On the one hand it might delabialize, as had already happened in many standard forms syllable-finally, and could happen prevocalically too (modern Zacapoaxtla has [kepa] for [k^{w}epa] "turn"). On the other hand, if prevocalic, the rounding might be transferred to the following vowel, yielding [k + rounded V]; standard [k^{w}iš], "perhaps," has become [koš] or [kuš] in some places. I presume that something analogous had happened in Benavides' speech, that his pronunciation was in fact on the order of [kuscomal].

Abbreviations. In the sixteenth through eighteenth centuries writers of both Nahuatl and Spanish allowed themselves great leeway in devising arbitrary abbreviations of frequently used words. It is true that they followed certain patterns, that some abbreviations hardly ever varied among skilled writers, and that Benavides was not exactly au courant, especially in such oddities as *Johp* (*Joseph*, often done *Josph*). But none of his abbreviations have any clear implications for speech. His *tt^o* is standard for *totecuyo* or *totecuiyo*, "our Lord"; in one instance the abbreviation is followed by the last portion of the word, *tt^{o}cuio*, and another time the word is written out in full, a rare occurrence in a Nahuatl notarial text.

Simple orthographic error. In older Nahuatl texts any deviance in a single letter or word that does not fit a known wider tendency or have parallels in the individual writer's practice is best left alone—not totally ignored, but filed in the memory to see if such a thing happens again. (One should somehow note even the most deviant-appearing phenomenon. After having seen thousands of examples of Spanish loan words in Nahuatl texts without any indication of an absolutive singular suffix, I came upon a single one with -*tli* added and went right by it as a meaningless oddity. Later I learned from modern dictionaries that a small class of loan nouns, mainly personal items normally possessed, in fact shows this ending in speech, and the very word of the deviant example is one such noun. I had to search through a huge corpus to relocate the example, *camisatli*, modern [kamisahtⁱi], "shirt." Later I found a few more attestations, most of words still bearing the suffix today.) Some deviances can be identified as most likely orthographic because they are of a type which frequently occurs and remain intractable even after all correspondences to speech have been investigated. They are also similar to orthographic and typographical errors we commit today. The most common slip in Nahuatl texts, the omission of one entire syllable (or less frequently writing it twice), happens not to occur here. Also frequent is the metathesis of individual letters, as here in *ncehimopalechuilis* (*nechmopalehuilis*, "he is to aid me"). True, metathesis is sometimes a valuable clue to speech, but it must occur in some pattern, and at a very minimum it must correspond to a pronounceable sequence in Nahuatl, which this example does not. An orthographic metathesis will also usually be the single exception to an otherwise uniform practice of the writer, as is also the case here. As with writers today, all types of orthographic error and especially omissions and repetitions occur with greatest frequency at line and page break and in material which has the nature of often-repeated formula. A special case of apparent orthographic error here is *alxado*, near the bottom; I take this to be Benavides' first try at writing *alexadro*, (*Alexandro*, *Alejandro*) as he did immediately afterward.

Lost or undecipherable portions. Many Nahuatl documents are missing some words at the margins or have holes of some size along the folds. Other times, because of such things as partial blotting of the ink, errors or extremely deviant usage on the part of the writer, or simple failure of the interpreter to fathom the intention, a portion of the text must be omitted. In the present case, I failed in several tries to understand what letters (two or three of them) were intended after *y*. . . toward the end of the document. While such gaps are regrettable, I do not see that they affect findings. The approximate sense can be reconstructed most of the time, and for linguistic interpretation the principle of a copious random sample is not changed at all.

In lieu of exhaustive analysis of the two very interesting companion documents to our main text, I will at least briefly indicate the situation in them as to syllable-final consonants. In a testament written by Leonardo de la Cruz in San Lucas in 1735, the following is the picture:

Standard	Leonardo de la Cruz
-tl	*-l* 8 times, *-tl* once (can be analyzed as syllable-initial)
-c	missing 17 times, *-qui* 8
-ch	missing once, *-x* once, *-h* once
-x	present twice, missing 3 times

-uh   missing 5 times
-s   present 24 times, missing 10 times
-l   present 11 times (plus the cases where it replaces *-tl*),
            missing 4

In other words, in this text weakening extends to all syllable-final consonants which have occasion to appear, making it even clearer than [1] for final
[t^l] is no isolated phenomenon, but rather part of a radical weakening of all
syllable-final segments. The use of epenthetic *i* [i] to preserve a consonant
which would otherwise be lost is also seen in this text, specifically with *-c*,
i.e., the writer puts either ∅ or *-qui*.

The third text, written in San Lucas in 1736 by Domingo Ramos,
approaches much closer to the standard, at least in parts of it. If one had not
seen the others, one might dismiss it as hopelessly arbitrary and contradictory, the only consistent deviance being *-l* for *-tl*. But looking closer, with
the previous two texts in mind, one sees that Ramos *either* gives the
standard form or deviates from it in the same directions as the others, so that
he can be said to share their tendencies. The following summarizes Ramos'
practice:

Standard	Domingo Ramos
-tl	*-l* 7 times
-c	present 15 times, missing 2 times, *-qui* 3
-ch	present 3 times, omitted 2 times, *-chi* once, *-x* 4 times, *-c* once.
-x	present 6 times (plus the 4 in which it replaces *-ch*)
-uh	omitted twice
-tz	*-s* (once) (i.e., apparently lenition of [t^s] to [s])

Overall, I hope that the above data and analysis strongly support the
position that deviances in older Nahuatl texts can deliver systematic evidence
on speech patterns. I emphasize that one must (and can) identify and discount abbreviations and orthographic error, and also disregard any isolated
case, drawing conclusions only from phenomena which repeat within a
writer's practice and preferably within the practice of many writers of the
same time and region, looking also to attestations of modern pronunciation
in that region as a point of reference. Under these conditions, I believe that
deviant spelling in older texts is potentially a prime source for historical
phonology.

For the present I will not enter deeply into the question of whether the
converse is true, that is, whether or not standard spelling tends to betray

standard pronunciation by the writer of the text. While I do not accept standard spelling as unequivocal evidence of pronunciation, I do believe that there tends to be a correspondence between the two. Note for example that one does not find -*l* for -*tl* in older Valley of Mexico texts, and correspondingly one finds only standard [tˡ] pronounced today. But what shall we make of variations between standard and nonstandard within the same or nearby towns or even in a single text, as with the third one discussed above? While I am far from being able to settle this question, let me suggest a hypothesis that seems to me consonant with what is known. I tend to think that the variations produced by a writer such as Domingo Ramos correspond to actual wavering between the standard and the nonstandard in speech; I would say that he is more in touch with the upper-class or formal tradition of speech than the other two, and tries to stick to it in his text, as in fact he does fairly well in the first part, but then increasingly slips back into more colloquial speech, influenced perhaps by the manner of speech of the testator.

As mentioned above, San Lucas was physically attached to the larger and richer San Antonio de la Isla; texts from San Antonio at this time are even more standard than those of Domingo Ramos—yet they do contain subtle hints of the same deviant phenomena alluded to above. My interpretation of this state of things is that in better-off and better-connected San Antonio the speech of the upper group was closer to the Valley of Mexico standard. In fact, texts from the larger Toluca Valley centers are more standard in general than those from smaller towns. From the latter seventeenth through the eighteenth century one sees in texts from the whole area what one could call a destandardization. I believe that what was happening was not a progressive phonological evolution but a change in which the upper groups, especially in the more important towns, who had spoken a quite standard Nahuatl, were increasingly adopting Spanish. (It is no accident that San Antonio's eighteenth-century church has a Spanish inscription on its façade, San Lucas' church one in Nahuatl.) Thus the more idiosyncratic, localized Nahuatl which had always been spoken by the lower-ranking members of society became more dominant. Finally localized speech took over to the extent that modern dialectologists presume a total uniformity for each "village," something I am sure was far from the case through the first two or three centuries after the Spanish conquest, in the Valley of Toluca or anywhere else in central Mexico.

Texts

Text 1. *Testament of Lucía María, San Lucas Tepemaxalco, 1731, written by Anastasio de Benavides.* (AGN, Tierras 2541, exp. 9, f. 6)

Jesus Maria Johp
Nica ytlasoMachuistocatzin y dios
tetatzin yn dios ytlasonpiltzin yn
dios Espiritu S^{n}to ma i mochichua
j$\bar{e}$ maria jos
- ax^{c}a viernes a 15 de junio de 1731
año Nica nicchichua notestame^{to} nechual nicocoxiqui Notoca Lusia maria Ca ninotlatlatilia noteotzin Notlatocatzin y tt^o dios nocychua ninotlatlatilia notlasomausnatzin Santa maria Nocychua ninotlatlatilia yn
S^{n}toti ycha S^{n}tati yn motemiltitica-
te ylchuicaqui Calitiqui nopa motla-
toltisque yn nechimotlapopolchui-
lisque yn notlatlacol yni onimo-
yoloytlacalchuili yn tt^{o}cuio gesus
Risto Ca ninocemaquilitzinnochua y
noyolia noanimatzin ytla ninomace-
chuis yntlasomiquilistzin yn tute-
cuio dios ypallechuiloca noanimatzin Ce misa Ynca Resposos nopa
mitos y ncehimopalechuilis noteopixicatzin padre ministro Ca Sann
ixiquichi niSonquixitia nocococatlatol Ynpa yaltepetzin S^{n}to S^a
Lucas EnBangelista ca yechuatzin-
tzin notestigos
- Yni centlamali Nitlanachuatitias
ce miltoli mani Cuahutenco nimaca-
tias nu^{x}puchi yntuca felisiana de la
Rus ychua Ce Cuscomal ynema ies
testigos
- yhua no niquitochua noermanotzin

Jesus, Mary, Joseph
    In the precious honored name of
God the father, God his precious
child, and God the Holy Spirit, may
this be done. Jesus, Mary, Joseph.
    Today, Friday the 15th of June
of the year 1731, here I make my
testament, I the sick person named
Lucía María. I implore my god and
ruler our lord God; I also implore
my precious honored mother St.
Mary; I also implore the male and
female saints who fill heaven to
speak for me and forgive me my
sins through which I have offended
our lord Jesus Christ, for I give him
my spirit and soul entirely. If I experience the precious death of our
Lord God, the aid of my soul will
be that one mass with responses
will be said for me; with this one
my priest, the father minister, will
help me. This is all; I conclude my
sick person's statement. My witnesses are:

    First I order that I am giving a
small field at Cuaxochtenco to my
daughter named Feliciana de la
Cruz, and also a granary will be her
inheritance. Witnesses:
    And I also say that my brother

D^n F^{co} marti nechimaquilis nohipo felisiana del + opuali Surco
yxitlahuateco y. . . nonemaqui
nicocoxiqui

don Francisco Martín is to give for
me to my daughter Feliciana de la
Cruz forty furrows at the edge of the
plain, the inheritance of me the sick
person.

Maiordomo Bernadino de S^{n}tia-
go fiscal de la S^{a}ta yllesia D^n
Leonisio Rafael aHde D^n fr^{co}
marti Retor alxado ju^o alexadro
E^{no} anastasio de Benabides

Majordomo, Bernardino de San-
tiago. Fiscal of the holy church,
don Dionisio Rafael. Alcalde, don
Francisco Martín. Rector, Juan
Alejandro. Notary, Anastasio de
Benavides.

Text 2. *Testament of Francisco Martín, San Lucas Tepemaxalco, 1735,
written by Leonardo de la Cruz.* (AGN, Tierras 2541, exp. 9, f. 33r-33v)

ju maria jucph
Yn ican itlasomaynstocatzin y dios
tetatzin y dios ytlasopiltzin y dio
epiritun santo ma y mochihua ca nehual nichiahua notestamento noca
fr^{co} martin ca ninoneltoquitia y
noteotzi y notlatocatzin y dios no
ihua notlasomaisnatzin sata maria
ma nopa motlatoltiz quimotlatlalis
yntlasomaiscenconetzin y ttyo jesu
sto nehmopolpoluhuilis y notlacoli
notlapilchiahua niahua ninotlatlatilia santomen y sa pedro y san pablo
moxtitzitzi apostelo[. . .] ma nopa
motlatolti[. . .] y quinnoyquilis no-
yoliatzi noanimatzi quimoyetenehui-
lis yn ahuicatl itin ma y mochia a-
me jesus maria jucph
- Ca no yahua nopaleahuiloca noanimatzi centel misias yahua ce resposos nopa motlatoltzinno padre guardia nica ypan ialtepetzi satun sa lucas Ebagelita notlaxilacalpa
- nin celtel y tlanahuatia ni caltzintli
nicati agustin de los ageles quimo-

Jesus, Mary, Joseph.
    In the precious honored name of
God the father, God his precious
child, and God the Holy Spirit; may
this be done. I, named Francisco
Martín, make my testament; I believe in my divinity and ruler God,
and also may my precious honored
mother St. Mary speak for me and
ask her precious honored one child
our lord Jesus Christ to pardon me
my sins and evildoing, and I implore the saints San Pedro and San
Pablo and all the apostles to speak
for me and take my spirit and soul
to praise him in heaven. May this
be done. Jesus, Mary, Joseph.

    Also for the help of my soul,
may the father guardian say a mass
with a response for me here in the
altepetl of the saint San Lucas E-
vangelista, in my district.
    First I order that (at) this house
(where) I am Agustín de los Angeles

telquipanilhuili santotin Ca hueltzin
Juan Bastista ca nema yes yhua solar quimochili mepapa tequtzitli

- cotlamatli nitlanahuatia ninomaquilia totlaxomaisnatzi de los ageles
yahua sa fr^co ynemaqu in agustin de
los ageles

- yetlamantli nitlanahuatia ninomaquilia totlasomaisnatzi de ahuada-
lope ca ynemaqu i jua batista yhua
ce san fr^co yahua sann aniotonio

- y natlamatli nitanahuatia ninoma-
quiliatia totlasomaahuinatzi ecarna-
sio ca ynemaq i geronimo miguel

- yn macuitlmatli nomaquilia ce
mili mani cuaxotenco calaqui xnax-
tli yei almo ninomaquilia agustin de
los agele quimochilis nepapa tequi-
tzitli ce chicaties notlatol
- yn chiqucetlamatli nitlanatia ce
mili mani yxtlahuateco ynemaq i
nosihua ytoca maria madalena
- y chicotlamatli nitlanahuatia ce
mili mani nixeahuila cepoali surcu
ynemaqui marcos nosobrino

- Chquey chice tlamatli nitlanahuatia ce machio ninomaquilia Agustin
de los ageles yehua ome acha yhua
asasado
- hinatlamatli nitlahuatia ce mili
mani san anitzin calbaro atzitlepa
onechmocalitia noCotzi catca ytoca
D fr^co martin ninomaqulia agustin
de los ageles quilemotequipanis ya
tzin S^rnora de s ageles opa quitias

is to serve the saints, (for Juan Bautista cannot?); (the house) and the
lot are to be his inheritance, and he
is to perform the various duties.

Second, I order that I give our
precious honored mother of the Angels and the saint San Francisco to
Agustín de los Angeles as his inheritance.

Third, I order that our precious
honored mother Guadalupe is the inheritance of Juan Bautista, along
with a San Francisco and San Antonio.

Fourth, I order that I give our
precious honored mother of the Incarnation to Gerónimo Miguel as
his inheritance.

Fifth, I give a field near the border where three almudes of seed can
be planted to Agustín de los Angeles; he is to perform the various
duties. My statement is to be valid.

Sixth, I order that a field next to
the plain is the inheritance of my
wife named María Magdalena.

Seventh, I order that a field at
(Nixehuillan?) of twenty furrows is
the inheritance of Marcos, my nephew.

Eighth, I order that I give a mule
to Agustín de los Angeles, and two
axes and a hoe.

Ninth, I order that I give a field
at San Antonio (Calvariotitlan?)
that my late grandfather named don
Francisco Martín left me to Agustín
de los Angeles; he is to serve the
Lady of the Angels; there he is to

cadela yhua xochil ca chicaties notlatol
- yahua quecomal ynemaqui juan
bastia centel
- yahua geronimo miguel o ce quecomal ynemaquis
- Ca ytzoqutia nocococatlatol ca ye-
ahuatzin notestigo

D⁰ llonisio Rafael   D⁰n atonio
de la crzu fiscal de la ta lesia   D⁰n
atonio de sa juan ald pasado   nicolas de santi alsin   lleonardo de la crz
esquiriban

Ax 1 de julio Axcan i xiahuil de
1735 años

(provide) candles and flowers. My
statement is to be valid.
And a grainbin is the inheritance
of Juan Bautista.
And another grainbin is the inheritance of Gerónimo Miguel.
I conclude my sick person's
statement. These are my witnesses:
Don Dionisio Rafael. Don Antonio de la Cruz, fiscal of the holy
church. Don Antonio de San Juan,
past alcalde. Nicolás de Santiago,
constable. Leonardo de la Cruz,
notary.
Today, 1st of July, year of 1735.

Text 3. *Testament of Agustín de los Angeles, San Lucas Tepemaxalco,
1736, written by Domingo Ramos.* (AGN, Tierras 2541, exp. 9, f. 35)

Jesus maria y Joseph
Yn iCa yntocatzin dios tetatzin yhua
dios ytlasopiltzin yn dios espiritu
sato yhua notlasomahuiznatzin sata
maria mochipa huel neli yxpochtli
ynic nopapan quimotlatlatiliatzinnos
yn itlasomahuizseteConnetzin yn
tt⁰ x̄t̄o ynic nexmopopolhuilitzin-
nos y nanima noyolia yn ixquich i
notlatlacol y notlapilchihuaz yn
itlatocachatzinCon yn ilhuicac yn
opa Cemicac quimoyectenehuilis-
tzinnos yeyca axcan lunes a 23 de
julio de 1736 años y nica nicchihua
nomemoria testameto nehual notoca
agustin de los ageles niCa notlaxila-
Calpa yn iCuac dios quimonequilti-
tzinnos y nanima noyolia ytla nino-
miquilis y notlalnaCayo onpa mo-
toCa yn iteoynchatziCon dios yhuan

Jesus, Mary, and Joseph.
In the name of God the father
and God his precious child and God
the Holy Spirit, and my precious
honored mother St. Mary, forever a
very true virgin, (I desire) that on
my behalf she implore her precious
honored one child, our lord Jesus
Christ, to pardon my soul and spirit
all my sins and evildoing so that it
will praise him eternally in his royal home in heaven, wherefore today, Monday, the 23d of July of the
year 1736, here I make my memorandum of testament, I named Agustín de los Angeles, whose home
district is here. When God wishes
my soul and spirit, if I die, my
earthly body will be buried in the
divine house of God and the house

ichatzinCon sato sa lucas auagelista
no niquitohua yn itechConpan yn
ipalehuiloca y nanima noyolia setel
misa yhua se respossos y Capa nito-
Cos yc nexmopalehuilis notlasoteo-
pixcatzin padre guardia

- ynic setlamatli nitlanahuatia no-
telpoch yntoca ju⁰ bactista nicnoca-
huilia Cali quimoquitlahuiz tlac-
panas tlapopoxhuis yhua yni solar
ynemaqui ninomaquilia ju⁰ bastista
quimotequipanilhuiz sata gelsia y-
hua yn mili mani yxtlahuateCon yc
quacxuCu nicnomaquili ju⁰ ba[. . .]-
tista quimochihuilis tequil yhua se
macho ynemaqui yhua se acha
- ynic ontlamatli nitlanahuatia
nosihua maria asosio nicnomaquilia
se quescomal yhua totlasonatzin de
loss ageles quimotepanilhuia yhua
se mili mani san atonio carballotitla
achi tlapaqui ayac a quixtili
quemania onechmocahuili no-
tlasotatzin omestiCacCac

- ynic yetlamatli nitlanahuatia notel-
poch ytoCa geronimo nicnomaquilia
[...] frascCon yhua se acha ynema[...] geronimo yhua noalbasia
leonardo de la Crus auh Ca quimoc-
tilisque nopilhuatoto yhua no
yehual noalbasia Dⁿ diego de los
satos auh Ca ye nictzoquixtia
noCohCoxCatla[...] nehual ni-
ConCoxqui Ca yehuati Ynique
notestigohua ynique Dⁿnastasio
benabides fiscal de sata gelessia Dⁿ
sebastia nicolas allde lixosi de la
crus regidor mayor roque medosa

of the saint San Lucas Evangelista.
I also say, concerning the aid of my
soul and spirit, a mass and response
(will be said for me), and as to
where I am to be buried, my precious priest the father guardian will
help me with it.

First I order that I leave to my
son named Juan Bautista the house;
he is to take care of it, sweep up and
provide incense, and I give him this
lot as his inheritance—he is to serve
the holy church, and I give Juan
Bautista the field at the edge of the
plain, at the border; he is to perform
the duties; and a mule is his inheritance, and an axe.

Second, I order that I give my
wife María de la Asunción a grainbin and our precious mother of the
Angels—she is to serve her—and a
field at San Antonio Calvariotitlan,
somewhat broken (divided in two?);
no one is ever to take it away from
her; my late precious father left it to
me.

Third, I order that I give my son
named Gerónimo (an image of San)
Francisco and an axe, as Gerónimo's
inheritance. And my executor is
Leonardo de la Cruz; he is to see to
my little children. And also don
Diego de los Santos is my executor.
I conclude my sick person's statement, I the sick person. These are
my witnesses: don Anastasio Benavides, fiscal of the holy church; don
Sebastián Nicolás, alcalde; Dionisio? de la Cruz, regidor mayor;
Roque Mendoza, majordomo; Juan

mayordomo ju⁰ pablo rafael rector
nehuatl onitlaCuilo domigo ramos
esños

Pablo Rafael, rector. I did the writing, Domingo Ramos, notary.

---

9. Care, Ingenuity, and Irresponsibility: The Bierhorst Edition of the *Cantares Mexicanos*

Bierhorst, John, transl. *Cantares Mexicanos: Songs of the Aztecs*. Stanford: Stanford University Press, 1985. xiii + 559 pp. including appendix, bibliography, and index.

Bierhorst, John. *A Nahuatl-English Dictionary and Concordance to the Cantares Mexicanos: With an Analytical Transcription and Grammatical Notes*. Stanford: Stanford University Press, 1985. 751 pp. including appendix and references.

Nahuatl, the primary indigenous language of central Mexico, is blessed with a written legacy unique among American Indian languages for its extent and time depth. One outstanding feature of that legacy is a body of songs set down mainly in the sixteenth century, the primary monument being the collection known as the *Cantares mexicanos*. The Cantares set contains well over half of all the known songs (91, some of which are song cycles) and greatly surpasses all other collections as to the variety of its materials and the sufficiency of its orthographic and other conventions. Ethnohistorians, cultural anthropologists, literary scholars, and others have long been interested in the texts, and several generations of scholars in Mexico and elsewhere, including some figures of high distinction, have devoted serious attention to them. Yet not until the appearance of the work now under review was there an adequate transcription of the Cantares mexicanos, or a complete translation of them into any modern language.

John Bierhorst's edition is thus distinctly a major event in Nahuatl studies, and it makes several very important contributions. It also has some outstanding faults. But first the contributions. Among them is a splendid transcription which for the first time makes the original Nahuatl of the entire Cantares easily accessible to scholars, arranged by the original units, reproducing the orthography as exactly as can be done in print, and spacing the letters into blocks following modern grammatical principles. The last part, a necessary but extremely difficult task (depending as it does on correct lexical and morphological analysis of texts of maximum complexity), is beautifully done. Though I would rearrange a few passages which I interpret differently, the transcription is in effect definitive. I have repeatedly checked suspicious-looking spots against a photocopy of the original and have yet to find a single error as to the reproduction of letters and diacritics. Some may exist, but overall the transcription is unusually trustworthy.

The translation too represents a large advance in many ways. Unlike previous major translations of this material, it scrupulously respects all the original units, allowing the reader to see the true structure of the songs. By virtue of being the first to survey the entire corpus systematically and simultaneously, Bierhorst has for the first time recognized many conventions of the Cantares vocabulary. His work has also profited from a great improvement in Nahuatl grammatical studies in recent years, involving the work of J. Richard Andrews (1975) and the rediscovery of Horacio Carochi, the great seventeenth-century grammarian. Bierhorst knows both well, and his translations show it. He also clearly has a gift of his own for understanding language, a subtlety and ingenuity that he has often exercised in an original fashion and with good effect. He has combed Spanish histories and Nahuatl codices for every scrap relevant to the Cantares. The texts are heavily sprinkled with the names of indigenous historical personages of central Mexico from both preconquest and early postconquest periods, and Bierhorst has had surprising success in identifying them. Some figures elude identification or remain unrecognized, and the identifications may not all stand the test of time, but the biographical information greatly enhances our understanding of the ethnic and historical dimensions of the texts and increases their general intelligibility.

Adding to the value of the edition is a large accompanying volume containing a dictionary-concordance and an analytical transcription of the Nahuatl. The former has entries for all words occurring in the texts, including proper names, and the latter allows one to see in detail how Bierhorst interprets the morphology and to some extent the syntax of individual passages. The concordance aspect, even though coverage is not exhaustive, will be invaluable for further research into the Cantares.

Bierhorst has written a substantial introduction containing much new material of great merit. His discussion of the organization of the songs is first-rate,[1] he has enlightening and reasonable things to say on the cloudy question of the drum beats meant to accompany the songs, and he establishes, to my satisfaction at least, that the texts in their present form originated primarily in the generation starting about 1550. Many deal with events and personnel of the Spanish conquest or the postconquest years, and the majority show some Spanish-Christian influence on vocabulary and concepts. In addition to all the reasons that Bierhorst adduces, the timing he proposes coincides perfectly with a general phenomenon, the flourishing of the partly Hispanized indigenous corporations of central Mexico in the second half of the sixteenth century. After the present edition, we can no longer treat the songs as virtually pure compositions of the preconquest period, altered only by the word "God" patched in over the names of indigenous deities. In an oral tradition, however, in which each singer often composes anew on the basis of a version already existing, in effect creating only a minimally new variant, the corpus could still be predominantly preconquest in ultimate origin.

Along with the new dating comes a different perspective on authorship. Bierhorst maintains that the (mainly preconquest) kings and lords who figure so largely in the songs, often speaking in the first person, are by no means to be taken as their authors. Such a title as "The song of Neçahualcoyotl," says Bierhorst, is best understood as "song about Neçahualcoyotl." Moreover, the songs usually make it clear that the main character is already deceased, much of the purpose of the composition being to exalt him and revive his memory. With those few songs where a composer is named, he proves to be distinct from the person or persons feted. Bierhorst puts much of the blame for the poet-king myth on the seventeenth-century Tetzcocan chronicler Ixtlilxochitl, who had little understanding of the songs and was intent on magnifying the fame of one of his ancestors. This has the ring of truth; I too, in totally unrelated research on sociopolitical organization, have found Ixtlilxochitl to be a great distorter of earlier phenomena, far less knowledgable and trustworthy than his immediate predecessors such as Tezozomoc and Chimalpahin.

I do think that Bierhorst goes too far in trying to expunge any tradition that poet-kings existed in preconquest times or later. The Cantares are saturated with royalty and high nobility. I would be surprised if kings and lords did not compose songs both before and after the conquest, and the persons exalted in the Cantares may well have done so. They may even have composed prototypes of some of the songs we know. They do not, however, appear to have composed the songs we know in the form in which they have come down to us. I agree with Bierhorst that the appearance of a personage as protagonist in a song is not prima facie evidence that he composed it, but on the contrary makes it more likely that he did not. Not all the uncertainties are resolved. For example, in the case of specific persons named as composing songs in the postconquest period, the main verb used is *tecpana*, "to order, put in order," which could very well apply to a (possibly very slight) rearrangement of an already existing composition. Whether there was a sharp distinction between composer and performer is something we still do not know. In any case, Bierhorst's work should bring about a considerable change in the traditional general position on the authorship of the songs.

Taken together, the contributions I have been discussing can be considered a legitimate breakthrough, that is, they put the study of Nahuatl song on a new level and will facilitate a new cycle of research, translation, and interpretation. These merits, however, are not destined to be the most frequent topic of public discussion in connection with the Bierhorst edition. It is Bierhorst's "ghost-song" interpretation that is bound to catch the eye of colleagues and lay readers alike. I regret the amount of attention that must be given here to this topic, but one has no choice, for the interpretation not only dominates the commentary and large sections of the introduction but has worked its way deeply into the dictionary-concordance and the translation itself.

Bierhorst calls all the compositions of the Cantares "ghost songs." According to him (pp. 3-4),

> the Aztec ghost song may be described as a musical performance in which warrior-singers summon the ghosts of ancestors in order to swell their ranks and overwhelm their enemies. . . In response to the music, ghost warriors from paradise, led by ancestor kings, supposedly came "scattering," "raining," "flying," or "whirling" to earth in the form of flowers or birds. . .

For Bierhorst a song's principal ancestral figure is the "muse," whom he sees as producing further ghosts (in Bierhorst's terminology "revenants"). The singer of the song may take a "song trip" to the heavens; living persons involved in the songs often die and ascend to heaven as "payment" for the "revenants." Eighty-six pages of commentary to the individual songs are devoted almost exclusively to explaining which persons are ascending or descending through the heavens, or have just done so, or are about to do so. Yet an unsuspecting reader who had not seen the introduction or the commentary might proceed indefinitely through the translation without the slightest notion of such heavenly traffic, resuscitation, and sacrificial death, for hardly any of it is explicit.

Inordinate skepticism, however, is not necessarily called for. In the North American West, the well known ghost dances of the plains Indians offer a close parallel to the Cantares as Bierhorst sees them, and Bierhorst as originally a translator of North American Indian song is quick to make the connection. Revitalization movements with similar notions have been occurring for centuries across the world and have appeared within the borders of Mexico as well. Moreover, Nahuatl incantations collected in central Mexico in the early seventeenth century speak openly of calling down gods and spirits to bring about cures and other desired effects, and sometimes the speaker seems to go into the other world to retrieve the spirit (as seen in the early seventeenth-century treatise of Hernando Ruiz de Alarcón). On the other hand, although millenarian movements, with unmistakable external manifestations, were endemic from the sixteenth century forward in the nonsedentary north of Mexico, and not unheard of in the more sedentary but isolated south, they were virtually nonexistent in the center, the land of the Nahuas. Revitalization phenomena are characteristic of people who feel that their sociopolitical units and whole way of life are in imminent danger of extinction. Such was not the case in central Mexico, where a network of local states survived the conquest intact as entities, with their essential mechanisms still functioning. Yet it must be admitted that Mexico Tenochtitlan, the former imperial center and the focus of the Cantares, was unique within central Mexico; it alone had been the unequivocal loser in the great shifts occurring through the conquest, and its reaction could have been different from that of other indigenous states.

One might ask how the often noticed lyricism of the Cantares can be reconciled with the notion of martial "ghost songs" in Bierhorst's sense. The apparent incongruity is not per se insurmountable. It was already understood that war is one of the main themes of the songs. With the entire corpus of texts now intelligibly transcribed before us, it becomes apparent that the great idiosyncrasy of Nahuatl song as it has survived is that in it the topics of war, the afterlife, and ethnic patriotism are associated not with epic narrative but with conventional elements of worldwide lyrical expression.

The validity, or the extent of the validity, of the ghost-song interpretation cannot be decided by arguments on a general plane. The issue must be dealt with out of the texts themselves; either the language to support such an interpretation can be adduced, or it cannot be. I will have to enter deeply, then, into matters of translation difficulty, translation error, and the reason for such error. I do not do so lightly or gladly. In the past I have committed egregious errors in translating older Nahuatl texts, and I expect to commit more in the future. Every Nahuatl translator of this century and the past has made deplorable errors; it is simply part of the process of trying to bring the understanding of at least one Indian language up to the standard for the major European languages, and we must have the freedom to reach into the unknown without ridicule. Moreover, as I have said above, I consider Bierhorst on balance a very good translator. Nevertheless, the ghost-song interpretation turns on specific translations and inferences, so they must be discussed.

The Cantares, for all their wealth, are a restricted body of material with very little context (imagine that we knew under two hundred European poems, no direct discussion of them, and very little closely related prose). Their syntax is unusual, masked further by a near-total lack of punctuation, and their vocabulary is obscure, much of it not in existing dictionaries. Translation of any of the more complex passages is something of a guess in the best of cases. But these general difficulties are only the beginning. The texts are shot through with vocables or nonsense syllables, sometimes in strings, sometimes in isolated syllables; sometimes between words, sometimes within words. They bear no special indicator, and the translator must decide what is a vocable and what is not. Many look a great deal like words or morphemes. *A*, *an*, and *aya* occur constantly; they can always be interpreted as *a(h)*, "not," and *aya*, "not yet." The result is that in large stretches of the text it is impossible to be sure which statements are positive and which are being negated. The recurring vocable *yehuaya* can be construed to contain *ehua*, "he rises or departs" (for an example, see pp. 228-29, verse 4). Elision of the vowel of the ubiquitous particle *in* leads to excess *n's* everywhere. *Can* can mean "where" or represent *ca in*, a nearly meaningless particle combination, or be a frequent error for *çan*, "just" or "but."

Nahuatl in general distinguishes clearly between direct address and third person forms, but in the Cantares such distinctions seem to be widely ignored. Especially, many nouns that one would expect to be in the vocative are not. A translator has little to go on and may easily fall into the multiplication of direct address, creating nonexistent repartee. In written Nahuatl of all kinds it is hard to identify the subjects and objects of verbs, and in the conditions of the Cantares it is often quite impossible (for examples of errors see the four-verse sample reproduced below). Essentially, I contend that given the present state of the art of translating older Nahuatl in general and the Cantares in particular, no interpretation is likely to prove valid which depends on a chain of subtle inferences abstracted from a given translation without considering the many alternate translation possibilities.

Perhaps I can give some sense of how easy it is to get apparently simple and basic things very wrong by giving some examples, shown on the table on the following page:

Nahuatl	Bierhorst's translation	A more correct translation
mahmana tlatzihui (pp. 228-29, verse 4)	the Enduring One, grow weary	get upset, grow weary
macac omeya yyollo (236-37, 10)	let no one's heart flow out	let no one doubt
tla xonahuia huehue-titlan xonmiquani 248-49, 18)	be pleasured then beside the drum—and move beyond	enjoy yourself, move over next to the drum
oncan xamanque yn pipiltzitzinti (256-57, 13)	the princes (lie) broken	the little children were shattered
ma ixquich tlacatl ma quimolnamiquili inic topampa tonehualoc (274-75, 9)	Let every man recall Him. For you arose on our be-half.	let everyone remember how he was tormented on our behalf.
at aoc tomatian in monamiccan mochi-huatiuh chalchiuh-elotl (308-09, 38)	maybe our time is up, and the green-corn ears, these jades, are to pass away— that they might be created.	perhaps we will no longer be alive when the emerald-colored new ears of corn (planted) last year mature
inteocuitlatlapal ica (314-15, 5)	gold-colored	with its golden wings
otonnexineque (320-21, 1)	We've cut off our hair.	They have Otomi-style haircuts.
onnemacoc (330-31, 20)	they who were swallowed	everyone surrendered
tonecoque ye nican (338-39, 97)	we've been required right here	we've arrived here
tlapia (340-41, 106)	is paying honor	is in charge
onixtlahuia in Mexicayotl (346-47, 17)	surrendered, then, is the Mexican nation	the Mexican nation comes into its own, receives its due
titotoliniao tle titocuepazque (384-85, 42)	how can we return if we're poor?	we are poor (afflicted). What is to become of us (what are we to turn into)?
ymixpampa hualehua (392-93, 5)	they're rising up against them	they're fleeing from them
chicopa (392-93, gloss)	on one side	seven times
oc no chicopa (394-95, gloss)	on the other side	seven more times

Bierhorst's versions, of course, are put to the service of ghost-song exegesis. In the passage here from p. 256, for example, he identifies his broken princes (actually small children) with the Magi, who are then said on no further evidence to have been killed and risen to heaven in a ghost-song exchange.

Nahuatl comes in a Spanish wrapping. The original grammars and dictionaries, and much else, are in that language, and one must approach Nahuatl through it. Rare is the Nahuatl scholar who did not learn Spanish first. With his North American experience, Bierhorst is different, and at the time when he did the bulk of the work for the present edition (things may already have changed, for he is good at languages) he did not know Spanish very well. This circumstance may actually have contributed to his originality, but it causes some problems in the dictionary and the translations. Bierhorst did not realize that the gloss *antaño* in Molina means "last year," causing part of the difficulty in the passage from p. 308 given just above. He did not understand the plain Spanish of either Molina or Carochi to the effect that *çan tequitl* with a verb means "to do nothing but what that verb designates," hence translates it (pp. 218-19, song 43, v. 7) as "oh but scarcely." He says (dictionary-concordance, p. 168) that *inehua* means "to strike a blow without aiming, hence to strike an ill blow," referring to Molina, who nevertheless plainly says that the meaning is "for a shot to miss what is aimed at."

Not only does Bierhorst immediately interpret whatever results he extricates from this thicket of difficulties in terms of ghost song notions, but he has consciously or unconsciously carried out extensive manipulations of the translation so that it will lend itself more readily to his interpretation. In the Cantares it is clear that mentions of flowers, songs, and birds often have additional reference to people, in Bierhorst's eyes usually "revenants." He extends such usage at will to almost any noun, and in this practice he is greatly abetted by his idea that the instrumental word -*ca*, often suffixed to nouns in the form of -*tica*, can be translated "as," as in *xochimaquiztica netotilo* (pp. 182-83, v. 2), which Bierhorst renders "all are dancing as flower bracelets" rather than the expected "with flower bracelets." No grammarian has ever noticed such use of -*ca* before, nor have I in extensive reading of various kinds of texts, nor do I find any evidence of it in the Cantares themselves. (For another example of the bad results of the "as" rendering of -*ca*, see the extended passage translated below.) Along the same lines, Bierhorst standardly translates -*yol* and -*yollo*, "heart," as "hearts," meaning a multitude of people, normally "revenants." To take one of a thousand instances, on p. 408-09, v. 43, Bierhorst renders *yc no yohuaye noyol* as "O my hearts!" I would respace this *ycnoyohua ye noyol* and translate it "my heart is troubled or desolate." "Heart" is not an ordinary noun in Nahuatl but is used to categorize a large set of idioms having to do with emotional states and the will. To find it constantly personified, and in the plural to boot, is shocking. Especially the *-yollo* form exhibits what is often called the sign of inalienable possession, meaning that the thing signified is an organic and inseparable part of the possessing entity itself. Even in the unlikely event that the word were to appear referring to persons in the plural, it would not fail to exhibit the plural possessive suffix, which it never does.[2]

Much the same effect is achieved in Bierhorst's translation by taking abstract nouns to refer to groups of people. In the Cantares, which strike me if not Bierhorst as one of the greatest tributes to noble companionship ever written down, words like *icniuhyotl*, "friendship," *coayotl*, "comradeship," *tecpillotl*, "nobility," and *teucyotl*, "lordship," abound. Bierhorst nearly always translates these words as "friends," "comrades," "nobles," and "lords," the persons referred to of course usually being construed to be that many more "revenants." Forms in *-yotl* can in fact be collectives and I have no doubt that in the Cantares they often are, but Bierhorst makes virtually no allowance for the strong praise of the abstract qualities that so impresses me, nor for the possibility that any persons referred to are primarily the present company, the audience of the song. A particularly egregious case of this sort of thing is on pp. 228-29, v. 1, where *xochimiquiztli*, "flower death," is translated as "flower mortals"; nothing justifies such treatment of an active deverbal abstract noun.

Bierhorst also resorts to translations which facilitate the great amount of ascending, descending, appearing, and disappearing called for by his interpretation. The reflexive *quetza*, meaning simply "to stand up," is usually translated "to appear" (e.g., pp. 234-35, v. 1). "Down" is often seen in the translation with no basis in the text whatever, as on pp. 352-53, v. 10, "bringing down" for *quihualaxitia*, a verb form which says nothing about up or down. On pp. 351-52, v. 1, *onmani* is translated "fall" (from heaven), although its meaning is "to spread horizontally, extend, etc." On pp. 362-63, v. 16, one of several such instances, the string *a y tzin* is translated without adequate reason as "down below"; elsewhere in the book it is rendered as a term of endearment.

God and the other world proliferate in the translation through a few simple devices. *Oncan* and *ompa*, both meaning "there," are usually rendered as "beyond." Sometimes this seems to be the true intention of the text, but for Bierhorst such a reading becomes automatic, even in cases when "there" merely anticipates or reiterates a specified location (as on pp 328-29, v. 3). With the slightest justification and in my opinion often without any at all, Bierhorst takes an unspecified subject or object (of which there are myriad) to be God, writing "He" and "Him" as on pp. 204-05, song 35, v. 1 (where I think that in fact some of the verbs already have specified subjects). Unidentified or unrecognized names of a descriptive nature are often taken to refer to the sun and hence to the deity. On pp. 236-37, v. 8, *quauhtlehuanitl* is rendered "Ascending Eagle," which the commentary tells us means the sun, but this in fact was the name of a king of Amaquemecan, the place to which these verses refer. A similar interpretation is given on pp. 318-19, v. 8, obscuring the fact that the Nahuatl clearly names Quauhtemoc, king of Tenochtitlan during the Spanish siege.

Bierhorst's central image is that of "revenants" being "whirled" down from heaven. A whole series of Nahuatl verbs frequent in the texts—*malina, ilacatzoa, ihcuiya*—are uniformly translated "whirl" even though their primary meaning is "to twist elongated matter." In the Cantares, flowers are the most usual objects of these verbs, followed by songs, and the senses that leap to the eye are "to entwine garlands of flowers," secondarily "to string together the verses of a song," and thirdly "to entwine and bring together the present happy company." In dictionaries and in usage generally, rarely do these verbs refer to free revolution (*ihcuiya*, "to gather up, collect, wind up" not at all to my knowledge); the only one of the set that often does mean to spin like a top is *malacachoa*, quite rare in the Cantares, and even it is a term coming out of weaving. So determined is Bierhorst to have whirling that on pp. 318-19, v. 5, he translates the verb *cuecueyahua*, not found in the dictionaries, as "whirl," though from its etymological affinities and its few known attestations elsewhere I think it probably means "to shine." To give an example or two, on p. 329, verses 15-16, I would say "twisting his garlands," not "whirling" them as Bierhorst does, and on pp. 196-97, song 29, v. 1, for *anquimalinaco anquilacatzoay in tecpillotl* I would say "you have come to entwine nobility, to twist it together (i.e., to bring together the fellowship of nobles)," not with Bierhorst "you've come to spin, to whirl, these nobles," the latter taken to be "warrior revenants."

Another need in the ghost song interpretation is for great amounts of creating, specifically of "revenants." Three devices of Bierhorst's go far toward supplying the need. First, innocently or not he consistently misconstrues the reflexive form of the verb *chihua*, "to make, do, engender, create." He is right that reflexives often have passive meaning even with personal subjects, but this is not equally true of all verbs. The reflexive of *chihua* is so much used in Nahuatl in the meanings "happen, become, grow," and others that it virtually never serves as a substitute for the passive in the sense of "make, create" (except perhaps in the special meaning "appoint, constitute"). Bierhorst speaks of creation nearly every time *mochihua* appears, never in my opinion correctly. Thus where on pp. 352-53, v. 5, he translates *tiquetzaltototl timochiuhtihuitz, spilito xanto* as "you come created, O Quetzal, O Espíritu Santo," I would say "Holy Spirit, you come transformed into a quetzal bird." The second device is the word *tlaocolli* or *tlayocolli*, almost always possessed, which appears frequently in the Cantares. Sometimes it indubitably means "sadness, pity, mercy" and is translated accordingly by Bierhorst, but far more often he renders it as "creation," deriving it from the verb *yocoya*, "to create, invent, fabricate." This derivation is entirely of his own devising; the patientive deverbal nouns from *yocoya* to be found both in the dictionaries and in actual texts are *tlayocoyalli* and *tlayocoxtli*. In my opinion, *tlaocolli* means "sadness" or "mercy" throughout the Cantares. The third device is that at will Bierhorst construes the verb *ihtoa*, "to speak (and related meanings)" as signifying "to create" ("revenants"), indicating the meaning by the translation "to utter." The objects of the verb are often invented out of the vaguenesses of the Nahuatl third person. On pp. 230-31, v. 9, Bierhorst translates *notlayocol a noconayaihtoa* as "He is my creation. I utter him." I would translate the passage as "I speak my sorrow."

A revitalization movement normally directs its hostility at an invading power, which it aims to destroy root and branch. Here the ghost-song explanation of the Cantares encounters a difficulty. The main enmity apparently shown in the texts is toward the traditional rivals of the Mexica, namely the other indigenous states of the region. Direct mention of Spanish lay personnel is not prominent, and no tirades against them occur; the Christian God, the Holy Trinity, and the Virgin Mary are well represented, along with some ecclesiastics, but the attitude shown toward them is at least superficially one of reverence. Bierhorst does some of his greatest stretching in the attempt to get the Cantares to produce statements radically hostile to Spaniards and Christian religion. Here is verse 33 on pp. 292-93, with Bierhorst's translation of it.

> Yn çan no iuh ye quichiuh Nozcacauhtzin oo apa hualhuetz ye tenoch-
>   titlani ymatiya ye yehua Malques
> My father's done it just for fun, and—with His knowledge—into the
>   water at Tenochtitlan he's toppled, he the Marquis!

The Marquis is Hernando Cortés, and Bierhorst claims in the accompanying commentary that Cortés was produced as a "revenant" in order to be destroyed, then carried to heaven as a sacrificial victim. I think verse 33

Samples of Transcription, Translation, and Commentary from the Bierhorst edition

The Nahuatl passage:[3]

1. Ye quilhuia yn icihuauhtzin in Acapepenatzin ahua Pille netle Mano cana, mano cana, achitzin xitechompehui toconizque, ye ma yhui ye ma yhuio notecuiyo oquichpillitzin

2. Ohuallaque in Pipiltin ye huexotzinco y Ton Xihuan y nelpiloni ye tlen conizque in Pipiltin mano cana Et[a]

3. Ye ca onihualah ca onicuiteyah ye ma xonmotlapalo ye cihuatzintle tla xiqualcuiya tla xictemacaya yn man copatica in man tacatica ya ma ya onihualo in teteuctin ayyo Et[a]

4. In notzinitzcanhuicoltzin ye ço huel quatzin tlapalhuacalxochitl y ma ycaya onilacatziuhtihuitz Notecotzin tla xiqualcui tla xictemamaca-ya Et[a]

Bierhorst's translation:

1. His woman says, "Down here, Reed Picker! Come, prince! Hail! Here! Here! Conquer a little something that we can drink! Let it be done, let it be done! My lord! O man-child! Down here!"

2. The princes have come. Huexotzinco's Don Juan Nelpiloni is the one these princes are to drink. "Here! *Here! Conquer a little something that we can drink! Let it be done, let it be done! My lord! O man-child! Down here!*"[4]

3. Oh yes, I've come; and I've set off to get him. Hail, woman! "Please do come get him. Please offer him up. Let him be dispatched as a *white man's* cup, as a *white man's* dagger. O lords!"

4. "Would that crimson basket flowers might come whirling on account of this delicious trogon cup of mine. Come get this lord, this man of mine. Please offer him up! *Let him be dispatched as a white man's cup, as a white man's dagger. O lords!*"

My own translation, which I am confident those who know Nahuatl will find more nearly correct:

1. Acapepenatzin says to his wife, "Lady, listen, please somewhere, please somewhere scare us up a little something to drink." "Let it be so, let it be so, my lord, manly noble."

2. "The nobles have come, among them don Juan Nelpiloni of Huexotzinco. What are the nobles to drink? Please somewhere, (please somewhere scare us up a little something to drink." "Let it be so, let it be so, my lord, manly noble.")

3. "I have come back; I went to get it (the drink)." "Step forward, dear woman, do bring it here and give it to people, whether in a (European) goblet or in a (European) cup. Let all the lords drink."

4. "My trogon jar is very pretty; let my tecomate (jar, pot) come being wrapped around with red basket flowers." "Do bring it here and distribute it to people, (whether in a goblet or in a cup. Let all the lords drink.)"

Bierhorst's commentary (pp. 510-11):

1. The singer informs us that a Huexotzincan woman is attempting to summon a Huexotzincan ghost, whom she addresses as Reed Picker (i.e., one who slaughters "reeds," or warriors). She wants him to come make conquests so that the Huexotzincans will have a little blood to drink.

2. The ghosts arrive, but they are Mexicans, not Huexotzincans; and their intended victim is Don Juan Nelpiloni (an Indian lord of Huexotzinco).

3. The leader of the Mexicans greets the woman and announces his intention to take Huexotzincan captives. The woman welcomes the Mexicans enthusiastically (as though she has no choice or as though she has mixed feelings about Huexotzinco's having collaborated with Cortés). She tells the Mexicans to go ahead and kill the Huexotzincan men, here called "daggers" (warriors) and "cups" (because their blood is to be drunk)—but the white man's words *copa* and *daga* are used.

4. The woman says she is glad to have her man killed, because in exchange she will receive a shower of Huexotzincan "basket flowers" (revenants).

plainly means something very different. Keeping in mind that in verse 32 someone is said to have drowned, I would translate the Nahuatl just above as follows:

> My father did the same; he fell into the water (canal) at Tenochtitlan in the time of the Marqués.

On pp. 308-09, verses 45-46, and pp. 312-13, v. 61, Bierhorst attempts to establish that certain passages through ambiguity and innuendo imply that Cortés is being hanged. But the reflexive verb form *piloa* being used merely designates certain kinds of motion and suspension, as opposed to the passive, which is used for hanging as a punishment, a distinction that Bierhorst ignores. Secondly, the fact that the protagonist of the song, the Chalcan ruler don Hernando de Guzmán, is here called just "don Hernando" sets up no ambiguous wording as Bierhorst claims, for it would not have occurred to anyone in his right mind in the New Spain of the second half of the sixteenth century that "don Hernando" could be an allusion to the Marqués del Valle, universally referred to either by his title (as in the Cantares themselves) or by his full name including surname.[5]

On pp. 382-83, v. 31, *Jesu Christo in maoc toconcuicatino* is translated "Jesus Christ...Don't sing for Him!" In fact, the form *toconcuicati(n)* is ungrammatical and as such meaningless. If one presumes that a *ti* was left out toward the end, the construction could in itself be either in the purposive-motion imperative, "let's go sing for Him," the more natural reading, or in the vetitive, as Bierhorst translates it. Bierhorst gives the reader no indication that there is any doubt whatever about the meaning. I think that both the context and certain grammatical considerations point to the alternative Bierhorst did not choose, the purposive-motion construction; the particle *oc* is associated with positive commands, and the verbal prefix *on-* frequently occurs together with the purposive. It is equally likely that *ca*, not *ti*, was omitted, which would make the form imperative and yield a translation "let's sing for Him." (I exclude the possibility of the second-person singular vetitive not only because of *oc* and the final *n* but because in the whole section the singer addresses a plural audience.)

Without all the kinds of legerdemain I have been describing, the translation would give a considerably different overall impression, and it would be much less amenable to the ghost-song interpretation. I hope that my piecemeal approach has managed to convey the message that because of unavoidable uncertainties, possibly avoidable errors, and systematic distortions, an interpretation that can reasonably be made of Bierhorst's translation is not necessarily (or even probably) a valid interpretation of the original text. Nothing can make the point as well, however, as a full sample of the apparatus. On two pages just above (152-53) I have therefore presented the following: the Nahuatl of a section of song 89 (pp. 410-11 of the edition), consisting of four verses; Bierhorst's translation; my own translation; and Bierhorst's commentary. I earnestly invite the reader to peruse these materials carefully.

It will be seen that Bierhorst's commentary is utter nonsense. In translating the four verses, he has misconstrued a good portion of the words of the original, gets the speaker wrong most of the time, and has not arrived at a version that makes sense; yet in a spirit of total irresponsibility, on this flimsy foundation he has built an imposing ghost-song fantasy, not a single word of which has any validity whatsoever. If all the translations in the edition were demonstrably as bad as this sample, the whole work would be a travesty. I repeat that I consider the work in general to be of inestimable value, but travesty is exactly the right word for the entire commentary section. Even if certain things in it should eventually turn out to be in some sense not too far off the mark, at the present juncture we have no reason to take any of it seriously except for the small portion dealing with factual background. The same applies to the sections of ghost-song exegesis in the introduction.

In my opinion, the best way to understand the songs is to operate on the presumption that the historical figures mentioned in them are mainly imagined to be speaking in their own time, not in the song-present (even if the song does in some sense conjure them up), and that the events referred to are the real original ones. Not only would this interpretation be consonant with the statements of several observers at the time (on whom Bierhorst heaps scorn) that the primary purpose of the songs was to remember past glories, but it makes the songs both more credible and more moving in translation. On pp. 318-19, v. 2, we find the following:

> Hualtzatzia in tachcauh in quauhtencoztli çan conilhuia in capitani ya o
> tonan ye malintzin y xacaltecoz acachinanco otacico
> Chief Yellow-Beak Eagle comes shouting. And Captain, or Mother
> Marina, says, "Yellow Beak, my lookout! You've arrived in
> Acachinanco!"

Bierhorst has his chief leaping down from heaven as a "revenant." I think, on the contrary, that this personage, who by Bierhorst's data was alive at the time, is arriving from his homeland to take part in the siege of Tenochtitlan. I would translate as follows:[6]

> The leader Quauhtencoztli comes shouting, but the captain, or doña
> Marina, says to him, "temporary quarters (*xahcalli*, huts) are to be

set up at Acachinanco (where the siege of Tenochtitlan is thought to have begun). You have arrived."

On pp. 249-41, v. 36, in the original and in the translation some Chalcans are said to have become Mexicans, Acolhuans, and Tepanecs. Bierhorst claims this means that Chalcan "revenants" were transformed into enemy "revenants." I think the reference is to the actual dispersal and loss of territorial units that took place in the Chalcan wars, the general topic of this song.

The ghost-song interpretation in Bierhorst's hands suffers from a serious logical and esthetic flaw. The Cantares are filled with the theme of impermanence, which Bierhorst refers virtually entirely to the brevity of the time the ghost "revenants" are supposed to have here on earth. Yet again and again throughout the songs, in a multitude of variants, one finds laments that we have only one time on earth, as on pp. 394-95, v. 2, *ayoppan tlalticpac*, which Bierhorst correctly translates "there's no second time on earth." But Bierhorst claims precisely that the figures have come to earth for a second time, and that the bewailing of transience has reference to that second time. Not only is this notion illogical, it trivializes a rich vein of lyricism in the songs. Consider passages like those on pp. 184-85, 350-51, or 372-73, which movingly speak of the impermanence of flowers, kingdoms, and human life, weigh the uncertainties of our future, and call for a moment of fellowship, dancing and song while we may. Such statements far transcend the ghost-song baggage.

Nevertheless, I do not categorically deny any possible validity of the ghost-song explanation with certain songs. For one thing, at present our understanding of the Cantares is too preliminary to deny anything categorically. After someone has done a second-generation complete translation, carefully assessing and annotating all discoverable translation alternatives instead of twisting everything in one direction, I will be fully prepared to reconsider the matter. For another thing, any composition mentioning some flowers and a person from the past can theoretically be interpreted as a ghost song in Bierhorst's sense if one is sufficiently uninhibited. For yet another, there are a very few passages in the Cantares (see pp. 326-27, verses 18-22, and 352-53, verses 7 and 8) where Bierhorst's exegesis actually corresponds closely to explicit, intelligible statements in the texts themselves. For still another, I think the Cantares are too varied to be subsumed under a single genre in any aspect except possibly structure, and that different interpretations probably apply in different cases.

Several aspects of the ghost-song apparatus can be appreciated and utilized by accepting them in a somewhat different sense. Having ghosts raining down bears a close affinity to reviving the memory of ancestors through song. I can readily see the importance of the figure Bierhorst calls the "muse." In his scheme, the "muse" produces "revenants"; I would say that a protagonist serves as the central figure around whom a world of memories comes flooding back. I agree that a great many Cantares passages speaking of birds and flowers have direct reference to noble warriors of the past, even if not "ghosts." I do not accept Bierhorst's doctrine of "payment," in which living persons are sacrificed in return for "revenants," but the term -patiuh, "price, value of something," does exist in the texts (e.g., pp. 314-15, v. 13) in a meaning as yet unclear to me, and its further elucidation is greatly to be desired.

The dictionary-concordance accompanying the translation deserves a longer discussion than I can give it. Anyone reading or translating Nahuatl song will find the work most useful; in its capacity as a concordance it will be indispensable. Yet it is treacherous, primarily because it incorporates Bierhorst's entire set of speculations on ghost-song vocabulary. Let the reader be aware that any gloss for which a specific reference is not given is, by his own statement, Bierhorst's invention out of experience with the Cantares. By no means all such glosses are distorted; I accept many that do not have to do with ghost-song terminology. In the long run, advance in the study of Nahuatl song calls not only for a concordance of words but for a complete concordance of the stock phrases of which the songs are made; Bierhorst's compilation is at least an important step in that direction.

As to the brief grammatical notes, which could as well be termed simply "translator's notes," they concern primarily orthographic variants and questions of usage. Their organization is chaotic, and Bierhorst seems unable to distinguish orthographic from phonological variation or to understand the principles of the latter at all, but as with most of his productions, the expert would do well to read this section carefully. Among forgettable material manifesting a considerable amount of error and caprice, one will find some acute remarks and original insights. For example, I agree entirely with Bierhorst that a main function of the purposive-motion forms is to indicate the carrying of an act to its completion or destination (dictionary-concordance, p. 710).

The Bierhorst edition of the Cantares leaves me grateful and impressed, but also in many respects unconvinced and exasperated. Although the book is a great boon to Nahuatl scholars, I fear that in the hands of the uninitiated, who will constitute the majority of its readership, it may do more harm than good, mislead more than instruct.

III. Historiography

10. Charles Gibson and the Ethnohistory of Postconquest Central Mexico

In December, 1986, I gave a talk "Charles Gibson the Ethnohistorian" as part of a memorial session in Gibson's honor, and afterwards some members of the audience were good enough to encourage me to publish it. I now do so, leaving out some (not quite all) of the more personal touches, while adding material to the final section on developments among Gibson's successors. At the session we did not fail to show our affection for a fine and unusual person, but above all we were trying to grapple with the significance of the remarkable, still very influential body of historical writing he produced. The task of comprehension is double. First, Gibson's work has such density and depth that it needs a certain amount of explaining in and of itself; in some quarters Gibson has been more recognized than understood. Second, he needs to be seen in the context of those writing before and after him. Before him, in his specialty, there was almost no one; we do not always realize the extent to which basic operating concepts of Mexican ethnohistory, taken for granted by everyone today, were new with Gibson. After him has come a small avalanche of research, not least because of his example, and in order to understand either Gibson's impact or the purpose and contribution of much recent work, the two phases must be brought into relation with each other. Perhaps, indeed, a thorough survey of postconquest Mesoamerican ethnohistory from World War Two to the present would do more toward helping us grasp the meaning of Gibson than a discussion specifically centered on him; so much has now been done that a stocktaking is called for in any case. But the time is not quite ripe, for the field is growing and changing too quickly. Several works now in progress will alter the picture appreciably within a very few years, and yet others stand behind them. Meanwhile, possibly the present piece can serve both to give some perspective on a giant of Mexican ethnohistory and to provide a provisional report on current directions in the field.

Gibson wrote many valuable articles and bibliographical works in some way related to Mexican Indians, but the two principal monuments he has left us are *Tlaxcala in the Sixteenth Century* and *The Aztecs Under Spanish Rule*.[1] These I propose to discuss virtually a chapter at a time, if the reader will bear with me. I will give what some might see as a disproportionate amount of attention to *Tlaxcala*, not only because it is somewhat neglected in comparison to *The Aztecs*, but because in some respects it is historiographically even more forward looking and directly relevant for today's practice than the later book.

I do not mean to tarry over the nature of ethnohistory as a subdiscipline. Gibson himself once said that he was prepared to define ethnohistory as the history of Indians. Not only will that suffice for present purposes, it expresses Gibson's inclination to include ethnohistory in the rest of history just like any other topical subdivision, using essentially the same methods and not isolating it from the larger corpus—views in which I heartily concur; though I and others of my contemporaries may appear more crossdisciplinary, interdisciplinary, or nondisciplinary than Gibson, this is a characteristic of the whole historical endeavor as it is evolving and not merely of ethnohistory. I have some qualms about "Indian" as a category in describing the indigenous inhabitants of the Western hemisphere, but some roughly equivalent category is needed, it is the one Gibson used, and it will serve here.

Tlaxcala

Gibson's *Tlaxcala in the Sixteenth Century*, appearing in 1952, was the first major study in the field of Latin American history to make Indians the primary focus and topic of discussion. One could of course say that the demographic work of Simpson, Cook, and Borah,[2] which was in full swing before the appearance of *Tlaxcala*, primarily concerned Indians, since tribute records were the archival and methodological core and only Indians paid tribute. And surely demography did enlighten us vastly about trends in the Indian world. At that point, however, macrodemography and aggregate statistics were the emphasis, with little or no direct study of the cultural patterns and structures which organized Indian life.

It is also true that Indians had loomed large in the general Spanish American historiography of the previous hundred years, but always indirectly, as the object of Spanish actions, attitudes, or policies, being conquered, converted, ruled, or argued about. In the work of Lewis Hanke,[3] which reached its fullest expression not long before *Tlaxcala* and surely influenced Gibson in more than one way, Indians appeared to come to the forefront, since their attributes were the crux of the matter, but the heroes and villains were still Spaniards; their stereotypes and partisan statements were the only source of information on the Indians. With Hanke the necessity of getting something more directly from and about the Indians became acute, since an opinion about the nature of something is not in a vacuum, but must be measured against whatever else can be found out about the object of the opinion. Hanke himself was becoming increasingly aware of this problem and spoke of the need of finding new sources to help solve it. But essentially hardly any progress had been made up to that time in understanding Indians after the arrival of the Spaniards. And by the same token the history written of Spaniards up until then was incomplete and often illusory. It was impossible to understand conquest, conversion, and rule without a good comprehension of the characteristics and participation of those who were acted upon.

In *Tlaxcala*, Gibson with one stroke brought the field past the doldrums of concentration on Spanish attitudes and actions and opened up the possibility of a thorough reinterpretation of early Spanish American history. Yet it was not a radical departure, operating rather in the framework of sources and approaches already developed within the field. Neither at this point nor later was Gibson deeply touched by anthropological concepts and methods. He mastered whatever the anthropologists wrote touching on his immediate topics, utilized the information, and gained their respect, but he acted within the specific tradition of early Spanish American history. The one potentially revolutionary aspect of his approach was the redirection of focus from Spaniards to Indians, asking of any source primarily what it said about Indian actions, motives, attitudes, and structures. Even this could be seen as something on which the field was converging. The regional focus, equally essential to the study's results, was new and progressive at the time, but not unparalleled. A movement was already under way to supplement countrywide or empire-wide studies, usually based mainly on records in Spanish archives, with projects concentrating on specific subregions and based on a larger quotient of American records, including documents found in the subregion itself. An example would be J.H. Parry's *Audiencia of New Galicia*. An immediate, automatic, and highly salutary result of this procedure was a greater realism and more weight given to actors on the local scene.

For the rest, Gibson largely used the sources and approaches that had gradually been evolving in Spanish American history for more than a century. He did so cumulatively; whether consciously or not, in his successive chapters he repeated the different stages through which the field had passed. Chapter 1, on the Spanish conquest, includes narrative material based largely on the same kinds of chronicles that had fed tales of conquest ever since William Prescott, and it follows the course of the campaigns in a broadly similar fashion, trying to determine exact routes and dates as well as to deduce the stratagems of the leaders. But aside from having no interest in romantic color and concentrating his attention on the Indian side, Gibson proceeded far more analytically than his predecessors (and indeed most of his successors) in the narrative line. He was able to show the Tlaxcalans following a rational course of action in their own self-interest without regard to other Indian groups but with much regard to their own position within the indigenous balance of power, and neither overestimating nor underestimating the Spaniards, but systematically testing them and then drawing prudent conclusions.

Chapters 2 and 3 are devoted to something approaching the type of institutional history that tended to succeed narrative history generally in our field after the 1920's. Chapter 2, Religious History, goes over the process of Christianization quite in the manner of Robert Ricard,[4] relying above all on Franciscan chronicles and correspondence with the crown and attributing a very broad, indispensable role to the friars themselves. Indeed, one could get the impression that this chapter is less of an advance than the previous one. We find for example the sentence (p. 39) "A large part of the success of Christianity in Tlaxcala was due unquestionably to the personal character of the friars themselves," and Gibson at times seems to say that a good part of the reason for problems and loss of momentum later was that the successors of the first generation were lesser. The inversion of focus is less full in the religious chapter than in the one on conquest.

A step beyond Ricardian church history is a detailed chronology of the construction of churches, the smaller as well as the larger, throughout the province of Tlaxcala, pieced together not only from chronicles but from all manner of administrative records both viceregal and local, leading to the establishment of a temporal pattern that dovetails nicely with developments in other dimensions of Gibson's interest. Both the general orientation of the chapter and the church construction section may show the influence of Gibson's mentor George Kubler, who in *Mexican Architecture of the Sixteenth Century*[5] had done a spectacularly thorough and sophisticated history of monastic church construction and in the rest shown himself to be an unreconstructed Ricardian. Most in the vein of Chapter 1 is Gibson's careful critique of the Tlaxcalan conversion legend, showing that the process was not quite as early, voluntary, total, and unanimous as the Tlaxcalans later convinced themselves it had been.

Chapter 3, on Spanish government, carries the type of history previously done on viceroys and Audiencias down to the level of the provincial corregidor. By its nature it cannot focus primarily on Indians, but through a careful reconstruction of the individuals and offices involved it shows the minimal nature of Spanish local government, its dependence on Indian structures, the generally cooperative relationship between the corregidor and the Tlaxcalan authorities, and the long-term ineffectiveness of the corregidor in enforcing important legislation in favor of the Tlaxcalans, especially the failure to stop the massive entry of Spanish stockraisers and obraje operators in the later sixteenth century.

Chapter 4, Indian Government, is the heart of the book and its contribution. Here Gibson goes beyond emphasizing the Indian side of a Spanish-Indian topic; all the people involved are Indians. This part of the work can still be considered institutional history of a kind, but it is at such a local level, deals with such different people and traditions, and marshals the careers of such a large number of individuals of less than the highest rank, that it seems something entirely new. The first section of the government chapter, a dynastic history of the rulerships of the four subkingdoms of Tlaxcala before and after the conquest, carefully worked up from diverse sources of which partisan genealogies are the largest, is significant in showing the continuation of these royal lines until they declined at the end of the sixteenth century. But the revolutionary feature of the chapter is the portrait of the Indian-manned Tlaxcalan municipal council, the region's primary corporate manifestation and main governmental organ, which reached its mature form by 1545-46 and thereafter remained little changed for the rest of the century.

Though organized and reorganized under Spanish auspices and ostensibly on the Spanish plan, the cabildo in fact, in its post-1545 version, diverged substantially from the Spanish model, reflecting indigenous structures and modes of organization, and it vigorously defended the corporate interests of Tlaxcala and its indigenous nobility. The carryover in personnel recruitment from preconquest times was overwhelming, and a tight group of high nobles from the four kingdoms kept the cabildo in their own hands across the whole century. Gibson demonstrated in detail and with clarity that the Spanish principle of officeholding, in which each holder represented himself, his family and friends, and a certain economic complex, but functioned at large, gave way to the indigenous principle whereby each individual officeholder represented a constituent part of the whole, and all such parts were in theory separate and equal, operating through division and rotation.

Not that Gibson wrote in so many words, much less emphasized, what I have just said. The Gibsonian manner included the discovery of many important new concepts and principles together with a strong reticence about expressing them overtly. Succinct generalizations are to be found buried in obscure paragraphs or not expressed at all, and only those who can deal with this aspect of Gibson's work will ever fully appreciate it and profit from its richness. At times, Gibson may not have formulated his findings even to himself as generalizations. Gifted with a strong instinct for significance and patterning, he was generous in presenting patterns and stingy in commenting on them. But in this case as in most, I have no doubt that he himself had formulated the basic principle in his mind. Consider his statement (p. 122) "Indian government . . . gave new meaning to certain purely American political concepts, adapting the quadruple divisions, for example, to the cabildo offices."

What struck Gibson more about postconquest local selfgovernment in Tlaxcala than its organizational principles, and what he expressed more forcefully, was the active part the Indians took in the process. They rejected anything that failed to suit them and eagerly took up anything that favored their interests and the preservation of their ways. At times Gibson in a rather inchoate way called this process Hispanization or acculturation, but the essence of his insight was that the Indians, remaining themselves, took an active part in the interaction of the two peoples, that their characteristics and decisions in large part determined what the Spaniards could and would do, and that arrangements concerning the Indians bore the Indians' stamp.

A Spanish protocol of the 1545 agreements on the constitution and operation of the Tlaxcalan cabildo helped Gibson grasp the situation, and so did a multitude of Spanish administrative records concerning Tlaxcala (like those found in the ramos Indios and Mercedes of Mexico's Archivo General de la Nación). But by far the most important documentary basis of this most important part of the work were the minutes of the cabildo of Tlaxcala, of which an entire volume is preserved, concentrated in the years between the late 1540's and the 1560's. Here were authentic expressions from within the Indian world which were strictly contemporary with events and lacked the flavor of reports or petitions to the outside.

The documents were, however, in Nahuatl, and Gibson later modestly professed not to know that language. Nevertheless, around the time of writing *Tlaxcala* Gibson worked hard on Nahuatl and was pleased with his progress.[6] In the book, several passages from Nahuatl annals, not transcribed or translated into Spanish or English to this day, are quoted at length, correctly, and rendered correctly into English. Thus Gibson did learn some Nahuatl while doing research on *Tlaxcala*; I believe he especially learned to recognize certain repeating formulas of the documentary genres he encountered. He seems to have gained a real but perhaps rather limited facility;[7] then by the time of *The Aztecs* he largely abandoned Nahuatl sources.

In the *Tlaxcala* project Gibson was aided considerably by the fact that the cabildo minutes have brief Spanish glosses or summaries, done probably in the early seventeenth century. Though the original categories of thought remain hidden and a large amount of significant detail is missing, from the glosses one can indeed gather the kernel of most cabildo sessions recorded. That Gibson was relying on the summaries is not in doubt; once or twice he repeats (relatively minor) errors committed by the commentator, most notably in the case of whether or not the tribute could be paid in money, where the commentator reported the negative votes but neglected to report that there were twice as many positive votes. Gibson did, however, make direct use of the cabildo minutes in a very fruitful way without needing much Nahuatl. The first portion of every session record lists the members attending, whose names are the same in either language, together with their offices, for which the Spanish loan words *gobernador, alcalde,* and *regidor* were used. Records of the yearly municipal elections are equally transparent and in addition give the affiliation of each official by subkingdom or *cabecera.* Gibson began compiling files on selected individuals and total membership lists for certain years, and on that basis was able to conclude not only that selection adhered faithfully to the principles of rotation and equal division among cabeceras, but that through repetition in office a quite small circle of nobles manned the cabildo, providing continuity and becoming adept in the ways of Hispanic-indigenous government.

The remaining parts of the book, Chapters 5 on Tlaxcalan Society and 6 on Privileges, Tributes, and Colonies, have interest, of course, but not on the same level as the section on Indian government. In the part on society Gibson had to go rather far astray from the main strengths of his sources, and in any case it is difficult or impossible to do justice to the topic without an inner understanding of social categories in Nahuatl. The social generalizations in this chapter include some thoroughly outdated and unacceptable statements, nearly the only thing in the book of which that could be said (points of detail, however, are fully reliable even here, as always with Gibson). Nevertheless, Gibson did grasp and convey the main characteristic of the situation, that society not only in some "villages" but in the broader province taken as a whole remained essentially intact. Seeing the energetic and often positive adaptations of the nobles and having little direct evidence of it for the commoners, Gibson tended to think that change at the lower levels of society was minimal, which today seems probably not so. In a sense, the image of passivity which Gibson corrected at the level of the leaders was tacitly projected onto the mass.

In the last substantive chapter, an elegant miscellany, the outstanding item is the description, mainly on the basis of Spanish administrative records, of the campaign of the Tlaxcalans to magnify the services they performed for the Spaniards in the conquest and thereby receive exceptional privileges and rewards. Here are the Indians successfully manipulating the Spaniards, waiting until memory of what actually happened was dim and then bombarding Spanish officials with propaganda year in, year out, playing one agency off against another and understanding fully that the easiest to impress were the most distant and most ignorant; hence the delegations to Spain. Gibson's work on Tlaxcalan booster campaigns had a large effect in the direction of changing the image of the helpless Indian generally. But at the same time Gibson did not fail to see and say that the privileges gained amounted to very little. As he observes (p. 169), "Probably the most striking conclusion to be derived from an analysis of the Tlaxcalan privileges is that they affected the practical affairs of the province to only a minor degree."

This balance of Gibson's is a crucial asset, enhancing his work's lasting value. Although a pioneer, he avoided excesses. He was clearly excited to be altering the image of the passive Indian, showing the conquest as something other than an immediate and unmitigated disaster for the Indian world, and even pointing to the optimism and prosperity of Tlaxcala in the decades of the mid-sixteenth century. But he was by no means blinded to the factors, above all the growth of the Spanish civil sector, which were giving the picture a decidedly different cast by 1600, and he made the evolution an integral part of his treatment. Thus the old inert Indian was not replaced in his work by the equally unrealistic active, creative Indian who is always right and always has to win. Gibson's balance is related to the fact that he was blessed with the ability not to think in polar opposites. He may never have said it in one sentence, but his work shows his understanding that change and continuity in the Indian world, rather than starkly contrasting elements, were overlapping and even reciprocally supporting aspects of a joint process. The Tlaxcalans accepted change in order the better to stay the same, and their adaptations in fact had much of the intended effect.

The balance and evenhandedness I have been talking about was essentially the same thing as Gibson's openness, apparent lack of preconceptions, and skepticism, which had much to do with the striking originality of his work. It was not that he in fact lacked preconceptions, the general baggage of the field at that time, but that he was more aware of them than others were, and he was prepared to and did test whatever notion he might be presented with against fresh and freshly viewed data for its validity. The most obvious fruits of this way of doing things were to be seen later in *The Aztecs*, but the procedure itself is just as marked in *Tlaxcala*. Some readers have misunderstood Gibson's work as stemming from a blind or mechanical empiricism, the opposite of a more theoretical approach. If we stop to consider, what often passes among us for theory is the manipulation of concepts. Such an activity is the prisoner of the inherited concepts; it is secondary to and dependent upon the process of generation of adequate concepts. Gibson was a challenger, demolisher, and ignorer of inadequate concepts and a strong force in developing more satisfactory and sophisticated ones, even though he was not much inclined to give them succinct formulation himself.

Nearly the first thing most readers notice about *Tlaxcala* are its extended appendices and bibliographical notes, which are gradually seen to be of a piece with the stunning thoroughness and care with which everything of any description is treated. In every case massive relevant materials are marshaled, to be examined closely and methodically in light of each other. Gibson's passion for detail and lavish use of it are famous. Let the Gibsonian mode not be thought of as myopic, mechanical list making. It was a creative activity in which Gibson surveyed all the small parts for their significance within the larger context and constructed new larger wholes, truly new because he confronted each item anew on its own terms and was alive to whatever configuration was taking shape before him. The appendices never fail to illustrate a point, and the bibliography is more notable for its judicious remarks than for its impressive extent and coverage.

Many years later, the full original *Relación geográfica* of Diego Muñoz Camargo turned up in a Scottish repository. A mere bibliophile or antiquarian might have felt his labor had been for naught. I think Gibson in fact hardly blinked an eye when told of the find. The discovery of a major new version of the writings of the most important chronicler of Tlaxcala neither affects the validity of Gibson's general bibliographical survey nor adds startling new information. Gibson surveyed the material before him exhaustively, but he did not necessarily aspire to cover literally all known and discoverable material. By the standards of those preceding him, he was neglectful of archives in Spain—concentration on American repositories was a conscious emphasis in line with what was going on in the field generally. Nor did he use the Tlaxcalan notarial records to any extent, though he was aware of their existence. Perhaps the time for notarial records had not quite arrived, or more likely Gibson surveyed some of them and saw that their primary subject matter was economic dealings among Spaniards.

If one is to complain that Gibson was too devoted to small detail, one should complain likewise about sculptors, painters, and violin makers, who in a similar way go lovingly over every minute aspect of their material with a gradually evolving larger whole in mind. I have often deplored in those around me the tendency to think of the main process of research, compilation, transcription, translation, and so forth, as drudgery, donkey work, mechanics, as opposed to some other process of insight and composition. Gibson understood that the two processes were one; insight and awareness must constantly be brought to bear on each new datum. He acted, however, not on some inculcated maxim, but, as it should be, out of inclination. He took joy in the work, in all aspects of it. Gibson's organic synthesis of detail without losing individual identity, particularly in his following of cabildo members, anticipated the career pattern history which was to have such an impact on the field in the late 60's, 70's, and since.

Looking at *Tlaxcala* as though it were written today, it mainly stands, quite aside from presenting a great deal of useful information that will be found nowhere else. Arthur Anderson, Frances Berdan, and I have recently brought out a quasi-documentary publication on the Tlaxcalan cabildo minutes which gives more systematic detail on many aspects and opens up the Nahuatl conceptual vocabulary but rarely challenges Gibson's data and findings.[8] On one basic point we did come to different conclusions, or at least resolved a question on which Gibson remained in doubt. In line with his universal skepticism, Gibson noticed that in the remaining record not much is said about the four-part division of Tlaxcala before the definitive constitutional arrangements of 1545. He therefore doubted at times (at other times taking the opposite position) that a thorough quadruple division was basic to the organization of Tlaxcala in the preconquest period, and he further doubted that beyond selection of officials it had anything to do with the operation of the province in post-1545 times, instead considering Tlaxcala to have been governed as a whole. Since the principle of equal subdivision, most especially by twos and fours, turns out to have been basic to sociopolitical entities all across central Mexico and beyond, we have little hesitation in considering it to have been a feature of preconquest Tlaxcalan organization. And as to the role of the four-part division in governmental operations, closer examination of the entire Nahuatl text of the cabildo minutes shows that everything major and minor was done separately in fours and by rotation, tribute workers for Tlaxcala City for example coming all from one subkingdom at a time, supervised by cabildo members from their own group. Inside the single chest where city valuables, funds, and papers were kept, one would find four separate accounts, and a single disbursement might come out of two or three of the separate funds. How to maintain some kind of overall unity was a frequent source of preoccupation of cabildo members.

Gibson saw that Tlaxcala was less exceptional on the central Mexican scene than it appeared. But he did tend to think Tlaxcalan patriotism and historical consciousness unusual. Today we have myriad examples of parallels for both characteristics, and they must be considered standard. So is the interpenetration of Spanish and indigenous governmental devices. Tlaxcala might seem something of an oddity as an extremely large and complex entity retained as a unit after the conquest, but in fact there were others, such as Huejotzingo and Xochimilco, and it is often from these well-documented larger situations that we must learn general lessons about the internal governance of Indian towns all over central Mexico.[9] Gibson's *Tlaxcala* thus has greater universality than the author was aware at the time of its publication, and we will be well rewarded if we keep it on our list of items of primary consultation in ethnohistorical matters.

The Aztecs

With *The Aztecs Under Spanish Rule*, published in 1964, no special recommendation is necessary, for as all know, the book to this day is the standard comprehensive work on central Mexican Indians from conquest to independence. It seems at first glance to cover everything conceivable, and since it embraces the whole Valley of Mexico complex, it was immediately recognized as equivalent to a macrostudy representative of all central Mexico if not more. Yet if we consider, it is like *Tlaxcala* in being regional, exhaustive, and based on records in America not Spain, and those attributes are crucial to its strength. For all its topical breadth the book is markedly corporate in approach. It actually contains less on individuals and internal functioning than *Tlaxcala*; no equivalent of the Tlaxcalan cabildo minutes appeared, nor has any appeared to this day. Most of the book is about that portion of the Indian corporate world visible in its contacts with Spanish officialdom. The sources of the critical portions of the work consist of a great variety of Spanish administrative records and corporate Indian litigation in Spanish courts. Unlike *Tlaxcala*, *The Aztecs* shows no appreciable impact of Nahuatl documents.

The corporations on which Gibson concentrated were neither on the imperial scale nor at the minimal scale of hamlet or *calpolli*, but at the all-important and up until then ignored middle level, which was the essential one for the Indians in terms of self-identification, which survived the conquest intact, and on which the Spaniards of necessity were to fasten in all their arrangements. More specifically, the corporations involved are the many local Indian states, usually on the order of city-state size, called by the Spaniards *pueblos* and by the Indians *altepetl*, that filled the Valley of Mexico and continued to be the basis of everything that happened for long after the conquest. Gibson implicitly rejected the category "village," which had been the standard definition of Indian sociopolitical units until then. He did not take up the Nahuatl term "altepetl" despite his laudable tendency to use original categories because it failed to appear very much in the Spanish sources he used. *The Aztecs* comes close to being a book on the altepetl that never uses the word. In fact, it does appear three times, of which once is in the glossary and once is a quote from a Nahuatl source. But Gibson did fully recognize the falsity of the tacit operating generalization that the conquest had destroyed Indian civilization down to the village level. Rather a complex entity on the order of a kingdom survived, and Gibson showed in depth how it was partially defined by a dynastic ruler and contained a set of separate constituent parts, each a territorial unit, each of which owed allegiance and tribute to the ruler.

The Aztecs is organized in large chapters each devoted to a massive topic carried chronologically over the whole time period covered, which gives the superficial reader an impression of timelessness, but is well suited to demonstrating in a great many dimensions the gradual continuum of change so characteristic of the period. The central chapters deal with the altepetl. What I consider the minor chapters do not. The core chapters show the altepetl in one guise after another as the framework for and determinant of nearly everything that went on outside the Spanish city for a long time after the conquest, thereby making sense of two or three centuries of Mexican history, in which until that time nearly the only thread of intelligibility was the demographic curve that had been worked out by the Berkeley demographers. Gibson's creative compilation, this time taking the form of mapping, was crucial to the process of laying bare the patterns. He kept track of the component parts of all the preconquest altepetl, the encomiendas, the parishes, and the postconquest municipalities, mapped them, and they all turned out to be the same. The succession of chapters that shows the coincidence of the different entities is perhaps the most majestic, powerful display in the Latin American historical literature, like a line of tall ships each in turn coming abreast and firing a broadside, one and then another and yet another. Of course, in his meticulous way, Gibson immediately noticed that the various types of entities were not literally, precisely, and universally the same, and he devoted endless space to documenting the differences, putting these chapters beyond the reach of the impatient and even tending to obscure the main message for the inattentive.

A strong chronological organization adds further force to the central heavy battery of chapters—Towns, Encomienda and Corregimiento, Religion, and The Political Town. That is, these chapters in order deal with different forms the basic entity took in chronological succession, spoiled a little it is true by the corregimiento, which should have come last, having been crowded in with the encomienda because it lacked the makings of a whole chapter itself. "Towns" sets up the entities as fully formed in the preconquest period. "Encomienda" shows that with some variation for well explained reasons, one altepetl with one ruler or *tlatoani* became one encomienda, that hence the units were determined by preconquest precedent and not by the administrative decision of Hernando Cortés or any official high or low. As a footnote, the corregimiento is seen to be a collection of these units, institutionally minimal and relying mainly on the Indian towns themselves.

"Religion" was especially revolutionary, turning the Ricardian world upside down. The chapter delivers the message not only that the parish is the same entity once again, using the already existing internal organization, but it is posterior to the encomienda and actually a function of the encomienda, which in turn was a function of the altepetl. These facts put mendicant activity in a proper context for the first time. For all except perhaps art historians, the Ricardian view of the church as sole and arbitrary creator of the postconquest social, cultural, and even political world of the Indians was now dead. An especially large amount of jurisdictional variation was noted between encomienda and parish, in large part because originally there were too many potential encomenderos and too few clerics to man parishes.

"The Political Town" shows the partial transformation of the altepetl into a modified Hispanic-style municipality with the powers of the rulership devolving upon the gobernador, other nobles filling the remaining offices, and the entire entity retaining full consciousness of itself, much as in the earlier story of Tlaxcala. "Tribute and Town Finance," large parts of "Labor," and a good deal of "Land" are extensions of the Political Town chapter, showing how various altepetl mechanisms were used and adapted. Of particular importance is a brief section in "Land" on *congregación*, not only showing that the program was far less extensive than earlier imagined and often a failure when carried out, thus leaving existing entities more nearly in place than once thought, but also allowing us to see that even where it was successfully executed it normally respected altepetl structure, that is, a congregación normally simply collapsed a given altepetl in upon itself, retaining its identity and the essence of its organization.

An especially significant segment of these chapters runs through the mechanics of procurement of temporary labor through the encomienda, repartimiento, and informal arrangements successively, showing the very small steps involved in each change and the lateness of the legal aspects in relation to any given change. Here a basic process of Spanish American history was seen for the first time as a continuum intelligible on its own terms, not as a puzzling succession of three unrelated stages defined in legal terms and in respect to crown intentions. (The only thing like it at that time was Woodrow Borah's explanation of estate evolution along a single line of developing demographic and economic forces.) It was in this section of *The Aztecs*, hidden in the middle of a paragraph (p. 235), that Gibson issued his immortal and forever valid statement that in Spanish American history law is a commentary on developments more than a shaping of them.

All the larger structures in the central Mexican countryside were some sort of permutation or adaptation of the altepetl except one, the large Spanish estate or hacienda. Gibson's treatment of the hacienda does not fall directly into line with the series of altepetl chapters, but it has equal significance. In this context, the true distinction between the hacienda and the other fixtures emerges clearly: its oblique rather than direct relation to the altepetl, its creation of new structures rather than simple adaptation of existing ones (see p. 333). In fact, although the hacienda had a strong effect on the Indian corporation, in a certain sense one could say that it does not belong in the book, and Gibson showed an awareness of this by not giving it its own chapter, dividing hacienda-related topics instead between Land, Labor, and Agriculture. Despite the scattering, the message got across; indeed, the part on the hacienda was more quickly understood and had more immediate scholarly repercussions than the true core of the book. Gibson's tracing of the process of Indian land loss and its accretion to the hacienda was no longer strikingly new. The new things were his picture of the hacienda as primarily oriented toward making a profit in the local urban market and of hacienda labor as still consisting even in the eighteenth century of more temporary workers than permanent, with owners by no means intent on maximizing the numbers of the more highly skilled and expensive resident laborers.

The implications of Gibson's hacienda research for the Indian world were great and clear, but the first scholarly reactions were more in the field of the history of Spanish enterprise. Gibson was as important as François Chevalier in setting off a torrent of hacienda studies which include some of the most distinguished and sophisticated work in the literature (and of which possibly we have now had enough for a while). All of it confirms Gibson's conclusions at the expense of those of Chevalier. Gibson's method, that is essentially his sources, also had an impact. The sources for the newest part of the hacienda sections are very different from the administrative records used for the Indian corporation. They consist almost entirely of internal hacienda records, especially majordomos' correspondence and payrolls, included in the Regla papers which Gibson inspected on a fortunate trip to Pullman, Washington. This was the first time a scholar with synthetic abilities and cognizant of the literature got at the hacienda from the inside; quite a few have done so since.

Coming to the minor chapters, there is the background piece Tribes (whose title causes no end of trouble), brought together quite unchanged from material then current among anthropological ethnohistorians, and most of the chapters The People, Agriculture, and Production and Exchange, which despite no small amount of precious archival detail are mainly devoted to summary of outsiders' synthetic accounts of things going on inside the Indian world, beneath the corporate level. These are all in all the most dated portions of the work, although some important trends are shown or hinted at. In his treatment of the evolution of maize and pulque production and chinampa agriculture, Gibson gave us all the materials we need for an important generalization he stopped just short of making explicitly, that Spaniards would take over direct management of any given activity even if fully indigenous, and even if the market was indigenous, at the point where it became sufficiently profitable to reward them, but they could be deterred to the extent that an esoteric and labor-intensive indigenous expertise was involved. The chapter The City, on the Indian community of Mexico City, is based on the same kinds of research as the mainline chapters and contains much potentially valuable material, but the approach of looking at the Indian corporation independently and not in close relation to Spanish doings is far less viable here, and in any case the subject is somewhat divorced from the rest.

With this we arrive at the conclusion, which the reader might think it superfluous to single out for discussion even in a treatment of *The Aztecs* as unrelenting as this one. But not so, for this particular conclusion, rather than merely summing up the main points set forth in the body of the work, stands in some respects at variance with it, and since over the years many scholars in other specialties have read the conclusion and nothing else, in some circles the concluding chapter has spread serious misapprehensions about the book's thrust. The great contribution of *The Aztecs*, compared to anything that went before it, was its display, on a very large canvas, of the lesson that Indian structures and vitality survived the conquest in a major way, affecting and often almost dictating whatever measures the Spaniards planned or enterprises they undertook. Ultimately, however, corporate decline appeared to be the outcome, and consequently the message Gibson proclaimed in the conclusion was one of exploitation, decline, and unparalleled drunkenness. The fact (to which I will return) that he had worked less on the eighteenth century than on earlier times left him more inclined to such views of the matter than he might have been otherwise, but in any case, though he successfully minimized its impact on the body of the book, he was always more than a little sympathetic to the Black Legend, and identification with a group he saw as downtrodden was an important part of his motivation, so that the tenor of the conclusion might have been much the same even if the research had taken a different course.[10] Whatever the reason, the variance or discrepancy remains. The conclusion does not do justice to the multitude of congruent insights revealed in the body of the study. It seriously retarded general comprehension of *The Aztecs* and even now often trips up readers who stumble upon the book unprepared. One positive contribution it made was to encourage William Taylor to approach the matter of indigenous drinking more systematically, with a resulting much clearer picture.

After Gibson

I now turn to the questions of the effect of *The Aztecs* on subsequent scholarship in Mexican ethnohistory and how such scholarship may be changing Gibsonian perspectives. The first main reaction to *The Aztecs* among prospective ethnohistorians was to give it a wide berth. Such a vacuum in the wake of outstanding work has been observed in the field both before and since. As successors gradually began to take heart, they have confirmed a great deal of the analysis presented in the body of the book, including, as far as I am concerned, all the points I mentioned above. And given Gibson's generosity with all manner of significant detail, as well as his munificence in giving references to parallel cases not used in the text, *The Aztecs* remains a crucial source book for new research on central Mexican Indians. I think it is fair to say that everything that has been and is being done in postconquest Mexican ethnohistory has been in some way planned around *The Aztecs*, to extend, complement, or test it, in effect to build on it.

After a decade or so of scrutiny, readers began to see that contrary to first appearances and just as Gibson himself always said, *The Aztecs* did not cover absolutely everything. One important characteristic of the book, despite the eighteenth-century hacienda analysis from the Regla papers and many interesting late-colonial details, is that it shares with *Tlaxcala* a strong sixteenth-century emphasis, especially if we think of the broader sixteenth century that in the indigenous world goes as far as the first two or three decades of the seventeenth. I have no complaint; one should begin at the beginning. If Gibson had covered the late seventeenth and eighteenth centuries as thoroughly at the level of primary research as he did the early period, he would have been in serious danger of never finishing, and somewhere along the line he must have realized as much. Now Gibson was a bold originator and skeptic only where he had inspected the ground minutely for himself; not being in quite that position for the eighteenth century, he reverted to the caution he habitually exercised when he did not have all the facts, and hence tended to accept readily the existing stereotypes of severe and unrelieved decline in the late period. He saw the extensive late fragmentation of the altepetl in this light, he spoke of the leveling and compression of indigenous society, he seemed in one part of the book (p. 181) to say that Indian notaries tended to fade out in the seventeenth century and later.

Sometimes consciously, sometimes more by chance, post-Gibson ethnohistorical researchers have often concentrated precisely on the eighteenth century, and all in all they have found less decline, more retention and continued vitality than *The Aztecs* would lead one to expect. Taylor, the best known of Gibson's students, has tended to work on the eighteenth century. His first book, *Landlord and Peasant in Colonial Oaxaca*,[11] primarily took up the estate history challenge of Chevalier and *The Aztecs*, but even so it is full of ethnohistory. The topic was chosen to complement the preceding central and northern Mexican research more geographically than temporally, but finding that the temporal center of gravity of the records fell in the eighteenth century, Taylor started with the more recent and worked his way back.[12] The Indians of Oaxaca turned out to have retained their lands and their dynastic rulers, remaining very much an active force in the region until the very end of the colonial period. Of course this in no way contradicted Gibson, but had rather every appearance of being regional variation, as to a large extent it actually was.

In Taylor's next book, *Drinking, Homicide, and Rebellion*,[13] the weight was again on the eighteenth century, perhaps to a large extent because of the nature of the Ramo Criminal of the Archivo General de la Nación. This time the Mexico City orbit was included as well as Oaxaca. Indian towns were shown to have continued to assert their rights in at times violent local protests and disturbances as they had done in preceding centuries. Although they made adjustments to the Spanish presence, Indians continued to show more or less normal patterns of homicide, and their drinking was seen to be in large part a continuation of now better understood preconquest practices, gradually adapted to new economic conditions and opportunities and assimilated to Spanish ways of using alcohol. It was not moderation in the

European style, perhaps, but neither was it a sea of demoralized drunkenness. Here the perspective of *The Aztecs*, especially as it appears in the conclusion, is strongly modified, and there can be no doubt that testing Gibson's formulation was part of Taylor's specific purpose in undertaking this project. As I mentioned above, the parts of *The Aztecs* being most revised, over and above the question of the eighteenth century, are often those having to do with more informal and internally oriented personal behavior rather than formal and externally oriented corporate behavior.

Drinking, Homicide and Rebellion also meaningfully extended the Gibsonian range of technical approaches, making it possible to penetrate beyond the corporate aspect to the inside of the Indian world and draw out significant pattern even without much information on the specific context, by subjecting different series of fragmentary data, widely scattered in time and region, to sampling techniques. Some of the most startlingly successful results are to be found in the section on homicide, in other words, in research on an activity of a highly informal, personal-familial nature. Both strictly statistical sampling and qualitative comparative analysis proved fruitful. Taylor's methodological example in this book is especially significant because homogeneous chunks of material on the postconquest indigenous world (other than reports, censuses, and parish records), generated in a single time and place, are extremely rare.

At present Taylor is in the late stages of yet another eighteenth-century project, a large-scale study of rural, mainly still Indian parishes and the Spanish priests who served them. Here as in his first book he goes beyond a too often hermetic ethnohistory to combine the histories of Spaniards and Indians, seeing them as they ultimately must be seen, in relation to each other. Gibson would have been (and doubtless in fact was) in favor of such an approach; late in his life he put years of effort into the history of Spaniards. But though *The Aztecs* in one sense is the history of the relations of the Indian corporation with Spanish officialdom, Spanish-Indian interaction as such, and especially at the level of the individual or small group, is hardly touched. The study of this topic in a manner other than superficial and fragmentary represents a major challenge for the near future; as important as it is, it is technically very difficult because most sources tend to be systematic about one group or the other, not both. The relatively humble Hispanics dwelling in originally Indian settlements, a vital focus of cultural contact, had no corporate organization, were marginal to Spanish hierarchies, and generated few records about their own activities per se.[14] Taylor has hit on a sphere combining Spanish-Indian contact with good documentation on both groups.[15]

Internal hacienda records, documenting another major point of contact between Spaniards and Indians, seem to provide no coherent view of the Indian side of things. Yet some hacienda research concerning the eighteenth century has reached deeply enough into Indian matters to help in the revision process. A notable example is that of John Tutino, who in working on haciendas of the Valleys of Mexico and Toluca in the late colonial period[16] found Indian towns standing up to Spanish estates in labor and land matters, generating vast amounts of litigation, even running an informal, volunteer labor recruitment system not unlike the old repartimiento, while municipal office was dominated by an upper group about the size of the old nobility, which also held far more land than the average. Recent work by Robert Haskett on Indian town government in the Cuernavaca district, based on Nahuatl as well as Spanish records, shows in much more detail and depth the continuation of gubernatorial dynasties, upper-group political dominance and relative wealth, and vigorous factional politics in the area's Indian towns.[17]

In the matter of Nahuatl notaries going into decline in the eighteenth century, as I and others continue to collect Nahuatl notarial documents, it begins to appear that more material may be preserved from the eighteenth century than from any earlier period, though it is true that a significant drop-off occurs around 1770 as Indians began to do more of their recordkeeping in Spanish.[18]

Everyone who has touched the topic has confirmed in greater or lesser degree the eighteenth-century fragmentation of the altepetl of which Gibson speaks, but some new work throws a different light on it. Stephanie Wood's recent dissertation on Indian corporations in the Toluca Valley[19] shows that the process of getting recognition of a new unit as an independent Indian town required a great deal of initiative and perseverance on the part of the Indians, that the entities still conceived of themselves as altepetl and functioned accordingly, and that their course of action was well suited to the conditions and often led more to an expansion or recovery on the part of the Indian world than to its simple fragmentation.

The second large thrust of recent ethnohistorical research, in addition to the full inclusion of the eighteenth century, is the opening up of mundane documents written in the Nahuatl language as a source.[20] These automatically get us inside the Indian world into a realm of individuals, internal interaction, indigenous concepts, society, and culture (essentially all the things that escaped Gibson's corporate approach and administrative sources), allowing us to fill in and often revise the matter in what I have termed the minor chapters.

Because of the nature and novelty of Nahuatl documents, a movement I sometimes call a New Philology has arisen. Most types of Spanish documentation are so well understood and so uniform that we generally march through them by the yard, taking skeletal notes, and we have long since abandoned the industrious document publication of previous generations. Nahuatl sources in turn are now demanding publication, and for several reasons the documentary phase in this case may be more than introductory and transitional. In line with preconquest traditions, postconquest Nahuatl alphabetical documents are far more declamatory and spontaneous than most of their Spanish counterparts, and on that count alone many of them can be appreciated only through a quite full reproduction. Since Nahuatl texts vary so greatly with time and region, much of their message is in their vocabulary and orthography, so that close comparison of full transcriptions is often called for. Moreover, we must explore the nature, conventions, and significance of several distinct documentary genres, and the only way to study a genre is to have full examples. The approach of tracing individual careers and small organizations, which has done so much for the social and cultural history of Spaniards and allows one to cut rapidly through large masses of documents, proves very difficult to apply with the Nahuas because, as already mentioned, documentary concentrations of requisite density are few indeed. Even when we have a thickly documented situation we find it hard to follow any but some prominent individuals through the sources with confidence because of the extremely small repertoire of names used in the Indian world. We are forced into broader studies and a more directly thematic approach. Yet Nahuatl documents, as numerous as they are, are not usually found crowded together in single volumes or dossiers. Publishing some of them gives scholars access to a corpus large enough for various kinds of wide-ranging studies without an undue amount of time lost in mere searching for examples.

For all these reasons, important Nahuatl documentary publications have been appearing and continue to appear. They include broad samplings as well as publications of single large documents or documentary caches. Of the former type are *Beyond the Codices* and the documentary appendix of *Nahuatl in the Middle Years*.[21] Of the latter are *The Testaments of Culhuacan*, *The Art of Nahuatl Speech*, and Eike Hinz's German edition of parts of the early Cuernavaca-region censuses.[22] The above mentioned *Tlaxcalan Actas* contains a detailed summary of a major document plus numerous selections.[23] As time has gone on, the commentary sections of the publications have become more elaborate. In *The Testaments of Culhuacan* a succinct comment precedes each testament included; in *The Tlaxcalan Actas* a large essay discusses sociopolitical organization and operation as revealed in the document; in *The Art of Nahuatl Speech* a preliminary study, including among other things a detailed analysis of the terminology of rank and kinship and the conventions of polite discourse, takes up approximately as much space as the transcription and translation. A mixed genre of document-plus-monograph appears to be evolving, in which equal attention is given to ethnohistorical "facts," the conceptual apparatus displayed in the document, and the text itself as an example of a certain documentary type.[24]

Gibson saw almost all of these items, often before their publication, and greeted them with increasing enthusiasm as he saw their potential. He was quick to note the documents' value in giving the reader something of the flavor of life among the Nahuas. If one is coming from *The Aztecs*, perhaps the most immediately surprising aspect of such material is the ubiquity of hints of Spanish influence in it, things that show Indians making Spanish cultural goods their own, betraying the extent of personal contact between the two peoples; such contact indeed proves to have been the motor of change in the postconquest Indian world.[25] *The Aztecs* because of its corporate emphasis and its thematic concentration on Indians has given many of its readers the impression, though I am quite sure Gibson did not intend it, that the Indians lived in great isolation.

When I first undertook Nahuatl philological work, my goal was to prepare myself for a general social and cultural history of central Mexican Indians in the postconquest centuries, using primarily sources written by the Nahuas themselves in their own language.[26] A decade and a half after its conception, the work is on its way to the public.[27] My original motivation had to do with my earlier writing on Peru.[28] My hope was to achieve a balanced perspective by applying the same methods of career tracing and concept analysis to the indigenous population, with similar results. Sources in the language of the population to be studied, an absolute must for such research, were not then much in evidence for the Andean region,[29] but were much more numerous in central Mexico. As I became more familiar with Gibson's writings, I began to see my project additionally as aiming to complement *The Aztecs* by giving a picture of the same sector from the inside and with attention to the indigenous conceptual repertoire.

But this is not the place to discuss a book many of whose main themes are summarized in the first chapter of the present volume; let us look at some other relevant scholarship. Much of the new Nahuatl-based research does not directly contradict *The Aztecs* but merely adds dimensions not previously seen. In S.L. Cline's recent book on late sixteenth-century Culhuacan,[30] based on a unique set of contemporaneous Nahuatl testaments, those dimensions are above all family, inheritance, household, and land. To take just one aspect, the organization of family land holdings proves to revolve around categories unknown to Gibson, including the distinction between house-land and all other land, and between inherited and purchased holdings. Here is a universe as complex and important as the altepetl at a different level, and indeed the principles of altepetl organization tend to repeat themselves at the household level.

In *Nahuatl in the Middle Years* Frances Karttunen and I approached cultural ethnohistory by using Nahuatl texts to study the impact of Spanish on the Nahuatl language over the colonial period.[31] Our method had much in common with that used by Taylor in *Drinking, Homicide and Rebellion*;[32] we compiled all the examples of Spanish loan words and other Spanish-influenced linguistic phenomena in all then known postconquest Nahuatl texts and used the results as a sample to be subjected to several kinds of analysis. One of the main findings was the existence of three successive clearly defined stages corresponding to the degree of contact between Spaniards and Indians (Stage 1 goes to ca. 1540-50; Stage 2 to ca. 1640-50; Stage 3 thereafter—see Chapter 1). I have since discovered that the stages correlate with the temporal patterning of developments in almost every dimension of indigenous life. Such perspectives, still in the process of being worked out, can help deepen our understanding of the nature of *The Aztecs*. The book is above all about Stage 2, which was the time of greatest corporate flourishing in the postconquest Indian world, lending a special appropriateness to the corporate approach that is employed. There is very little on Stage 1, the first generation that to a large extent eluded Gibson's methods and sources and threatens to elude Nahuatl-based research equally. I have already commented on the fact that little of the material (other than that on the hacienda) concerns Stage 3.

Of course at times the new-style research is bound to bring about more direct revision of some details in *The Aztecs*. Despite having shown the continuity at the level of tlatoani and gobernador and having seen much broader continuities in local government in *Tlaxcala*, in *The Aztecs* Gibson took the position that the cabildo beneath the level of the governor was a new Spanish creation.[33] Haskett, in the work mentioned above, using Nahuatl election documentation and cabildo membership lists compiled on a large scale, is able to show organization and behavior betraying preconquest survivals at all levels of the cabildo.

Perhaps the single result of Nahuatl-based research that has the largest potential for putting *The Aztecs* in a different perspective has to do with the principle of organization of the entity so crucial to the whole book, the

altepetl as I have been calling it. In speaking of the entire unit Gibson
mainly used the term "town," which can be interpreted in various ways and
poses no real problem. When it comes to internal organization, Gibson's
basic categories are *cabecera* or capital and *sujeto* or subject settlement.
These were so central to Gibson's thinking that he sometimes calls the
whole altepetl a *cabecera-sujeto* unit rather than a town. Without a doubt
the Spanish records fully justify Gibson's usage and interpretation. But
when we turn to Nahuatl documents speaking of political organization, we
find that "altepetl" means the whole entity, and terms exist for constituent
parts, what we usually call calpolli; but there is no word for a dominant part
ruling the other parts, nor does such fit into the general scheme of organization by a symmetrical arrangement of independent parts, of which Tlaxcala
is a good example. The implications of the discrepancy between Spanish
and Nahua ways of looking at Indian organization are too large to go into
here. I have made some statements on this matter,[34] and the dissertation of
Susan Schroeder[35] contains a detailed analysis of political concepts in the
writing of the Nahuatl annalist Chimalpahin. Generally speaking, Gibson's
accounts of events and trends are unaffected, but the mental organization of
the indigenous political world is clearly not captured in *The Aztecs*.

An important contribution in this respect is the recent dissertation of
Rebecca Horn on Coyoacan in the period I am calling Stage 2.[36] Horn
shows that there were several entities inside the Coyoacan district which are
termed "altepetl" in Nahuatl records, and that with time these received
varying degrees of recognition as separate political or ecclesiastical jurisdictions. A thorough-going internal division classed all constituent districts
of Coyoacan as belonging to one of two halves, each of which for a
long period supplied half of the larger municipality's officers. The kind of
second-generation mapping Horn has done, going in much more detail over
a smaller area than Gibson and taking into account the categories surfacing
on the Nahuatl side, is a technique full of potential, and if others follow her
example, it will be possible to refine and extend the overall Gibsonian map
very considerably.

The Aztecs also has implications for other parts of Spanish America.
Andean ethnohistory, for all its development in certain aspects, has until
now lacked an adequate explanation of the relation between indigenous units
and Spanish-introduced structures. The process of compilation and mapping
is now finally under way, especially in the work, still in progress, of
Thierry Saignes on Upper Peru. The results put one in mind of central
Mexico; surely Saignes and others must have been aware of Gibson's
example. And Nancy Farriss must have had the intention of doing for the

Yucatan region something on the order of what Gibson did for the Valley of Mexico. Her work on the Yucatecan Maya is comparable to *The Aztecs* in scope and scale.[37] It is much more sophisticated anthropologically and also retrieves more information on internal functioning (in this somewhat like *Tlaxcala* but more extensive), and it does greater justice to indigenous thinking. It does not, however, map the indigenous entities a la Gibson; that remains a task for the future, along with the corresponding analysis of the structure of sociopolitical units and its ramifications. *The Aztecs* also figures as a point of reference in Farriss' comparisons between Yucatan and central Mexico, which has the effect of making Yucatan seem rather more unique than it would if compared with the most recent post-Gibson research.[38]

Thus the work that Gibson helped stimulate is bringing changes. But as models, starting points, and sources of ideas, facts, and references, *The Aztecs* and *Tlaxcala* will continue to enlighten us for a long time to come.[39]

11. A Vein of Ethnohistory: Recent Nahuatl-based Historical Research

Less than twenty years ago, very few mundane Nahuatl texts of the sixteenth to eighteenth centuries were known to scholars, and when some began to come to light, they were anything but easy to understand. Attaining a reasonable mastery of the language and conventions of the texts was distinctly a collective effort. In the early stages of my quest for comprehension I was helped greatly by anthropologists and linguists whose collaboration I sought.[1] Before long I formed in addition an ongoing informal seminar to work over Nahuatl texts of interest. Most of those attending were my own graduate students, but if this was instruction, it was also learning. Often I was only a step ahead of the students, if that. Many times we all had to admit defeat in the attempt to understand given words, phrases, or whole passages, and the one to hit on the solution to a particular puzzle was not always myself.[2] If I supplied many of the texts, the students too supplied some from their own research trips and library searches.

Over the years, some outstanding participants in the documents seminar have gone on to produce important scholarship in which Nahuatl texts were the primary source, or at least one of the primary sources. In each case, as one would expect, the first step has been a dissertation, followed by the publication of related articles and work toward a book. One such book has appeared, two others have been accepted for publication at this writing, and plans for further books are being vigorously pursued. The movement is thus in midstream. Few people, I think, are at present aware of its full extent and overall thrust, or of the relationship between the various works associated with it. My intention here is to provide an overview as a guide for prospective readers and a preliminary indication of the kinds of results being achieved. The scholars I will be speaking of are of course individuals, each approaching a special topic in a special way, and I doubt if they would appreciate being thought of as members of a school. In view of that individuality (which indeed has contributed to the complementarity that after all tends to tie them together as a group), in the following pages I propose to discuss briefly, one after another, the work of five authors, in the order in which their dissertations were completed, adding a few general remarks at the end.

S. L. Cline. *Colonial Culhuacan, 1580-1600: A Social History of an Aztec Town.* Albuquerque: University of New Mexico Press, 1986.[3]

Early Latin American social history in general has drawn great strength from, and indeed has sometimes been identified with, studies which broach a large variety of interlocking themes and have a mass of mundane records as the primary source, but in compensation are sharply restricted temporally and spatially (prima facie, that is; the significance of such work is still usually very broad). But the nature of extant indigenous sources has made it hard to use this approach in Nahuatl-based historical writing, and practitioners have mainly adopted other techniques.[4] Because of the existence of a unique set of sixty-five Nahuatl testaments from one time and place—the Valley of Mexico altepetl of Culhuacan around 1580—Cline has been able to produce a study of the classic type while staying within the field of indigenous-language research.[5]

With *Colonial Culhuacan*, Cline has achieved a series of firsts: first full-length monograph on postconquest history of Mexican Indians based on Nahuatl sources; first overall ethnography of a central Mexican indigenous community in a time period before the twentieth century; first book to present a thorough, newly researched treatment of postconquest Nahua life at the household level; first to study postconquest land tenure thoroughly in that context,[6] or to investigate petty money dealings and local indigenous traders of the postconquest period, or to give a comprehensive assessment of the role of women in the indigenous community, or to pay systematic attention to naming patterns. Other scholars are now engaged on similar or related enterprises, and still others will follow, but Cline's study should remain of interest as a major reference point, concisely pinpointing the situation in a late sixteenth-century indigenous community which is far better documented than most are ever likely to be.   The book is also easy and entertaining to read, for not only has Cline kept her prose and organization straightforward and inserted many apropos quotations from more familiar material in the Spanish chronicles and Sahagún, but she has, above all, richly illustrated her points with examples from the Culhuacan testaments. The latter provide marvelous material for the purpose, but it took much effort and insight to find, among the myriad possible passages, the best ones on so many different topics, and to recognize the subtleties of their meaning. For this reason the book can serve scholars as an invaluable guide to their own further research in the Culhuacan collection. On the other hand, Cline's study would be an admirable choice for someone who wants to do some initial, exploratory reading in postconquest Mexican ethnohistory. The sense of closeness to the lives of real people is heightened by Cline's using one Angelina Mocel and her relatives to illustrate an impressive number of topics throughout the book. Cline says it all in a paragraph of her conclusion:[7]

> Information about sixteenth-century Indians of any town is frag-
> mentary at best. In the Testaments of Culhuacan, we have one of
> the best sources from the people themselves. The insights we have
> into people's lives give us the sense of dealing with real personal-
> ities. Diego Sánchez, who lay dying from a knife wound inflicted
> by a black man, tried to take care of his brothers and sisters. Ana
> Juana attempted to protect her son's inheritance against her good-
> for-nothing third husband. Luis Tlauhpotonqui made a futile effort
> to collect debts owed to his deceased, wheeler-dealer father. Doña
> María Juárez was worried about the sales of land to Spaniards.
> These are not merely interesting anecdotes. When placed in con-
> text, they illustrate dynamics of social relations and the process of
> cultural change.

Just what are these dynamics and processes of change? In general, Cline finds in everyday life in late sixteenth-century Culhuacan a phenomenon that all of us who are working with Nahuatl sources quickly recognize, that in nearly every dimension there was far more continuity from the preconquest era than once thought, but on the other hand that Spanish elements were pouring into and in some sense altering local culture; yet the two were somehow proving compatible in the main. To discuss these matters on Cline's primary ground, household life and the land regime, would take us too far. Let us look at some smaller topics (smaller in this context, for they are of great inherent significance).

Testaments are not the best source for a history of the higher levels of municipal government, but Cline has done marvels at the lower levels. She has recognized by their repeated appearance that the *albaceas* (executors), despite their Spanish title and function, were not chosen ad hoc by individual testators in Culhuacan, but were municipal officials empowered to carry out all testaments, a situation apparently with preconquest roots of some kind. Moreover, these same functionaries might appear also as "deputies" or constables, betraying the versatility or lack of specialization that we find everywhere among the lower officers of Nahua municipal governments. Through scrutinizing some of the executors' own testaments, Cline has deduced that the executors and their cronies the notaries often held on to assets intended for masses or other purposes—a type of behavior which might have its origins on either the Nahua or the Spanish side.

With very little to go on, Cline has ferreted out some *pochteca*, heirs of the preconquest merchants or traders of the region. They manifest several presumably traditional indigenous traits: their place in society is middling; they form a tight intermarrying circle and often hand their activity on to the next generation; they are mobile and may change altepetl residence or marry across altepetl. At the same time she has shown that they had extensive money dealings, including loans, giving credit, and maintaining current accounts, that they sometimes used Spanish partnership arrangements, and that possession of a horse or mule was perhaps their strongest single diagnostic characteristic.

Names abound in testaments, and Cline has applied extensive analysis to the large number contained in the Culhuacan collection. At this time both indigenous and Spanish names were still in use, with rapid movement in the direction of the latter, which all in all denoted higher rank. The system was becoming quite complex, capable of showing a large number of distinctions. Though names of Spanish origin were employed, the manner of their use was not Spanish. One of the clearest examples is with naming women. Not only did many women still bear the traditional Nahuatl order names, the Spanish names chosen for them also showed less variety than did men's, as before the conquest. Cline's book contains a great deal of information and insight concerning Nahua women (over 42 percent of the testators were female), and as in this instance they are seen as an integral part of the society, with their special roles and traits duly noted, but not at the expense of forgetting the many things they shared with men as members of the same culture, and particularly in the daily life context dominant here.

In my own researches I have found comparable (not always identical) phenomena in many corners of the Nahua world at many different times. Used with care and sophistication, Culhuacan is a good microcosm.[8]

We should not forget the source of Cline's study, the Culhuacan testaments themselves, for Cline has participated in an edition (Cline and León-Portilla 1984) which includes them all in transcription and translation, with a brief commentary to each.[9] Cline has produced a most valuable analysis of this corpus in her book, but I am sure she would not say that she has exhausted their significance. I feel that I have not done so either, despite having pored over them again and again (in addition to all that Cline has done) in work on *The Nahuas*. It seemed to me that whenever I had a new idea, or found a hint of an unknown process in some remote part of central Mexico, I could usually find a good illustration of it in the Culhuacan testaments. In general, Nahuatl wills dating from the late sixteenth century, when Spanish writing skills had become second nature, yet Nahua loquacity was still strong and preconquest genres still lay just beneath the surface, tend to be especially informative and colorful.[10] Yet I somehow doubt that sixty-five wills from another Nahua community of the time would turn out as rich, fascinating, many-dimensional, and inexhaustible. The Testaments of Culhuacan are a bible of postconquest Nahua social life. And not only scholars, I find, can enjoy reading them.

Stephanie G. Wood. "Corporate Adjustments in Colonial Mexican Indian Towns: Toluca Region, 1550-1810." UCLA doctoral dissertation, 1984.

On a research trip to the Mexican archives in relation with her senior thesis, before she had begun graduate study, Stephanie Wood met William Taylor, who referred her to some interesting documents on Indian disturbances or uprisings in the Valley of Toluca in the eighteenth century. She went on to produce an extensive research paper that contained the germ of her later dissertation.

Wood's dissertation project was conceived with the work of Gibson and Taylor very much in mind. Neither had devoted special attention to the Toluca Valley, populous and centrally located though it was. Studying a valley neighboring the one which is the locus of Gibson's *Aztecs* allowed for confirmation and generalization of many of Gibson's findings. The primary thematics, however, concerned questions of decline versus vitality in the postconquest Mexican indigenous world. Gibson had concentrated on the sixteenth century and tended to see the late colonial period as a time of deep decline in the Indian world (see Item 10); Taylor had found vitality continuing through the whole period but had concentrated above all on Oaxaca, to the south and outside the Nahua culture area.[11] Wood set out to see if, as she already suspected from her beginning research, strong Indian corporate vitality continued through the eighteenth century in the Mexican heartland as well. She has found that it did, though the energy is especially evident in smaller corporate groups splitting off from larger ones, so that Gibson was by no means simply wrong. But part of the movement involved settlements which had entirely disappeared and in some cases may never have existed. Moreover, the fever for corporate recognition in the eighteenth century spread to new communities associated with Spanish rural estates and mines, inhabited by Hispanized and even non-Indian people, which nevertheless quite often succeeded in establishing themselves as formally recognized Indian towns.

Beginning her research with the eighteenth century, where, after all, the weight of the Tolucan documentation falls, Wood found herself following one issue after another back in time, in some cases as far as the mid-sixteenth century. In general, she shows that in the first half of the colonial period Indian corporations were rather passive and complacent about various types of reorganization and encroachment by Spaniards, which left them more intact than was once imagined. In the second half of the period, under greater pressures, they became more aggressive and waged often successful campaigns to defend corporate rights.

Note that Wood's study at its inception had no particular orientation toward Nahuatl-language work. The basic sources for most of the research just described were Spanish-language records of litigation and Spanish administrative activity, just as with Gibson. The campaigns for community status are seen primarily in the Spanish (and Gibsonian) conceptual language of *cabecera*, *sujeto*, and *pueblo* (and indeed, when functioning in Spanish courts the Indians themselves had to use these terms). In the end, however, Nahuatl records showed their usefulness in the project, adding an important dimension. Wood found examples of Nahuatl documents of the type often called "primordial titles," embodying boundary definition, history, legend, and overall self-assertion of some Nahua entity. I too had located and studied a regional cache of such texts, from the Chalco region (Item 3); Wood was able to find nearly all the same salient characteristics in her samples, establishing the widespread uniformity of the genre. This aspect of Wood's work reinforces the themes of the other part; here too we see continued vitality, now in the cultural realm, with a traditional indigenous corporate ideology expressed in the indigenous language, and at least partly in relation to the same legal campaigns for autonomy.

As in the struggles for community recognition, however, not everything was simple retention; the titles as such were a new genre, a new cultural creation of indigenous people in the late seventeenth and early eighteenth centuries, for in the Toluca region as elsewhere, earlier examples are not to be found. Oral legends had no doubt existed all along, as well as bits of Nahuatl written narrative done close to the events, but the particular amalgamation of such elements appearing in the titles, couched in a popular, colloquial Nahuatl of the late period, was new, a sign of cultural vitality if there ever was one.

Wood has done much to refine our notion of the titles genre. Beneath the corporate façade she has discovered evidences of factionalism in the communities, and at times a closer relation to historical facts than appears on the surface. Coming from the titles proper, she has approached the puzzling

"Techialoyan" codices—highly pictorial, done on indigenous paper, aiming in general at an archaic impression—and has established them to be a sub-variety of the normal titles, though with much less authentic local content, much more specifically geared to supporting autonomy campaigns in Spanish courts. Wood continues to work on translating and comprehending both standard titles and Techialoyans, and she has done several articles on such topics.[12]

Since Wood had defined her project in corporate terms and had found a wealth of relevant material, the type of mundane Nahuatl document that throws so much light on individuals and household life did not come much into play. Nevertheless, she was fully aware that such texts could be used to expand the scope of her study, turning it into a general history of the indigenous world in the Valley of Toluca during the time covered, so she collected all the indigenous-language testaments from the region that she came upon. In this way a corpus came into being that demands comparison with the Testaments of Culhuacan, and is actually by now more voluminous. The Culhuacan testaments were a unit from the beginning, which gives them one sort of unique value, and they concern a single time and place, allowing an unparalleled view of standard, recurring structures and concepts in one uncontestably real situation. Wood's collection lacks these qualities, but has several most useful and complementary qualities of its own. Since it ranges over a longer time period and a larger (though still closely defined) region, it can be used as prima facie evidence of the generality of certain phenomena and also of trends in their variation over time and space. It is specifically complementary to the Culhuacan collection in that the latter is from the late sixteenth century, whereas nearly all of Wood's material is from the seventeenth and eighteenth centuries. Wood has already begun producing articles resting on compilations from the Toluca wills on topics such as gender in religion,[13] and research of this type will doubtless greatly enrich the book to which we look forward.

Susan Schroeder. "Chalco and Sociopolitical Concepts in Chimalpahin: Analysis of the Work of a Seventeenth-Century Nahuatl Historian of Mexico." UCLA doctoral dissertation, 1984.

Of the five works I am discussing here, four are predominantly social in orientation (two actually have "social" somewhere in the title). That is, though they may investigate matters as diverse as political struggle, local government, dynastic continuity, land tenure, inheritance, or the organization of jurisdictions, they abstract patterns under these rubrics from a multitude of closely observed individual cases, seen in documents done close to the time and place and naming specific real people and locations. Schroeder's work is quite different; although her topics—the historical evolution of a cluster of Nahua kingdoms and the nature of Nahua sociopolitical terminology—fit easily into the general range, she is studying not a variety of discrete, often disparate sources, but one vast all-encompassing source, the writings of the greatest of the Nahua annalists, Chimalpahin. Schroeder is in the first instance asserting, for example, not that the history of the Chalco kingdoms actually took such and such a shape, but that Chimalpahin says it did. The pattern she seeks is in Chimalpahin's statements and hence was presumably in his mind. Thus Schroeder's work is in one sense intellectual history in the classic manner. Yet the ultimate interest here is not Chimalpahin's opinions only. The views of Chimalpahin take on such significance because in all the corpus of Nahuatl writing his annals represent the only thorough historical treatment of a major political complex and the only full example of Nahua sociopolitical terminology in use in actual texts. Chimalpahin must serve as the primary answer to the scores of Spanish writers of the sixteenth to eighteenth centuries who saw Nahua history and political organization in European terms and who until recently determined our view of these matters. Thus Schroeder's study is akin to Wood's work with primordial titles; she too is doing a sort of general cultural history, seeking features of the Nahua mind and its evolution, though in the writings of a single individual rather than of several.

Finding pattern in Chimalpahin was no small task even if he is but one individual. As with other Nahuatl annals, his histories consist primarily of short accounts of certain specific events, inserted under the year of occurrence, with no other organization.[14] Although he is reflective for a Nahuatl annalist, he mainly sticks to the creed of this most laconic of genres: never consciously analyze; never summarize; never define terms. Chimalpahin's language is beautiful but so complex and unparalleled in other extant texts that his oeuvre has never been well or fully translated. Schroeder's ambitious research plan involved massive compilation of all mentions of every political entity, every individual, and every relevant term, together with its explanatory context, which was then translated as far as that could be achieved. This meticulous research has left an important residue in the dissertation in the form of tables of kingdoms, subkingdoms, rulers' titles, and genealogical/chronological kings' lists, as well as the many crucial passages culled from Chimalpahin, reproduced and translated, which stud the pages of the work. I understand that these features are, fortunately, to be preserved in the book version of the study soon to appear with University of Arizona Press.

One of Schroeder's major achievements is having unraveled Chimalpahin's version of Chalco history, producing a quite unified, if intricate, account of the political history of the many Chalco kingdoms from their inception to Chimalpahin's time. This task, however, was but a preliminary to the elucidation of the overall mental organization of the complex as Chimalpahin (implicitly) viewed it, making crucial hierarchical distinctions. Greater Chalco consisted of four large realms, theoretically ordered by the sequence of their foundation and distributed geographically to the cardinal directions. These four entities in turn were divided into several kingdoms each, each with its own ruler (or sometimes two), ordered by the same chronological principle. The subkingdoms then each contained a set of the familiar calpolli. Schroeder's analysis puts us in a position to understand a given entity's place in the overall scheme and thus interpret properly such things as reports of interdynastic marriages or wars between kingdoms. But it does far more than that. The structure of not a single other large political complex in all of Nahua central Mexico is as well or fully portrayed in original sources as Chalco is in the writings of Chimalpahin. Chalco is our best microcosm for the organization of Nahua political life, that is, for how that organization was conceived by the people involved. We can be sure that Chimalpahin idealized, and also that he simplified, for known entities of the Chalco region fail to appear in his scheme, but the general nature of that scheme remains clear and full of meaning for the analysis of Nahua political life before and after the conquest.

A second part of Schroeder's work, if anything even more transcendent than the first, analyzes the key concepts Chimalpahin uses in speaking of political history. It emerges clearly that for Chimalpahin, as for other Nahuas, the governing entity and framework is the altepetl, and not either a larger imperial structure nor the smaller calpolli, as previous generations of scholars tended to think. Chimalpahin's notion of what constitutes an altepetl is not startling. The interesting thing is the vision of altepetl nested within altepetl. Chimalpahin seems to have no special term for a complex altepetl, but he calls a constituent kingdom within a complex kingdom a *tlayacatl*. In Chalco, no king (tlatoani) has a jurisdiction larger than a tlayacatl. The name Chimalpahin employs has not been found in other Nahuatl sources, nor has in fact any other comparable term, but using Chimalpahin as a guide we can recognize the phenomenon everywhere we look in central Mexico. Chimalpahin also throws much light on rulership. A rulership (*tlatocayotl*) pertains to an altepetl and can survive beyond the end of the dynasty that holds it; each rulership is characterized, indeed virtually defined, by its polity-specific title. At a lower level, similar titled lordships, though without sovereignty, existed in the various calpolli. These are but some of Chimalpahin's terms and meanings, constituting an entire political vocabulary which is much richer than (and considerably at variance with) common parlance in relevant scholarly circles today.

In my work on *The Nahuas*, I had occasion to examine the Nahuatl sources for political systems in a series of widely scattered subregions; Tlaxcala, Tulancingo, Cuauhtinchan, Tetzcoco, Coyoacan, and Mexico Tenochtitlan are only some of the most prominent and best documented.[15] Variation in detail exists, and there appear to be some quite meaningful differences between the eastern and western parts of the Nahua macroregion. But everywhere one sees the elements and principles of Chimalpahin's portrait of Chalco, which remains the richest, most systematic single Nahuatl source for matters of the conceptualization of sociopolitical organization. Without it, working out the larger picture would have been an immeasurably more difficult task.

Many other topics await investigation in Chimalpahin's annals, a vast repository of Nahua concepts and culture in pre- and postconquest periods; Chimalpahin the individual, as writer and as person, also calls for investigation. Schroeder is in fact presently at work on some of these matters.[16]

Robert S. Haskett. "A Social History of Indian Town Government in the Colonial Cuernavaca Jurisdiction, Mexico." UCLA doctoral dissertation, 1985.

A revised version of Haskett's dissertation is due to be published in the near future by University of New Mexico Press. While the book will be more polished and tightly integrated, it will also of necessity omit much valuable material in the dissertation, so that those with a research interest will probably continue to consult the first version as well as the second. (Readers wanting a quick overview should consult Haskett's summarizing article.)[17] The dissertation form of the study is a monumental work, taking the broadest possible view of an already broad topic; there are few dimensions of ethnohistorical interest on which Haskett does not dispense some insight, new fact, or valuable confirmation.

The research strategy of the project involved the choice of an arena, the Cuernavaca jurisdiction (most of modern Morelos), which despite its proximity to the Valley of Mexico, its demographic weight, and its importance in the central Mexican economy had not yet attracted much in the way of ethnohistorical study, whether based on Spanish or on Nahuatl sources. On the other hand, the Cuernavaca jurisdiction held promise as to documentary resources because it belonged to the domain of the Marqués del Valle, for which, all in all, fuller records are preserved than for areas directly under royal government. Most of the documentation is in the section Hospital de Jesús of the Archivo General de la Nación, much feared by researchers, and rightly so, for the chaotic state of its contents, but Haskett forged ahead and ultimately found what he was looking for.

As to thematics, Haskett wanted to counteract descriptions of indigenous municipal government that in the main were too oriented to the Spanish view of it, often the formalistic view embodied in general ordinances. Haskett wanted, above all, to see local government as it appears in records produced by the people involved, and he wanted to see it in operation rather than as a static form. His main point of departure was, naturally enough, the work of Gibson. Actually, Gibson presented two rather distinct models. In *Tlaxcala* (see Item 10), having examined a single cabildo in action, partly on the basis of Nahuatl records, he showed strong carryover from the preconquest period in terms of personnel and principles of operation, so that in this case postconquest municipal government was seen to be an amalgam substantially altered from its Spanish form. In *The Aztecs*, apparently feeling that Tlaxcala was exceptional, Gibson reverted to the then more standard position that beneath the level of the governorship (where he was highly conscious of the continuity), the cabildo offices were strictly Spanish, and the indigenous tradition of office at this level was lost. It was this view that tended to become orthodox.

Haskett attacked the problem by compiling lists of membership of many cabildos over substantial stretches of time (Cuernavaca and Tepoztlan are most fully accounted for, but there is systematic information on many others). He has produced the most massive, detailed, and realistic account yet available of the constituent parts of postconquest indigenous local government in central Mexico, and he has gone much further than any predecessor in showing these parts in action. He also covers an admirably long time period. Relatively little was found for the sixteenth century and very early seventeenth, but thorough coverage proceeds uninterrupted from then until the very eve of Mexican independence. The product of archival fate, this chronological distribution nevertheless turns out to be a perfect complement to Gibson's work. As to the theme of preconquest continuities or their absence, Haskett's findings resemble those of *Tlaxcala* more than those of *The Aztecs* and go much further, chronologically and in other respects. Although the names of most of the offices may be new, Haskett repeatedly shows practices which continue those of the preconquest period in hardly disguised fashion. He also shows that frictions continued to be of the same type as before the conquest, based on rivalries between constituent parts of the entity or between noble lineages, or both.

It had often been said, and Gibson too inclined to that view of the matter, that the Indian nobility and ruling dynasties quickly disappeared after the conquest; yet by following officeholding patterns and property holding, Haskett demonstrates not only the indefinite persistence of a nobility or select predominant group, but the existence, over periods of many decades and in some cases more than a century, of dynasties and dynastic factions in recruitment to the highest municipal office, the governorship. Since the study is by no means restricted to municipal affairs in the narrower sense, Haskett is able to show through new evidence, in branches of interest as diverse as language, estate formation, commerce, and material culture, that the upper levels of Indian society at once retained preconquest goals, traits, and mechanisms, and absorbed a great deal from the Spaniards, as it suited their purposes. Officials at the highest level were often, as we might expect, especially skilled in Spanish language and other Spanish lore, or even racially mixed, the better to deal with local Spanish authorities, but Haskett lets us see that even they were in many ways authentic members of the indigenous community (betrayed not least in their frequent conflicts with those very Spanish officials with whom they were allied). The study provides us with a great deal of effective ammunition to combat those who hold that the Indians of central Mexico were quickly deprived of their culture, or that Indian corporations were ever static, isolated, or egalitarian.

The very core of Haskett's sources consists of Nahuatl records—complaints, petitions, statements of defense, wills, and above all election lists—but each of these typically come as detached items surrounded by many pages of Spanish litigation, from which Haskett gleaned essential background and facts. The most notable of his archival feats was the discovery of an entire new Nahuatl documentary genre, the municipal election report, consisting of a mainly formulaic section of introductory rhetoric, followed by a complete list of that year's new officers. Haskett has not only exploited the lists for their names but analyzed the texts both stylistically and linguistically, finding reminiscences of preconquest rhetorical formula as well as considerable Spanish influence on the concepts and language used.[18]

Rebecca Horn. "Postconquest Coyoacan: Aspects of Indigenous Sociopolitical and Economic Organization in Central Mexico, 1550-1650." UCLA doctoral dissertation, 1989.

Some years ago when I was avidly collecting older Nahuatl documents from all possible points of origin across central Mexico, it was rather a source of annoyance to me that so often they would turn out to be from Coyoacan.[19] Whether it be because of the Marquesado connection (as with Haskett), or the fact that Coyoacan was close to Mexico City and target of one of the first pushes by Spaniards into an area outside the capital, or for some other reason, the old altepetl of Coyoacan seems to be blessed with more extant Nahuatl texts than any other single comparable entity. Horn has taken advantage of this wealth to return (in this like Cline) to social history's tradition of intensive studies of limited localities where the same individuals and entities may be seen repeatedly and the different dimensions of interest quickly illuminate each other.

In recent decades the various disciplines that in any way impinge on the study of Indians have converged, intermingled, and at times become nearly indistinguishable. I still think that historians have the great advantage of being the most flexible in their ways of gaining understanding, in adjusting to what they find before them. Horn approached Coyoacan with an open mind, prepared to consider all the material available and utilize its potential for answering questions of current ethnohistorical interest. Two rather separate blocks of records soon began to stand out, and she judiciously built on them. The first, already known in large part but not analyzed, was a rather extensive set of records, many but not all in Nahuatl, concerning Coyoacan local government and high officials, with the names of a great many subunits, settlements, or locations. The second, for the most part discovered and first examined by Horn herself, was what appears to be the largest number of Nahuatl-language land transactions preserved for any subregion.

Horn saw the first block as a unique opportunity to carry mapping of sociopolitical units, of the type with which Charles Gibson made such a large contribution to the understanding of central Mexico, to a more local level, employing Nahuatl records and concepts as well as the kinds of records Gibson had used. This was also tantamount to dealing with the organization of a major complex altepetl, comparable to what Schroeder had done through Chimalpahin, but this time using a varied documentation and portraying the entity at the level of social reality. Gibson's accomplishment had been to map all the altepetl of the Valley of Mexico; he called them cabecera-sujeto units, or pueblos, or towns, and was content in the case of each unit to indicate, in the Spanish fashion, one "cabecera" and several "sujetos." This method was adequate for his purposes, but he himself was aware that many "sujetos" were omitted, and above all, nothing was shown about the internal ordering of the altepetl.

In her research on the organization of Coyoacan, Horn was greatly helped by her corpus of Nahuatl land sales. Here a great many apparent simple toponyms were identified as *tlaxilacalli* (the unit most moderns know as calpolli), and above all, they were placed within an altepetl which was not the overarching domain of Coyoacan but an intermediary entity, what Chimalpahin would have called a tlayacatl. Horn was able to identify the expected four of these subaltepetl, plus another, recently acquired, which was rather outside the scheme. With the aid of modern maps and crossreferences in the documents, she was able to map the approximate dimensions of the constituent altepetl and place most of the tlaxilacalli within them. Returning to the level of macro-records, she noticed that when, in the seventeenth century, new and smaller parishes were created inside the general Coyoacan jurisdiction, they bore a close relation to the sub-altepetl. The Spaniards had thus originally ignored its inner complexity in dealing with Coyoacan; yet the subentities continued to function on their own all along, and when, further into the postconquest period, decentralization was felt appropriate, they reemerged.

Coyoacan also had some form of dual organization, with two parts called Acohuic (apparently "upper") and Tlalnahuac (apparently "lower"). Since some lists of lands and market groups were organized by these categories, Horn was able to determine with a high degree of certainty which tlaxilacalli belonged to which and thus to locate the Tlalnahuac and Acohuic districts on her general map of Coyoacan. One result of this detailed work was to establish that, as one might expect, Coyoacan offices were often systematically divided between the two great districts, half going to each. Another result was very much unexpected. Tlalnahuac and Acohuic did *not* coincide with the division into four constituent altepetl, two in each. Rather Tlalnahuac was a rich, populous, low-lying strip along the eastern edge of the Coyoacan domain, occupying parts of two of the sub-altepetl, while the remaining parts of those two plus all of the other two fell into Acohuic. It appears, then, that two different and competing principles of internal organization were operative in preconquest Coyoacan and continued in operation in postconquest times, at least for many decades.

All these aspects of the organization of Coyoacan are of interest not only because Coyoacan happened to be a large and important realm, but because the procedures used have filled in large gaps in Gibson's style of mapping and given qualitatively different results at the altepetl-internal level.[20] We can expect to find similar things wherever we can produce similar evidence on a specific altepetl. Horn's results are all the more significant because equally well documented situations are extremely rare.

The land research that Horn has done may seem to have produced less striking results, but this is primarily because she had more predecessors in that department. Her work on the topic deserves attention because of the large size of the base of Nahuatl land texts she is dealing with, allowing her to refine concepts even where they are already known and somewhat understood. She has carried out a minute study of the documentary characteristics of Nahuatl bills of sale and includes a chapter on the conventions of the genre, with the implications for actual land transfers. Two of the results of Horn's land-related studies will bear mention here. Her bills of sale contain convincing evidence that the Nahuas were still assessing taxes on the basis of land, as they had always done, well after the Spaniards had gone over to emphasis on a uniform per capita tax. Second, Horn discovers a complex process in which at first traditional Nahua landholding concepts are pressed into use in new situations brought on by the Spaniards, and then in a second step the appropriate Spanish concept may be adopted, but much affected by, if not identical to, the original Nahua notion. Horn's prime example is that of *huehuetlalli* and *patrimonio*. At first the Coyoacan people would call a piece of land huehuetlalli (land held a long time in the family) as a pretext for selling it under the Spanish system; some later documents then substitute the Spanish word "patrimonio" (patrimony) at this juncture, clearly still with the same meaning, to those issuing the statement, as "huehuetlalli."

Horn's work stands in a complementary relation to some of the other studies considered here; that with Schroeder has already been mentioned. The substantial section in Horn's dissertation on officeholding is comparable on a smaller scale to Haskett's research, with some similar conclusions, and the time periods of the two fill in for each other, one beginning systematic study almost where the other leaves off. Horn's land-related research tends to show, in a general way, that most of what Cline describes about land and land concepts (chinampas aside) holds true for Coyoacan and for a rather longer time period, and thus may be viewed as not mainly peculiar to Culhuacan around 1580, but with a wider range of applicability. The time period of Horn's work, 1550-1650, is very interesting from the point of view of Nahuatl-based historical studies generally, for it is virtually identical with what I call Stage 2 (see Item 1).

Part of Horn's original motivation in undertaking her project was to include both Spaniards and Indians within its scope, since Coyoacan was the site of much early Spanish activity. She found the Spanish presence as strong as she had expected, but her research specifically on the Spanish side was still in progress when the dissertation was completed. She is now at work in Spanish records on the Coyoacan Spaniards and intends to produce the first book of primary research in which Indians and Spaniards are both studied head on, as integrated with each other as possible, and at all events inside the same covers.[21]

*   *   *

If I put *The Nahuas* (which may be represented for the moment by Item 1 in this volume) in the same bin with the five works just discussed, we can use the corpus so formed as the field of reference for some brief considerations about Nahuatl-based historical writing in general. First, in view of the title of the present book, let us examine further the question of the relation of things Spanish to this kind of history (some aspects of the matter were already discussed in Item 10, pp. 176-77). Three quite different facets are involved: Spanish cultural elements in Nahua life, sources in Spanish, and the history of Spaniards.

All the authors have uncovered abundant evidence of the presence of elements of Spanish origin in postconquest Nahua society and culture, and they are finding the Nahuatl materials available to be an adequate basis for an analysis of the role and evolution of these elements in the indigenous context.[22] All agree that Nahua culture was not obliterated, but all also agree that Spanish influence[23] in the indigenous culture is a major part of the overall story of the Nahuas from the time of the conquest forward. Essentially, there is no problem here. Nor is there any large problem with using Spanish sources in conjunction with Nahuatl-language materials, or even instead of them, when necessary, and there are whole classes of topics for which it is in fact necessary. It remains true that only sources in indigenous languages can reveal indigenous concepts to us. Once the essential conceptual vocabulary is grasped, a Spanish document can give us a relevant "fact" as well as a document in Nahuatl. Among the authors in consideration here, Schroeder had literally no occasion to use Spanish sources and Cline only one somewhat peripheral block, in both cases because a massive unitary Nahuatl corpus was at the heart of their respective projects. But Haskett, Horn, and myself have made a great deal of use of the Spanish records (often litigation) surrounding and explaining Nahuatl texts, and Wood's study, in its present form, rests *mainly* on Spanish documentation, which did not prevent the integration of a significant section based on texts in Nahuatl.

The large problem and challenge remains the task of integrating the actual history of Spaniards themselves, for as active and adaptive as the Nahuas were, it is hardly likely that the elements of Spanish origin we are finding in indigenous culture got there entirely as a result of indigenous people reaching out to take them. Indeed, my work in *The Nahuas* and the related projects has led me to the conclusion that it is precisely contact between the two peoples that made the engine move. Yet in not a one of the studies in question here (Schroeder may be absolved because of her mainly preconquest scope) are Spaniards more than peripheral characters, seen outside their own context when seen at all. Perhaps the method Horn has adopted in her ongoing research is at least a partial answer: study in Spanish sources the very Spaniards who are in direct contact with the particular Indians one is studying in indigenous sources, and hope that the connection emerges.

I have spoken of a New Philology in connection with the editions of Nahuatl texts that have been appearing (see Item 10, p. 178). But the term had perhaps just as well be applied also to the works of substantive analysis being discussed here. Cline's *Colonial Culhuacan* and *The Testaments of Culhuacan* (Cline and León-Portilla) are not really separate enterprises; in a way, the book of analysis is as bound up with texts as is the edition of the original documents. Every one of the studies being considered either provides a substantial documentary appendix or repeatedly excerpts and paraphrases certain texts, or does both. Other philological tools are also at work here. Many of our authors use something on the order of linguistic analysis, and they also show concern for idiom, usage, and the meaning of individual words. They are very aware of documentary genre and prone to genre analysis. Not only is a genre with its conventions the prism through which we see our topics, but the nature and evolution of the genre is an important part of the history we are aiming at. Cline devotes a chapter to the nature of the testament, Wood a section to "titles," Haskett a chapter to the genre of election records he discovered, Horn a chapter to bills of sale, and I a chapter and a half to a whole gamut of genres.

One associates this kind of methodology with cultural, intellectual, or literary history. Indeed, what began as "social history" is becoming ever more "cultural history."[24] Our authors originally, I think, all thought of themselves as continuing the tradition of a kind of social history that had a golden age in the early Latin American field in the late 1960s and the 70s.[25] Some may still so conceive themselves, and with good reason. Emphasis continues to be on including all the people and all the phenomena, not forgetting the ordinary and everyday, for they form a context without which the allegedly exceptional cannot be comprehended. The refusal to take things at face value, whether it be formal institutional structures or articulated rationales, has not abated. The social history with which we began always had two sides: establishing patterns through synthesis of the diverse action of individuals and small organizations, and attention to key concepts appearing as words and phrases in the sources relating to those individuals and organizations. What is happening is that the emphasis is changing from the first activity to the second; but just as the second was vital to the earlier work, the first is still an important part of the current type of research.

The nature of Nahuatl sources has had much to do with the change, but something parallel has been happening in the early Latin American field generally, and also even more widely. It would have and should have happened, I think, even if there had been no indigenous people in the history of Latin America and no sources generated by them.[26] But whatever our perspective on it, a move in the direction of broadly more cultural investigation has been on its way for some time and continues to gather momentum.[27]

The Nahuatl-language historical movement has now made a substantial corpus of varied texts available in comprehensible form and has gone far, in several complementary directions, toward using them to build a more adequate version of the history of central Mexico in the three centuries or so after the conquest, as well as vastly enriching our understanding of what must have existed in the area in the late preconquest period. As we reach a certain plateau, the most urgent intellectual task, on a par with the need to integrate the history of Indians and Spaniards, is to gain perspective on the Nahua historical literature—now without anything remotely resembling a peer in the Western hemisphere—by studying other New World peoples in similar terms, if that can be done. There is some indication that it can be done in fact, and the work has already begun.[28]

IV. Spaniards

12. Spaniards among Indians: Toluca in the Later Sixteenth Century

The Toluca Valley, high and spacious, lies immediately to the west of the great valley of Mexico, yet the mountain barrier separating the two basins has always permitted the existence of cultural differences. In later pre-Hispanic times Toluca was the home of the Matlatzinca, an Otomi-related people, in contrast to the Nahuatl speakers of the central valley. Finally in the last century before the Spanish conquest, Nahuas from the Valley of Mexico invaded the Toluca area and proceeded to occupy it with unusual thoroughness, on account of its proximity and its richness as a maize-producing region. Settling in the valley in substantial numbers, they molded the dispersed Matlatzinca to their own more nucleated residence pattern. Nahuatl speakers were dominant, though apparently far from the most numerous group, by the time the Spanish conquerors arrived and began to assign different parts of the valley to individual Spaniards in encomienda. A large portion of the area and population went to Cortés himself, later to be incorporated into his seigneurial estate. European rule did nothing to alter the valley's domination by Tenochtitlan-Mexico City. Now as before, the capital was the main destination of valley tributes and surplus products, with the addition of a new, lesser market in the silver mines of Temascaltepec and Sultepec, off to the southwest.[1]

As the year 1600 approached, after more than half a century of effective Spanish presence, in the third Spanish generation, the Valley of Toluca was still Indian in many senses. A majority of its inhabitants spoke various Indian languages; the main settlements were the same that had already existed in preconquest times; maize agriculture was still the basis of life; and the region was considered by the Spaniards to belong to the Indian commonwealth rather than the Spanish. The councils of all the valley towns, including that of the principal one, Toluca itself, were composed solely of Indians. The highest judicial-executive officials in the valley were of the type whose jurisdictions by original intention was primarily over Indians (*corregidores de indios* in the parlance of some).

Yet when fray Alonso Ponce visited Toluca in 1585 on an inspection tour of Franciscan establishments, he was greeted in the provincial capital not only by the Indians, but by "the many Spaniards who reside there." The aide who recorded his journey for him wrote that the Valley of Toluca was "very fertile in maize and fodder for livestock of all kinds, and so there are many stock farms (*estancias*); they raise many pigs and make marvelous hams that are famous in all New Spain."[2]

In what follows I mean to present a detailed study of the functions and structure of the Spanish community of the Toluca Valley in the time around 1580 to 1600, using for illustration a series of life sketches synthesized from Tolucan notarial and trial records. The deeper purpose is to study the manner and rate of growth of provincial Mexican society (and indeed these processes were much the same in all areas of Spanish America which originally had a population base of well organized, agricultural Indians). My interest therefore extends beyond the Spanish and Hispanized population of the valley to the social and cultural impact of that group on the Indians, and to the Indians themselves, whenever the records of the Spanish community render them visible.[3] The survey will begin with the earliest, in 1600 still most basic manifestation of Spanish society in the valley: the estates.

Estate types

In the whole Toluca Valley at the end of the sixteenth century there was to all appearances nothing approaching a fully developed hacienda, in the sense of a large relatively consolidated landed property, run under one management, monopolizing large areas and centered on a well built up nuclear settlement or plant. The evolution of estate forms was in an intermediate stage, and the general picture was one of diversity, fragmentation, and truncation. In the early years of Spanish occupation, estates in regions like Toluca were thoroughly dominated by the encomenderos, who though relying more on tribute collection than on production by themselves, kept almost all rural Spaniards in their direct employ as tax collectors, foremen, or stock watchers. With the expansion of a Spanish society and economy, the type of humble Spaniards who had worked for the encomenderos often tended to make themselves independent as small-scale stockmen or farmers. When successful, they would try to build up their own managerial hierarchy and complex of interests, approximating the almost eternal principles of Hispanic estate organization.

Around 1580-1600 in Toluca, the humble agriculturalists had appeared, but the elaboration of their estates was far from complete. There was a large gap between the many-dimensional estates which were based on an encomienda, with headquarters in Mexico City, and the smaller, simpler, more local enterprises, which were more purely agricultural and had humbler ownership. The two types were at this time not in very direct competition. Encomenderos sold some of their tribute maize to the local stock growers;

they sometimes leased their lands, equipment, and stock to humble local farmers rather than manage them directly; and their own poorer or illegitimate relatives were an important element in the growing class of locally based estate owners.

Encomienda estates. All the encomenderos of Toluca in the time of which we speak appear to have had the same general characteristics. They were citizens of Mexico City, where they maintained their usual residence. Without exception they owned land and kept stock in the vicinity of their encomiendas. Almost all seem to have been grandsons or sons of the original holders; the first holders themselves conformed to a certain type. Not among the very earliest conquerors, they tended to be "settlers" (*pobladores*), dependent on Cortés for their prominence. Licenciado Juan Gutiérrez Altamirano had family connections with Cortés, and helped administer the Cortés estate; Juan de Sámano had powerful friends in Spain and achieved Cortés' favor through that avenue. Thus Cortés turned the Valley of Toluca almost into a personal enclave, containing not only a large section of his own private preserve, but the encomiendas of some of his closest associates. How long the Cortés association remained functional is hard to say, but a lasting effect was that some very important families had their main assets in Toluca.

Of these families the best documented are the Sámanos. The originator of the Mexican branch was named Juan de Sámano like the secretary of Emperor Charles V, his relative and namesake. Arriving in the early 1520's, he received the encomienda of Zinacantepec, just west of Toluca; he sat on Mexico City's council and was its chief constable. His successor in both the encomienda and the chief constable post was his eldest son (also Juan de Sámano). He had a second son who did not inherit the encomienda, but, as family prestige mounted and usage began to distinguish many sons of the conquerors in title, did become a "don," don Carlos de Sámano; don Carlos was later at one time or another chief constable of Mexico City, warden of the fort of San Juan de Ulúa, governor of Yucatan, and in 1601 one of Mexico City's alcaldes.[4]

The encomendero of Zinacantepec from the early 1580's into the seventeenth century was the first holder's grandson, don Juan de Sámano (Turcios), citizen of Mexico City and one of its alcaldes in 1603.[5] Don Juan was married to doña Inés de Carvajal, of a famous family of conquerors, the Alvarados.[6] He signed his name in the fluent, elegant style of the very well educated around 1600, more cursive, even, and with larger characters than the signatures of the previous two generations; doña Inés could sign almost equally well. In the externals as in all else, don Juan was a full member of the highest circle of Mexican society. On the occasion of certain important transactions don Juan came to Toluca in person, but much of his local business was done through subordinates. Once he even stayed in Mexico City while doña Inés was in Zinacantepec. Don Juan's principal local representatives were Jusepe Martín, his chief majordomo, and Juan de Sámano (without "don"), a relative.

Zinacantepec had a nominal 1,191 tributary Indians around 1598, which made it one of the two or three largest in the Toluca Valley, and comparable to the larger grants in the jurisdiction of Mexico City in general.[7] The tributes in maize were a very substantial asset. Presumably most were sold into the Mexico City market in some fashion, but don Juan also sold them to local inhabitants like Juan Nieto, stockman and tanner, and used them as security in large credit transactions.

Don Juan held land in the district of Zinacantepec, but it would appear that his holdings were not vast, and not necessarily expanding. Indeed, he sold some lands granted him in the area to humble local Spaniards. The principal landed property of his that appears in the sources was a quite modest farm (*labor* or *heredad de labor*) on the way from Zinacantepec to Toluca; don Juan kept it leased out much of the time to local Spanish residents. While we do not know its exact size, the terms of the lease and the appurtenances of the property serve to define it sufficiently. In 1585 don Juan leased the farm to a Miguel González for three years, at 250 pesos plus 20 fanegas of maize per year. On the property were two adobe houses, a black slave, and ten yokes of oxen with plowing apparatus. Another lease is known from the year 1593, showing the property little changed and the terms of the lease almost the same. The lessee this time was Juan Esteban, an illiterate farmer (*labrador*) who had lived in the immediate vicinity of Zinacantepec for years. The lease was for three years again, with Juan Esteban paying 333$\frac{1}{3}$ pesos a year. The houses and the twenty oxen were still there; the slave was not mentioned, but there were now some pens and 150 pigs. Somewhere in the valley don Juan also had sizable herds, and presumably an estancia where they ran; in 1593 he sold 116 colts to one stock trader, and 200 steers for slaughter to another. His stockraising thus far outweighed his agricultural undertakings in extent and value.

The records reveal little about the activities of Jusepe Martín, the estate's chief steward, except that he was responsible for such things as the delivery of the just mentioned stock, and was apparently acquiring some land for himself in the Zinacantepec area. In all probability he spent a great deal of time shuttling back and forth between the capital and the valley in the course of carrying out general management of the estate's affairs and thus

was not exactly a full-time resident of the valley. A better documented
figure is don Juan's relative Juan de Sámano, present in the valley from
1585 to 1593 at least. Several factors—his lack of the title "don," his
subordinate position to don Juan, and his residence and citizenship in the
Valley of Toluca rather than Mexico City—all hint that Juan was a poor
relation, probably illegitimate and conceivably mestizo.

Without fuller knowledge of the whole context we cannot always tell
when an individual is acting for himself and when he is representing others.
But it is reasonably clear that Juan de Sámano, while serving the Sámano
estate as a trusted, high-level administrator, was building up a position
specifically for himself in the Toluca Valley. He was a literate man, with a
signature as good as don Juan's except that it was in a standard, by that time
slightly old fashioned sixteenth-century style, rather than in the new metro-
politan-inspired style of don Juan. Juan's position relative to don Juan's
appears most clearly in a document of 1585, in which don Juan empowers
Juan to buy, sell, and borrow in his name, and to represent him in litigation—the standard powers given an administrator.

Juan's own interests can be seen in the following details. In 1591 he
bought a mulatto slave woman; in the same year he had a free mulatto
working for him at the very reasonable salary of 100 pesos a year. The
man, Juan Melchor de Dueñas, had a beautiful signature. Sometime before
1592, Juan acquired some lands well off to the south of Zinacantepec, on the
slopes of the great volcano, the Nevado de Toluca. Not long after that he
bought an estancia that had belonged to Peribáñez de Gamboa (see below),
in the drier northern region, putting both properties under mortgage (censo)
and selling back much of the stock on the new property to the former
owner's widow. The property near the volcano, described as "dos medios
sitios de estancias," was devoted mainly to pigs. In 1593 Juan made a binding four-year company contract with an Alonso Hernández, an arrangement
that almost amounted to a lease. Juan contributed the land and 100 sows,
while Hernández contributed another 100 and all the active work; the profits
were to be shared equally. Whether people like Juan de Sámano and Alonso
Hernández are to be considered actual employees of the Sámano estate or not
is a debatable question. Certainly they were in a semi-dependent relationship to it, and constituted a part of the total complex.

In addition to a clearly subordinate relative such as Juan, don Juan de Sámano had other kin more nearly his equal, who also gravitated at times
toward the estate. A don Alonso de Carvajal, probably the brother or cousin
of don Juan's wife doña Inés de Carvajal, accompanied don Juan to Zinacantepec in 1593. Above all there was the previously mentioned don Carlos

de Sámano, don Juan's uncle, who during his lifetime held several posts of national importance. Don Carlos was don Juan's senior and in a sense the more prominent person of the two, but was not in the direct line of succession for the Sámano encomienda. Nothing could be more natural than that don Carlos should be named alcalde mayor of Ixtlahuaca, the northern jurisdictional district into which Zinacantepec fell despite its proximity to Toluca. It is not known when don Carlos occupied the post, or when he left it, but he was alcalde mayor in 1585, apparently making Zinacantepec his residence. Thus the Sámanos in that year had a three-pronged family hold on Zinacantepec: the heir occupying the encomienda, the uncle serving as highest local administrative authority, and the illegitimate relative seeing to local agricultural aspects. Of course the archetypal purity of this set of relationships must have been a comparatively rare occurrence, and even with the Sámanos it did not last long (though don Carlos did acquire land near Ixtlahuaca). But it only makes more visible the degree of influence that encomenderos of this time must often have exercised over the magistrates of their districts, given the extensive intermarriage of the encomendero group, its concentration in Mexico City, the impermanence of the magistrate's position compared to the encomendero's, and the fact that the magistrates, so often second sons, were generically the social inferiors of the encomenderos.

The relation of the Sámanos to the Indians of Zinacantepec is discernible only in the broadest of terms. A certain attempt at tutelary dominance, which could be posited in any case, may be inferred from hints such as the fact that some of the most important indigenous leaders of the region bore the name of Sámano, like the don Juan Vásquez de Sámano who was "cacique y gobernador" in 1570, or an Indian noble don Carlos de Sámano in 1591. Aside from this we have the mere knowledge that a good portion of the town's surplus maize was going to the Sámanos as tribute. Otherwise, both the demand and the acculturative impact of the Sámano estate would seem to have been moderate but persistent. Juan de Sámano and a few other estate administrators, with their mulatto or other subordinates, must have resided ordinarily in Zinacantepec, requiring servants and supplies. Don Juan's heredad might have employed from half a dozen to a dozen Indian families on a permanent basis, with larger numbers coming at harvest time. Juan's pig estancia will hardly have required so many, and don Juan's herds would normally be watched by slaves or humble Hispanics, with a small number of Indian helpers.

The encomienda estates of Toluca at this time were mature variants of the classical Iberian estate in that they comprehended the full social hierarchy, extending from city to country, and branching into various locally profitable endeavors. Neither markets, competition, nor long evolution yet pushed them into consolidation or attempts at monopoly; they were content to leave much land in Indian hands, while profiting from maize production mainly through tribute and purchase; they did not yet amass lands or insist on complete and direct monopoly of a given area, but tolerated other Spanish enterprises within their own spheres, and were even prepared to lease properties to the small agriculturalists.

Though the Sámano interests were extensive, they were probably not the largest of the kind. The Altamirano encomienda included an even greater number of nominal tributaries (2,299 in Metepec, Calimaya, and Tepemaxalco in 1598), and the Altamirano men made even more resplendent marriages. Don Juan Altamirano, the first holder's grandson, was a knight of the Order of Santiago, and married the daughter of the second don Luis de Velasco, viceroy of Mexico and Peru.[8] Their estancia at Atenco seems to have been a larger, more intensive, directly-run operation than anything the Sámanos had. In 1594 the Altamiranos sold 1,000 steers, 1,000 cows, and 2,000 calves from the Atenco estancia to a merchant. The sale was negotiated by an Hernando de Altamirano Saavedra, without "don," who was a valley resident. Atenco had other Spanish and mulatto employees. Don Juan Altamirano's uncle Juan Alonso Altamirano was also at times present in the valley; in 1584 he was serving as alcalde mayor in Metepec. Thus the Altamiranos appear to have had much the same division of functions among heir, uncle, and poor relative as the Sámanos.

Other Toluca encomiendas are even less well recorded, but we do know that Gaspar de Garnica, second-generation encomendero of Tlacotepec,[9] had an estancia in the valley. The Muñoz de Chaves family had some sort of estancia in the jurisdiction of their encomienda of Jiquipilco. The usual assortment of relatives was present, with at least one Spanish employee. Jiquipilco was a secular parish rather than a Franciscan one, and the local priest had so many accounts and dealings with the encomendero of Jiquipilco that he must be considered his representative. Though in the third generation, the encomendero of Jiquipilco was still plain Pedro Muñoz de Chaves without "don," because of the plebeian flavor of the family's founder, the Maese de Roa, and probably also because of less than prospering fortunes.[10]

Properties of plebeians. At the opposite end of the spectrum from the estates of the encomenderos were small holdings like the strip (*pedazo*) of land owned by illiterate Diego Mejía de Lagos (doubtless Portuguese) just to the west of Toluca. It had a small house, only six oxen and three plows, and Mejía owned no slaves. The total value of the property was no more than 300 pesos, and after Mejía's death it was leased for 32 pesos a year. Nevertheless, this made a stable basis for a life. Mejía lived on the same spot for years, and arranged his daughter's marriage to an equally humble farmer who continued in the area and cared for his surviving children after Mejía died.

A defining characteristic of non-encomendero farmers and stock growers was relative marginality in the Spanish world; they were often illiterate, of humble social origin, late arrivals in Mexico, foreign (especially Portuguese), or all of these things put together. Some were apparently mestizo, though it is hard to prove. Their relative position and social profile, then, corresponded exactly to that of the estancieros or rural employees of the encomenderos of the conquest period.[11] They were indeed merely estancieros grown independent, and in many cases they were still in semi-dependence. The above Mejía's son-in-law was the lessee of don Juan de Sámano's heredad. Like their antecedents the estancieros, the small farmers and stockmen lived in the countryside, on their holdings, or perhaps in a nearby Indian settlement of some size, or at most in the town of Toluca.

How many non-encomienda properties might there have been in the valley in the years around 1600? Various observers exclaimed over the number of both owners and stock.[12] To count the holdings listed in the records proved unfeasible. First there is the question of whether the various estancias, sitios and caballerías of a single owner constituted separate properties. Sometimes they did. Inexact descriptions and changes of hands through inheritance and sale render precise identification impossible. After reaching a total of some fifty apparently separate estates long before exhausting even the relatively small sample of documents that I studied, I came to the conclusion that I could not control duplication. I am left with a strong feeling that there were more stock enterprises (estancias) than wheat or maize farms (heredades, labores). They were in all parts of the valley from south to north, east to west, with sheep predominant in the dry northern part of the valley, and pigs mainly in the center and south. One indication of the relative density is that many of the holdings abutted on others. My general impression is that there were scores of Spanish holdings with some kind of buildings or improvements, and that it would not have been possible to find a place anywhere in the valley that was more than three or four miles distant from some Spanish agricultural enterprise, though the concentration must have been greatest in the immediate area of Toluca and Zinacantepec.

Pig farming. Within the category of non-encomienda holdings, there were subtypes and variations in scale. Today renowned for its sausage, the

Valley of Toluca already had a reputation for hams and bacons, and many of
the estancias were mainly pig farms. An example is the estate of Antonio
Tavera (the name is still known in Toluca), a first-generation immigrant
born in Lisbon, Portugal, who died in Toluca in 1580. Tavera had lived for
a time in Mexico City, and even owned a house there. After settling in
Toluca he married a local girl, Catalina Pérez, whose family had been in the
area for three generations; her father, a stockman and muleteer, left her a
substantial inheritance which probably went far toward getting Tavera
started. Tavera's main holding was a "labor de pan" near Toluca. At his
death there were 250 pigs and 14 oxen on it. Tavera had a black slave woman, but it is not clear whether she was connected with the pig farm or not.
He took a Melchor González into his service to help run the operation;
finding him more than satisfactory, he arranged for González to marry his
natural daughter, and the new in-laws made an unwritten partnership agreement. It does not seem that there were any houses on the farm; none appear
in the estate inventory. Tavera and his family lived in a house he owned in
the center of Toluca, near to the fountain. While he was not outfitted in
truly luxurious style, he did have silver, china, and pewter service, much
good linen, 20 paintings or images, and 24 books in Spanish and Latin.
Here as in several other cases, the valley estates were contributing directly to
the Spanish urban community in Toluca.

Sheep shearing. The northern part of the valley was very propitious for
sheep. One way for a humble man with little capital to profit from the
sheep business was to concentrate on herding, shearing, and marketing the
animals of others, rather than owning land and animals directly. This was
the procedure of illiterate Francisco Martín Albarrán, prominent in the
Toluca Valley for decades. In 1581 he was farmer of the valley's tithes. In
1585 he was simultaneously operating on lease an estancia of Pedro Sánchez
Farfán at Coyotepec, with 2,000 sheep, and the estancia of the Cortés estate,
from which he sold 1,000 muttons (previously shorn) to the mines of
Sultepec. He also bought wool in large amounts, doing the shearing himself, as when he acquired the wool of 3,000 lambs on the Altamirano estate
of Atenco. Here again we see how the Toluca growers and farmers at once
served the great estates and used the relationship to become independent.
Albarrán must have had a fairly large staff, as implied by the Spanish
shepherd who worked for him at the high salary of 300 pesos per year,
supplying his own horses. Another, less well documented figure, who took
on lease the sheep belonging to the Indian hospitals of Ixtlahuaca and
Jiquipilco in 1591, was a Francisco de Pliego (or Priego). Pliego could
make his signature, unlike Albarrán, but so crudely that he too was certainly

illiterate. These two must have been the originators of the Albarráns and Pliegos who have remained so important among the locally prominent families of Toluca into the nineteenth and twentieth centuries.[13]

Herding. Some of the stockgrowers in the northern end of the valley were developing quite impressive complexes. Manuel Váez, an illiterate Portuguese, raised sheep in the Ixtlahuaca area in the 1580's and 90's. He had Spanish employees and a black slave, and aside from three "sitios de ganado menor" in Ixtlahuaca and Jiquipilco, he owned another estancia off to the west in the Maravatío area, towards Michoacán, with 300 goats and 300 pigs. Adjoining this property he maintained an inn. In 1585 he did not know how many sheep he owned, but they seemed to outnumber the 3,000 he had on lease from a doña María de Zayas. He had at that time just sold 700 lambs. He also leased out some of his estancias to others. Váez seems to have maintained his residence in Ixtlahuaca, though he hoped to be buried in Toluca; he was becoming enough of a man of influence that despite his small education he often stood in for the alcalde mayor of Ixtlahuaca on an interim basis.

Sheep were not the only possibility in the north. Miguel Hernández, a Spaniard born in the Maestrazgo of southern Extremadura, and apparently illiterate, called himself "criador de ganados." His principal business was raising horses; in 1591 he branded about 100 colts and 25 mules. Though he had several land claims, his main estancia was at Amanalco in the far west of the valley (in the jurisdiction of Malacatepec, which was in turn in Ixtlahuaca), where he had a house which seems to have been his usual residence. He considered himself a citizen of Malacatepec, even though he did own a house in Mexico City. He had married in the valley and had several grown children, some of whom he had already set up in life with part of his own holdings.

One of the most successful and pretentious of the plebeian stockraisers was a Miguel García de la Banda, a sheepman in the Ixtlahuaca area with a considerable assemblage of grown children, employees, and slaves. In 1593 he sold 4,000 lambs to a citizen of Tula. He seems to have been literate, and though his own wife was without the "doña," his son and namesake married a doña Leonor de la Cueva, and his daughter was called doña Ana de la Banda.

Estates of marginal gentlemen. If the stockmen and farmers of the Toluca Valley were mainly plebeians reaching up, there was also a certain amount of movement in the other direction. We have already seen how the relatives, particularly the illegitimate or poor relatives, of the valley's enco- menderos were seeking an independent position within the family estates.

The same pressure impelled other marginal aristocrats to seek refuge and opportunity in the country. A major example was Alonso de Villanueva Cervantes, second son of the important conqueror Alonso de Villanueva, one-time secretary of Cortés. Villanueva Cervantes had a large estancia somewhere in the Ixtlahuaca district. In 1604 his total worth was estimated (with probably exaggeration or error) at 100,000 pesos.[14] His orientation and manner of operation approximated that of the encomenderos, for he had a majordomo who carried the main burden of his affairs; he was a citizen of Mexico City, and owned houses and stores there. Yet he was reputed to reside mainly in the Toluca Valley, and he was certainly there at least a good deal of the time. In 1593 he served for a while as alcalde mayor of the Ixtlahuaca district.

The most suggestive of such cases was that of Peribáñez de Gamboa, the legitimate son of conqueror Cristóbal Martín de Gamboa. Cristóbal Martín had been something of a plebeian, and Peribáñez must not have been the eldest son, since he held no encomienda. Also his mother, Cristóbal Martín's wife, had been an Indian woman, and apparently a commoner rather than one of the Indian noblewomen a few conquerors married.[15] The records never call Peribáñez a mestizo, and indeed there is some doubt whether contemporaries really considered mixed products of a legitimate marriage to be mestizos. Nevertheless, his heritage had its effect, visible not only in his retirement into the country, but in the strong Indian element in his valley establishment. Peribáñez had not given up all pretensions. He was a citizen of Mexico City, and hoped to be buried alongside his parents in the capital's hospital of Nuestra Señora de la Concepción, where he made a very large endowment (3,000 pesos) for a chaplaincy. The elements of his estate were standard enough. He lived on his heredad San Miguel, near Jiquipilco, where he had a house and the usual ten yokes of oxen, and he also owned an estancia San Antonio on the Lerma river, with hundreds of mares and colts. He had a standard number of two black slaves, and his nearest Spanish neighbor, illiterate Esteban Hernández, had almost become his dependent; after Peribáñez' death Hernández managed the estate.

All of this was to be expected. More unusual was the location of a semi-luxurious household with many amenities (though little valuable furniture) on the farm itself, rather than in Toluca, Ixtlahuaca, or even Jiquipilco. Most notable of all was the strength of the Indian strand running through the whole operation. Peribáñez took the uncommon step of marrying an Indian noblewoman of Jiquipilco, doña Cecilia de Rojas. She brought him only a small piece of land in dowry, but must have helped improve his relations with the Indian council of Jiquipilco, from whom he often bought maize. The ordinary language of the household must have been Nahuatl or Otomi, since doña Cecilia after twenty years of married life still had to call on an interpreter when transacting legal business. Not so doña Cecilia's brother don Pedro, who was constantly in Peribáñez' company; don Pedro could sign his name as well as any Spaniard, and spoke such good Castilian that he often did official interpreting, for his sister among others. From Peribáñez he had assumed the surname Gamboa. Peribáñez' marriage produced no children, but he brought up an Indian girl in his house, leaving her a legacy, and also boarded two small daughters (probably mestizo) of his friend Esteban Hernández. The estate also had a strong Indian element in its management. Whereas most stewards and supervisors mentioned in the Toluca area records were Spanish, mulatto, or black, Peribáñez' estancia San Antonio had two Indian overseers (*capataces*), called Pablo González and Mateo Vásquez. Nevertheless, it should not be imagined that Peribáñez' indigenous affinities were a manifestation of any Indian patriotism. He left doña Cecilia in full control of his liquid estate only on condition that she should marry some "honorable Spanish person."

The estates which dotted the Tolucan landscape and brought a Spanish presence into remote corners of the valley can be seen as a response to the valley's environmental potential; they can be seen as an adjustment to a still intact, maize-growing Indian population. But they are also in a sense a creation of Mexico City, which stimulated production as the main market, while its inability to absorb the whole flow of immigrants from Spain, or the growth of new generations of Spaniards and mestizos, impelled people of varying degrees of marginality to leave the capital for areas like Toluca.

Industrial and commercial activity

Neither Toluca's Indian communities nor its rather dispersed and often marginal Spanish population represented a very attractive market. Mexico City and Puebla were more favorable locations for such industrial development as the local Spanish economy could support. Yet it was natural that someone should try to take advantage of the valley's stockraising to process its products on the spot for the markets of cities or mines. Toluca thus saw a very modest growth of shops (*obrajes*) turning local wool into serge and other inexpensive cloth, and of tanneries to process valley-grown hides.

Textiles. Surviving records show only three operators of textile shops (*obrajeros*), and we cannot be quite sure that all of them were functioning at the same time: Juan García Carrillo in 1584 and 1585, Alonso de la Peña from 1585 to 1593, and Juan Domingo in 1591. The shops all seem to have been in Toluca itself. Only García Carrillo is fairly well documented. He was the son of another local obrajero, Juan García Rodrigo, who though preparing to go into retirement at this time, occasionally stood as guarantor of a debt for his son, or acted in his name. As so often in such cases, the son's signature was far better written than the father's. The only measure we have of the volume of production are some wool purchases. In two separate transactions in 1585, García Carrillo bought 1,372 arrobas (ca. 25 lbs. per arroba) of wool from a local merchant, for a total of 1,886$^1/_2$ pesos.

As to labor, there is some evidence about the types employed, if not the numbers. Some slave labor was used, or at least Juan García bought a black slave in 1585. The Garcías also made written contracts in the course of the year with three Indian workers, one from Mexico City, one from the Toluca Valley town of Tlacotepec, and one from Toluca itself.[16] The contracts varied. The most skilled weaver operated on a piecework basis, promising to weave and finish 24 "pieces" of sackcloth or serge in a year at 2 pesos each, paid as he produced each piece, or a total of 48 pesos. If he finished early he could leave, but if not he would have to stay on until the 24 pieces were complete. The other two workers got half the pay, 20 and 19 pesos respectively, plus food, and were simply obliged to weave at a loom for a year. Unlike the first, these two received most of their pay in advance, 14$^1/_2$ and 16 pesos. One of the contracts mentions that the Indian was to live at the obraje, which was also García Carillo's house.

Something more about the Toluca obrajeros' procedures can be deduced from a contract entered into the same year of 1585 by illiterate Alonso de la Peña. Peña bought 200 arrobas of black and white wool from Juan Nieto, a local stock trader and tanner, on credit, and also borrowed 50 pesos in coin. He agreed to pay back gradually in fulled sackcloth (*sayales*) of three types: blue, black, and blue and black, the latter being the most expensive. Nieto was to go on lending him money to supply and pay his workers.

Tanning. If the picture of the obrajeros is incomplete, that of their fellow processers the tanners is even more so.[17] A shoemaker (*zapatero*) and long-time Toluca resident called Francisco González el viejo is the clearest figure. Probably literate, he and his wife Leonor Suárez lived in a house he owned in central Toluca; not far out of town he had an estancia. That he owned a tannery is not certain, but he did run one for the corregidor of Toluca in 1591, processing several hundred cow and goat hides at a time. The building in which the tannery was housed was on the road from Toluca to Zinacantepec. It had two vats, and the plant belonged to the Juan Nieto just mentioned. Nieto never called himself a shoemaker or tanner, and was active in trading wool and stock from as far away as Michoacán. But we can deduce an interest in tanning from a 1585 document in which Nieto hired a shoemaker together with his apprentice. The shoemaker was a free mulatto, illiterate Juan Pérez de Ribera, and his unnamed apprentice was an Indian. The terms were good for Pérez de Ribera: 200 pesos for a year of work, plus meals for himself and his helper, and a 12-peso horse to ride. He received a 20-peso advance, and after that he was to be paid in instalments.

Another possible tanner was a Spaniard by the name of Gonzalo Ruiz. In 1585 Ruiz paid 26 pesos to release an Indian, Pedro Jacobo, who was trained as a tanner, from the corregidor's jail. Pedro was to remove the debt by working at his trade at the rate of 7 pesos a month, with two other local Indians standing good for him. There was also something on the order of a tannery at Tenango in the southern part of the valley in 1591, run for the profit of the corregidor. A Pedro Rodríguez, shoemaker, who was in operation in Toluca in 1585, also probably did more tanning than shoemaking. European crafts for local consumption appear to have been very weak. No blacksmith appears, though there must have been at least one, nor does any tailor;[18] the only carpenter in evidence was a newly arrived Spaniard who promptly entered the service of another person for 150 pesos a year. Toluca must have been dependent upon Mexico City for a large part of its craft services.

Mercantile activity. In the matter of commercial development, there was clearly a place for a class of people who would sell and move products of the valley's estates toward the capital and the mines, and there was also room for some selling of goods from the outside in Toluca, though to a very limited market. It seems that commerce was mainly in the hands of traders based in the valley, perhaps because the movement was more from Toluca to Mexico City than vice versa, and also because the trade was not so intensely profitable that Mexico City merchants would rush to monopolize it. Indeed, the professional merchant of the type common along the trunk line, in Mexico City, Puebla, Veracruz, or Zacatecas, was not a characteristic figure in the Valley of Toluca, despite the high degree of commercialization. One or two people like Sebastián de Goya, who bought and sold wool, livestock, and trade goods, and financed the operations of one of Toluca's corregidores, were polished professionals who probably emerged from Mexico City circles. But only three or four traders appear with the label of merchant (*mercader*).

The valley's most prominent merchants, the Rodríguez Magallanes family (probably originally Portuguese, to judge by the name and their many Portuguese connections), were local people who found their way into commerce from humble beginnings. The elder Francisco Rodríguez Magallanes could hardly make a signature; his son, Francisco Rodríguez Magallanes el mozo, was far better trained—the same phenomenon as with the García family of the obraje. Francisco the younger ran Toluca's principal general store, where he sold all kinds of merchandise (cloth, soap, thread, etc.) in both small and large amounts, and did much supplying of estates. He occasionally made medium-sized loans (150 pesos). He also bought up slaves, horses, and valuables at auctions, then resold them. But it appears that at least as important a part of his business was large-scale buying and selling of valley products. He often acted in company with Toluca citizen Diego Rodríguez de Solís, who was an entrepreneur and financier, but not a declared merchant. It was these two who made the above-mentioned sale of over a thousand arrobas of wool to obrajero García Carrillo in 1585. Francisco Rodríguez acquired from a citizen of Toluca 1,000 arrobas of *nacascolo*, an indigenous dyeing and tanning material, to be delivered in the capital. He also bought 200 pigs and 300 arrobas of tallow from local estate owners, as well as other smaller lots. Perhaps his largest venture of 1585 was to enter a partnership whereby he and a local stockman named Antonio González took a three-year lease on a large sheep estancia in the valley, with over 10,000 head, belonging to a Mexico City hospital.[19] Francisco Rodríguez won the lease in public bidding in the capital; doubtless he contributed finances, his partner the work.

Pig trading. Since the valley had pig farms, it also had pig salesmen. This was the role of Sebastián González. He was of the same type as the lowly farmers, an illiterate immigrant from the area of Ciudad Rodrigo in Spain. But instead of growing animals, he traveled about the country buying and selling them, apparently specializing quite strictly in pigs. He bought them from many sources, including from Toluca Valley Indians, and made buying trips as far as Michoacán. Fattening the pigs sometimes involved him in purchase of maize from Indians and others, but he owned no land. To sell, he traveled often to Mexico City, and to the mines of Temascaltepec. He had dealings with various pork sellers (*tocineros*) of the capital.

Despite his constant travel and lack of land, González had roots in Toluca. Near Toluca's Franciscan monastery he owned a substantial house, the residence of his wife, one of his daughters and some of his grandchildren. He had supplied dowries for two of his daughters (1,500 pesos for one of them), and it was only bad luck that one of his sons-in-law had fled his family and returned to Castile. At his death in 1581, Sebastián's gross worth was very considerable, 6,000 pesos.

Mule trains. Sebastián González had a good deal in common with that other perennial valley type, the muleteer (*arriero*), who was also a mover of goods. In fact, González owned four pack mules and a saddle mule, along with the black slave that so often accompanied a pack train. His son-in-law Francisco Pérez, who by no accident was from the same hamlet in Spain as González, was apparently a full-fledged muleteer. When he died in 1585, his main assets were a horse, a musket, and seven pack mules with their equipment. Some estate owners had their own pack trains.[20]

Petty trade. Another type ubiquitous in the Spanish Indies was the small dealer, peddler, or trader in odds and ends (sometimes called a *tratante*). Elsewhere I have defined the type for Peru in the conquest period. These small traders were frequently foreigners, that is, true foreigners rather than Portuguese, who for many purposes may be considered hardly more than unusually marginal Spaniards. Late sixteenth-century Toluca had a perfect exemplar of the type in Juan Antonio de Venecia, who admitted to being born in Venice as his name indicates. His excellent signature indicates a certain education, but whether because of Spanish stereotypes or because of his own inclinations, he made his living by various petty dealings, using his house in Toluca as a tavern and store. The dimensions of his business can be surmised from his purchase of a cask of sherry from Francisco Rodríguez Magallanes (above), on credit, "to be delivered to my house at your risk," or from the large cauldron he kept in his house to make soap, or from his numerous small debts and credits, in amounts from 3 to 30 pesos. Juan Antonio owned no agricultural properties. In the most remote areas of the Spanish empire, every Italian managed to find another, and here it was no different. Juan Antonio married Francisca Hernández, daughter of a Miguel Corso (Corsican) who seems to have lived in Juan Antonio's house.

Toluca's processers and sellers could be considered two different groups, but had much in common. Both tended to be based in Toluca itself rather than in the countryside. Both apparently got an earlier start than did plebeian farmers and stockraisers outside the encomienda. Whereas almost all the plebeian agriculturalists of the later sixteenth century were immigrants, among the obrajeros and merchants of Toluca we see at least some second-generation figures. The sequence of development was first the encomienda estates (now often in their third generation), then provincial commerce, then independent plebeian agriculture; all had a strong tendency toward stability, up to this time at least.

The official community

The principal purpose of Spanish secular government in Toluca, originally, was to mediate between the capital and the valley's Indians, by collecting tributes and adjudicating Indian disputes and offenses. However, the encomiendas did much of the tribute collection and the Indian communities largely settled their own internal disputes. The official organization was left with little to do but maintain itself. By the latter part of the sixteenth century local officialdom was mostly concerned with the legal business of the valley's Spanish community, and dealt with Indians mainly as they were employed by or came into conflict with the local Spaniards. Usually there was a separate head of government for each of the valley's two main jurisdictions, Toluca (the more densely populated, including the center and south of the valley) and Ixtlahuaca (north and west, but extending as far south as Zinacantepec). The chief officials in each district rotated quickly, but among their subordinates there was far greater continuity. The corregidores and alcaldes mayores rarely brought many people into the valley with them. Each in turn depended on a persisting structure, consisting of deputy, constable, notary, and interpreter, who were stable members of the local Spanish community. In the case of the Toluca district, which will be used as our example because of fuller documentation, all the minor officials lived in the town itself.

The deputy. The person most frequently serving as deputy (*teniente de corregidor*) in Toluca was Pedro Millán, who acted in that capacity for all the corregidores from 1580 to 1594 at least. A long-time resident, he was about fifty years old in 1586, and owned a house in the center of town. He was a notary by profession, and in 1591 affirmed that "I maintain myself by my work, because I have no other income than what I bodily earn by the diligence of my person as a notary public." His registers have not survived, however, and the issuing of public documents was probably not his principal concern. He traded at auctions and frequently served as executor of testaments for local residents; nothing could be more symbolic of his general function than the fact that in 1591 he liquidated the estate of corregidor don Martín Velásquez, who had died in office. Millán had no standing appointment, not even with any one corregidor, but was named deputy on an interim basis as needed. This could mean either a short trip to represent the corregidor in one of the valley towns, or standing in for a few days at Toluca while the chief toured the valley, or taking full charge for weeks at a time when the corregidor was in Mexico City. Throughout 1585 Millán presided in the corregidor's court considerably more frequently than Agustín de Hinojosa, the official occupant.[21]

Another such figure was Francisco Pérez de Vargas, a notary who operated in Toluca in company with his relative Diego Pérez de Vargas for some years. Around 1590 he came into increasing prominence, until after Velásquez' death he served as teniente for apparently about a year, while a new permanent occupant was being named. At any given time there were at least two or three notaries officiating in Toluca, any one of whom might record proceedings in the corregidor's court or serve briefly as teniente. The notaries changed frequently, but at least three families of them, with the names Pérez de Vargas, Solórzano, and Mojica, had more than one representative and took root in Toluca.

The constable. For a time an illiterate Diego Martín was the corregidor's chief constable (*alguacil mayor*), but in 1585 he was gored by a bull during celebrations in Toluca's square, and is heard of no more. His competitor, Francisco Cherinos, both preceded and outlasted him, serving repeatedly as executor, constable, or chief constable for various corregidores from 1582 to 1593 at least. In 1591 and probably at other times, he was at the same time acting as a steward for the corregidor's private interests. He was a literate man, and before 1584 he married the Toluca-born María de Flores.

The interpreter. Of all these figures the Indian court interpreter, Juan Serrano, was the most stable, or at least most consistently present. Though he may appear somewhat unusual, he is actually a good example of a frequent, important phenomenon, the Indian who used his mastery of Spanish skills to gain entry into the Spanish world. Serrano could sign his name beautifully, sometimes in the version "Juan Serrano del Valle" (of the Valley of Toluca, presumably); there can be little doubt of his literacy. One wonders whether he was of plebeian origin or from the indigenous nobility. His lack of the "don" would indicate the former as more probable. Whenever a delegation came to the corregidor from one of the Indian councils, or when a Spaniard made a contract with an Indian, or Indians testified in litigation, Juan Serrano did the interpreting. He appeared in this role as early as 1570, and continued to officiate at least through 1585. Generally he stayed close to Toluca and left the hinterland to others; on these occasions, it often proved that the Tolucan constables and notaries could interpret for themselves if necessary.

It would perhaps be too much to say that Serrano had already become a full-fledged member of Tolucan Spanish society. His marriage partner is unknown. But he had certainly gone a long way toward acceptance among Spaniards. The notaries scrupulously refrained from calling him an Indian, instead referring to him as a citizen (*vecino*) of Toluca like the long-term Spanish residents. Indeed it was only by chance that I was able to confirm

that he was an Indian at all. Serrano's specialty was translating from
Nahuatl, and this sufficed for the great majority of cases. At times it was
necessary, however, to call in an Indian named Lucas de Vitoria who could
translate Otomi; once when both were present the notary made a slip and
referred to the "Indian interpreters," letting the secret out. Serrano appeared
not only in documents concerning Indians, but was considered an adequate
witness to transactions between Spaniards, and even once signed in place of
a Spaniard who was unable to do so for himself. Serrano probably owned a
house in central Toluca, but there is no direct evidence of it. He did own a
valuable property to the west of the city, a wheat or maize farm (*heredad de
pan llevar*) complete with house and pens. In 1582 he leased it for three
years to Diego Mejía de Lagos (the illiterate Portuguese dirt farmer, above)
for 350 pesos a year. A Juan Serrano el mozo, who must have been his
son, was also called a citizen rather than an Indian, and owned land in the
valley in 1585.

The lawyer. Another member of the local legal establishment was
Gaspar de Ribera, *procurador de causas*, or untitled court lawyer. Though
this was not an official position, Ribera had a practical monopoly of the
function of representing both Indian councils and individual Spaniards of
every variety, from 1582 through 1594 at least. The only apparent inter-
ruption to his undisputed reign was the one-time appearance in the records of
an Agustín Ramírez, procurador de causas, in 1591. Ribera also sometimes
served as interim notary for the corregidor. There was not a titled lawyer
with a university education (*letrado*) in the whole valley, as litigants repeatedly asserted. Titled lawyers of Mexico City would sometimes send an
underling to Toluca to carry on a suit; the latter had to run back and forth to
the capital for consultation. Indeed, the most serious cases often began and
ended in the capital, with only the evidence-gathering taking place at Toluca.
Even a skilled physician had to be sent for from Mexico City when a
prominent person was seriously ill; in 1591 a physician and surgeon from
the capital was charging 20 pesos for each day of absence from there. Thus
Toluca was even more dependent in the upper professional sphere than in the
crafts.

The corregidor. The stable official complex just outlined, with its
almost corporate unity and continuity, was headed by a shifting chief
magistrate/administrator. There were at least seven heads of government,
and probably more, at Toluca in the years between 1580 and 1600, three
with the title of corregidor and the rest with that of alcalde mayor. Those
presiding at Ixtlahuaca were consistently called alcalde mayor. All the
known Ixtlahuaca magistrates, and at least three of those of Toluca, were

members of Mexico City encomendero families. It seems that Mexican-born Spaniards were the norm for the more usual, quasi-interim appointments, while appointments meant to last longer often went to peninsular Spaniards, and indeed in some cases originated in Spain. The Toluca post was the more important and the larger plum. While no one appears to have presided at Ixtlahuaca more than a year or two, appointments at Toluca twice lasted at least three years, and another would have done so if the occupant had lived.[22] Some of the men sent to Toluca were close to being administrators by career. Agustín de Hinojosa Villavicencio, corregidor around 1584-1586, was employed in 1591, with the title of "teniente general," in conducting Tlaxcalans north to new settlements in Chichimec territory. His wife, doña Ana de Ovalle, was daughter of the royal factor in Guatemala City, where Hinojosa may have held some post previously.

The corregidor or alcalde mayor of Toluca was supposed to be within the hierarchy of the Cortés estate. However, in the 1580's, perhaps because of the political troubles of the Cortés family in the mid-sixteenth century, there was hardly any mention of the Marqués del Valle. Toluca was generally spoken of merely as being in New Spain, and the corregidor had his authority simply "por su Majestad." From 1590 the connection seemed to come somewhat alive again; at least the estate paid the corregidor's salary, and by the end of the century the Marqués del Valle was being mentioned more frequently at the head of documents.[23] Nevertheless, the corregidores and their subordinates seem to have acted no differently whether they were working for the Marqués del Valle or for the king, so we may leave that factor out of account.

Very little of the ordinary procedure of the corregidores can be surmised from the notarial and trial records which make up the bulk of the Toluca documentation of this time. For history, it is fortunate that one of them died in office, bringing about the preservation of a body of documents (a will, memoranda, claims, statements, liquidation proceedings) that give a good picture of at least the economic role of a corregidor in local society. The example cannot be held up as quite typical for Toluca, because it was on an unusually grand scale. But many of the processes must have been the same no matter who was corregidor, and some do not depend on the intervention of the corregidor at all.

Don Martín Velásquez was born in Iscar near Valladolid, in Old Castile, and seems to have had connections with the royal court, since his nearest relative was a doña Isabel de Salcedo who lived in Madrid, and he had acquaintance with the households of noblemen like don Juan Manrique. Spanish royal authorities named don Martín corregidor while he was still in

Spain, before he had ever seen the Indies. Special importance must have attached to the appointment, since don Martín was corregidor of both Toluca and Ixtlahuaca, with a salary paid partly by the Cortés estate, partly by the royal treasury. He left Seville in 1589 with a fleet that also carried a new viceroy for New Spain. Already he was loaded down with debts—to his sister, to a friend, to a Madrid hosier—and had intentions of using his post for his own economic advantage (a part of his behavior not only necessary but expected). In Seville he made his first commercial investment, in company with a Mateo Vásquez de Acuña, who was also going with the fleet and is elsewhere described as a "merchant of Castile," though at that time he was already a citizen of Mexico City. Don Martín and Mateo Vásquez together bought 172 yards of Milanese cloth from a Genoese merchant for 6,020 silver reales (some 750 pesos), payable in two years or with the next fleet. In all probability, the expected profits from don Martín's corregimiento were the basis of the credit, while Mateo Vásquez arranged the purchase, transport, and sale. It later proved that don Martín did not even know to whom the money was owing. The cloth was probably sold in Mexico City. Except for four casks of wine he sold in Toluca, there is no evidence that don Martín or any other corregidor of this time tried to sell anything for use or consumption in the valley, either to Spaniards or to Indians.[24]

In Havana and Mexico City don Martín accumulated further debts, so that he was in need of acting quickly to improve his fortunes by the time he arrived in Toluca in 1590. He brought with him a Martín Blasco, his steward, and another employee as orderly and aide; whether they accompanied him all the way from Spain is not known. Beyond these two, he had to make use of the familiar local machine: Millán and Pérez de Vargas as tenientes, Cherinos as constable, and the ordinary notaries. All of these people served him in both private and public capacities. Pérez de Vargas and Cherinos bought maize for him, while his hired man Francisco de Zamora became receptor of fines.

Don Martín's basic method in trying to profit from his stay in Toluca was a simple and standard one. He used his official position to obtain various kinds of credit; with that credit he participated in the local Spanish processing industry and bought Indian maize, both activities being oriented toward the outside markets of Mexico City and the mines. The governmental accounting procedures of the time made it relatively easy for him to do this. In the absence of banks, warehouses, and civil servants, it was not expected that an official would have all the money and goods entrusted to him physically under lock and key at any given moment. His signature that certain goods or money had been received merely constituted his personal obligation to deliver them at a future, often indefinite or distant date. Nothing prevented his treating the assets as his own in the meantime. For a corregidor in a provincial town, there was nothing to check such manipulation, and the local administrative machine would quickly teach him how to do it.

One apparent opportunity would be to trade with the tribute maize coming from such Indian towns as were not in encomienda. If don Martín did this, no evidence of it remains. Liquid revenues were even easier to manipulate, and here the evidence is ample. The main money revenue of the corregimiento came from *penas de cámara* (fines for mainly minor offenses) and the more substantial *alcabala*, or sales tax. Though provincial tax collection was spotty indeed, officials in the Toluca Valley made a serious effort to collect a tax on large, publicly known sales of stock, wool, hides, or maize. As to the fines, don Martín apparently treated them as pocket money, meaning to make the amounts good later. The sales tax offered a different sort of opportunity. Since large stock sales and the like were often on a credit basis, the sales tax, which could amount to 200 or 300 pesos, might be the largest immediate outlay on the buyer's part, and if cash were needed, might make the sale impossible. The corregidor could remove the necessity for cash, extending credit at no expense to himself, simply by entering the tax on the books as paid, and accepting the buyer's private obligation to pay him later. The corregidor might receive his return in interest, in a share of the goods sold, or in the good will and cooperation of the buyer.[25] This part of the deal is hidden from direct sight. But when don Martín died in early 1591, after certainly less than a year in the valley, he already owed the crown over 2,000 pesos "in alcabalas, penas de cámara, and other things." No misconduct was charged, and when don Martín's estate paid off the debt, the matter was considered closed.

Alcabala manipulation was one of the principal advantages don Martín had to offer his perhaps most important local collaborator, merchant Sebastián de Goya,[26] with whom he entered into a general arrangement. Goya advanced goods (above all cowhides) to don Martín, as well as small amounts of money to his employees for ordinary expenses. In return don Martín did favors for Goya such as deferring payment of a 200-peso tax on a large stock sale, still outstanding when don Martín died. Don Martín also sometimes reversed the procedure and actually lent money to Goya when any was available—probably out of royal funds. Thus Goya once lost badly in gambling with some local friends (apparently including the corregidor himself), and don Martín lent him 150 pesos.

As far as can be seen, don Martín was putting at least as much capital and effort into exploiting the Spanish estate economy as the Indian maize economy. Mainly through Goya, he acquired a large number of hides for two tanneries he began to operate. This was done under the administration of his steward Blasco, of course, with the actual tanning done by experts. One of these establishments was in Tenango; it may have been more a slaughterhouse and storing place than an actual tannery. The other was the tannery of Francisco González, referred to above. The volume was considerable; between August 1590 and January 1591 don Martín bought some 1,200 cowhides, most at 7 reales (seven-eighths of a peso) each. There were goatskins in smaller numbers. The tanning was well under way before don Martín died. He also had on hand 420 salted cow tongues and 14 arrobas of tallow. But the tannery business dominates his personal accounts.[27]

The other branch of don Martín's commerce was to buy up maize grown by valley Indians, obviously with the intention of reselling it, though his early death left his marketing plans unclear. He did most of his buying from the Indian towns as corporate entities, the transactions being signed in each case by the governor (*gobernador*) and council members. Don Martín's agent in this was Francisco Pérez de Vargas, his frequent teniente. At don Martín's death, Pérez de Vargas had in his possession signed declarations of the councils of six valley towns, obliging themselves to deliver a total of 1,100 fanegas of maize at 5 reales per fanega.[28] If the statements are to be taken at face value, the councils had already received their money in advance.

Though this wholesale, corporate buying accounted for the bulk of don Martín's maize, he also instigated some petty trading that is of equal interest from the viewpoint of the history of social organization. Through Blasco the steward, and Francisco Cherinos the constable, don Martín distributed to the "Indian traders" of Toluca ("los indios rescatadores de esta villa") some 80 pesos with which to buy maize for him. Thus there was a class of Indians devoted primarily to petty commerce, probably making the circuit of village markets as well as trading in the large general market of Toluca itself. Some ordinary Indians, therefore, must have been selling part of their maize individually for cash. Through this avenue don Martín acquired 140 fanegas, most of it at the same price as from the corporations, but some cheaper by a real per fanega.

The corregimiento or Spanish civil administration had a certain importance in that the members of its lower staff were an increasingly stable part of the Spanish urban population of Toluca; through their legal services they facilitated the operation of the valley estates and the movement of both Spanish and Indian products to outside markets. The corregidor himself was a figure of little moment, pushed by his staff into the steps of his predecessors, not rooted enough to serve the community very well as a ceremonial head. Don Martín Velásquez had fine clothes and expensive saddles, and kept three mounts; but his personal entourage was limited to two men, he was unmarried, and he owned neither house, land, nor slaves.[29] The corregidor's need to make quick profits did serve to increase credit somewhat: this and his own entrepreneurial activity gave a certain stimulus to the Spanish estates and the outside market economy, but did not result in any form of endeavor that was not already going on independently.

Ecclesiastics. Quite distinct from the rest of the official community was the ecclesiastical component. Rather than being concentrated in Toluca proper like the other elements, it tended to spread thinly over the valley, with one representative in a given town as the norm. (The Franciscans were a partial exception, as we will see.) The ecclesiastical network of the valley was in its origins a part of the encomienda system, built on Indian provincial structures. Though never quite achieved, the general aim was to have one ecclesiastic stationed in each encomienda's local center, which would at the same time be that vicinity's principal indigenous settlement. This structure was still visible in the latter sixteenth century, though there was by now ecclesiastical representation in important valley settlements whether encomienda towns or not. Six valley curacies appear in the surviving records of the time (probably there were more than that in fact), and there were four Franciscan establishments.[30]

Curates. With the secular priests of the valley, the relationship to the encomienda went considerably beyond residence patterns and original structure. Of the four priests for whom some coherent career information is available, at least two were of encomendero families of Mexico City.[31] This is indicative of a tendency to use the rural benefices in the same way as the corregimiento, to furnish an outlet for the cadet sons of important families of the capital, only one of whom could hold the family encomienda. Thus the position of encomendero was both socially and economically superior to that of parish priest. As we have already seen, the priest sometimes acted as a local representative of the encomendero's interests. All the priests were participating in the Tolucan estate economy in the same way as the encomenderos.[32] And though they had to live mainly in the country, the priests like the encomenderos looked to the capital rather than to Toluca. In Mexico City were their relatives or other associates, with whom they were in constant contact, and for them the culmination of a successful career would be advancement to the cathedral chapter of the archbishopric of Mexico. They were educated men. They had beautiful signatures, and three of them had earned the baccalaureate; perhaps indeed all of them were university-educated, for the title "Bachiller" by this time had such little prestige that its holders often dropped it or used it inconsistently.

The best documented of the rural curates is a Francisco de Aguilar Martel, *beneficiado* of Jiquipilco for years before his death there in 1594. Details from the inventory of his possessions can suggest some of the contours of his life. The estate was liquidated by his legitimate brother Pedro de Salazar Martel, who was with him when he died; other brothers lived in Mexico City. One of these was probably the Baltasar de Salazar, citizen of Mexico City, who owned an estancia somewhere in the northern half of the valley and sometimes farmed the valley's tithes. This in turn makes it likely that both were close kin of Antonio de Salazar, canon of the Mexico City cathedral, who was responsible for tithe administration. Curate Aguilar had a bundle of papers at his home in Jiquipilco recording transactions with Canon Salazar. He also had an account book of his dealings with Pedro Muñoz de Chaves, Jiquipilco's encomendero.

Aguilar owned a considerable amount of property in and around Jiquipilco, much of it bought from the encomendero family. His household in Jiquipilco was not modest. Though he had little furniture, his varied personal effects filled several chests, and itemizing them took four pages of paper. He kept three horses and a mule, and two black slaves (though these may have been associated more with his agricultural properties). This does not imply a lack of priestly diligence on his part, of course, and the elaboration extended to religious necessaries. Among his possessions were two rich vestments, a painting on wood of Christ carrying the cross, and a library of 32 volumes. All the books were on religious topics; most were in Latin, several in Nahuatl, and a few in Spanish. Aguilar had three landholdings in the valley, of which the only one apparently being actively worked was an "estancia y labor" named San Mateo.

What was the impact of a person of Aguilar's type on the local society of a place such as Jiquipilco? Since Spanish estate owners living nearby would be of humble origin, and the lord of the encomienda was usually absent, Aguilar was the local society's highest-ranking permanent Spanish resident, in terms of education and social connections.[33] Clearly he would have great influence with Jiquipilco's Indian council. Much of his time, however, must have been devoted to managing his affairs, and in this aspect he was little more than a standard cog in the Spanish machinery. His effort to mold the behavior and beliefs of his indigenous parishioners was apparently serious and sustained, but its acculturative power was reduced by Aguilar's mastery of Indian languages (so that he did not need to use

Spanish), his isolation from others like himself, and his probable frequent absence consorting with his associates in the capital.

Friars. The religious of the valley's four Franciscan monasteries made up a corps considerably different from the rural secular priests, though in some aspects deep affinities can be glimpsed or surmised. Information on basic characteristics of the Franciscans does not necessarily appear in the notarial and trial records that are the source of this study. The Franciscans definitely stood apart from the economic, commercial, and legal network we have discussed above. About their agricultural activity there is no better evidence than some passing, highly colored remarks in the official Franciscan histories and reports, where the monasteries of the valley are said to have had gardens and orchards with every imaginable European fruit or crop, naturally all in the most flourishing state.[34] The only example given, however, is peaches. One is left with the impression that the Franciscans had little to do with the main branches of valley agriculture. From the total lack of any documentary reference in the many land transactions recorded, it is clear that they did not hold estancias in the usual fashion, nor is there any record that they employed stewards or leased any property.

The allocation of the Franciscans' standard Toluca Valley contingent of ten men (one might estimate the valley's secular priests at about the same number) was four in Toluca and two each for Zinacantepec, Metepec, and Calimaya. At times there was really only one friar at Zinacantepec (and presumably at the other two sites). Thus though there was a nominal equality between the four foundations, each having its own father guardian, in fact the Toluca house was to a certain extent the center of a Tolucan subprovince. Aside from the inequality in number of friars, the monasteries of Metepec and Calimaya were characterized in 1585 as old and small, while the one at Zinacantepec was not yet finished.[35] This clustering of the Franciscans around a Tolucan center distinguished them from the secular priests, who had little or no internal organization, each looking straight to Mexico City.

The notarial records contain one very strong and concrete manifestation of the Toluca house's ascendancy, in an episode replete with interest of various kinds. In 1594, the Indian community of Zinacantepec agreed to pay for the construction of an elaborate gilded altarpiece (*retablo*) for the local Franciscan church. A sculptor or carver (*escultor*) of the capital, by the name of Juan Montaño, was to build it in Mexico City. The total cost was 2,350 pesos, all to be paid by the nobles and commoners of Zinacantepec. This was a massive amount. Even if we should assume that fray Juan de Ulloa, father guardian, who was present as a witness, had forced the arrangement on the unwilling Indians at the cost of severe reductions in their manner of life (and there is no reason to make such an assumption), the transaction still implies considerable economic potential for Zinacantepec's Indian community. It also implies either great influence on the part of the father guardian or a very strong feeling of identification with the monastery church on the part of the Indians, or, most likely, both concurrently. A second aspect is the dependence on the capital and on secular Spaniards for elaborate art work. The building of this retablo is a far cry from the commonly imagined picture of friars directing local Indians in masterpieces of art. Here the only physical contribution planned for the Indians of Zinacantepec was carrying the finished product back from Mexico City. Of course trained Indians probably did much of the work in Montaño's Mexico City shop, but that is another matter. To return to the clarification of the relationship between the Franciscan monasteries in the valley, the important thing about the agreement from that point of view is its repeated reference to the already existing retablo in the Toluca monastery, on which the one in Zinacantepec was clearly to be patterned.[36]

On the basis of the documentation used for this study, I am unable to contribute much to existing knowledge of the role of the Franciscans among the Indians, except that the friars were very likely ultimately responsible for the reasonable level of literacy among the nobles on the Indian town councils, and they must have had something to do with the large numbers of Indians whose surnames were taken from saints or prominent friars. Even concerning the Franciscans' role in the Spanish world, it is only for Toluca proper that one can piece together some information from the chronicles and certain references in the notarial records.

The Franciscan monastery of Toluca was the least "colonial" establishment the valley could show in any branch of life, in the sense of being comparable or not to the same sector in Mexico City. For perhaps thirty years until his death in 1577, the famous linguist and preacher fray Andrés de Castro, who had studied theology at Salamanca, lived in the Toluca monastery.[37] Another noted resident was the Franciscan historian fray Gerónimo de Mendieta, author of the *Historia eclesiástica indiana*, who functioned there in the 1560's, and probably also later.[38] In 1585 there was a newly organized theological seminary in the monastery, by all indications the only one at the time in the whole Franciscan province of central Mexico. This was apparently not intended to be more than a temporary arrangement, however, something on the order of a spiritual retreat; the seminary is not mentioned again.[39]

The Franciscan establishment in Toluca was beginning to serve as a cathedral-like religious center for the Spaniards of the valley. Some of the more wealthy were still being buried in Mexico City, and many had masses said for their souls in the capital's churches, particularly at the cathedral's altar of Nuestra Señora del Perdón. But increasingly Spanish residents of the valley, including those who lived and died in remote parts of it, requested burial in the Tolucan monastery and endowed masses there. The Franciscans had long since begun to serve the local Spanish urban community of Toluca. The church and monastery were on the main square, and except for the adjoining house of Martín, the monastery's Indian constable, seem to have been surrounded mainly by Spanish residences. In previous decades fray Andrés de Castro had already preached a separate sermon on Sundays for local Spaniards; the friars also served as the Spaniards' confessors,[40] and many local Spaniards belonged to the monastery's sodalities (*cofradías*) of the Holy Sacrament, Holy True Cross and Incarnation of our Lord.[41] Little evidence appears on whether or not the friars had kinship ties with other Spaniards, either in Toluca or in Mexico City, as the secular priests did. Later, such ties would be strong, but at this time those few friars whose origin is known were born in Spain.[42] Also the Franciscans in Mexico shifted frequently from one part of the country to another, Mendieta himself being a good example. All in all, the Franciscans were contributing more than the secular priests to nucleation of the valley's Spanish community. Despite their noncommercialism, they had affinities with Toluca's urban commercial and official sectors, while the curates were associated more with the estate system.

Mestizos, mulattoes, and blacks

Mestizos. In the above I have already given several examples of the role of mulattoes and blacks, but some more direct discussion of Hispanized auxiliaries and intermediaries may be useful. The most puzzling feature of the Toluca documentation, on the face of it, is the nearly total lack of mention of any people called mestizos. Since the common denominator of the Spaniards of Toluca was marginality, it is surprising to find those marginal members of Spanish society, the mestizos, so little in evidence. The very few so described turn out to be abandoned figures, crippled or orphaned. There was lame Diego, mestizo, without a surname, who was the occasional employee or servant of pig seller Sebastián González (above); at his death González still had not paid Diego three pesos he owed him. Or there was Lázaro Navarro, mestizo, a boy of fifteen in 1598, who had lost both his father Cristóbal Navarro and his mother Lucía, an Indian woman of

Toluca. He had become the servant and amanuensis of notary Francisco Pérez de Vargas (above) and thus was acquiring a better education than a mestizo waif might ordinarily expect.

Even allowing that the largest number of mestizos should be where there were the most Spaniards (Mexico City), and that the proliferation of mestizos may be a later phenomenon than once thought, it seems to defy common sense that there should be more mulattoes than mestizos in the Toluca Valley. The apparent explanation is that most of the mestizos who were born in or entered Toluca were being reabsorbed among the Spaniards. One may suspect that many of the valley representatives of the encomendero families were mestizo, but in the absence of baptismal records or more wills like that of Peribáñez de Gamboa, this is impossible to prove. Also the wills of valley residents are full of mentions of natural daughters who received dowries, and doubtless managed to marry impoverished newcomers, as in the example of pig raiser Antonio Tavera's daughter. It is fair to presume that many, probably almost all of these natural children were mestizo. Nevertheless, in Toluca, with such a strong first-generation and immigrant element, the time of the mestizo had not yet come. After another twenty years the picture must have changed considerably in this respect.

Blacks and mulattoes. Assessing the role of the clearly-labeled free mulattoes is less difficult. Theirs were the same low-level, low-prestige, but often skilled, responsible, or supervisory tasks that had been the domain of blacks and mulattoes ever since the conquest period.[43] Mulatto shoemaker Juan Pérez de Ribera, with his 200 pesos a year and his Indian helper, could stand for them all. There were also mulatto estate foremen and hired hands, as well as mulatto muleteers, some working for Spaniards and some owning their own mules. Some were illiterate, while some could sign painfully, and some signed exquisitely; their pay scale also varied, in the same general range as for humble Spaniards. A mulatto named Gaspar de Maluenda, who did some sort of agricultural work, lived in Toluca for many years in the house he owned next to Pedro Millán the notary and Francisco González the shoemaker, until he finally sold out in 1582 for a good price, 330 pesos. In contrast to the frequently seen free mulattoes, free blacks were very rare. The only one appearing in the records is a Juan Grande who bought some small items at an auction in 1592. An endless procession of blacks and mulattoes, slave and free, were pressed into service as criers at auctions, etc., according to the demands of Spanish custom. Most of them never appear in the records more than once, and no truly professional black town crier is known.

Slaves were numerous, mainly black with an occasional mulatto; owners gave little apparent regard to their ethnic origin, or whether they were Mexican-born or not. The women were frequently house servants; most of the men, as the reader will have noticed, were scattered all over the valley on farms and estancias. Hardly a good-sized property was without its one or two black slaves—but never more than that. The mere manner of their distribution tells us that they cannot have been mainly responsible for the actual labor of agriculture, that their function must have had to do with maintenance or supervision.

Some hint of how these people lived, along with much insight into the general position of mulattoes and blacks, is contained in some litigation carried on in 1584 between a mulatto woman, Agustina Sánchez, and a prominent Toluca citizen named Francisco Gómez Maya, chief of a numerous clan of Spanish (or more probably Portuguese) stockraisers, farmers, and traders. Agustina Sánchez, usually called just Agustina mulata, was suing Gómez Maya for wages, while he in turn accused her of theft, ingratitude, and misconduct. Agustina was a free woman, but for a decade she was married to Juan Zape, Gómez Maya's black slave; to judge by his name Juan was probably born in the Sierra Leone region of West Africa.

Gómez Maya owned a stock farm (estancia de ganado menor) of which sheep were the main asset, but which was devoted also to a diversified agriculture. Named Jicaltepec, the estancia was near San Pablo (Autopan, doubtless from Nahuatl Atocpan), an Indian hamlet or barrio in Toluca's immediate jurisdiction, some three or four miles to the north of the town, on the Lerma river. Juan Zape and Agustina Sánchez lived together on the estancia, she fixing his meals and washing his clothes like any wife for a husband (by the standards of that period). At this time she dressed mainly in the style of an Indian woman. She and Juan must have been able to speak fluent Nahuatl or Otomi, or both, as well as Spanish. As all trial witnesses agreed, Gómez Maya was always in Toluca, and hardly ever came to the estancia, while Juan and Agustina lived constantly in the country and came to Toluca only for Sunday mass or on holidays. Juan was clearly in charge of the estancia; "there was no one there to serve."

After a time, Juan and Agustina modified their way of life. While he continued his residence on the estancia, she went to live in the neighboring Indian village of San Pablo, in the house of an old Indian woman named María Xochitl. The plan was that Juan would come once a week to bring supplies; Agustina, with presumably better facilities and more help, would prepare his meals and send them to him. However, Juan brought quantities of mutton, bacon, cheese, maize, salt, chile, and even wool, and Agustina developed the practice of selling the excess for cash to San Pablo's Indians through the agency of María Xochitl. Naturally Agustina and Gómez Maya had different opinions as to the legitimacy and volume of such transactions.

Juan's death around 1580 put an end to these arrangements. Probably Juan died of the great pestilence of those years, which also affected Agustina, for she was in Gómez Maya's house in Toluca many months, recovering from extreme debilitation. After she was well, her position in the Gómez Maya household was very ambiguous. She had long been a dependent; she now received free bed and board, washed the family linen, and guarded the house when the family went to mass. But she was not content to be a servant. The Gómez Mayas claimed that she used the interval when they were at mass to steal wool and sell it to Indian women who came to the house. However that may be, Agustina had indeed become an Indian trader through her years at the estancia (unless she had been one even before that). Though she had begun to dress more richly, completely in the style of a Spanish woman,[44] she still spent much of her time in the country. She often came to San Pablo to stay with María Xochitl, bringing meat, cheese, and wool from Toluca for María to sell. By now she was accustomed to attend the periodic markets ("tianguis" in the Spanish records, from Nahuatl *tianquiztli*) in the many hamlets around Toluca. All this brought increasing tensions with the Gómez Mayas, and finally she broke with them, married a local mulatto named Miranda, and began to sue them for wages in return for services done.

The story of Juan Zape and Agustina Sánchez reveals once again that despite the multiplicity of their activities, blacks and mulattoes in thickly-settled areas like central Mexico or Peru almost always, in one form or another, played the role of intermediaries between Spaniards and Indians, a function still unchanged in the Toluca area in the third generation of Spanish occupation. A final symbol of that function might be Agustina's friend Angelina Paxan, born in Cuauhtitlan in the Valley of Mexico, who was considered a mulatto woman, being half black, half Indian;[45] she was the servant of a Spaniard and had lived in Toluca for fifteen years, but she gave legal testimony in Nahuatl rather than Spanish.

Indians

Only a small proportion of the Tolucan notarial records and court proceedings of the years 1580-1600 deal with Indians in any direct way. Given an indisputable, overwhelming continuity of Indian language, residence pattern and agriculture from the still recent time of conquest, there is no better way to arrive at some sense of the social dynamics of the Indian population than to estimate the probable impact on them of the Tolucan Spanish community described above.

Servants. By the general norms of the Spanish Indies of the time, the valley's several hundred Spaniards, mestizos, mulattoes, and blacks would have required at least that many Indians to serve them, clean their houses, work in their kitchens, and groom their horses. Such Indians, located not only in Toluca proper, but in secondary centers like Ixtlahuaca and Zinacantepec, and also on the Spanish rural properties, were on their way to becoming permanent Spanish dependents, outside the Indian communities and heavily exposed to Spanish techniques and language. None of the main activities of the Tolucan Spaniards—neither stockraising, obrajes, nor tanneries—called for large amounts of short-term, unskilled labor, of the type usually channeled through the *repartimiento* (draft rotary labor) at this time.

Repartimiento labor. Indeed, the records make no mention of an internal valley labor repartimiento, though there must have been some such obligation, to help plant and harvest crops for the minority of true farmers, and also for the pig raisers, who grew some of their own fodder. The only repartimiento appearing in the records is the one for the mines of Temascaltepec, which were far from Mexico's largest or richest. The labor draft was administered not by the corregidor of Toluca, but by the alcalde mayor of the mines, who sent a constable into the valley to collect the Indians. Sporadically from 1582 to 1629 the Indian council of Toluca appealed for enforcement of a viceregal decree that repartimiento Indians in Temascaltepec should be paid wages for the days of their journey, that the miners' blacks should not steal their food, that they should not have to carry ore in their blankets, work on Sundays and holidays, or go into the actual diggings—all of which prohibitions were repeatedly violated.

Skilled and other permanent workers. But the main Spanish demand was for a smaller number of more permanent workers; servants, shepherds, weavers, and tanners.[46] The most skilled, the weavers and tanners in Toluca, must have been very few, but we do know that such people were present, as seen above. In the case of one large estancia there is also specific mention of that permanently resident corps of Indian shepherds (see note 19) which must have been a feature of most such Spanish properties. Indians were also working for Spaniards as muleteers, and there was an Indian silversmith in Toluca.

It is a notable, though expected, fact that many of the servants and skilled Indian workers came from outside the valley. The silversmith, a Francisco de Frías, was from Mexico City; so was one of the weavers.

There were servants from as far off as Puebla to the east and Chiapas to the south. Some of the muleteers were born in the nearby mining towns. It was these same people who were most likely to be Spanish speaking or *ladino*.[47]

Almost all of the work contracts between Spaniards and Indians at this time concern Indians with some special skill or qualification, or at most females who served as housekeepers. It is apparent that contracts with most resident Indian servants, stockwatchers, etc., were not being formalized. And indeed the amount of money involved would hardly have warranted it. Even the skilled Indians rarely got above 30 or 40 pesos a year, less than half the pay of the most humble Spaniard or mulatto; permanent work of a less skilled nature can hardly have commanded more than perhaps 15 to 20 pesos in cash.

While debt was often involved in the work contracts, deliberate and large-scale attempts to use debt to try to hold workers were not in evidence. First of all, some contracts involved no advance or a small advance (see the first of the weaver's contracts discussed above). Very often the Indian had been jailed for theft, loss of valuables, or debts to another party, and the new employer redeemed him by making good the debt or loss. That the debt per se was not the primary holding device can be seen in the fact that the Indian employee often had to present other Indian residents as guarantors. These characteristics can be seen even in the contract that approaches most closely to the (now antiquated) notion of agricultural "debt peonage" of all those in the Toluca records of this time. In 1594 in Zinacantepec, the illiterate, non-Spanish speaking Indian Luis Nicolás agreed to work for Spaniard Juan Esteban, an equally illiterate, marginal agriculturalist of the area, who was then leasing the encomendero's maize, wheat and pig farm (see above). Certainly the destiny intended for Luis Nicolás was to guide one of the farm's yokes of oxen. Luis Nicolás was to work off a $16^3/_4$ peso debt at the rate of 2 pesos a month, or 24 a year. But Juan Esteban had not advanced him that amount, nor sold him goods. Luis was already in debt, owing $6^1/_4$ pesos to a merchant of Toluca, 7 pesos to a relative of the encomendero, $2^1/_2$ pesos to the deputy alcalde mayor; he owed Juan Esteban at that point less than a peso. An Indian of the noble class, don Juan de Tovar, the only literate member of the trio, guaranteed Luis' presence until the obligation should be removed.

Independent activity. Some Indians in and around the valley were operating in independence both of Indian communities and Spanish employers. They, too, often came from outside, or had connections with the outside. The most outstanding example was an Indian Jusepe Martín, trader in pigs, a citizen of the Santa Catalina subdistrict of Mexico City, who appeared in Toluca in 1585 and bought 115 fattened pigs from corregidor Hinojosa for no less than 1,035 pesos, half to be paid in 40 days, and the rest in 80. (Transactions between Spaniards often gave the deadline for payment in days in even tens, but 40 and 80 are round numbers by preconquest standards, making it appear that the purchaser was still operating in terms of the indigenous vigesimal system and its twenty-day months.) Jusepe Martín did not know Spanish, and could not sign his name. With a person like this operating on such a scale, one cannot help thinking of the *pochteca* or long-distance Nahua merchants of preconquest times, even if pigs had been introduced by the Spaniards. Some local Indians also sold pigs to Spaniards. Some Indians owned mules; a Pablo de la Cruz, who could sign his name reasonably well, bought two mules from a Spaniard in Calimaya in 1585, for 55 pesos. He must have been operating as a muleteer on his own.[48] So was Indian Bartolomé Gutiérrez, born in Zinacantepec, who had another Indian in his hire, taking mules back and forth to the mines of Sultepec. It seems likely that the nobility also participated directly in the Spanish economy; when don Francisco de San Cristóbal, gobernador of Zinacantepec, sold 66 pigs to a local Spaniard, he presumably did so for himself rather than in the name of the community.

Maize and markets. Individual sale of maize for cash at the local markets was a persistent feature of the valley's economy. It was carried on in part by a class of near-professional traders or rescatadores, referred to above in connection with corregidor don Martín Velásquez, who used them to acquire maize for resale outside the valley. In that case the sales were petty, but the total amount could be very considerable. In 1594 the viceroy, in an attempt to control the price of maize in Mexico City, named a judge to go to Toluca, repress the rescatadores, and license Spaniards who would buy maize in the various valley markets and bring it to the Mexico City granary for sale.[49] Whether the Toluca market was as renowned and rich as it has since become; whether transactions were predominantly cash, credit, or barter; and just what was the nature of the products sold, are all questions that the records leave unanswered. But we may say that at least some products of the Spanish estate economy were being traded, and that some cash buying took place. The general tianguis was held in Toluca's main square as would be expected, and by 1591 it was a Friday market, as it has been ever since.[50]

It still appears that more surplus Indian maize was reaching the Spanish economy through the Indian community corporations than through private trading. The corporations not only delivered tribute maize to the local officials or the encomenderos, but made commercial sales to Spaniards, of which those to the corregidor in 1591 are the most fully recorded (see above, and note 28). The communities sold both to local stockraisers and to buyers from outside the valley.[51] Payment in advance of the harvest seems to have been the norm for these transactions. Sometimes there was conflict between the desire to sell and the necessity of paying tribute. In 1585 the Cortés estate seized 800 fanegas of maize belonging to the Indian community of Toluca, claiming that amount to be owing as back tributes; the Indian council regained possession with a local Spaniard as their guarantor in case a final higher court decision should go against them. Though the records sometimes refer to the "maize of our community," there is little information on the important question of whether such maize was cooperatively grown on land set aside for that purpose, or whether it was grown individually and then collected. The Capulhuac trial (see below) refers once to the "milpa de nuestra comunidad," hinting at a common field in that case.

Pulque. Another form of Indian enterprise was producing and selling the native alcoholic drink pulque for local Indian consumption. Though illegal, the pulque trade flourished in all Indian towns. When things were slack, the corregidor could always make some money by touring the countryside and fining *pulqueros* in what amounted to a desultory liquor tax. In 1593 alcalde mayor Alonso Valadés, accompanied by perennial constable Cherinos and a notary, went on an inspection tour of the central and eastern part of the valley, to combat pulque and check on fulfillment of a viceregal order that Indians should raise chickens. Not a single chicken was found anywhere, but all the towns and villages had from 3 to 30 producers of pulque who sold their product in their houses from large jars, and freely admitted the offense. They received a standard fine of 15 reales, perhaps the value of the contents of two of the large jars, since the usual price was a real for a big pitcher and half a real for a small one. Most were able to pay, but at one little place where almost the whole population was selling pulque, there was not enough money, so the corregidor agreed to be content with the 46 pesos they could raise among them, which came out to a little over 10 reales each.

In the town of Atlapulco (considered a *cabecera*), some pulqueros from the surrounding district were already in the public jail. They were interrogated individually, and a list of them can help give us some notion of what sort of people pulque sellers usually were. From the barrio of Almaya were Miguel García, councilman (*regidor*) and Alonso de Aguilar, chief steward of the local church (*fiscal*). From the barrio of Taxcaltitlan came Lucas Tebyatl and Melchor Tux,[52] both *tepixques* or ward chiefs. From Tianguistengo came Antón de León, cantor in the church, and Juana Tlaco, a widow. One single person, Lucas Hualacitl of Taxcaltitlan, was a tribute-paying commoner (*macehual*). Thus it would appear that mainly people of some position were selling pulque, perhaps because of greater exposure to Spanish monetary commercialism, perhaps because they had a greater need for cash than others, but most likely because their position made it easier for them to influence others to buy.

Spanish law. At least a few local Indians were beginning to use the forms and agencies of Spanish law to settle their internal affairs. We find them, like Spaniards, not hesitating to throw each other in jail for debt. Some of the nobles legalized their inheritance of land through formal statements of mutual recognition. One case involved tension between noble and commoner over their respective rights. A dispute arose in 1593 between don Juan Bautista, a noble of Zinacantepec, and an Indian couple named Pablo Nicolás and Juana. Pablo and Juana had been occupying a house and lot in Zinacantepec, along with some maize land; they had built additions to the house, and finally claimed it as their own. But don Juan asserted the property was his, having belonged to his grandparents before him. The upshot was that Pablo acknowledged don Juan's possession, and don Juan paid 2 pesos for the improvements. Here, although the noble won the larger point, we also see persons from the lower sector of the indigenous world gaining some redress through the use of outside leverage.

Indian names. In the absence of fuller information on the Indians, discussion of even so apparently external a matter as their names can help advance our knowledge. All Indians by now had Spanish Christian names, and many had surnames in Spanish as well. Yet there was a separate naming system, and a majority of Indians bore names which would have been recognized as belonging to indigenous people even if notaries did not consistently add the epithet "indio." Most of their first names were shared with the Spaniards, though some, like Pablo, were almost exclusively Indian property. It was the surnames that were quite distinct. The three most common types were: Nahuatl names; names taken from Christian saints or dogma; and Spanish first names as last names (arising generally from abbreviation of a saint's name as a surname). Indians of the nobility often bore the surname of prominent friars (Castro, Mendieta) or of the local encomendero family (Sámano in Zinacantepec, Altamirano in Calimaya). A certain number of Indians bore simple Spanish patronymics like Hernández or Gutiérrez. These things surely have a social and cultural meaning, though interpretation cannot be unambiguous. Clearly the priests and friars were originally responsible for the religious names. It is tempting to think that the patronymics were often assumed from the humble local Spaniards for whom many Indians worked; it is definitely true that Indians from

outside the valley often bore Spanish plebeian surnames. The proportion of
the name types varied from one group to another, and from place to place.
Thus the prominent Indians of Toluca bore mainly saints' names; most of
the ordinary population of the smaller, remote settlements still had
indigenous surnames.[53]

Language and literacy. A command of the Spanish language was
apparently still rare among the Indians of the valley, including the nobles
and councilmen, and even the Spaniards' servants and skilled employees.
Looking through the records, one might be led to suspect that the interpreters were insisting on the speaking of Indian languages to preserve their
jobs. But numerous isolated cases where "indios ladinos" spoke for themselves show that there was little reluctance to recognize Spanish-speaking
ability where it existed. It would appear that the ordinary language for
Spanish-Indian discourse must have been Nahuatl, or else there simply was
remarkably little Spanish-Indian discourse, with mulatto, black, and mestizo
intermediaries carrying the main burden of communication between the
sectors (probably very few of the first-generation Spanish and Portuguese
immigrants achieved much in the way of learning indigenous languages).
As honeycombed as the valley was with Spaniards, no large-scale, speedy
process of direct mass Hispanization was taking place. As to literacy, ordinary Indians were innocent of writing skills; the Indian employees of the
Spaniards were little different. Even among the nobles and councilmen not
everyone could write, though I never saw a case of an Indian entitled "don"
who could not somehow scribble his name. While the evidence does not
extend beyond signatures, there is much to be deduced from that alone.
Some of the autographs are fluent and impressive; several of the Indians
were able to vary the signature with the occasion, adding "alcalde," "fiador,"
or "testigo" as appropriate. There are several indications of an ability and
inclination to write phonetically, as with the Indian don Carlos de Sámano,
who, since his own language did not distinguish the pronunciation of *c* and
g, signed his name "don Garlos." Though a minority accomplishment, the
ability to write was spread widely over the valley, and every Indian town had
its two or three council members who could sign their names and who
doubtless kept Nahuatl records, the later loss of which must be lamented.

Indian councils. Though Toluca was a *villa* (town) and the others only
pueblos, the recognized larger settlements of the valley all had the same
political organization: a gobernador (almost always "don"), who from
fragmentary evidence seems to have been replaced almost as quickly as the
rest of the council; one or two *alcaldes ordinarios* or judges; some regidores
or councilmen; and an alguacil or constable. Often additional nobles

(*principales*) joined this group on important occasions; the council ordinarily consisted totally of Indians who were or passed themselves off as nobles, for in the documents we see often the words "the councilmen and other nobles."[54] This sort of organization was not confined to the important towns which were headquarters of a parish or an encomienda. Indeed, the Spaniards seemed uninterested in distinguishing the rank of towns. Even those settlements which were considered barrios, directly dependent upon larger entities, had their councils. The "pueblo o barrio" of Cuapanoayan, somewhere near Ocoyacac and too small a place to be included on a corregidor's tour, nevertheless had its gobernador don Juan Buenaventura and its alcalde. At the lower levels, some at least of the towns had officials with the title of *tepixque* or *tepisque* (Nahuatl *tepixqui*, "keeper of people"), a carryover from preconquest times.[55]

Familiarity with Spanish legal practices was also quite widespread. In 1584 the council of Capulhuac in the east of the valley waged an adroit battle against the encroachment of a Spanish farmer, although the outcome of their effort is not known. The Spaniard was able to get a grant in the Capulhuac area of some land that seemed to be out of use. But before he could begin exploitation, the Indians hastily put in an irrigation ditch and planted beans. The Spaniard complained, and the corregidor arrested the main figures of the Indian council, but they claimed they were ignorant of the grant and had been in active possession all along. Thereupon they were set free to go to Mexico City to consult with their lawyer, Licenciado Villanueva (remember the Villanueva Cervantes who was deeply involved with valley affairs). Though authentic representatives of Indian interests, the councils were always being subjected to local Spanish influence of various kinds: from the resident priests and friars, from the encomenderos, and not least from the estancias and farms that shared the countryside with them. The weakest point in the Capulhuac council's case was that several Spanish and mulatto employees of nearby estancias had seen the Indians digging the irrigation ditch after the Spanish claimant had already been given possession.

Coexistence more than acculturation. The Indians of the Toluca Valley retained immediate control of the region's primary asset, maize agriculture, and were in the culturally strong position of a majority on its home ground, retaining its own language. Though a formidable complex of Spanish structures penetrated the whole valley and impinged upon Indian lives in every aspect, we cannot but be impressed with the remaining extreme marginality of the Indians from the point of view of the Spanish world, and the apparently slow penetration of Spanish cultural influence into the Indian core. All quick Spanish social and cultural influence that one can detect in records of the kind used here is tied closely to the literal insertion of Spaniards into the area, or to the literal detaching of Indians from the community milieu to be thrust into the context of Spanish structures. The example of the Tolucan Indians of this time implies a greater role for the simple accretive growth of Spanish-mestizo-mulatto society, and a lesser role for acculturation or diffusion, than I for one had previously imagined to be the case.

Toluca as a Spanish province

Despite the residence in Mexico City of the encomenderos and the Indian character of the formal municipal government, Toluca by 1580-1600 had become in the essentials a "Spanish" town, much like any other in Mexico. Its social-economic organization was no different from Mexico City's. In each case the wealthiest and most influential residents were Spanish, clustered in the center of town, and pushing the Indians, many of whom were their employees and dependents, toward the edges. Around each town lay a hinterland of Indian settlements and Spanish estates, of which each was the commercial-legal center.

Of course Toluca was markedly provincial. Its Spanish population was chiefly involved in the production, processing, and movement of goods toward the Mexico City market. This of itself would not necessarily mean total dependence, but combined with the capital's proximity, it resulted in a still rudimentary development of the Spanish professions and crafts during the latter sixteenth century. The nearness and predominance of Mexico City were the ultimate reason why Toluca remained formally an Indian town. Toluca's provincial character showed itself above all in the nature of the Spanish inhabitants. Fray Gerónimo de Mendieta was perfectly correct when he asserted that most of the Spaniards who lived among Indians were of little account, "de poca suerte."[56] That is, they were the new immigrants, the humble, the poor, in all ways the marginal members of Spanish society, who of necessity sought an opportunity away from the capital in a less competitive situation.

In the Tolucan case, a very strong Portuguese element was present, particularly in agricultural activities, but penetrating into commerce as well. This was apparently quite a general phenomenon in the provinces; Woodrow Borah has noted the importance of Portuguese farmers, estate managers, and muleteers in the Tulancingo region around 1640.[57] That the Portuguese were already so numerous and well established in the Toluca Valley by 1580 indicates that the influx of Portuguese nationals had little to do with the union of the Spanish and Portuguese crowns, but was rather part of an overall secular pattern of emigration from Iberia to America. The importance of immigration into the valley should not be taken to mean that the Spanish community was transient; most adult Spaniards, both newcomers and native, made local marriages, almost always to Spanish women born in the vicinity.

The tendency of the encomendero families to look to and reside in Mexico City left the plebeian stockraisers as the valley's wealthiest permanent residents. While the stockmen tried to emulate the encomenderos in many ways, they did not follow them to the capital. Rather they were by 1600 showing an inclination to make the town of Toluca their seat. It would appear from the later dominance of families like the Albarráns and Pliegos that the Mexico City aristocrats continued to retreat from the area (without giving up a strong role in its economy), and the plebeian stockmen gradually became the local aristocracy, up to a point, always with tacit recognition of the preeminence of Mexico City. Even in 1600 they were beginning to seek honors and titles in a modest way.

Toluca's situation thus had yet another standard provincial characteristic, great stability. All over Spanish America the rate of turnover of personnel was greatest, and the rise and fall of fortunes was quickest, where there was great wealth, in places such as the capitals, the mining towns, or important entrepôts.[58] It cannot be mere coincidence that rare names like Pliego, Albarrán, Tavera, and Arratia have persisted in Toluca over the centuries. The framework established in the sixteenth century continued unchanged in the mid-eighteenth. Villaseñor y Sánchez, writing at that time, tells us that maize and pig products for the Mexico City market were still the basis of the economy. Toluca was still an Indian municipality, with its Indian gobernador and council; the Franciscans still held forth on the plaza. But within this framework a quiet revolution had taken place, for the town now held 618 families of Spaniards, mestizos, and mulattoes, to 412 families of Indians.[59] The implications of this situation for the rest of the valley can well be imagined.

From the Tolucan case one can deduce that any area of sedentary, maize-growing Indians within the orbit of a major Spanish center would attract a group of humble Spanish settlers by the second or third postconquest generation, and that this group even though not vast in numbers would become in many ways the region's social and economic upper class, gradually giving the local Indian governments an increasingly fictional character if taken as representing the overall regional social and economic structure.[60] We would expect the strength of the provincial Spaniards to be greater in Toluca, near the Hispanic population and market power of Mexico City, than it was in remote Oaxaca, and greater in Oaxaca than in yet more remote Chiapas. But everywhere we must be prepared to recognize the early active penetration of secular Spaniards, Spanish auxiliaries, and Spanish forms into the Indian countryside as the principal cause of social and cultural change in the provinces.

13. The Magistrate of Zacualpan

To the west of the highland Valley of Mexico, which has held the capital and social-economic center of the country from preconquest times until today, lies the yet higher and cooler Valley of Toluca; south of that, past the great Tolucan volcano, the land falls off into a maze of lower mountains and ravines where the Spaniards in the years after the conquest discovered silver deposits and established some mining camps or towns, of which Taxco was the largest and Zacualpan one of the smaller. By the latter sixteenth century there were ore refining mills at Zacualpan using the same mercury amalgamation process as at Taxco or at the even greater northern sites such as Zacatecas, so that Zacualpan, like them, had its *alcalde mayor* or chief magistrate to collect revenues, regulate mercury supplies, and maintain order.[1]

During the early 1590's some complaints were heard about the doings of the then alcalde mayor, a Diego de Santa Cruz Orduña; Santa Cruz even came once to Mexico City to testify in his own behalf, but that failed to put the matter to rest. On Thursday, the 18th of June, 1592, the viceroy of New Spain secretly commissioned a Mexico City notary to go to Zacualpan and take testimony as official receiver of evidence. Such things were hard to keep secret, however; almost immediately the alcalde mayor's brother-in-law, an influential Mexico City resident, got wind of the impending visitation and hastened off to warn Santa Cruz. Measured in a straight line, Zacualpan is only some sixty or seventy miles southwest of Mexico City, but the terrain puts straight lines out of the question, and in the sixteenth century the trip took three or four days. By Monday the 22nd of June, the brother-in-law had arrived, and the alcalde mayor was scurrying about making preparations: giving the keys of the royal chests to their proper custodians; stamping the *coronilla* or property mark of the crown on bars of silver that had been left without it; pressing the miners to pay deferred duties.

By the time the receiver and his aide left Mexico City on Tuesday the 23rd, a lieutenant of the alcalde mayor was hurrying back north from Zacualpan to Ixtapan (on the edge of the district toward the capital) to look out for him and send word of exactly when he was to be expected. Though the lieutenant told the Indians of Ixtapan to be on the watch, he seems to have napped considerably himself, and he nearly missed his man. On Friday afternoon the 26th, on the edge of town, he became aware of a Spaniard on a horse, followed by another rider, a small Chichimec (that is, an Indian of the north country), and a third Indian leading a packhorse which carried the bedding. They said they had come from Mexico City and were accompanying a gentleman who had gone ahead. The lieutenant rushed on into the center of town and found the receiver at the priest's house, claiming to be going only as far as Malinaltenango, on private business; but not deceived, he quickly wrote a letter to his chief and sent it off by an Indian messenger.

So when the receiver got to Zacualpan on Saturday the 27th of June, things were all ready for him, as he soon came to realize. Nevertheless, he took testimony from the alcalde mayor's obliging enemies and had the accounts examined (though by accountants whom the alcalde mayor himself suggested). The viceroy and high court in Mexico City took no strong action against the magistrate as a result of the investigation; instead, he continued for a fairly normal three-year term until November of 1593, when in Zacualpan's public marketplace another notary proclaimed a *residencia* or official review of his actions in office.

Papers from both investigations have come down to us. For all their incompleteness, unintended bias and intended deception, they tell us much about the manner of accommodation of various potentially conflicting elements. If we mistakenly took royal directives literally, we would suppose officials of the importance of an alcalde mayor to be single-mindedly dedicated to collecting royal revenues and regulating local economic activity in the crown's interest. But in effect, participants in the local economy, lower officials who were also local figures, and upper officials coming from the outside all allied to their respective individual economic advantage, not in any full-scale opposition to the imperial government, but in a general tacit agreement which served the locals first and larger governmental interests second.

Zacualpan was more a district than a town, and its mines and small camps were scattered about over the very broken terrain of the jurisdiction. When the receiver came in 1592 he found that "most of the witnesses who have to be examined are at their refineries, in the camp of Atizapan and in other ravines and in places a league distant and more." A little off to the south was "the camp below," Texicapan, which had a church and a square and rivaled Zacualpan. In the whole area there may have been some fifteen to twenty *haciendas de minas* or silver refining mills with their accompanying underground diggings, since a total of 22 "miners" or *mineros* appear in the 1592-93 records (by and large the term "minero" was synonymous with "mill operator," and many of those so named specifically mentioned their enterprises; see Table 1). Production in 1591-92, as measured by the amount of silver taxed, was at an average annual rate of close to 22,000 marks—hardly a fifth of the rate of the great Zacatecas mines in those years, but still appreciable.

Each miner standardly employed a *mayordomo* or general manager and under him several Spanish technicians, accountants, and foremen; these directed a crew of quite skilled permanent workers (some of them black slaves and some Indian wage workers) and a much larger number of carriers and diggers (mainly Indians, some of them on short-term tribute labor obligation) who made up the enterprise's *cuadrilla* or gang. A miner had constant need for ready cash, to pay his staff, build and maintain stamping mills and other equipment, and make crucial purchases: from the crown, mercury, and from private individuals reagents, maize (the staple of the Indian workers), and other supplies.

Both supplies and credit for the local miners came in good part from merchants who maintained stores in the two main camps of Zacualpan and Texicapan. Eleven or twelve merchants (depending on one's criterion) are named in the 1592-93 investigations, compared to the 22 mining entrepreneurs (see Table 2). Some were well educated and well capitalized, some were more marginal in both respects, and one was actually illiterate, but all did much the same things. They sold general merchandise from Mexico City in their stores, which were usually taverns as well—part of their business was with the overall camp population including Indians. The core transactions, however, especially for the better established merchants, tended to be larger ones into which they entered with mine operators, selling them supplies in large lots, and sometimes giving them credit or lending them money, or both at the same time. Some merchants kept mule trains which went back and forth to Mexico City, though there were also independent muleteers.

As to the mine operators, none were entirely illiterate, but neither did most of them have pretensions to high birth or connections. Mainly they were good ordinary Spaniards in their 40's and 50's who had come to own a mill through a lifetime of work in the industry (compare Table 1). Prominent among them were the Gómez brothers, a whole faction in themselves: Bernardino Gómez, in his later forties, operator of one of the largest enterprises in the area; Gregorio Gómez, about 40, also an important miner until his mill building collapsed; and Martín Gómez de Peralta and Gómez Sotelo, in their early thirties, still dependent on the older brothers and not above getting into fights. The Gómezes tended to act as if they owned the whole area, demanding respect and preferential treatment from merchants and officials, and they had been known to have former employees beaten up for

Table 1.

Miners of Zacualpan in the time of Diego de Santa Cruz Orduña

Name	Description	Age in 1593, where known
Alonso Alvarez Alderete	citizen (vecino) and miner (minero)[a]	34
Lope de Angulo	miner	50
Antonio de Betanzos	miner, has refinery in Texicapan, lives there	43
Toribio Díaz de Güemes	miner	57
Martín Flores	citizen and miner, resident in Texicapan	50
Bernardino Gómez	citizen and miner	46
Gregorio Gómez	citizen and miner	40
Juan Gómez Corchón	citizen and miner at Texicapan, son of Alonso Gómez, miner	35
Martín Gómez de Peralta	citizen and miner	30
Rodrigo López	citizen and miner	60
Alonso de Nava	citizen and miner	61
Benedito de Novera	miner, majordomo for Agustín Guerrero	50 or over
Bartolomé Romero	miner	44
Juan Sánchez de Gamboa	citizen and miner	30
Pedro Sánchez Marín	citizen and miner	
Juan Bautista de Orozco	citizen and miner	
Bartolomé de Santa Cruz Aguilar	citizen and miner	33
Gómez Sotelo	miner	30
Lorenzo Suárez (de Figueroa)	citizen and miner	57
Capt. Antonio Velásquez	citizen and miner	55
Juan Velásquez de León	citizen and miner	25
Don Amaro Velásquez	citizen and miner	23

[a]It may be that those called "citizen and miner" usually had their own refineries, while those called only "miner" usually ran refineries for others.

wanting back pay. These were to be the greatest enemies of the alcalde mayor. His greatest supporters, on the other hand, were the Velásquezes. Their holdings may have been no larger than those of the Gómez brothers, but they were the only family at the mines to bear certain titles indicative of social pretension and position. The father was Captain Antonio Velásquez, and the son, don Amaro Velásquez, not only was the only Spaniard in the entire region with the title of "don," but his beautiful signature betrayed an aristocratic education in Mexico City; there was also another young member of the clan who was a miner, Juan Velásquez de León, probably don Amaro's cousin.

Merchants, miners, and their employees accounted for the bulk of local Europeans, but some few grew livestock for mine supply, practiced service trades, or were petty dealers in various other local materials and, like the Portuguese *tratante* Gaspar González, did not earn the title of "merchant" (*mercader*). Around the square of Zacualpan, near the *casas reales* or royal building where the alcalde mayor had his residence and headquarters, there lived some people with accounting and other skills who depended on helping with local governmental work as well as serving the mining economy directly. Precious few inhabitants were not caught up in mining in one way or another. The more established miners and a few other Spanish residents married (sometimes to each other's daughters) and raised families. There was therefore room for a schoolmaster, one Juan de Fromesta, "master of teaching boys." But he too went into accounting and keeping keys, and eventually became official distributor of Indian labor in the district. A second generation was coming of age, sometimes a fancier version of the first like the already mentioned don Amaro Velásquez, who was "citizen and miner of Zacualpan" as his father was; another group, at a lower level, ran together and drew the older generation's disapproval for going "gambling and whoring around these mines."

In the camps and mines, people of varied ethnicity—Spaniards, mestizos, blacks, mulattoes, and Indians—rubbed shoulders in a context where the Spaniards, though often not a majority, set the tone. In this ambience even the Indians were frequently not strictly local, but from a radius of fifty miles or more in all directions, and sometimes from even further afield. The rough wet forests of the area from Taxco west had never been a major area of indigenous settlement. Nevertheless, there were some Indian municipalities with their own town councils and lands, liable to the alcalde mayor in the crown's name for certain obligations—royal tribute, road repair, short-term mine work—but otherwise locally autonomous. One such community, the smallest, was at the original site of Zacualpan (Nahuatl Tzacualpan, "where the pyramid is"), not far from the mining town named after it; Ixtapan (Nahuatl Iztapan, "among salt"), on the main road to Mexico City, was another, and Tonatico (Nahuatl Tonatiuhco, "place of the sun") was a third. The first two felt pressures from the constant traffic between the mines and the capital, but the people of Tonatico, off the usual route, claimed that no one bothered them. The Indians of these towns and others from farther away

Table 2.

Merchants of Zacualpan in the time of Diego de Santa Cruz Orduña

Name	Description	Age around 1593, where known
Sebastián de Bohorques	merchant (mercader) with a store	35
Antonio de Gaviola	merchant, Basque	50
Gaspar González	petty trader (tratante), Portuguese	53
Juan de Hornaz	citizen and merchant	
Juan Núñez de Safi (Zafín)	merchant, tavernkeeper	35
Alonso Lucero	citizen and merchant	
Gaspar Martínez	has a store at the mines	27
Diego de [Menoz?]	merchant, has store at the mines	36
Ortuño de Novia	merchant, has store in Texicapan	45
Juan Ortiz de Frías	has a store of merchandise at Texicapan	45
Bernardino de la Puente	citizen and merchant	32
Lope Rodríguez Carvallo	merchant, resident, tavernkeeper	

also took part in the mining supply business, coming as individuals with maize and ore-refining salts, which they sold in the marketplace to whoever would buy them.

As in the Toluca Valley (and elsewhere), any new alcalde mayor arriving in Zacualpan for his three- or four-year term had to operate through local officials and quasi-officials who had been there before he came and stayed after he left. The same two or three figures were aides, accountants, and custodians of the keys for one alcalde mayor after another. The notary public, who had the monopoly of legitimizing major transactions of any kind, was a prime member of this local semiofficial community, and with time in any such situation tended to become de facto head of it. Gerónimo de Tovar, the notary of the early 1590's, had been in Zacualpan for over twenty years. He had married off one of his daughters to an important miner, and his son Francisco, though one of the local young rowdies, also stood in for his father as clerk and notary on occasion. Diego de Santa Cruz, when he first came in as alcalde mayor, was to ally himself with Tovar and listen to his counsel, and through his whole term he would often, during periods of absence from Zacualpan, name him *teniente* or deputy to carry out all his functions, just as with his exact counterpart Pedro Millán in the Valley of Toluca.

As an influence on the alcalde mayor, Tovar was probably the most important local person. But within the formal hierarchy, and measured as a power rather than as an influence, the more prominent figure was Juan de la Peña, *alguacil mayor* or chief constable. The nature of the post of chief constable varied greatly from place to place; in Zacualpan it was auctioned off among persons considered qualified, who were generally already local residents and who held it for periods of time rather longer than the terms of the alcalde mayor. Peña seems to have entered office not long before Santa Cruz Orduña, but he was still there (if under fire) in 1595, two years after the latter vacated. There was also a considerable social distinction between the two posts. The chief constables were more plebeian. A predecessor of Peña's had been the relative of a barber. As to Peña himself, his signature was as modest as the approving epithets his supporters gave him, "honest man," "honored person," and the like, never breathing a word about gentle birth. The chief constable was intended to be the principal executive arm of the alcalde mayor. He also maintained the jail, and appointed and directed one or more lower constables, who were responsible among other things for forcible debt collection—a vital function where credit was so important and business failure frequent. While there is no certain indication that he was a native of Zacualpan, Juan de la Peña had lived in the area for at least a quarter of a century. For years before becoming constable he had maintained residence at Texicapan, carrying on various kinds of entrepreneurial and supply activity, though he was not exactly a merchant. He owned a mule train and sent it to distant salt flats for reagents, or to good agricultural areas for maize, in either case to be sold to the miners. He owned two different small bakeries where Indians prepared for sale loaves of wheat bread that were "the worst and smallest sold in these mines," according to an enemy. A black slave woman of his, aided by Indian employees, sold quarters of fresh beef in the marketplace. It is not entirely clear whether at this time Peña's house was also a tavern, inn, and store; at any rate he had quite an establishment, with many family members, guests, slaves, and employees.

Even after Peña acquired the constable's post he seems to have continued to spend most of his time at Texicapan, and when the alcalde mayor was gone, Peña would serve as his deputy in that camp. Indeed, buttressing his economic position there would seem to have been his main purpose in becoming constable in the first place. On taking office, he disguised his activities slightly to avoid the appearance of conflict of interest. The mule train was sold (to good friends and possibly fictitiously), while the dealing in reagents and maize continued. Peña entered into partnership with a Juan Ortiz de Frías, who ran for the both of them a general merchandise store and tavern not far from Peña's house. The bakeries and meat business went on as before. By some accounts Peña also lent money at interest to miners, but with him this was far from being the core activity that it became with the alcalde mayor.

At the time of the visitation, there were a few complaints of the constable's neglect of duties and precautions, especially with the jail: "the jail of these mines is nothing; all it is is a little room about to fall down, and the blacks and Indians they arrest can take the roof off, and it's not a jail or anything else, and it has no shackles except the stocks, and it's impossible to guard anyone in that jail"—not to speak of having Indian men and women together.

But most of the charges leveled at Peña had to do with use of official influence to further his private economic interest. Whether the accusations were well founded or not (and they were more or less successfully ignored), they are indicative of ways in which minor local officials often gleaned advantage from nearly salaryless and not very honorific posts. Enemies charged that Peña had the marketplace of Texicapan moved so that it would be next to his tavern. (The reply was that the front door of the church, looking onto the old plaza, had fallen into disrepair and become dangerous, so it was shut up and the side door used as the main one, with the plaza being moved correspondingly. The move itself and its effect for Peña were not denied.) The constable was said to have taken strong action against the sale of pulque (the staple indigenous alcoholic drink) to the Indian populace, except for tolerating one Indian pulque dealer established next to his house and selling for him. Similarly he was supposed to have confiscated all the wine measures in town to prevent Christmas carousing, except that he left the measures in Ortiz's store untouched. He was said to assure himself of the very best meat at the official butchery concession, and to warn Indians in the marketplace to buy his meat and wine and no other. When Indians came from afar to sell maize and salt, he is supposed to have encouraged them to sell at impossibly high prices, then at the end of the day bought up their unsold stocks for resale, with the result that Indian sellers stopped coming to the mines. Peña and witnesses friendly to him challenged most of this, and established that the Indians continued to come selling supplies at moderate prices, but they made little attempt to deny the extent of Peña's business activity.

To return to our protagonist the alcalde mayor, beneath the technicalities of officeholding and trading in silver his story is a classic and simple one: a marital and financial alliance between the highest local official and the strongest local social-economic interest, in order to facilitate and make more profitable reinvestment in the local economy. Diego de Santa Cruz Orduña was a man of about forty at the time when he was alcalde mayor of Zacualpan, and was considered by his friends to be an "important person, hidalgo and cavalier." From several indications we can conclude that he was born in Mexico City of a line going back to the early conquerors of New Spain, the kind of family that one would expect to be, by the late sixteenth century, aristocratic and well established, with a tradition of holding encomiendas. Both of the alcalde mayor's surnames, Santa Cruz and Orduña, occurred among the conquerors, and surely we can connect him with a namesake who was a citizen of Mexico City at around the same time, had a licentiate's degree in law, and was "son and grandson of the first conquerors of New Spain and Mexico City." But if there was any encomienda in the immediate family, Diego must have been a younger son who did not inherit it. Second sons and other non-inheritors in these circles might enter the clergy or the law, or they might go from one area to another undertaking short-term local judicial-administrative assignments like the magistracy of Zacualpan. Thus Santa Cruz may well have held other such posts previously, though that is not known.

Concurrently with receiving the Zacualpan appointment, Santa Cruz made a splendid marriage, probably his first despite his maturity, for a family's younger sons had a hard time getting established, and generally only the established married. The bride was doña Isabel de Salcedo Legazpi, also of old Mexico City families on both sides. To understand the essence of the marriage, however, we need to know that doña Isabel's brother was Ruy López de Salcedo, encomendero of Zacualpan and Tenancingo (a sizable Indian town just to the north of the Zacualpan area on the way to Mexico City). The double encomienda was not a very large one in terms of tribute-paying population, with only a little over 600 Indian tributaries in both areas put together. Moreover, the then encomendero was a citizen and resident of Mexico City rather than of Zacualpan, just as his predecessors had been before him. Yet in a sense he was Zacualpan's leading social-economic figure. Above and beyond its base of a steady tribute income, an encomendero family had the advantage of having been prominent in its area from the first years after Spanish occupation; and in addition to primacy it had a steadiness and generational depth not matched by other kinds of local interests, especially in a place where the main local activity was something as up-and-down as silver mining. The family would have its head in Mexico City (or other large city), but it would keep younger or poorer relatives and employees in the encomienda area and make whatever investments there which seemed most appropriate to the family's long-term interests. The encomendero family had an unmatched prestige in its traditional area, not hard to turn into official influence and economic advantage, and it had official perquisites of considerable economic potential beyond simple tribute revenue. For example, the encomendero of a mining area had first call on buying small lots of silver refined by means other than amalgamation, and Indian mine workers and other small operators produced substantial amounts of such silver.

Whatever the exact source of the wealth, the Salcedos were able to give doña Isabel, and hence her husband, a very impressive dowry, by most accounts 22,000 pesos in silver coin. The entire nominal annual production of the Zacualpan silver refineries was worth only some seven times that much, about 160,000 pesos. Santa Cruz and doña Isabel took 5 or 6 thousand pesos to the mines with them when they first went out in fall of 1590, then the rest came from the capital city in two or three instalments after some months. The whole amount became a revolving fund to be lent to Zacualpan's miners at interest. Surely the entire arrangement was a package deal. The Salcedos must have already counted on Santa Cruz being alcalde mayor of Zacualpan before they agreed to the marriage; they must have intended from the beginning that the dowry be lent to miners. The nature of the return on their money is not known to us. They may have been silent partners in some of the mines, perhaps those of the Velásquezes; they may have received important favors from the alcalde mayor, such as undertaxing their non-refinery silver purchases; they may have received a percentage of the alcalde mayor's lending profits, or used him as a channel for further profitable loans; they may even have discounted the dowry, giving Santa Cruz in fact 16,000 (as some versions have it) instead of the nominal 22,000, knowing that at some future time the Salcedos would recover the larger amount. However it was, they clearly viewed the arrangement as vital to their interests; otherwise at the time of the 1592 visitation the encomendero would have sent a messenger, not rushed off to Zacualpan in person.

Hardly were Santa Cruz and doña Isabel settled down in Zacualpan's royal building than there appeared an urgent need for their capital. The dean and leader of the Gómez brothers, Bernardino, was deeply in debt to the immediately preceding alcalde mayor, Gaspar de Valdés, and was on the point of being hauled off to debtor's imprisonment in Mexico City (sending the owner to distant prison was often the final ruin of a mining enterprise). A loan of 1,500 pesos saved Gómez, and then Santa Cruz and his wife continued with loans for current expenses until Gómez owed them over 7,000. Almost the same occurred with Lorenzo Suárez, another of the largest miners of the region, who owed money to the previous alcalde mayor and to other persons as well. Santa Cruz arranged a loan for him from a priest residing in another district, then went on to lend him, eventually, as much as he had Bernardino Gómez, perhaps more. And so it went. The pair lent Pedro Sánchez Marín 12,000 pesos, Rodrigo López 6 or 7 thousand, another miner 2,000, another 1,000, and at least five others unknown a- mounts. Indeed, there is little reason to doubt a witness' statement that they lent money to nearly all the miners in the jurisdiction. It is hard to tell in many cases whether the amounts mentioned are totals of many small transactions (some of them trades rather than loans) and thus count the same money more than once, or are actual accumulated debt. What is clear is that Santa Cruz and doña Isabel were reinvesting.

The terms of the loans were standard for the time and place, of just the type that merchants in the mines frequently made. The miners had a great need for coin or reales (8 reales to a peso); the silver they produced was in principle negotiable once it had been taxed and given the official stamp, but the large ingots could not be broken up to pay wages or to make incessantly necessary small purchases. The primary form of lending was that the lendor gave the debtor reales coming from the mint in Mexico City, expecting payment in stamped silver within a varying term, most often between 40 and 60 days, discounting the silver by five reales per mark. At the mint, a mark of refinery silver was worth about $7^1/4$ pesos, or 58 reales; in loans, the lender gave only 53 reales for each mark to be paid back (the same discount applied in straight trades of reales for silver). Of course, silver was better than nothing at all; if the lender was out of reales but had stamped silver on hand, he lent this, to outer appearances without interest. But the effect was the same. Since he received the full 58 reales in return, he gained over the de facto lower value of silver in the camps, and imposed on the debtor the transportation charges to Mexico City, risks, minting fees, commissions, and the like.

Thus Santa Cruz and doña Isabel most often gave reales for silver, and only occasionally large amounts of silver for future reales. Apparently much of the lending and trading was done bit by bit, day to day, as the miners needed cash, with no documentation more binding than a receipt or an entry in an account book. One of the younger Gómez brothers told how he would go for Bernardino to the alcalde mayor's house and get 15 or 20 marks' worth of reales for current mining expenses, sometimes paying in silver immediately. The pretense was maintained that doña Isabel alone was doing the lending. When debts accumulated beyond a certain point, the debtor would grant a formal letter of obligation, mentioning only doña

Isabel as the creditor. The obligations specified payment dates, but in fact
there was much stalling. Bernardino Gómez undertook in June 1591 to pay
1,027 marks by the end of August of that year. Instead he went along
delivering small amounts from time to time, entering them on the back of
the contract. By June 1592 he had paid only 170 marks, by March 1593
something over 500 marks, by November of that year 625. Much still
remained to pay when Santa Cruz left Zacualpan, transferring the debt to a
Captain Maldonado (a relative of the encomendero and possibly the
incoming alcalde mayor). Of course this was an extreme case, in which the
alcalde mayor's eventual loss of patience and attempts to force collection of
debts to himself and others embittered the Gómez' to the point where they
made serious accusations against him, and during the latter period of his
term they went months without speaking to him.

When Santa Cruz had accumulated enough silver through repayments, he
would send it off, either by a merchant's mule train or with a Juan
Melgarejo who was close to being his employee, to be changed into reales
in Mexico City by his standing agent there, a mestizo merchant and cacao
dealer named Pedro de la Palma, who was stationed near the Dominican
monastery north of the capital's main square. After the trade at the mint, the
reales were sent back to Zacualpan to be reinvested. Santa Cruz seems to
have maintained a steady open account with Palma, since on one occasion
he was able to command a draft of 1,000 pesos without sending along any
silver.

Nearly all of the above activity could have been carried out in much the
same style by any individual fortunate enough to have 20,000 pesos in cash.
In what way was it advantageous to be alcalde mayor? Perhaps the largest
single factor was that the alcalde mayor was in ultimate charge of such local
debt collection machinery as there was. And then, the mere fact that he was
first instance judge of all local disputes and person chiefly responsible for
the distribution of short-term Indian tribute labor among the miners, as well
as royal tax collector, made him a figure whom miners might want to please
by borrowing from him rather than from others and by paying him back
promptly.

But the office afforded much more specific quasi-legitimate means for the
magistrate-lender to further his business and help his clients. A miner paid
a 5 percent royal tax on all silver he presented for stamping; he also paid the
crown 110 (after October 1591, 100) pesos for every hundredweight of
mercury he consumed (an expense usually some four times as large as the
tax). As to the tax, the only pressing obligation on the alcalde mayor was
to send it all in to Mexico City in time to make the more or less yearly

fleet for Spain. Within that limit, there was nothing to prevent him from accepting acknowledgments instead of silver, and indeed up to a certain point he was encouraged to do so, since crown officials had no desire to ruin miners and reduce their own revenues. As to mercury, mercury payment schemes were so complex and so frequently changed that they were even easier to manipulate than the silver tax. As a result, the alcalde mayor was in a position to extend important credits without interest when he saw fit. On the one hand this helped his debtors and made his loans more attractive. On the other, the alcalde mayor could defer payment to the king while taking cash or silver repayment of his loans for himself, hastening his rate of reinvestment. Santa Cruz was frequently accused of this shady though not blatantly illegal practice, which he of course denied.

Related practices merged into the area of the frankly illegal, though some of them would have been essentially no more detrimental to the crown than the deferred payments. The alcalde mayor could simply take the king's silver and trade with it, being sure that the proper amounts got to the capital city on time. There were, it is true, certain obstacles to this sort of manipulation. When any silver accrued to the crown through duties or payments, the alcalde mayor was to stamp it with the *coronilla*, signifying crown ownership, before placing it in the royal chest. Santa Cruz failed to observe this regulation strictly, leaving at times half of the king's silver without the property mark; he told subordinates he left the mark off the smaller pieces so that they could be used for making change. Though this rings a bit hollow, there is no doubt that previous alcaldes mayores had done the same.

The second obstacle was the existence of multiple keys and locks to the royal silver chest. There were three important repositories in the thatch-roofed, partly adobe royal building: off to one side, the mercury storeroom; in an outer chamber of the alcalde mayor's dwelling quarters, a chest with the royal marking irons; and further within, in his bedroom, the chest for the silver of the king. For each repository there were three keys, all three needed for opening; the magistrate was to keep one, the notary a second, and an elected delegate of the miners' community the third. In point of fact, except in times when a visitation loomed, the alcalde mayor seems to have kept all the keys to the mercury and the silver himself, and shared only those to the marking irons. Even these were usually in the hands of semi-dependents who lived close by. In the case of the mercury and silver keys, Santa Cruz long refused to give them out unless the authorized holders would offer financial sureties, which they in turn refused to do. In his second year Santa Cruz saw to it that a nephew of his was elected miners' delegate, but he failed to give the keys even to him, most of the time. As damning as this may seem, once again there is no doubt that predecessors in the office had followed exactly the same practices, and as to the key to the marking irons, it was the miners themselves who petitioned that their forever absent delegate be relieved of it and it be given to someone closer at hand so that they could mark silver when they needed to.

There was actually an even simpler way to get around the problem of the king's chest—not to put the silver there in the first place. One witness said that in all the times he had been at the royal building he had never seen anyone open the chest for the crown's silver, that the alcalde mayor simply put what he had collected for the king in his own room.

Santa Cruz was accused on one instance of a potentially truly serious type of disservice to crown interests: conspiring to have silver miss the fleet so that he could continue to trade with it. Witnesses claimed that when the important miner Lorenzo Suárez came to present over 600 marks of silver, during the time when fleet preparations were going on, Santa Cruz rejected it, saying it was too poor (that is, with too high a content of the lead used to make large bars adhere). Then on the very day after the shipment of crown silver for Mexico City had left, Lorenzo Suárez' Indians were seen to approach the royal building bearing a number of big silver bars, and there was great murmuring on the square. Though Suárez himself denied that the alcalde mayor had anything to do with the timing, the receiver of evidence openly expressed his suspicions to the contrary.

When merchants lent money to miners, they almost always combined this activity with sale of supplies of various kinds. The advantages to the lender were many; he could force goods onto the cash-hungry miner that the latter did not really need, he could disguise the true interest rate by charging prices higher than he otherwise would, and above all he could become the steady general supplier or *aviador* of a certain miner clientele. The alcalde mayor certainly seems to have understood the attractiveness of such procedures. In the early part of his term he brought in significant amounts of maize to sell, and he supplied Bernardino Gómez with 150 bushels of reagents. Then for the later period we hear little of these enterprises, leaving us to conclude that the magistrate gradually decided it was better, in his position, to concentrate on money lending and liquidity.

We have already seen that Santa Cruz brought doña Isabel with him to Zacualpan and that she had a much more than ornamental part in their overall plan. Other relatives came as well, and they too found some place in the scheme. In the first months of the alcalde mayor's tenure, the most prominent of these was Melchor de Legazpi, a nephew (or other junior relative) of doña Isabel's. He seems to have been intended for the role of

Santa Cruz' principal aide, alter ego, and active business representative. He lived in the royal building and was frequently deputy when Santa Cruz was gone. It was he who at first did most of the trading in reales with the miners, though people understood that it was for the alcalde mayor "because he was young and poor and didn't know when payment was due on the reales he gave." Several times he took a merchant's mule train to the Valley of Toluca to buy maize, which he stored in a room next to the alcalde mayor's place and sold to the miners. But despite his impressive start, Melchor did not work out well. He began to presume on his connections, borrowing horses and money from local people and telling them his senior relative would approve and pay them back, when such was not the case at all. Santa Cruz argued with Melchor and removed him from the silver trade. Long before the magistrate's term was out, Melchor had left Zacualpan. Someone said he had gone—perhaps half-exiled—to "China" (that is, the Philippines).

Another person with family ties to the alcalde mayor was Juan Sánchez de Gamboa, miner of Zacualpan, who was married to the magistrate's niece. It is not known how long Sánchez de Gamboa had been at the mines, and the records shed little light on his role. More in the forefront was Bartolomé de Santa Cruz Aguilar, in his early thirties, nephew of the alcalde mayor, or to be precise nephew once removed, son of Diego de Santa Cruz' first cousin. Bartolomé came to Zacualpan before the alcalde mayor had been there a year and bought (doubtless with financial help from his relatives) a refining plant already in operation. The very next year, 1592, the alcalde mayor convinced the miners (or enough of them, for there was some difference of opinion) that they should elect Bartolomé as one of their two delegates (*diputados*), posts which ordinarily rotated among the best established of their number. One miner believed that Santa Cruz did it "to honor his nephew and make his reputation, since he was so newly arrived in these mines." It was also advantageous to have one of the miners' principal official representatives in one's pocket, and further, as we have seen, there were considerations of access to keys. Bartolomé was still delegate and still operating a mine in late 1593, when the alcalde mayor left office.

This then was the substance of the commercial and familial complex which Diego de Santa Cruz integrated into the operation of the office of alcalde mayor of Zacualpan. There were yet other formal and informal perquisites of the post that worked in a general way to his advantage. The chief magistrate was usually a respected member of Mexico City society; that plus his various powers made his home (especially if he was married) the natural focal point of the mining town's social life. The alcalde mayor was expected to entertain. Santa Cruz did so, and also allowed (or perhaps organized) gambling on these occasions. Different people told it differently. According to some, the alcalde mayor charged so much a pack of cards, and the miners lost thousands of pesos to him. It was claimed that Bernardino Gómez alone lost 2,000 pesos, a good starting point for the great enmity if true. Someone else estimated the grand total of the losses at 300 pesos. Don Amaro Velásquez said that "on holidays the citizens of the mines, some of the important ones, would come together at the house of the alcalde mayor and play at cards"; they would send out to the store for the cards, and little money was involved.

An undisputed informal prerogative of the alcalde mayor was to take a little for himself in "long weights" when he weighed and marked silver; some did complain, however, that Santa Cruz abused the privilege. Another practice was that when the alcalde mayor granted possession of a mining claim or settled a dispute over one, the party or parties involved would voluntarily donate (usually to doña Isabel) "two picks" (*dos picos*) in the mine, that is to say, the product of two Indians working in the mine every day. If the donation failed to come voluntarily, Santa Cruz would send someone around with a pointed request. Often the two picks would be sold back to the miner for sums reaching 200 pesos, in what amounted to a fee or rake-off for granting possession (circumventing official directives that the maximum fee for this service should be 2 pesos). Another source of petty money was the road repair fund. The person holding the official butchery concession in Zacualpan was obliged to give the alcalde mayor up to 200 pesos a year for needed repairs of roads and bridges. Since horses, mule trains, and people on foot were the main traffic, there was no huge need for improvements, and anyway one could have the Indian communities do necessary road work for virtually nothing, so that, as one witness said, the magistrates had always spent the 200 pesos however they wanted.

Other prerogatives were related to the alcalde mayor's role as principal royal authority over the Indian communities of the district. One small emolument was that Indian litigants always gave him presents of fowl and fruit, just as they had done with their own judges in preconquest times. And as with their own rulers they were prepared to help construct and maintain his house (i.e., the royal building). In fact, however, they did not always donate their services, for the accounts show several instances of substantial pay to Indian artisans and day laborers for construction work on the royal building. The privilege Santa Cruz used most liberally was that of re-questing Indian bearers, sometimes to bring things from the surrounding area to Zacualpan, but more especially to go from Zacualpan to Mexico City. As often as once a month he sent off parties of from three to eight

Indians bearing honey, salt, boxes of candles, and boards for his house in
Mexico City, which he seems to have kept open in addition to his residence
in Zacualpan. Accounts varied as to the bearers' pay; estimates of what
private individuals paid for sending an Indian to Mexico City as bearer or
messenger went from 6 reales to 16, and Santa Cruz himself was said to
have paid from 6 to 12 (perhaps different amounts at different times). The
essential advantage to him seems to have been not that bearers cost him
nothing but that he could command them at will.

We need not presume that absolutely all alcaldes mayores at mining
camps carried on large-scale lending to the miners, nor that they were as
elaborately and irrevocably tied to local interests as Diego de Santa Cruz
Orduña was. Still, we have seen that his general procedures in many ways
varied little from those of his predecessors, and that the immediately preceding occupant of the office had also been a large lender. Nothing Santa
Cruz did came as a shock to his superiors in Mexico City. A high court
judge reviewed the papers from the 1592 visitation, which showed all of
Santa Cruz' activities in full bloom, and concluded that though there were
violations of the letter of the instructions as to marking and guarding the
king's silver, carrying on trade, and deferring payments, nevertheless the
crown had received its due, at least from fleet to fleet, and there was no need
for punitive action beyond having the alcalde mayor pay the costs of the
visitation. Santa Cruz' record was indeed a very good one when it came to
having the silver delivered by fleet time; for the fleet of 1591 he came
within 150 pesos of the amount due, and for the fleet of 1592 he actually
delivered a 2,000-peso surplus, probably the unintended effect of some
sudden change in regulations or prices (compare Table 3).

On consideration, it seems entirely possible that the package deal aspect
of the alcalde mayor's arrangements extended to the high Mexico City
officials who made the appointment, that is, that they were aware of Santa
Cruz' marriage, the size of the dowry, and its probable use, and that Santa
Cruz' solvency was a condition of their appointing him. It was all very
well to let penniless magistrates in remote non-revenue-producing districts
pilfer from the king to scrape together a bit of capital, but this would not do
where royal revenues were counted in the thousands of pesos and royal
monies circulated in the tens of thousands. The alcalde mayor needed to be
well enough off that he was somewhat immune to the grossest of temp-
tations. Not even Santa Cruz' enemies accused him of substantial outright
stealing, saying he was too rich to need to do such a thing.

Table 3.

Zacualpan silver production, mercury sales, royal taxes, and treasury remittances under the administration of Diego de Santa Cruz Orduña, 1591-92

Silver marked	Peso value	Corresponding amount of mercury used	Mercury value and price	Royal twentieth	Remittances to treasury
(Oct, 1, 1590 to March 19, 1591 for the 1591 fleet:)					
11,721 mks, 5 oz	84,862	101 cwt, 83 lb, 5 oz	18,531 ps at 110 per cwt	4,243 ps, 1 r	13,305 ps, 5 rs (April, 1590)
(March 19, 1591 to Oct. 26, 1591 for the 1592 fleet:)					
12,611 mks, 4 oz	91,300	109 cwt, 57 lb, 9 oz	19,941 ps at 110 per cwt	4,565 ps, 1 r	1,362 ps (April 26, 1591) 7,257 ps (Sept. 7, 1591)
[(Oct. 1, 1590 to Oct. 26, 1591:)					
24,333 mks, 1 oz	*186,162*	*211 cwt, 50 lb, 14 oz*	*31,472 ps*	*9,808 ps, 2 rs*	*21,924 ps, 5 rs]*
(Oct. 27, 1591 to April 27, 1592 for the 1592 fleet:)					
10, 789 mks, 1 oz	78,110	93 cwt, 74 lb, 3 oz	15,508 ps, 6 rs, at 100 per cwt	3,905 ps, 4 rs	3,702 ps (Nov. 16, 1591) 3,717 ps (May 9, 1592)
[(Oct. 1, 1590 to April 27, 1592:)					
35,122 mks, 2 oz	*264,272*	*305 cwt, 25 lb, 1 oz*	*46,980 ps 6 rs*	*12, 713 ps, 6 rs*	*29,343 ps, 5 rs]*
(July 4, 1592 [incomplete]:)					8,854 ps,7 rs

mk = mark; p = peso; r = real

The type of lending Santa Cruz engaged in was certainly tolerated—in view of its prevalence one might even say encouraged—by high crown officials. Credit supplied by merchants was irregular in supply and, if there is anything at all to the constant wails of both miners and officials, it was unduly disadvantageous to the miner. Most of the miners of Zacualpan heaped praise on Santa Cruz and doña Isabel as their saviors; essentially only those who had trouble paying back complained, and they only until such time as they could pay. At the very end of Santa Cruz' time the

Gómez brothers had made some progress in paying, and then even they showed signs of coming around. If it had not been for the chronic problems of the Gómez interests, extending through the terms of at least three magistrates, there would very likely never have been any serious questioning of Santa Cruz' activities at all.

Some said that the alcalde mayor had hurt the merchants, even driven them out of the business of lending and extending credit. This seems a great exaggeration. Merchants continued to demand forcible collection of debts which miners owed them in sums up to 1,000 and 1,500 pesos. The miners appear to have needed and used all the loans and credit that both magistrate and merchants could supply. But the alcalde mayor, endowed with the largest lump of capital, which was also the most readily reactivated because of the prerogatives of the office, had the steadiest supply. As one miner said, "sometimes the merchants in the camp had no reales, and you could get them from doña Isabel."

Thus despite apparent aspects of dubious legality, Diego de Santa Cruz' term in office was used, with crown tolerance, for the reinvestment of a large amount of money (doña Isabel's dowry), ultimately derived from the Zacualpan mines, back into those mines, to the profit of the alcalde mayor and the encomendero family, and to the economic advantage of Zacualpan's mine operators.

Abbreviations

AGN Archivo General de la Nación, Mexico City.

ANS *The Art of Nahuatl Speech: The Bancroft Dialogues*, ed. by Karttunen and Lockhart.

BC *Beyond the Codices*, by Anderson, Berdan, and Lockhart.

CH Works of Chimalpahin, Zimmermann edition.

FC *Florentine Codex: General History of the Things of New Spain*, by Sahagún, trans. by Anderson and Dibble.

NMY *Nahuatl in the Middle Years*, by Karttunen and Lockhart.

TC *Testaments of Culhuacan*, ed. by Cline and León-Portilla.

The Nahuas *The Nahuas After the Conquest*, by Lockhart.

TA *The Tlaxcalan Actas*, by Lockhart, Berdan, and Anderson.

Notes

Preface

[1]Where I felt it necessary or advisable, I have made changes in the previously published items to reflect the subsequent evolution of my ideas or newly discovered relevant facts, and I have also made certain stylistic and terminological adjustments. The emendations, however, are overall of little moment.

[2]*The Nahuas After the Conquest: A Social and Cultural History of the Indians of Central Mexico, Sixteenth through Eighteenth Centuries*, forthcoming with Stanford University Press.

[3]I refer to Anderson, Berdan, and Lockhart 1976 (BC); Karttunen and Lockhart 1976 (NMY); Lockhart, Berdan, and Anderson 1986 (TA); and Karttunen and Lockhart 1987 (ANS). These, together with Cline and León-Portilla 1984 (TC) and the present volume, belong to a circle of books indispensable for those who would study *The Nahuas* deeply.

[4]A somewhat comparable, if rather more specialized essay is my "Some Nahua Concepts in Postconquest Guise" (Lockhart 1985). I considered including it here, but finally decided that the bulk of it is subsumed either under *The Nahuas* or under one of the various items here, and that it should be omitted in the name of avoiding excessive duplication. Even so, it contains certain formulations not seen elsewhere, and it was the place where I first enunciated my notion of Double Mistaken Identity. I recommend it especially for introductory purposes.

[5]In a very important way the statement by Frances Karttunen and myself on the organizing principles of Nahuatl song, "La estructura de la poesía náhuatl vista por sus variantes" (Karttunen and Lockhart 1980) would fit with Part II, despite not being by myself alone. See also the discussion of eighteenth-century Nahuatl, with an accompanying text, in Karttunen and Lockhart 1978.

1. Postconquest Nahua Society and Culture

[1]Preserved in the special collections department of the library of the University of Texas, San Antonio. The Nahuatl document, reversed, is used as a cover for a piece of Spanish litigation dated 1584 and may in fact date from a few years earlier. See the transcription and translation in the appendix of Lockhart, *The Nahuas*.

[2]Gibson 1964. Nahuatl-based scholarship is adding to the insights of this monument and changing many perspectives on it, but its core analysis remains valid.

[3]For example, compare FC, 8: 42.

[4]A transcription and translation of this document, together with substantial commentary, will be found in Item 4 of the present book. The text

is also referred to frequently in *The Nahuas*.

[5]ANS, pp. 141-43. The publication includes a complete transcription and two English translations of the entire set of speeches, together with a comprehensive preliminary study.

[6]I have discussed the genre at some length, using examples from the Chalco region, in Item 3 in this volume, and in a more general vein in *The Nahuas*, Chapter 9. See also Wood 1984, Chapter 8, for related material concerning the Toluca Valley.

[7]The best example of annals of the earlier type is CH. Aspects of the work are studied in Schroeder 1984. See also the discussion of annals in Chapter 9 of *The Nahuas*.

[8]Frances M. Krug is presently nearing completion of a doctoral dissertation on the late colonial annals of the region of Tlaxcala and Puebla.

[9]Major published collections include BC (with some translations now outdated in certain respects); NMY; TC; and TA.

[10]Here as in much of what follows I am summarizing some of the conclusions of *The Nahuas*. See also Cline 1986.

[11]Karttunen and Lockhart 1980 contains a thorough study of the structural aspects of Nahuatl song; the modular principle in art is mentioned in McAndrew 1964, p. 199.

[12]The topics of the preceding three paragraphs are discussed also in Lockhart 1985 and in Item 2 in this volume. See also BC.

[13]See Karttunen and Lockhart 1978, and also Item 2 in this volume.

[14]The following description of the stages summarizes, interprets, and sometimes expands on material in NMY. A full-scale yet succinct treatment of the process is Karttunen 1982, and an updated, extended discussion is in *The Nahuas*, Chapter 7.

[15]The great lexicographer fray Alonso de Molina notes in the "Avisos" to both halves of his *Vocabulario* (1571) that he includes Spanish words and compounds incorporating Spanish words because Nahuatl speakers used them and had no other words in their own language for those meanings.

[16]I now return to summarizing aspects of *The Nahuas*.

[17]The legal and institutional side of these developments receives extensive coverage in Gibson 1964, Chapter 9.

[18]Compare Haskett 1987 and Wood 1984, and for Stage 2 TA.

[19]A superb transcription, an in a way good but unreliable translation, and an unacceptable interpretation of the largest such collection are published in Bierhorst 1985.

[20]See Kubler 1948, McAndrew 1964, and Peterson 1985.

[21]Frances Karttunen (1985) has done research showing that phenomena corresponding to Nahuatl's Stage 3 appeared in the Mayan language of Yucatan only in the course of the eighteenth century, well behind the central Mexican schedule. Hunt 1976 and Farriss 1984 demonstrate a more general relative retardation of developments in Yucatan, in both Spanish and indigenous spheres.

[22]Lockhart 1985, p. 477. One could find many formulations. The essence of the matter is that each side naively underestimates the complexity

and idiosyncrasy of phenomena as seen from the other side and imperviously marches ahead in its own tradition.

2. Complex Municipalities

[1]Gibson 1964, p. 65.

[2]Gibson was fully aware of the composite states and himself contributed a great deal to our understanding of them.

[3]Gibson 1952.

[4]TA. Where not otherwise specified, all statements about Tlaxcala rest on data contained in this publication.

[5]Tulancingo collection (1), in Special Collections of the UCLA Research Library, a collection of modest size especially notable for its Nahuatl documents from the sixteenth, seventeenth, and eighteenth centuries. The materials are arranged only by folders and lack foliation. Where not otherwise specified, all statements about Tulancingo rest on data contained in this collection. UCLA's Tulancingo collections, valuable as they are, represent only a small portion of the archive of the Tulancingo alcalde mayor's office, reputed to be virtually intact and in private hands (see also Item 6 in this volume).

[6]See Carrasco 1963, 90.

[7]Vetancurt 1697, p. 63.

[8]I have as of the present not arrived at a satisfactory analysis of the relevant phrase, which occurs as "nauhcoco calpoli" and "(ypan) calpolli nauhcoco," but it does clearly contain "calpolli" and "nauh-," "four." See also Text 2A of Item 6 in this volume and the commentary to it.

[9]The situation as to indigenous government in the Tlaxcalan region in the eighteenth century remains to be investigated in detail.

[10]Several considerations lead to the conclusion that Tlatocan had precedence. Torquemada and Vetancurt both mention Tlatocan first. Normally the conquering, invading group (Tlatocan) becomes the upper half in dual organization arrangements, the conquered (Tlaixpan) the lower. "Tlatocan" means "where the ruler is." "Tlaixpan" is ambiguous; though it can mean "in front," it can also mean "facing, opposite," which I take to be the sense here; that is, Tlaixpan would be "the other one."

[11]See Schroeder 1984.

[12]See *The Nahuas*, Chapter 2, for a more detailed presentation.

[13]Carrasco 1963, pp. 85-91.

[14]Even that one may have still been using an indigenous name part of the time; I suspect that on Table 1 Juan de la Cruz and Juan Tlacochteuctli were the same person.

3. Corporate Self and History

[1]The Nahuatl text of his works is published in CH.

[2]Gibson 1975, pp. 320-21.

[3]The only instance I have seen of outsiders calling the town anything but

Zoyatzingo is reference in the title of neighboring Atlauhtla to "San Adonio Sihuatzinco."

[4]See Garibay 1970, p. 138.

[5]Zoyatzingo:

y quactlac yn atlacon textexcala
in the woods, the ravines, the crags...

Atlauhtla:

quauhtla yn atlaco y tetexcalco yn oostosqui
in the woods, the ravines, the crags, the caves...

[6]Nowhere in the documents is the Virgin of Guadalupe even mentioned, except as the name of one of the barrios of Atlauhtla.

[7]Kirchhoff, Güemes, and Reyes García 1976.

[8]The Spanish word *solar*, "lot," found a home in Nahuatl very early as *xolal*, which probably was not recognized by later Nahuatl speakers as a loan. In the Zoyatzingo text (f. 175) it appears not only incorporated into a verb but with the first syllable reduplicated to indicate distributive meaning, something usually likely to occur only with a fully assimilated root: "nexoxolaltecon," "laying out of various lots occurs." See also Text 2A of Item 6 in this volume, and the commentary to it.

[9]Paso y Troncoso 1939, 6: 5.

[10]Even the elaborate sixteenth-century narration of the conquest in the twelfth book of Sahagún's Florentine Codex concentrates overwhelmingly on the perspective from Tenochtitlan, with especially strong emphasis on Tlatelolco, where Sahagún's informants lived. Sahagún 1950-82, Book 12 (2d. ed.).

[11]One must admit that circumstances combined to make things hard for the provincial reporters. *Atlitic*, "inside the waters," was equally applicable to Mexico City and Spain. Spaniards were in the habit of saying merely "the Marqués," meaning Cortés as Marqués del Valle; yet Velasco was the Marqués de Salinas.

[12]This text is excerpted and discussed in more detail in *The Nahuas*, Chapter 9.

[13]The principal deviation has to do with the letter *c*, which is often intruded or omitted, or used in place of *u*, *uh*, or *n*, or replaced by *s* even to represent [k]. Something similar is sometimes seen in Toluca Valley texts (see Items 7 and 8 in the present volume).

4. And Ana Wept

[1]Chapters 3, 5, and passim, in addition to inclusion of the text in the appendix.

[2]Gómez de Cervantes 1944, p. 135.

5. The Testimony of don Juan

[1]Substantial scraps can also be found in some historical annals.

[2]ANS, Hinz 1987.

[3]See the preliminary study to ANS.

[4]A mundane dialogued text in a somewhat similar register, from much the same time, showing many of the same characteristics, happens also to be from the Tetzcoco region; see the document presented in Item 4 of this volume. Some letters in a comparable vein, however, are from Mexico City, as will be seen below.

[5]AGN, Vínculos 279, exp. 1, ff. 126r-127v, part of a set of Nahuatl texts having to do with the indigenous rulers of Xochimilco and their descendants. The exact date of don Juan's testimony was May 23, 1586. I first became aware of the section reproduced here in a group of photocopies kindly provided me by S. L. Cline at a time when I was hungrily acquiring all the Nahuatl documents I could get my hands on.

[6]See Horn 1989, pp. 76-85.

[7]See ibid., p. 83.

[8]See ANS, pp. 29-30.

[9]See ibid., pp. 59-60.

[10]See ibid., p. 33.

[11]As in the Dialogues, the term *teuctli*, "lord," is applied to persons of high rank regardless of gender, and as there in most cases, it appears in the vocative in the frozen form *totecuiyoe*, "our lordship," using the first person plural as a possessor and an archaic form of the noun stem. See ibid., pp. 38-39. (By way of qualification, let it be noted that in the present text this item appears once without either the archaic stem form or the abstractive ending *yo-*, and that in the Dialogues it is used more in the plural than in the singular.)

[12]See ibid., pp. 24, 44, 101-02.

[13]BC, Documents 32 and 33.

[14]Ibid. See also Tezozomoc 1949, passim, for extensive reports of intermarriage among the nobility of the Valley of Mexico, from a Mexica point of view.

[15]ANS, p. 101.

[16]For example, CH; BC, Documents 1-2, 4, 29-31.

[17]The form "nomemoria testamento," with but a single possessive prefix, shows us that the two terms were probably being treated as a single unanalyzed unit.

[18]The text contains an interesting detail on the orthography of loan words. Certain Spanish terms were so common that almost all Nahua writers, especially those as well educated as the one who penned this text, always put them on paper in "correct" form no matter how they pronounced them, thus "san," "sant", or "santo (s^{to})" even though the *s* was pronounced as a Nahuatl *x*. This phenomenon is commented upon in *The Nahuas*, Chapter 8, and also in ANS, p. 102, with further remarks to the effect that it is mainly in unusual texts such as the Dialogues or the Nahuatl song collections that one sees phonetic writing of formulaic terms. I still find this to be true overall, yet the present mainline mundane text does have one counterexample, "xant lucas" for "sant lucas." Even this case is probably a slip. Though the *x* seems dominant when one views the word in the

original, an *s* is there too, probably written over the *x* as an attempt at correction.

[19]See ANS, p. 45.

[20]See the discussion in *The Nahuas*, Chapter 8.

[21]BC, Document 4. Another possible reference to doña Juana de Guzmán in this publication is to be found in Document 20, dated 1575 in Coyoacan, in which a Juan Alvaro declares that he had exchanged land with, among others, "doña Juana in Xochimilco" (that is, doña Juana was in Xochimilco, not the land).

6. Tulancingo

[1]It was so classified, at least, during the time I was working with it. This set is distinct from another group of Tulancingo documents held in the same place, mainly concerning a later period and without any Nahuatl texts.

[2]For a brief discussion of these characteristics see TA, pp. 31-32.

[3]Folder 1, documents dated Nov. 20, Nov. 24, and Dec. 11, 1570.

[4]TA, Selection 6 (pp. 76-77).

[5]Vetancurt 1697, 4: 63, confirms that Xaltepec belonged to the second "parcialidad."

[6]See the discussion of these matters in *The Nahuas*, Chapter 5.

[7]One *-co* could be the locative suffix, but this leaves the other unaccounted for. The word also occurs in some tribute records in the Tulancingo papers. See Item 2 in this volume, note 8.

[8]See the discussion of these matters, including this very case, in *The Nahuas*, Chapter 6.

[9]In the body of the document don Josef de San Juan is given as one of the alcaldes, perhaps the notary's error out of habit. Likely don Josef was ill or recently deceased and had been replaced temporarily, for in the signature section we see instead don Antonio Mejía, "interim alcalde for Tlaixpan."

7. Language Transition

[1]See BC for representative Nahuatl texts of the colonial period. Further texts and a discussion of the processes involved in Nahuatl's gradual adaptation to Spanish are in NMY.

[2]Nahuatl was not the only indigenous language spoken in the Valley of Toluca; it is likely that there were more native speakers of Otomanguean tongues than of Nahuatl. Yet only Nahuatl was written in the region, and the texts over a period of some two hundred years show the idiosyncrasy and relative consistency of an actual spoken dialect. After about 1600 all testimony by Indians of the southern Toluca Valley was given in Nahuatl, as far as I am aware, until at the end of the colonial period some began to testify in Spanish. As will be seen, the deviances in Toluca Valley Spanish texts by indigenous persons all relate directly to Nahuatl linguistic and stylistic characteristics.

Yolanda Lastra de Suárez and Fernando Horcasitas give much evidence of the survival of Nahuatl as a spoken language in the central and southern Valley of Toluca as late as the twentieth century in Lastra de Suárez and Horcasitas 1978, 185-250. See also Lockhart 1981, which establishes connections between eighteenth-century Tolucan texts and present-day speech as attested in Lastra and Horcasitas.

Whether Nahuatl was the first or second language for the writers of the texts, it was the operative one. I fully expect that the phenomena dealt with in the present study will be found to be closely parallel to those in areas where Nahuatl was nearly the sole indigenous language, as in the Valley of Mexico or the Puebla region.

[3]Preserved in AGN, Tierras 2541, expediente 11, f. 3. I have standardized the segmentation and capitalization and resolved a small number of overbars as the intended alphabetical letter, but have made no other change.

[4]For comparison see Documents 14 and 17 in BC; Document 10 in NMY; and especially Karttunen and Lockhart 1978, 153-75.

[5]Not underlined in Text 1 is the element *que*, marked with an asterisk for identification. One of the few basic changes that appear to have taken place in Nahuatl with respect to loan phenomena since 1800 is the use of the Spanish loan particle *que* to introduce dependent clauses. In colonial texts, only the calque *tlein* ("what, which") has been documented to date, and that only in certain restricted idiomatic uses (see NMY, pp. 45, 50). If the *que* here were taken at face value, it might be construed as the earliest so far authenticated dependent *que* in a Nahuatl text: *otlananquililique*, "they answered"... *que*, "that"... *ma momaca ynin D[s] ypiltzi*, "this child of God should be given..." One could also construe the *que* as the Spanish optative particle "let," identical in use and meaning to the Nahuatl *ma* just following it; such duplication and reinforcement through use of similar Spanish and Nahuatl elements simultaneously has been a transitional device in the introduction of loans into Nahuatl since the sixteenth century. Nevertheless, although I am by no means sure that one of these explanations may not be the true one, there is yet another possibility which would not involve postulating any Spanish element here at all: that the writer has made one of the most frequent mistakes seen in Nahuatl texts, the omission of a syllable when two consecutive syllables are identical. The intention would have been *quema ma*, "yes, let..." In fact, in view of the rarity of *que* in colonial Nahuatl texts, I lean strongly toward the third hypothesis.

[6]Much the same use of *quenami* and *i-ca* are to be found in a document of Amecameca (in the Valley of Mexico) written in 1746; See Karttunen and Lockhart 1978. The uses of *pia* and *pano* are also standard in late colonial Nahuatl; see NMY, p. 45.

[7]Some of these characteristics, seen in texts too numerous to refer to here, are: absolute suffixes in *-l* instead of *-tl* (*nehual* instead of *nehuatl*, "I," *amal* instead of *amatl*, "paper"); *c* where in standard Nahuatl one would expect *-uh* (*cuactenco* instead of *cuauhtenco*, "at the edge of the woods"; *quitepectiaya* instead of *quitepeuhtiaya*, "he went scattering"; *nicmotlatlactilia* instead of *nicmotlatlauhtilia*, "I implore"); preterites which are neither

reduced nor have *c* added (*onicmaca* instead of *onicmacac*, "I gave him"; *onicasi* instead of *onicasic*, "I took him"; *onicchihua* instead of *onicchiuh*, "I did it"; verbs ending in two vowels, on the other hand, have standard preterites). Other apparent deviances are widespread in older texts of central Mexico: *u* for *o* even when the vowel is short; merging of *ch* and *x*; *-mo-* as the first person reflexive prefix, among others. The strange-looking form *tuchpa* for *tixpan*, "in our presence," involves the common elements of *u-o* and *ch-x* merging, *n* omission, and elision of *i* rather than *o* at the *to-ixpan* juncture, the latter phenomenon being unusual because the *i* is long and not generally elided. I will not enter here into the important question of how many of these characteristics reflect speech and how many might be orthographic only. I will also not attempt to discuss apparent irregularities in the Nahuatl text exhaustively, asserting only that they all exemplify common trends for the time and place.

[8]Preserved in AGN, Tierras 2533, exp. 8, f. 2.

Spanish texts of eighteenth-century Mexico, including the most highly competent and erudite, lack any consistent system of capitalization, punctuation, or stress marking. Spelling approached today's norms, but *b* and *v* alternated freely, as did *i* and *y* for [i] and even *y* and *ll* for [y], as well as *s* and *c/z*, with preference for the former, and *qu-* and *cu-*, while *u* could be used for *b/v* and *v* could be used for *u*, especially in the word *uno*, *x* was common for modern *j*, and some consonants were spelled double at will. Any *h* could be omitted (except before *u*), and some usage inserted an *h* at will before any word-initial vowel.

Except for a few deviant spellings which may reflect pronunciation, the orthography of late eighteenth-century Spanish texts by Nahuatl speakers falls within the then obtaining norms—itself a fact worthy of note. In reproducing Texts 2, 3, and 4, I have standardized the capitalization (retaining the original *R*, which then meant the trilled or double consonant) but have left the punctuation (mainly lack thereof) and spelling exactly as they are in the originals.

Dho was the standard abbreviation of *dicho*; all the abbreviations used in the texts are perfectly normal Spanish usage of that time.

[9]From ca. 1640-50 forward, Nahuatl's formula for borrowing Spanish verbs has been to take the Spanish infinitive as a stem and add *-oa*, which inflects like any Nahuatl verb of the class ending in two vowels, becoming *-oz* (*-os*) in the future tense. In an actual Nahuatl sentence there would be obligatory prefixes which are missing from the form in this text.

The text includes several examples of a nonstandard or intruded *n*, a trait highly characteristic of colonial Nahuatl documentation although not especially so of parallel Spanish texts (see NMY, pp. 8-13). All in all, in Nahuatl texts *n* seems to represent the weakest detectable segment, subject to frequent intrusion because of Nahuatl's tendency to divide any intervocalic consonant into a weak syllable-final and strong syllable-initial segment (see Karttunen and Lockhart 1977, pp. 1-15). In the present case, the writer, having no grasp of the operation of the Spanish plural, is aware only of two extremely weak word-final segments in Spanish pronunciation, [s] and [n], which are present at mysterious times, and which he vacillates in giving as *s, n,* or zero, indifferently.

[10]Preserved in AGN, Tierras 2533, exp. 3, f. 22.

[11]For example, an original Spanish will by Juan Pedro, municipal notary of San Lucas Tepemaxalco (or San Lucas La Isla, or San Lucas Alistla, or San Lucas el Chiquito), in the Calimaya region, dated 1779, can be found in AGN, Tierras 2541, exp. 9, f. 8. A translation by the same Juan Pedro made in 1783, of a Nahuatl will done by a predecessor of his and dated 1731, can be found in ibid., f. 7. Another, made in 1784 of a will of 1762, is in AGN, Tierras 2533, exp. 2, ff. 21-22.

[12]There are two cases of phenomena other than loan words which may have been Nahuatlisms spreading at least into the Spanish of fairly humble people in the countryside. One is the use of the reflexive pronoun with the past participle employed as adjective, especially in *llamádose,* "called, named," where standard usage requires its omission despite its use with the infinitive and present participle. This form had spread as far as some provincial lawyers and court translators of the Toluca area, people who were not usually native speakers of Nahuatl. I suspect that the form did indeed originate among the Nahuatl speakers, whose uncertainties about the Spanish pronoun system will become apparent below, but I have no way of knowing for sure that *llamádose* is not simply a Spanish provincialism. Whether Nahuatl in origin or not, the form fits in neatly with the Nahuatl pattern of retaining marks of reflexivity in derived forms such as impersonals, participles, and deverbal nouns.

The second phrase is surely Nahuatl in origin, the uncertainty in this case being as to whether or not it had spread into provincial Spanish more generally. A common term for the future in Nahuatl is *moztla huiptla,* "tomorrow (or) the day after tomorrow." In translations this ordinarily appears not as some straightforward Spanish way of saying "in the future" but as *mañana o esotro día,* a phrase so set that it is sometimes seen elided to *mañana osotro día.* Its currency among Nahuatl speakers using Spanish is not in doubt, but I am not positive that it had really penetrated provincial Spanish because I have yet to see it in an independently generated text (though court translators with no other noticeable Nahuatlisms do use it).

[13]AGN, Tierras 2533, exp. 2, ff. 21-22, San Lucas Tepemaxalco, 1784. These cases involve indirect objects. At the moment I have no examples in which the obligatory *a* with a personal direct object is omitted, although I am sure it happened.

[14]AGN, Tierras 2616, exp. 7, f. 7, Huitzitzilapan in the jurisdiction of Tianquiztenco, date uncertain.

[15]Another apparent hypercorrect *a* in Text 4 is in the phrase *como lo dira a senores governadores pasados.* I believe that this corresponds to standard Spanish *como lo dirán los señores gobernadores pasados,* but the passage may be open to other interpretations as well.

[16]AGN, Tierras 2541, exp. 9, ff. 1-4.

[17]See note 13.

[18]See note 16.

[19]See note 13.

[20]AGN, Tierras 1501, exp. 3, Santa María de la Asunción in the Calimaya district, 1772.

[21]See NMY, p. 26.

[22]See note 13.

[23]The latter phrase seems to need *lo que*; a standard Spanish rendering might be something like *lo que más se ofrece, eso también lo da.*

[24]See note 13.

[25]AGN, Tierras 2541, exp. 9, f. 8, San Lucas Tepemaxalco.

[26]Preserved in AGN, Tierras 2541, exp. 11, f. 5.

[27]At the root of the awkward and incomplete phrase *este pedaso que le yso el difunto vn bien y buena obra* is the Nahuatl verb *tlaocolia* "to give someone something as a favor." *Vn pedasito solar*, without *de*, follows a Nahuatl phrase type; another *de* is somewhat similarly missing between *costara* and *Resibo*. *Yo escriui* lacks a *lo* which is always present in standard Spanish texts; the reason is that in the corresponding Nahuatl one uses an indefinite object prefix *-tla-* (*onitlacuilo*, from *icuiloa*, "to write"), which in effect becomes part of the stem so that the entire construct has the feeling of an intransitive verb, accurately conveyed into Spanish as *yo escribí.*

The spelling *poxecion* probably reflects the status of the word as an older loan into Nahuatl, from the time when Spanish *s* was a retroflex [ş] usually becoming [š] (written *x*) in Nahuatl loans; (see Karttunen and Lockhart 1976, p. 5). The spelling *tepihque* is neither the standard Spanish *tepisque* nor the standard Nahuatl *tepixqui*. Perhaps the *h* is for *ch*, as often occurs in eighteenth-century Nahuatl texts; in Text 1, *ch* occurs frequently where *x* is expected. *Onde* instead of *donde* is standard provincial Mexican Spanish of the time, and while *agia* instead of *haya* is not quite, one does see *(h)aiga*, *(h)ia*, and other variants of a form which seems to have been in flux in the everyday speech of ordinary people.

[28]See note 16.

9. Cantares Mexicanos

[1]Though the terminology is changed, Bierhorst's analysis in every respect follows that first put forth in Karttunen and Lockhart 1980. Bierhorst does us a serious disservice (p. 121) by including that article in a list of items which according to him do not attempt to challenge the basic assumptions of Angel María Garibay. Much of our view of Nahuatl song has also been incorporated into León-Portilla 1983, a major statement to which Bierhorst does not refer; probably it appeared after the Bierhorst edition was already in production.

Despite describing the structure of the songs adequately, I do not think Bierhorst gives structure enough importance. Even granting the tenets of his ghost-song interpretation (and as will be seen below, I do not), his commentary on the individual songs is far too linear to be consonant with their true nature. Nor does he at all take into consideration the fact that a pair of verses is most often a topical as well as a formal unit.

[2]The Cantares do have an unusual form -yolyol, which Bierhorst eagerly takes to be a plural. I do not know what it is; it is neither a normal distributive nor a normal plural. Formally it looks like the noun bound to itself, "one's heart-heart," conceivably "one's heart of hearts." In the texts it seems to function the same as -yol, as the subject of verbs indicating emotional state, as on pp. 248-49, v. 2.

[3]I have done the following respacing: changed icihuauh tzin in verse 1 to icihuauhtzin; ma nocana to mano cana (three times, once in verse 2); and oquichpilli tzin to oquichpillitzin. In verse 1, I take it that ahua Pille in an earlier version was cihuapille; the confusion of a and ci is a common error in sixteenth-century texts. However that may be, the vocative ending on Pille tells us unambiguously that a man is speaking at that point. On the other hand, the lack of the -e vocative at the end of the verse tells us that a woman is speaking. In verse 3, Bierhorst misreads taca as Spanish daga, "dagger," rather than as taça, "cup," forgetting his own admonition that the cedilla is often omitted. He apparently takes onihualo as the passive of ihua, "to send," rather than as an impersonal of oni, "to drink," which would be defensible except for the context; to my knowledge, however, the verb lacks the connotation "to dispatch, kill" that he gives it. In verse 4, Bierhorst misreads notecotzin as related to teuctli, "lord," when in fact it is the possessed form of tecomatl, "tecomate," with an n missing. In the same verse, Bierhorst and I agree that quatzin is the original's mistake for qualtzin.

[4]Bierhorst uses italics to indicate (1) material understood to be repeated but not actually written out in the original, and (2) editorial supplements in the translation. Let me add that the crude North American term and concept "white man" is entirely out of place in a sixteenth-century Mexican context.

[5]High-ranking personages in the Spanish world were in general often referred to, with no disrespect, simply by "don" and their Christian name, as one might call don Antonio de Mendoza, first viceroy of New Spain, "don Antonio." But the great conquerors who went through life without the "don" and received it only along with high titles after the conquest were never so addressed; Pizarro and Cortés were both known afterwards mainly as "Marqués," and never as "don Francisco" or "don Hernando," although they might be referred to on occasion with "don" plus the whole name including Christian name and surname.

[6]I have some uncertainties concerning the translation of xacaltecoz, but I am sure Bierhorst's reading is not right. As Bierhorst is aware, the captain is Cortés and doña Marina (whose title, however, Bierhorst did not recognize) is his interpreter.

10. Gibson and Ethnohistory

[1]Gibson 1952 and 1964. I regret not being equipped at present to list and comment on Gibson's other relevant writings, for they would reward the attention.

[2]For bibliography see Cook and Borah 1971-79.

[3]The book to be singled out is, of course, Hanke 1949.

[4]Ricard 1933. I have often marveled that such a fine book should have had such a pernicious influence (which it continues to have on many to this day).

[5]Kubler 1948. I think that Kubler had more influence on Gibson's prose, scholarly methods, and general outlook than any other single person.

[6]According to a much appreciated personal communication from Mrs. Alice Gibson.

[7]The truth is that this describes all of us moderns who purport to be scholars of older Nahuatl.

[8]TA.

[9]See Item 2 in this volume.

[10]The conclusion contains one of the very few instances of unclear thinking (as opposed to underformulation) that I have observed in Gibson's work; on p. 403 he seems to take the point of view that "exploitation," as used in political and moral debate, is an empirical category. It is a great tribute to Gibson that feeling as he did about the relationship between Spaniards and Indians, he could write with such serenity, explore areas having nothing to do with that concern, and come to many conclusions pointing in the opposite direction from the main thrust of his beliefs (as in the question of hacienda labor). The only place in the body of the work where I have felt that Gibson's attitude shows through is in his treatment of encomienda abuses (pp. 76-80). The things Gibson speaks of here are surely unpleasant, especially as they are portrayed, but they are also part of normal encomienda economics, in Mexico as elsewhere. In contradistinction to his work on the hacienda, here Gibson does not lay bare underlying patterns nor make new (and necessary) distinctions.

[11]Taylor 1972.

[12]Taylor, personal communication.

[13]Taylor 1979.

[14]Several recent ethnohistorical researchers have started out with some notion of drawing Spaniards deeply into their treatment and in the end have largely concentrated on the Indian side. Perhaps two phases of investigation are needed; once the indigenous situation of a given time and region has been deeply studied, it should be possible for someone concentrating on local Spaniards to construct an integrated picture containing both elements.

[15]In a demographic vein, Cheryl Martin (1985) has done much to combine the history of Spaniards and Indians. Borah (1983) has published a book which complements Gibson by showing more of the Spanish side of the interaction between high officials and Indian corporations.

[16]Tutino 1976.

[17]Haskett's article (1987), substantial as it is, only sketches out themes dealt with in depth in his dissertation (1985), which has been revised and will be published as a book. His massive research has produced a large-scale portrait of Indian local government in action, seen from the inside, in a major region of central Mexico across more than two centuries, with much new information on the social and economic life of the officeholding sectors as well. For a more detailed discussion see Item 11 in this volume.

[18]For examples of eighteenth-century Nahuatl and some discussion of its characteristics see NMY (pp. 112-21) and especially Karttunen and Lockhart 1978. See also Lockhart 1981 and BC (pp. 72-77, 96-97, 100-09). It is my opinion that as impressive as it is, the now emerging mass of eighteenth-century Nahuatl material has gained from the vagaries of archival preservation and trends in litigation and that if we had all the Nahuatl ever written, the late sixteenth and early seventeenth centuries would be seen to have produced more pages per year than any other time.

[19]Wood's dissertation (1984) is in the main quite Gibsonian in conception, being a large corporate study using primarily Spanish administrative records, with special attention to new corporate formations. The topic was chosen in part to extend the thrust of *The Aztecs* both temporally and geographically and to complement the work on other regions of Taylor. A most interesting portion of the dissertation deals with Nahuatl "primordial titles" and forgeries of Spanish land documents. For more detail see the discussion of Wood's work in Item 11 of this volume.

[20]This movement has taken place primarily in the United States and under the rubric of history, though not all participants have been in history departments. The overwhelming bulk of the work, to tell the simple truth, has been done by a circle including myself, some valued close colleagues, and some equally valued students of mine, several of whom have by now also become colleagues. I am by no means unaware, however, of the contributions of persons associated with anthropology. Their interest has often been primarily in the preconquest period, but their use of postconquest materials has put them on a path converging with ours. They have brought useful materials to light and added to the scope of the movement. To discuss this rather distinct corpus and examine the relations that should and do exist in Mesoamerican research between history and anthropology (which I view as speech communities, reading clubs, and the artifacts of certain research techniques rather than as intellectually distinct "disciplines") would be a major undertaking, and I defer it to the future. For now I will merely mention the names of some of those who have made significant contributions: Luis Reyes García; Pedro Carrasco; Fernando Horcasitas; Herbert Harvey and Barbara Williams; Hanns Prem and Ursula Dyckerhoff; Louise Burkhart. Of these Reyes has moved the furthest toward full-scale postconquest Nahuatl philology and Nahuatl-based ethnohistory, and work he is now doing on Ocotelolco (Tlaxcala) is bringing him yet further in that direction. I by no means intend to say that I think scholars should concentrate on one kind of source and do either one period or the other. Rather, the difficult-to-attain ideal would be to treat the four centuries or so center ing on the conquest as a single period to be studied in a unified fashion by all means available. One reason for a rapprochement is that postconquest Nahuatl documentation is the most powerful still unexploited resource for learning more about the culture, society, economy, and politics of the late preconquest period.

Miguel León-Portilla, Jorge Klor de Alva, Thelma Sullivan, and John Bierhorst, approaching from the general direction of intellectual history, religion, and literature, have also impinged meaningfully on the world of postconquest Nahuatl documents (the versatile Klor de Alva is an anthropologist as well).

[21]*Beyond the Codices* (BC, Anderson, Berdan, and Lockhart 1976) served its purpose in introducing a large number of people to mundane Nahuatl documents. It remains a meaningful selection (no one collection could be fully representative), and in its transcriptions errors are few and minor. The translations, however, many being the first ever published of their type, and done by scholars who, without predecessors, were just cutting their teeth on everyday postconquest Nahuatl, contain a large number of errors, most of them reasonably insignificant, but some of central importance to a given document's contents. Plans are being made for a much revised second edition.

On the other hand, the documentary appendix of *Nahuatl in the Middle Years* (NMY, Karttunen and Lockhart 1976), although bearing the same publication date, is in fact a later product. The first stages of apprenticeship were past by the time these translations were made, and they are quite error-free; I am at present aware of only one or two small outright mistakes.

Any translation from older Nahuatl, however, should be viewed as provisional, and a full-scale reexamination will practically always bring about emendations that go beyond the trivial. Yet I do not want to shake readers' confidence either; in translations in which I have been in any way involved in the last ten years, especially in the more familiar genres, gross uncertainties mainly affect certain lexical items of a highly specific or technical nature, whose dubiousness is often highlighted, and the general sense can be trusted not to change much in future revisions.

Smaller documentary publications throwing light on additional genres are Karttunen and Lockhart 1978, Lockhart 1980 and 1981, and though it does not reproduce any full samples, Lockhart 1982.

[22]TC; ANS. These two publications are in the Nahuatl Studies Series of the UCLA Latin American Center, of which I am series editor. Further documentary publications planned for the series and already being worked on include an edition of two of the most important of the Tlaxcala-Puebla annals, by Frances Krug and Arthur Anderson, and a volume of the Cuernavaca-region censuses beyond those published by Hinz, by S.L. Cline.

The two recent Hinz publications (1983) are up to date in every respect; that is, the transcriptions and translations are generally excellent, and they are accompanied by much introductory analysis. The same is true of Hinz 1987, which only recently came to my attention. One should not forget in this connection Andrew and Hassig's edition of Ruiz de Alarcón (1984). Though the original document is mainly in Spanish, it is most valuable for the Nahuatl incantations it contains, here doubly transcribed and translated, with a large explanatory apparatus.

[23]TA. The full document has been published in a Spanish edition (Celestino Solís et al., 1985); the transcription is essentially reliable, although certain things are respelled, and while the translation is generally good, it ignores many large questions that remain about meanings. The explanatory

apparatus is rudimentary; there is, however, a large analytical index. The two publications complement each other.

[24]It is increasingly hard to know whether the scholars producing these volumes should appear as editors or as authors.

[25]I am aware that the phrasing used here appears to make the Spaniards the prime movers, when actually both cultures were equally necessary to bring about the ensuing results, but in the present context I want to point out that a systematic, multi-generational, multidimensional process would not have taken the form it did at the time it did without the presence of Spanish persons and patterns among the Indians. Change was already going on among the Nahuas before the conquest, of course. The Spaniards unleashed much quicker and more obviously linear kinds of change by their interaction with the indigenous people. They did not themselves determine the nature of that change, however, for the results were determined equally by the attributes of the Nahuas and the closeness or distance of the two cultures on a large number of points. Consider how differently things turned out in the North Mexican mining districts, though they too were inundated by Spaniards.

[26]At some point I lost the feeling that philology was mere preparation and now think that it can produce artifacts of immediate and lasting value to a fairly wide readership and is a good vehicle for certain kinds of very subtle and innovative cultural-linguistic research.

[27]The most comprehensive introduction to the themes of the book is Item 1 in this volume.

To mention some relevant work in progress, Frances M. Krug is nearing completion of a dissertation on the late colonial Nahuatl annals of the Tlaxcala-Puebla region. Juan López y Magaña, having done an MA thesis on Juan Bautista de Pomar's life and writing, using Nahuatl documents on Pomar's activities, is now working in a similar vein on Diego Muñoz Camargo, looking toward a dissertation which will treat the two mestizo chroniclers as a type. Related pieces are appearing among the published proceedings of the 1985 Oaxaca Conference of Mexican and American Historians (Sánchez et al. 1990). Stephanie Wood, whose dissertation was discussed above, continues to work on primordial titles and Techialoyan codices; several articles with very new material and insights are on the way. Robert Haskett has begun a project on the Taxco mine repartimiento from the indigenous perspective, and S.L. Cline for some time has been collecting materials and writing preliminary pieces on Xochimilco, a vast and little understood entity which cries out for close investigation. Both of these projects will doubtless go far beyond the sphere of Nahuatl documents, as they should.

[28]Lockhart 1968 and 1972a.

[29]This may have been an illusion. George Urioste has in his possession copies of some late seventeenth-century Quechua documents from central Peru that are closely comparable to Nahuatl materials; they imply that Quechua was routinely written by native speakers in at least some parts of the Andean region and arouse the hope that larger caches will yet surface.

[30]Cline 1986. The testaments are the ones published in TC.

[31]NMY. The mass of known postconquest mundane material in Nahuatl has more than doubled since the appearance of this monograph in late 1976, but so far the new data bear out the original analysis. For a succinct and readable restatement see Karttunen 1982. Chapter 7 of *The Nahuas* goes back over the ground in considerable detail, expanding and updating it as well as presenting it anew. Karttunen 1985 initiates the important task of studying the same processes in other indigenous languages, in this case Yucatecan Maya, with the comparison to Nahuatl made explicit.

[32]Neither work influenced the other directly. Our publication appeared a little earlier, but by that time Taylor's project was far advanced.

[33]*The Aztecs*, pp. 172-73.

[34]Lockhart 1985, pp. 469-71, Item 2 in this volume, and *The Nahuas*, Chapter 2. See also Haskett 1987.

[35]Schroeder 1984. A significant related article by Schroeder is to appear in an anthology being edited by Herbert Harvey for University of New Mexico Press. See the discussion of Schroeder's work in Item 11 of this volume.

[36]Horn 1989. Horn also makes very substantial contributions in the area of land tenure on the basis of a large corpus of Nahuatl land sales and related documents, continuing the process (which began with Cline, Harvey, and Williams) of expanding the Gibsonian categories and elucidating them. See the more detailed discussion of her work in Item 11.

[37]Farriss 1984. Comparisons between *Maya Society* and *The Aztecs* could usefully be extended to great length. I am struck by the fact that (possibly because of the nature of the local archives) Farriss has made less use of civil sources and greater use of ecclesiastical sources than Gibson did, which gives things a very different slant. Farriss has also made good use of some indigenous-language sources and studies, but the indigenous-language aspect is not central to either book.

[38]Considering that Farriss' work had been in gestation for quite a while, one cannot really complain about her having relied on Gibson alone. But it is now high time for a halt to the general practice of using *The Aztecs* as a complete and self-contained description of indigenous central Mexico in the postconquest centuries.

[39]I have updated descriptions of ongoing work referred to in the original version of this piece in 1986, but I have not added analysis of anything else published since then. Among relevant subsequent works are Burkhart 1989, García Martínez 1987, Gillespie 1989, Gruzinski 1989, and Pastor 1987. Of these, Burkhart's book represents a large contribution to Nahuatl-based historical studies.

11. A Vein of Ethnohistory

[1]Especially Arthur J. O. Anderson, Frances Berdan, William Bright, and Frances Karttunen.

[2]I remember fondly an occasion when Robert Haskett was the first to re-

cognize a strange form in a Nahuatl document as a version of Spanish *imagen,* "image."

[3]Although the work appeared as a book in 1986, it grew out of Cline's 1983 UCLA dissertation, entitled "Culhuacan, 1572-1599: An Investigation Through Mexican Indian Testaments." At the time this provisional version represented a large accomplishment, but it is now entirely superseded by Cline's book and by TC.

[4]Compare Item 10, pp. 178-79.

[5]One associates these studies with the exploitation of a variety of types of sources, each giving a different perspective, and that of course is unattainable in the present case. Yet a large body of testaments represents a considerable variety in itself: sixty-five testators at as many different instants, going back over a related subject matter from a slightly different perspective each time, with the additional variable of the different notaries' styles. Social history's characteristic activity of synthesis and typology on the basis of numerous related fragmentary data is very much at work here.

[6]Cline anticipated this aspect in her article, Cline 1984. Others had already studied Nahua land tenure more in isolation.

[7]Cline 1986, p. 169.

[8]I wish to give special recognition to Cline's work in producing an appendix listing all the Spanish loan words in the Culhuacan testaments. It represents one of the largest additions made in years to our factual knowledge of the process of Nahuatl's incorporation of Spanish elements, and as such I have made prominent use of it in *The Nahuas,* Chapter 7.

[9]The first edition quite quickly went out of print. A second is being prepared, with a more satisfactory outward appearance than the first (technical problems prevented the use of an adequate type face). Certain mainly minor errors of transcription and translation are also being remedied.

[10]See *The Nahuas,* Chapter 8.

[11]When Wood was conceptualizing her project, Taylor 1972, which dealt with Oaxaca alone and continued Gibson's corporate emphasis, was the main point of reference. Taylor 1979 then appeared, with much material on the Nahua center as well as Oaxaca, and far more attention to individual behavior, but for Wood the die was already cast, and in any case Taylor still did not (having no occasion to) study the Valley of Toluca as an entity.

[12]See Wood forthcoming 1 through 4.

[13]See Wood forthcoming 5.

[14]Günter Zimmermann performed a task of great importance when he rearranged the bulk of Chimalpahin's writing in one chronological sequence in his (Nahuatl-only) edition (CH).

[15]See *The Nahuas,* Chapter 2.

[16]See Schroeder 1989. Schroeder forthcoming is a useful summary of the main points of the dissertation and book. See also my treatment of Chimalpahin the annalist in *The Nahuas,* Chapter 9.

[17]Haskett 1987.

[18]Haskett has also made use of some of the texts written in an ostensibly strange Spanish by Nahuatl speakers in the very late period. In the vein of

some work done independently by myself (see Item 7), he has not only extracted facts from such materials but begun to inquire into the patterns of the language, their origins, and their meaning.

[19]BC is dominated by Coyoacan documents, most of them from a collection in a volume of Tierras in the AGN, but others from UCLA's McAfee Collection, in which again the Coyoacan thread is strong. The only known large sheaf of Nahuatl documents in the Archivo de Notarías of the Distrito Federal proved to concern Coyoacan. Carrasco and Monjarás 1976-78 contains all Coyoacan material, a fuller reproduction of the source sampled in BC. When the Bancroft Library at the University of California, Berkeley, recently acquired a set of Coyoacan hacienda records, it proved to contain the largest known collection of Nahuatl bills of sale, all from Coyoacan.

[20]Wood and Haskett are also engaged in mapping related to their projects, but as I understand it their efforts, because of the nature of their studies and the materials available, tend to be valley-wide and generally more like Gibson's in scope.

[21]Horn is also working on local Nahuatl records of various kinds to broaden the view of indigenous life in Coyoacan beyond the areas of government, jurisdictional arrangement, and the economy.

[22]Spanish influence plays little role in Schroeder's study because the part of Chimalpahin she is analyzing relates primarily to the preconquest period; in her article Schroeder 1989 she deals precisely with Spanish religious influence on Chimalpahin.

[23]The presence of something Spanish among the Nahuas by no means is always best described as "influence." Often one could better speak of convergence, or active exploitation of foreign elements by the Nahuas, or adaptation and transformation. For simplicity, I will let such alternatives lie for now.

[24]I put these terms in quotes to emphasize their crudity; a long discussion would be needed to elucidate their meaning in general usage and in the early Latin American field in particular, and to broach the difficult question of whether or not there is really any difference of principle between them.

[25]It was then that Bakewell, Bowser, Brading, Russell-Wood, Schwartz, Spalding, Taylor, and myself came on the scene. I have described much of the movement in Lockhart 1972b, a piece which now needs updating in certain respects. I have in fact prepared an updated version but have not yet given thought to publishing it.

[26]I advocated and half predicted the development of a cultural/conceptual history, far wider than traditional intellectual history, in Lockhart 1972b.

[27]Very indicative is the change in Wood's work which took place half way through her dissertation research. Likewise Haskett has added a great amount of cultural analysis to an originally more social theme. In my own *The Nahuas*, the first four substantive chapters are more social, the next four more cultural (increasingly so), and the order of appearance is also the order in which the chapters were written. Important almost completed dissertations by Frances Krug and Juan López y Magaña are dominantly cultural

(see Item 10, note 27). Barry David Sell has done a vast amount of preparatory work toward a dissertation which will be devoted in the first instance to the philology of ecclesiastical Nahuatl texts of the sixteenth and early seventeenth centuries. Dana Leibsohn, a doctoral student in art history at UCLA, has at present made substantial progress toward a study of the so-called Historia Tolteca-Chichimeca (Kirchhoff et al. 1976) which will for the first time concentrate equally on the visual and the linguistic components of the Nahua communication system, examining the important relation between the two.

[28]Frances Karttunen has published a provisional but most enlightening and suggestive study of Yucatecan Maya in the postconquest centuries in relation to Nahuatl, finding all in all a similar process but a slower tempo (Karttunen 1985). My doctoral student Matthew Restall proposes to do a broad ethnohistory of Yucatan in the sixteenth to eighteenth centuries on the basis of Maya sources. I too have dabbled in Yucatecan Maya and am interested in comparative research on the region.

Kevin Terraciano, my doctoral student, has undertaken the courageous project of ethnohistorical research on the Mixtec region on the basis of sources in Mixtec that he has located, although he is without predecessors and very nearly without instructors in the language or formal instructional materials in its sixteenth-to-eighteenth-century form.

The Andes and Quechua loom as a case clearly parallel to that of central Mexico and Nahuatl and fully separate from it (as Yucatan is not). It always seemed as if no older mundane indigenous texts would be forthcoming from that region, but possibly we were wrong (see Item 10, note 29). I have learned a little Quechua (forgotten at the moment) and did some preliminary works with texts, which proved fascinating.

On this whole question of establishing the implications of the Nahua case through wider investigation see the final portion of Chapter 10 of *The Nahuas*.

12.   Toluca

[1]See Durbin 1970 for a presentation of the very little that is known of the valley's preconquest history. Anyone who is under the misconception that the Spaniards originated any new settlements in the Toluca Valley should consult Durbin's lists and maps of preconquest towns, pp. 16-26. All that the new Spanish rulers did was to rearrange the towns with central squares and straighter streets, sometimes moving the location a short distance onto flat ground, as in the case of Tenango. In many cases not even that much change was undertaken. Descriptions of Tenango, Sultepec, and Temascaltepec around 1580 are in Paso y Troncoso 1906.

[2]Ponce, p. 75. In Tenango in 1582 and in Temascaltepec in 1580, Toluca was actually considered to be a Spanish town, or "pueblo de españoles" (Paso y Troncoso 1906, 3, 18).

[3]I went to Toluca in 1969 in the course of a general survey of central Mexican provincial archives. In Toluca I hoped to find a great deal of direct

career information on Indians; while I already suspected the importance of the provincial Spaniards, there turned out to be far more data on them and far less on the Indians than I had imagined. I cannot express strongly enough my gratitude to Lic. Morelos García Alvarez, then Notario Público Número 1 of Toluca, whose establishment on Avenida Villada at that time contained an immensely valuable run of notarial and judicial records from the sixteenth century until today. Lic. Morelos allowed me to sit for some three weeks in a corner of his private office, thumbing pages and taking notes, while he conducted his business.

The documentary base of the present study consists of two large volumes in Lic. Morelos' archive, one entitled "Expedientes, 1560-1599," and the other in the section "Protocolos," entitled "Juan de Morelos, Juan Sedeño, Matías Pinto, Juan de Yniesta, 1591-1599." The documents of the first were mainly issued in Toluca, those of the second mainly in the Ixtlahuaca district. Despite the differentiation in title, both volumes contained a mixture of notarial documents and judicial proceedings. The documentation tends to concentrate in the years 1582, 1585, and 1591-94; since many people appear at both the earlier and the later dates, the records provide a general perspective of more than a decade. In view of the fact that almost all the life sketches draw on both volumes; that neither volume had internal pagination; and that no other sources are employed extensively in this study, I have decided not to make citations in detail, it being understood that the relevant data come from the two volumes in question. Whenever any other source is used, it is cited explicitly. Lic. Morelos' archive, I have been informed, was later moved to the archive of the state of México in Toluca, but I have never had occasion to search it out and can give no details.

[4]Dorantes de Carranza 1902, pp. 290-291; *Actas de cabildo del ayuntamiento de México*, records of the year 1601; Boyd-Bowman 1968, 73.

While there may have been a slight general tendency by the time period of the study to use the terms "don" and "doña" more liberally in Mexico than earlier, the principle of invariability had not changed at all (for a discussion of usage in the conquest period see Lockhart 1968, pp. 35-37.) That is, the name of a person titled "don" or "doña" never appeared in speech or writing without that title as long as he or she lived, nor did a person without the title ever receive it on occasion. There is not a single slip, error, or variation from this principle in the whole of the Toluca documentation. The presence or absence of "don" was still considered enough to distinguish two namesakes from each other, as in the case of the separate individuals Juan de Sámano and don Juan de Sámano, below. This usage is preserved throughout the present article, and the reader is invited to note the presence or absence of the title in each case, because specific comment in all instances would too greatly burden the text. It is a significant fact, for example, that corregidor Agustín de Hinojosa was not entitled "don."

The criteria of title distribution in the Toluca area in the time dealt with were still those of the conquest period, except that the encomenderos were assuming the "don" in the second generation; by the third generation the "don" was standard for males of the main branch of an encomendero's family, but still not conceded to some whose plebeian antecedents were not quite forgotten. The merchants, entrepreneurs, and plebeian estate owners of the Toluca valley of course did not bear the "don," nor did their women have the "doña," except that by the 1590's the daughters of one or two ranchers with growing wealth and pretensions were beginning to assume it. Almost all Spaniards connected with the valley and entitled to "don" or "doña" lived in Mexico City. For Indians, "doña" was used by women of prominence following criteria that cannot be ascertained in the restricted number of cases; only the most important men of the noble class were called "don," though there was some inconsistency.

[5]*Actas de cabildo de México*, records of the year 1603.

[6]Dorantes de Carranza 1902, pp. 196, 290-91.

[7]Francisco del Paso y Troncoso 1940, p. 36.

[8]Paso y Troncoso 1940, pp. 36, 38, 41; Dorantes de Carranza 1902, pp. 287-89.

[9]Paso y Troncoso 1940, p. 8.

[10]Dorantes de Carranza 1902, pp. 305-06; Paso y Troncoso 1940, p. 43 (with "Muñoz" mistakenly given as "Núñez"). Diego de Ocampo Saavedra, the encomendero of Ocuilan in the south of the valley, had a brother Juan Arias de Saavedra, who was a citizen of Mexico City, but was living in Toluca in 1586. Ocampo Saavedra had the encomienda through marriage. An illegitimate descendant and namesake of the original encomendero, Cerván Bejarano, was also a citizen of Toluca, married into the Gómez Maya family. See Dorantes de Carranza 1902, pp. 440, 444, and Paso y Troncoso 1940, pp. 36, 39.

[11]See the chapter in Lockhart 1968 entitled "Encomenderos and Major-domos," and also Lockhart 1969. The estate pattern in the Valley of Toluca fits perfectly into the framework of description and interpretation therein contained, and constitutes further evidence.

[12]Aside from Ponce, see the references in García Martínez 1969, p. 140.

[13]For some examples of this prominence, along with some mythology about the families' origin, see Salinas 1965, pp. xiv, 83, 84.

[14]Dorantes de Carranza 1902, pp. 435, 436.

[15]Her first name was Francisca, without the doña which was accorded to the women of the cacique class. Her surname in the copy of Peribáñez' will appears to be "Solxutl," possibly a form of the common Xochitl or Sochitl (Flower). She was born in the town (pueblo) of "Totutepeque," which could be any of various similarly named Mexican towns and hamlets, but there was a small settlement by the name of (San Pedro) Totoltepec just a mile or two north of the town of Toluca.

[16]The Mexican Indian had a name, Diego Suárez (Juárez), that could have been Spanish (although Juárez was very common among Indians), while the Tolucan Indians had "Indian" names: Francisco de San Juan (saint's name for a surname) and Miguel Melchor (two first names). None could sign.

[17]Along with the obrajeros for the wool of sheep and the tanners for the hides of cattle, there could well have been a group specializing in process-ing pork products. The passage quoted from a traveler at the beginning of

this article implies that Toluca exported hams and bacons as well as pigs. But in the records, sales of the animals are far more common than of the products. Such sales of bacon as there are are made by the pig raisers themselves, as when one Miguel González, a second-generation farmer and stockman, sold 100 arrobas of bacon to a trader in 1585 (for 230 pesos).

[18]In 1590 corregidor don Martín Velásquez' servant Francisco de Zamora had to take a pair of his master's black velvet trousers to "Palomares, gorrero" in Mexico City to be mended.

[19]Mexico City's hospital of Nuestra Señora de la Concepción owned the estancia of Mestepec in the western part of the jurisdiction of Ixtlahuaca. In 1585 it had 10,400 sheep: 7,734 ewes two years and over, 1,200 yearling lambs, and 1,166 suckling lambs, and 300 rams. Two black slaves had charge of the stock, and were included in the lease. They apparently rode the estancia's two mares. There were also some Indian shepherds, whom the lessees were enjoined not to try to remove. The estancia had on it a house described as large and very well covered with thatch, with four rooms and as many doors. The lessees were to pay 790 pesos, 3 reales at the end of each year, or 76 pesos per thousand.

[20]Pack trains, as the principal means of transporting goods, were a frequent sight in the valley. Selling them could be a major business. In October, 1535, a Juan Sánchez Caballero, citizen of the mines of Tlalpujahua (some twenty miles west of Atlacomulco) sold four sets of ten mules to as many well known citizens of Toluca, two sets at 400 pesos each and two sets at 500 pesos each.

[21]The Ixtlahuaca district equivalent of Pedro Millán were notaries Juan Sedeño and Juan de Morales, who often served as teniente, and lived in the area through the terms of several alcaldes mayores.

[22]The magistrates of this time known to me through the records I studied are as follows. Toluca: 1581, don Luis Ponce de León, alcalde mayor; 1584, 1585, and 1586, Agustín de Hinojosa Villavicencio, corregidor; 1590, 1591, don Martín Velásquez, corregidor (also of Ixtlahuaca); 1592, Gaspar Ortiz Magariño, alcalde mayor; 1593, Alonso Valadés, alcalde mayor; 1596, 1598, Luis Flores de Villamayor, corregidor. Ixtlahuaca: sometime before 1590, Lorenzo Porcallo de la Cerda; 1585, don Carlos de Sámano; 1590, 1591, don Martín Velásquez (also of Toluca); 1591, 1592, don Pedro Lorenzo de Castilla; 1593, Alonso de Villanueva Cervantes; 1594, Alonso Gómez Cervantes. In three cases, Valadés, Porcallo, and Castilla, either the magistrates or their exact namesakes held encomiendas in the Mexico City jurisdiction. Porcallo was at the same time a citizen and miner of Sultepec. A Juan Farfán de Lizarrazas was called ambiguously "alcalde mayor del valle" in 1582. Though the reference was made in Toluca, Ixtlahuaca may have been meant, for the northern jurisdiction was entitled "Ixtlahuaca y valle de Matlatzinca." In 1584 Farfán de Lizarrazas was alcalde mayor of the mines of Temascaltepec. Also in 1584, Juan Alonso Altamirano was "alcalde mayor del pueblo y partido de Metepec," at the same time that Hinojosa was corregidor of Toluca. Whether Altamirano was a deputy, or the two jurisdictions were separate, I do not know.

In addition to this, in 1582 a Francisco de Avila was corregidor in Tenango, at the extreme southern end of the valley (Paso y Troncoso 1906,
pp. 1-7). Avila's title was simply "corregidor por su majestad en este
pueblo," and the context gives the strong impression that he was not simultaneously serving as corregidor of Toluca. Moreover, the arrangement
seemed to be a relatively permanent one, for on the Tenango public square
were the "casas reales para el corregidor," distinguished by a studded double
door and a second-story gallery with four stone arches. Yet the corregidores
of Toluca, particularly don Martín Velásquez, often acted as though Tenango
were within their jurisdiction.

²³This had also been the practice in the time before the 1580's. A
document of March, 1566, when Juan de la Torre was alcalde mayor, refers
to "esta villa de Toluca que es del ilustrísimo señor don Martín Cortés,
Marqués del Valle."

²⁴The famous *repartimiento de mercancías* is largely a phenomenon of a
later time, when goods were more plentiful and rural buying power was
greater.

²⁵Agustín de Hinojosa Villavicencio also made this a frequent practice.
When the amounts were large he had the transaction notarized, the debtor
frankly saying that the debt was to Hinojosa for tax which the latter had
already declared he had received. The sales tax burden rested formally on the
seller, but usually devolved by mutual agreement onto the buyer.

²⁶I have seen no document that actually labels Goya a merchant; when he
is identified at all it is merely as a citizen of Toluca. But as mentioned
above, he had more elaborate mercantile training and more commercial
connections in Mexico City than the declared merchants of the Rodríguez
Magallanes family, and I do not hesitate to call him a merchant.

²⁷There is some indication that previous corregidor Hinojosa may have
preceded don Martín in the tannery business, since a few of the tanned hides
left by the latter had once belonged to the former. Another resource of
Toluca that don Martín attempted to exploit at least once was the Nevado de
Toluca. His partner Goya paid half a peso to some Indians who carried ice
from the volcano to Mexico City.

²⁸The towns were Zinacantepec, Tlacotepec, Tlachichilpan, Jiquipilco,
Ixtlahuaca, and Atlacomulco.

²⁹Don Martín might have acquired more of these things later, of course,
if he had lived. Agustín de Hinojosa brought at least his wife to the valley
with him, though no further definite sign of a retinue appears. We may
assume that there were rather imposing "casas reales" on the main square,
combining living quarters for the corregidor with some courtrooms or offices. The records contain no specific mention of them, however.

³⁰The documents I have studied contained references to permanent curates
(*beneficiados*) in the following six valley towns in the 1580's and 90's:
Almoloya, Atlacomulco, Ixtlahuaca, Jiquipilco, Jocotitlan, and Tenango.
Another was in Tenancingo, just beyond the valley limits. Durbin 1970, p.
95, mentions a curate in Jalatlaco, and a joint curacy for Atlapulco,
Capulhuac, Ocoyacac, and Tepehuejiyaca in 1569.

[31]One of these was Francisco de Aguilar (below), connected with the Salazars, prominent in Mexico City since the famous royal factor Gonzalo de Salazar. The other was Bachiller Cristóbal Cervantes Santa Clara, beneficiado of Ixtlahuaca at least from 1592 through 1594. The surnames of Cervantes and Santa Clara were both well known among the encomendero families. Cervantes had a brother, citizen of Mexico City, who was the namesake of the important figure of the conquest period, Bernardino de Santa Clara. Thus Cervantes must have been a close relative of his somewhat older contemporary, the noted mestizo chronicler Pedro Gutiérrez de Santa Clara.

[32]A priest's salary, paid by royal officials, was only a beginning toward making a living. Alonso Rodríguez Ugarte, beneficiado of Almoloya, received a salary of 130 pesos a year. Most mulatto hired hands made as much.

[33]Durbin 1970, p. 95, mentions Francisco de Aguilar as curate of Jiquipilco in 1569. If it was the same man, as seems probable, he lived at Jiquipilco at least 25 years.

[34]Ponce, p. 75.

[35]Ponce, pp. 75-76.

[36]The details of this agreement should be interesting to historians of art. Juan Montaño agreed to: hacer un retablo para la iglesia deste pueblo, el cual ha de ser de nueve tableros, diez con el que ha de estar detrás del sagrario, que ha de ser dorado lo que descubriere del sagrario, las columnas y frisas y bancos según y conforme está el retablo de la villa de Toluca, con columnas redondas y con sus guardapolvos dorados, y la talla estofada; en el tablero del lado de Evangelio la Anunciación de Nuestra Señora, al lado de la Epístola el Nacimiento de Nuestro Señor; en el segundo cuerpo, al lado del Evangelio San Lorenzo y San Esteban, en medio un San Francisco como está en el retablo de Toluca, en el lado de la Epístola Santa Catalina y Santa Clara; en el tercer cuerpo, en el lado del Evangelio la Resurrección como está en la villa de Toluca, en medio un San Miguel de figura redonda como está en el sagrario, en el lado de la Epístola la Ascensión de Nuestro Señor Jesucristo; y en el tablero más alto un Cristo crucificado con San Juan y María y la Magdalena, y por remate un Dios Padre de medio relieve, y dos Virtudes encima con sus insignias; a los lados deste tablero ultimo... From this point the document, which is in the legajo "Juan de Morales, ..., 1591-1599," is badly torn and deteriorated.

The 2,350 pesos were to be paid in three instalments: 350 pesos upon obtaining the viceroy's license; 250 pesos within 30 days after Christmas, 1594; 750 pesos at Christmas, 1595; 1,000 pesos when set up in Zinacantepec. Montaño was to have the retablo finished to the satisfaction of experts and delivered within a year and a half. There is no certain indication that the altarpiece was actually completed.

Parties to the agreement were a large number of "indios y principales," of whom only the town council members and the fiscal of the church were mentioned by name. Of these, four were able to sign: the alcaldes, Antón García and don Rafael Nicolás, and the fiscal, Martín Nicolás, the three of whom signed very well indeed, adding their positions to their names; and a Diego de (Dueñas?), who signed less well, but still not crudely.

The portal of the cloister of Zinacantepec was also a simplified imitation of the one in Toluca. See Salinas 1965, p. 48, n. 15.

[37]Mendieta, 4: 160-62.

[38]Letters written from Toluca in 1562 and 1565 are the usual guides for dating Mendieta's presence there; see Salinas 1965, p. 35. Mendieta's own writings show a close familiarity with Toluca at a later time, however. Also there is a hint, though not quite an unambiguous one, in his tale of a Pablo Hernández, Indian, who served him faithfully as fiscal of the Tolucan church. On Pablo's death Mendieta intended to set up a commemorative stone over his grave, but gave it up considering how many worthy people lay buried simply, including fray Andrés de Castro in that very church of Toluca. This should put the incident after 1577, but there remains the possibility that the mention of fray Andrés was a later reflection. Mendieta does not appear in the Tolucan record of the 1580's and 90's, but in view of their incompleteness and small informativeness on Franciscans, that is not a certain indicator. There are constant reminders of Mendieta in the form of Indians with his surname, including one literally called Gerónimo de Mendieta. Whatever Mendieta's activities in the Toluca area, he did not "found" the settlement of Calimaya, as some think (see Francisco Esteve Barba 1964, p. 173). Calimaya was not only a tribute-paying entity in the time of the Aztecs, but had been a Matlatzinca settlement before the Aztecs came (see Durbin 1972, pp. 19, 21).

[39]The passage in Ponce, p. 75, is as follows: "había a la sazón en aquel convento estudio de teología y muchos estudiantes; cuando no le hay moran en él de ordinario cuatro religiosos."

[40]Mendieta, 3: 124; 4: 160-62.

[41]In 1585 the latter brotherhood, whose majordomo was the humble Spanish pig raiser, Calisto de León, held a mortgage (censo) on a local house owned by another Spaniard of Toluca, at the rate of $24^1/_2$ pesos income a year.

[42]There is a hint that Mendieta may have brought some relatives with him. In Toluca in 1572 Pedro de Celada, merchant, born in the "merindades de Castilla la Vieja" in a place called Villarcayo (?), married Catalina de Benavides, legitimate daughter of Martín de Arratia, a Basque who was a local citizen, and Catalina de Soto. Two Franciscans, guardian fray Andrés de la Puebla and fray Miguel de Carvajal, were witnesses to Celada's recognition of the 1,000-peso dowry. Celada soon died, but not before the pair had a daughter, María de Celada. After marrying again, Catalina de Benavides died in 1582; she left to María de Celada 50 pesos, plus 75 pesos already left her by her aunt, *Gerónima de Mendieta*. Since María was of full Spanish descent on both sides, Gerónima must have been Spanish rather than one of the friar's Indian namesakes. The probability of a connection is increased by the fact that all these people were from the north of Spain, the region of Mendieta. The name Arratia, by the way, continued to be borne by prominent people of Toluca into the national period.

[43]Most of what is said in the chapter on blacks in Lockhart 1968 is applicable to the blacks and mulattoes of Toluca in the later sixteenth century.

[44]The standard desciption of what she wore when in the habit of a Spanish woman was: *fredellín de paño, sayas, jubón, cobija, ropa blanca.*

[45]She was recorded as a "mulata hija de india." This was the standard usage; the term "zambo" was not yet current (if it ever was), and many people then considered mulattoes were a mixture of African and Indian.

[46]One Indian butcher (*carnicero*) also figures in the Toluca records. Named Josefe Luis, he was a resident of Toluca proper, and died by 1592, leaving a widow, Magdalena Tlaco.

[47]This is not at all surprising in view of the history of the mines and the Indians' activities there. The 1580 description of Temascaltepec asserts that there were originally no Indians at all near the site, that the first of them were brought from elsewhere by the Spanish settlers, and that the Indians there at that time had come from many different parts of the country to work in the mines. Some of the Indians of Sultepec at the same time were said to have horses and use them to transport goods like the Spaniards; others were merchants dealing in both Indian and Spanish products. Paso y Troncoso 1906, pp. 13, 17.

[48]Despite the extreme frequency of this surname, one cannot help wondering if we do not see here the beginning of the de la Cruz dynasty of Tepemaxalco in the seventeenth and eighteenth centuries (see *The Nahuas*, Chapters 4 and 6).

[49]*Actas de cabildo de México*, 12: 9. The passage speaks once simply of "el tianguis," implying the dominance of the market in Toluca itself, then specifically mentions "los tianguis del dicho valle," conceding some importance to the smaller markets as well. The hoped-for sale price of maize in the capital was 12 reales per fanega, which may be compared to the 4 and 5 reales the Indians got from the corregidor in 1591. Gibson 1964, p. 453, mentions Mexico City prices of 10 reales in 1588, 11-12 in 1594, and 10 in 1597.

[50]Toluca auction proceedings of March 15, 1591, are headed by the words "en la plaza pública desta villa y tianguis general de hoy viernes. . ." Putting the market on Friday must have been an innovation of postconquest times, since the preconquest calendar did not have a seven-day week.

[51]Around 1591 a relative of the alcalde mayor of the mines of Zacualpan, off to the south, bought a quantity of maize in the valley of Toluca, estimated variously from 80 to 500 fanegas; a merchant of the mines came for it with his mule train. Retail maize prices at the mines were said to be running 17, 20, and even 24 reales the fanega. Archivo General de la Nación, México, Ramo Criminal, vol. 4, ff. 38, 42, 140. For more context see "The Magistrate of Zacualpan," Item 13 in this volume.

[52]"Tux" is the equivalent of Nahuatl *toch(tli)*, "rabbit," but I am not sure of the original of "Tebyatl." Perhaps *teoatl*, "large body of water"? "Taxcaltitlan" is Tlaxcaltitlan. "Hualacitl" just below is good Nahuatl, "one who arrives here (from elsewhere)," as is "Tlaco," "the one in the middle," among the most common names for a woman.

[53]For example, the distribution of a group of 23 nobles, council members, and other prominent Indians representing the Toluca community in 1584 was: saints' names, 12; other religious names (de la Cruz, etc.), 3; friar's name, 1; Spanish plebeian names, 4; first names as surnames, 1; Indian names, 2. The distribution of names among 35 Indians of the small settlement of Huitzitzila (?) was: Indian names, 21; Spanish plebeian names, 7; first names as surnames, 3; encomendero's name, 1; friar's name, 1; saint's name, 1; other religious name, 1. Nearly all the Indian surnames were identifiably Nahuatl, such as Huitzil, Chalchihuitl, Panmiquitl, Chicomecoa. One person had the word "mexicatl," Mexica, added after his name. I now realize that Toluca Indian naming practices were those of central Mexico generally. See *The Nahuas*, Chapter 4.

[54]The word "cacique" no longer appears in the Toluca records of 1580-1600. The only reference I saw was from 1570, when don Juan Vásquez de Sámano, then 56 years old, was "cacique y gobernador del pueblo de Zinacantepec."

[55]The greater retention of preconquest titles and offices at a lower level is a general phenomenon. See Gibson 1964 p. 182, and *The Nahuas*, Chapter 2. The Toluca representatives referred to in note 53 received the generic appellation of "tequitlatos," tribute collectors or ward heads.

[56]3: 158.

[57]Borah 1967, pp. 386-98.

[58]Alfredo Castillero (1967) notes the social stability of the western Panamanian region after the demise of the Veragua gold mines, compared to the quickly shifting families in Panama City.

[59]Colín 1955, pp. 45-46.

[60]Neither a corporate history of Indian communities, even as broadly conceived and on as grand a scale as Gibson's, nor social and cultural research on indigenous-language materials depicting the internal life of those communities, in the manner of myself and others more recently, can be accepted as the full history of the countryside. They are not even the full history of Indians, for the local Spanish presence was directly and indirectly one of the most important factors in the Indians' lives. Ultimately there is no alternative to an approach which studies all provincial phenomena, both people and structures, equally, without excluding any, accommodating all within a single framework of explanation and interpretation. I find myself in total agreement with the statement of Alfredo Castillero (1970, p. 66): "el estudio de la campiña...no debe ser...objeto de la etnohistoria, sino de la historia propiamente dicha."

13. Magistrate of Zacualpan

[1]The documentary basis for the present piece is to be found in Archivo General de la Nación, Ramo Criminal 4, ff. 21-399, being the investigation records alluded to above. Paso y Troncoso 1940, pp. 36, 40, identifies the encomienda of Ruy López de Salcedo; ibid., pp. 77-78, contains references to Licentiate Diego de Santa Cruz Orduña. See Dorantes de Carranza 1902,

passim, for a considerable amount of background on the Salcedo, Legazpi, Santa Cruz, and Orduña lineages. Gómez de Cervantes 1944, pp. 138-63, is a description of the silver mining industry written at just Santa Cruz's time and by a person with all the same general characteristics. Bakewell 1971, p. 241, gives the late sixteenth-century Zacatecas production figures and provides much other meaningful context. Note that the full value which Gómez de Cervantes (p. 148) specifies for a mark of refinery silver, 7 pesos and 2 reales, agrees entirely with calculations carried out on the Zacualpan records, but is much less than the 65 reales that Bakewell (p. 211) reports on the basis of Zacatecas data.

Glossary

Alcalde (Sp.)
A first-instance judge who is at the same time member of a municipal council (cabildo).

Alcalde mayor (Sp.)
Chief magistrate in a given area, appointed from outside; here, generally the chief Spanish judicial and administrative official in a jurisdiction embracing several altepetl; often used interchangeably with corregidor.

Altepetl (N.)
Any sovereign state; in central Mexican conditions, generally the local ethnic states the Spaniards were to call "pueblos." They became municipalities after the conquest and are occasionally called "towns" in this book.

Audiencia (Royal Audiencia) (Sp.)
High court, here the one residing in Mexico City and with jurisdiction for all New Spain.

Caballería (Sp.)
A land grant of moderate size intended for intensive agricultural use.

Cabecera (Sp.)
Term for what the Spaniards quite incorrectly perceived as a head town or ruling capital within the altepetl; opposite of sujeto.

Cacique (Sp. from Arawak)
Indian ruler, tlatoani; in late colonial Spanish, any prominent Indian.

Callalli (N.)
"House-land," a household's central agricultural plot, associated with its residence.

Calpolli (N.)
Constituent part, subdistrict of an altepetl. Generally seen written as "calpulli," following Spanish custom.

Chinampa (Sp. from N.)
Artificial raised plot for intensive agriculture built up in shallow water.

Coatequitl (N.)
Rotary draft labor for the altepetl.

Cofradía (Sp.)
Sodality, lay religious brotherhood.

Compadre (Sp.)
Ritual coparent; refers to the relationship between the true parent and the godparent.

Congregation; (Sp. congregación)
Resettlement (here of indigenous people) to achieve greater nucleation.

Corregidor (Sp.)
Often used as a synonym for alcalde mayor (q. v.), though at times indicating a higher rank.

Corregimiento (Sp.)
The jurisdiction or office of a corregidor.

Don (Sp.)	High title attached to the first name of a male, like "Sir" in English, masculine equivalent of "doña."
Doña (Sp.)	High title attached to the first name of a female, like "Lady" in English, feminine equivalent of "don."
Encomendero (Sp.)	Holder of an encomienda grant.
Encomienda (Sp.)	Grant (nearly always to a Spaniard) of the right to receive tribute and originally labor from the population of an altepetl through their existing mechanisms.
Estancia (Sp.)	A private landholding, usually consisting of one large grant, most often devoted to livestock.
Fiscal (Sp.)	In this context, church steward, the highest indigenous ecclesiastical official in a district.
Gobernador (Sp.)	Governor; in this context, an indigenous person filling the highest office of the altepetl, exercising many of the powers of the preconquest ruler (tlatoani).
Governor	Here, a gobernador.
Heredad (Sp.)	See *labor*.
Huehuetlalli (Sp.)	"Old land," patrimonial or inherited land.
Labor (Sp.)	An intensively cultivated smallish agricultural property.
Macehualli (N.) pl. macehualtin	Indigenous commoner.
Maguey (Sp. from Arawak)	Agave, source of the drink pulque and of fibers for various uses.
Merced (Sp.)	(Land) grant (the document or act of giving it).
Mesoamerica	Term used mainly among anthropologists for the area from central Mexico south to Guatemala containing "high" cultures with a great many common elements; used primarily with reference to the preconquest period.
Mestizo (Sp.)	Person of mixed Spanish and indigenous ancestry.
New Spain	The large jurisdiction centered on Mexico City and embracing much of present-day Mexico; also used more broadly for the whole general Mexican region.
Obraje (Sp.)	Any factory-like shop or works, here specifically an establishment for manufacturing textiles.
Obrajero (Sp.)	Owner or operator of an obraje.
Parcialidad (Sp.)	Spanish term for each of the larger subdivisions of a complex altepetl.

Peso (Sp.)	The primary unit in larger monetary transactions, consisting of eight reales or tomines.
Pilli (N.), pl. pipiltin	Noble.
Pochtecatl (N.), pl. pochteca	Professional indigenous merchant active in interregional trade.
Posesión (Sp.)	Proceedings giving someone formal possession of something, usually land.
Pueblo (Sp.)	Spanish term for an altepetl, but also applied to any identifiable indigenous settlement.
Real (Sp.)	A silver coin worth one eighth of a peso.
Regidor (Sp.)	Councilman, one of the members of a cabildo.
Repartimiento (Sp.)	System of temporary labor procurement whereby draft rotary labor from the altepetl was divided on a short-term basis among many Spaniards.
Sitio (Sp.)	"Site," the specific area granted as an estancia.
Stage 1	The time from 1519 to 1540-50 when Nahuatl did not yet borrow Spanish words other than names, and structures in general were little changed.
Stage 2	The time from 1540-50 to about 1640-50 when Nahuatl borrowed Spanish nouns and the indigenous corporation underwent large adjustments.
Stage 3	The time from about 1640-50 forward when Nahuatl began to borrow verbs and particles as well as nouns from Spanish and to be more deeply affected in idiom and grammar as bilingualism grew and the indigenous and Spanish populations were in greater daily contact.
Sujeto (Sp.)	Outlying subject hamlet; term used by Spaniards for constituent parts of the altepetl under the quite false impression that they were simply ruled by a cabecera.
Teniente (Sp.)	Deputy.
Teuctli (N.), pl. teteuctin	Lord, titled head of a lordly house (teccalli) with lands and followers.
"Titles"	Documents purporting to establish the right of an altepetl to its lands in Spanish times, usually done in Stage 3, containing in addition to accounts of a border survey various historical material, much of it legendary.
Tlatoani (N.), pl. tlatoque	Dynastic ruler of an altepetl.

Tlaxilacalli (N.)	A more common name for a "calpolli" or altepetl constituent, especially as a territorial unit.
Tlayacatl (N.)	In this context, a sub-altepetl with its own tlatoani inside a complex altepetl, which usually lacks a single dominant ruler.
Tomín (Sp.)	A coin or value worth one eighth of a peso; in Nahuatl became a term for coin, cash, or money generally.

Bibliographical Appendix:
A roster of the items in the present volume

1. "Postconquest Nahua Society and Culture..." A preliminary version was given as part of a lecture series on Mexican ethnohistory at Smith College in 1986, and the piece evolved further as my "standard talk." It was rewritten in Spanish in 1988 and is now forthcoming in *Estudios de Cultura Náhuatl*, no. 20, as "Los nahuas después de la conquista según las fuentes en náhuatl."

2. "Complex Municipalities..." Written in 1985 for the Conference of Mexican and North American Historians. Published in 1991 in *Ciudad y campo en la historia de México*, ed. by Ricardo Sánchez, Eric Van Young, and Gisela von Wobeser, 2 vols. (México: Instituto de Investigaciones Históricas, Universidad Nacional Autónoma de México).

3. "Views of Corporate Self and History..." Written in 1978 for a Stanford conference on the ethnohistory of Mesoamerica and the Andes. Published in 1982 in *The Inca and Aztec States*, ed. by George A. Collier et al. (New York: Academic Press).

4. "And Ana Wept." Written in 1978-79. Published in Spanish in 1980 in *Tlalocan*, 8.

5. "The Testimony of don Juan." Prepared for this volume in 1990 (the text having been transcribed earlier).

6. "The Tulancingo Perspective..." A skeletal version, without commentary to the individual documents, was assembled for an anthropological symposium in 1978. The final version was prepared in 1990 for this volume.

7. "A Language Transition..." Written in 1979. Published in 1988 in *Smoke and Mist: Mesoamerican Studies in Memory of Thelma D. Sullivan*, ed. by J. Kathryn Josserand and Karen Dakin, BAR International Series 402 (Oxford, B.A.R.). Unfortunately the piece as published was significantly mistitled, and a substantial portion of the body was omitted by simple error.

8. "Toward Assessing the Phoneticity of Older Nahuatl Texts..." Written in 1979-80. Published in 1981 in *Nahuatl Studies in Memory of Fernando Horcasitas*, ed. by Frances Karttunen, Texas Linguistic Forum 18 (Austin: Department of Linguistics, University of Texas at Austin).

9. "Care, Ingenuity, and Irresponsibility..." Written for *Reviews in Anthropology* in 1986, but since the piece grew far too long, its publication was greatly delayed. The present volume was already in production when it appeared (vol. 16 [1991], pp. 119-32).

10. "Charles Gibson and the Ethnohistory of Postconquest Central Mexico." First done for a memorial session honoring Gibson in 1986, then rewritten and extended in 1987. Published in 1988 as no. 9 of the Occasional Papers Series of the Latin American Institute of La Trobe University, Melbourne, Australia.

11. "A Vein of Ethnohistory . . ." Written in 1990 for this volume.

12. "Spaniards and Indians . . ." Written in 1970-71. Published in Spanish in 1975 in *Estudios sobre la ciudad iberoamericana*, ed. by Francisco de Solano (Madrid: Consejo Superior de Investigaciones Científicas, Instituto "Gonzalo Fernández de Oviedo") (a special number of *Revista de Indias*). Unfortunately the Spanish translation suffers from a great many deficiencies. The reader may wish to see in addition a later piece I wrote on Toluca (published in 1976 in *Provinces of Early Mexico*, ed. by Ida Altman and James Lockhart, Los Angeles: UCLA Latin American Center Publications); it abstracts a series of patterns about city-province relations and social evolution in general from the same data, but does not replace the more specific examples and processes illustrated in the piece included here.

13. "The Magistrate of Zacualpan." The archival research was done in 1969. The piece itself was then written in 1977-78 for an anthology for which it proved to be unsuited, so that it remained unpublished until now.

Bibliography

Actas de cabildo del ayuntamiento de México. México, 1889-1916.

Anderson, Arthur J. O., Frances Berdan, and James Lockhart.
1976 *Beyond the Codices.* Berkeley and Los Angeles: University of California Press.

Andrews, J. Richard.
1975 *Introduction to Classical Nahuatl.* Austin: University of Texas Press.

Bakewell, P. J.
1971 *Silver Mining and Society in Colonial Mexico: Zacatecas, 1546-1700.* Cambridge, Eng.: Cambridge University Press.

Bierhorst, John, transl. and compiler.
1985 *Cantares Mexicanos: Songs of the Aztecs.* Stanford, Calif.: Stanford University Press.

1985a *A Nahuatl-English Dictionary and Concordance to the Cantares Mexicanos: With an Analytical Transcription and Grammatical Notes.* Stanford, Calif.: Stanford University Press.

Borah, Woodrow.
1967 "The Portuguese of Tulancingo and the Special *Donativo* of 1642-1643." *Jahrbuch für Geschichte von Staat, Wirtschaft und Gesellschaft Lateinamerikas*, 4: 386-98.

1983 *Justice by Insurance: The General Indian Court of Colonial Mexico.* Berkeley and Los Angeles: University of California Press.

Boyd-Bowman, Peter.
1968 *Indice geobiográfico de 40 mil pobladores españoles de América en el siglo XVI.* Vol. 2. México: Editorial Jus.

Burkhart, Louise M.
1989 *The Slippery Earth: Nahua-Christian Moral Dialogue in Six-teenth-Century Mexico.* Tucson: University of Arizona Press.

Carochi, Horacio, SJ.
1983 *Arte de la lengua mexicana con la declaración de los adverbios della.* (Facsimile of 1645 edition, with introduction by Miguel León-Portilla.) México: Instituto de Investigaciones Filológi-cas, Instituto de Investigaciones Históricas, Universidad Nacio-nal Autónoma de México.

Carrasco, Pedro.
1963 "Los caciques chichimecas de Tulancingo." *Estudios de Cultura*

Náhuatl, 4.

Carrasco, Pedro, and Jesús Monjarás-Ruiz, eds.

1976-78   *Colección de documentos sobre Coyoacán.* 2 vols. México: Instituto Nacional de Antropología e Historia, Centro de Investigaciones Superiores.

Castillero Calvo, Alfredo.

1967   *Estructuras sociales y económicas de Veragua desde sus orígenes históricos, siglos XVI y XVII.* Panamá: Editora Panamá.

1970   *La sociedad panameña: historia de su formación e integración.* Panamá.

Celestino Solís, Eustaquio, Armando Valencia R., and Constantino Medina Lima, eds.

1985   *Actas de cabildo de Tlaxcala, 1547-1567.* México: Archivo General de la Nación.

Chimalpahin Quauhtlehuanitzin, don Domingo de San Antón Muñón.

1963-65   *Die Relationen Chimalpahin's.* Ed. by Günter Zimmermann. 2 vols. Hamburg: Cram, De Gruyter & Co.

Cline, S. L.

1986   *Colonial Culhuacan, 1580-1600.* Albuquerque: University of New Mexico Press.

Cline, S. L., and Miguel León-Portilla, eds.

1984   *The Testaments of Culhuacan.* UCLA Latin American Center Nahuatl Studies Series, 1. Los Angeles: UCLA Latin American Center Publications.

Colín, Mario, ed.

1955   *Toluca: Crónicas de una ciudad.* México: Secretaría del Trabajo.

Cook, Sherburne F., and Woodrow Borah.

1971-79   *Essays in Population History.* 3 vols. Berkeley and Los Angeles: University of California Press.

Dorantes de Carranza, Baltasar.

1902   *Sumaria relación de la Nueva España.* México: Imprenta del Museo Nacional.

Durbin, Thomas E.

1970   "Aztec Patterns of Conquest as Manifested in the Valley of Toluca." UCLA doctoral dissertation.

Esteve Barba, Francisco.

1964   *Historiografía indiana.* Madrid: Editorial Gredos.

Farriss, Nancy M.

1984   *Maya Society Under Colonial Rule.* Princeton: Princeton

University Press.

García Martínez, Bernardo.

1969   *El Marquesado del Valle.* México: El Colegio de México.

1987   *Los pueblos de la Sierra: El poder y el espacio entre los indios del norte de Puebla hasta 1700.* México: El Colegio de México.

Garibay K., Angel María.

1970   *Llave del náhuatl.* 3d ed. México: Porrúa.

Gibson, Charles.

1952   *Tlaxcala in the Sixteenth Century.* New Haven: Yale University Press.

1964   *The Aztecs Under Spanish Rule.* Stanford, Calif.: Stanford University Press.

1975   "Prose Sources in the Native Historical Tradition." In Robert Wauchope, gen. ed., *Handbook of Middle American Indians,* 15 (*Guide to Ethnohistorical Sources,* part 4, ed. Howard F. Cline et al.): 311-21.

Gillespie, Susan D.

1989   *The Aztec Kings: The Construction of Rulership in Mexica History.* Tucson: University of Arizona Press.

Gómez de Cervantes, Gonzalo.

1944   *La vida económica y social de la Nueva España al finalizar el siglo XVI.* México: Antigua Librería Robredo.

Gruzinski, Serge.

1989   *Man-Gods in the Mexican Highlands: Indian Power and Colonial Society, 1520-1800.* Stanford, Calif.: Stanford University Press.

Hanke, Lewis.

1949   *The Spanish Struggle for Justice in the Conquest of America.* Philadelphia: University of Pennsylvania Press.

Haskett, Robert S.

1985   "A Social History of Indian Town Government in the Colonial Cuernavaca Jurisdiction, Mexico." UCLA doctoral dissertation.

1987   "Indian Town Government in Colonial Cuernavaca." *Hispanic American Historical Review,* 67 (1987), 203-231.

Hinz, Eike, ed.

1987   *Discursos en Mexicano.* Acta Mesoamericana, 1. Berlin: Verlag Von Flemming.

Hinz, Eike, Claudine Hartau, and Marie-Luise Heimann-Koenen, eds.
1983   *Aztekischer Zensus. Zur indianischen Wirtschaft und Gesell-*
          schaft im Marquesado um 1540: Aus dem "Libro de Tributos"
          (Col. Ant. Ms. 551) im Archivo Histórico, México. 2 vols.
          Hannover: Verlag für Ethnologie.
Horn, Rebecca.
1989   "Postconquest Coyoacan: Aspects of Indigenous Sociopolitical
          and Economic Organization in Central Mexico, 1550-1650."
          UCLA doctoral dissertation.
1991   "The Sociopolitical Organization of the Colonial Jurisdiction of
          Coyoacan," In *Ciudad y campo en la historia de México*, ed. by
          Ricardo Sánchez, Eric Van Young, and Gisela von Wobeser. 2
          vols. México: Instituto de Investigaciones Históricas, Univer-
          sidad Nacional Autónoma de México.
ms.   "Indian Women in Mexican Parish Archives: Naming Patterns
          in Seventeenth-Century Coyoacan." Paper presented at the
          Pacific Coast Branch of the American Historical Association,
          Portland, Oregon, August 1989.
Hunt, Marta Espejo-Ponce.
1976   "The Processes of the Development of Yucatan, 1600-1700."
          In: Ida Altman and James Lockhart, eds., *Provinces of Early*
          Mexico. Los Angeles: UCLA Latin American Center Publi-
          cations.
Karttunen, Frances.
1982   "Nahuatl Literacy." In: George A. Collier et al., eds., *The Inca*
          and Aztec States. New York: Academic Press.
1985   *Nahuatl and Maya in Contact with Spanish.* Texas Linguistic
          Forum, 26. Austin: University of Texas Department of Lin-
          guistics.
Karttunen, Frances, and James Lockhart.
1976   *Nahuatl in the Middle Years: Language Contact Phenomena in*
          Texts of the Colonial Period. University of California
          Publications in Linguistics, 85. Berkeley and Los Angeles:
          University of California Press.
1977   "Characteristics of Nahuatl Resonants." In: *Proceedings of*
          the Southwest Areal Language and Linguistics Workshop V, ed.
          by Bates Hoffer and Betty Lou Dubois. Trinity University, San
          Antonio, Texas.
1978   "Textos en náhuatl del siglo XVIII: Un documento de Ame-
          cameca, 1746." *Estudios de Cultura Náhuatl*, 13: 153-75.

1980   "La estructura de la poesía náhuatl vista por sus variantes." *Estudios de Cultura Náhuatl*, 14: 15-65.

1987   Eds. *The Art of Nahuatl Speech: The Bancroft Dialogues.* UCLA Latin American Center Nahuatl Studies Series, 2. Los Angeles: UCLA Latin American Center Publications.

Kirchhoff, Paul, Lina Odena Güemes, and Luis Reyes García.

1976   *Historia tolteca-chichimeca.* México: Instituto Nacional de Antropología e Historia.

Kubler, George.

1948   *Mexican Architecture of the Sixteenth Century.* New Haven: Yale University Press.

Lastra de Suárez, Yolanda, and Fernando Horcasitas.

1978   "El náhuatl en el norte y occidente del Estado de México." *Anales de Antropología*, 15: 185-250.

León-Portilla, Miguel.

1983   "Cuicatl y tlahtolli: Las formas de expresión en náhuatl." *Estudios de Cultura Náhuatl*, 16: 13-108.

Lockhart, James.

1968   *Spanish Peru, 1532-1560.* Madison: University of Wisconsin Press.

1969   "Encomienda and Hacienda: The Evolution of the Great Estate in the Spanish Indies." *Hispanic American Historical Review*, 59: 411-29.

1972a   *The Men of Cajamarca: A Social and Biographical Study of the First Conquerors of Peru.* Austin: University of Texas Press.

1972b   "The Social History of Colonial Latin America: Evolution and Potential." *Latin American Research Review*, Spring 1972.

1980   "Y la Ana lloró." *Tlalocan*, 8: 21-34. (First printed version of Item 4.)

1981   "Toward Assessing the Phoneticity of Older Nahuatl Texts: Analysis of a Document from the Valley of Toluca, Eighteenth Century." In Frances Karttunen, ed., *Nahuatl Studies in Memory of Fernando Horcasitas.* Texas Linguistic Forum, 18. Department of Linguistics, University of Texas at Austin. (First printed version of Item 8.)

1982   "Views of Corporate Self and History in some Valley of Mexico Towns, Late Seventeenth and Eighteenth Centuries." In: George A. Collier et al., eds., *The Inca and Aztec States.* New York: Academic Press. (First printed version of Item 3.)

1985   "Some Nahua Concepts in Postconquest Guise." *History of*

European Ideas, 6: 465-82.

1991a   "Complex Municipalities: Tlaxcala and Tulancingo in the Sixteenth Century." In: *Ciudad y campo en la historia de México*,
ed. by Ricardo Sánchez, Eric Van Young, and Gisela von
Wobeser, 2 vols. México: Instituto de Investigaciones Históricas, Universidad Nacional Autónoma de México. (First
printed version of Item 2.)

1991b   "Care, Ingenuity, and Irresponsibility: The Bierhorst Edition of
the Cantares Mexicanos." *Reviews in Anthropology*, 16: 119-
32. (First printed version of Item 9.)

forthcoming 1: "Los nahuas después de la conquista según las fuentes en
náhuatl." *Estudios de Cultura Náhuatl*, 20. (Earlier version of
Item 1.)

forthcoming 2: *The Nahuas After the Conquest: A Social and Cultural
History of the Indians of Central Mexico, Sixteenth through
Eighteenth Centuries.* Stanford, Calif.: Stanford University
Press.

Lockhart, James, Frances Berdan, and Arthur J. O. Anderson.

1986   *The Tlaxcalan Actas: A Compendium of the Records of the
Cabildo of Tlaxcala (1545-1627).* Salt Lake City: University
of Utah Press.

McAndrew, John.

1964   *The Open-Air Churches of Sixteenth-Century Mexico.* Cambridge, Mass: Harvard University Press.

Martin, Cheryl E.

1985   *Rural Society in Colonial Morelos.* Albuquerque: University
of New Mexico Press.

Mendieta, fray Gerónimo de.

n.d.   *Historia eclesiástica indiana.* 5 vols. México: Editorial Chá-
vez Hayhoe.

Molina, fray Alonso de.

1970   *Vocabulario en lengua castellana y mexicana y mexicana y
castellana* (1571). México: Porrúa.

Parry, J. H.

1948   *The Audiencia of New Galicia in the Sixteenth Century.*
Cambridge: Cambridge University Press.

Paso y Troncoso, Francisco del, ed.

1939   *Epistolario de la Nueva España*, 6. México: Antigua Librería
Robredo.

1940   Ibid., 13.

1906   *Papeles de Nueva España: segunda serie, geografía y estadística,*
           7. Madrid: Sucs. de Rivadeneyra.
Pastor, Rodolfo.
1987.   *Campesinos y reformas: La mixteca, 1700-1856.* México: El
           Colegio de México.
Peterson, Jeanette Favrot.
1985   "The Garden Frescoes of Malinalco." UCLA doctoral disser-
           tation.
Ponce: see *Relación.*
Relación del viaje ... de fray Alonso Ponce ... Excerpt in Miguel Salinas,
           Datos para la historia de Toluca. México, 1965.
Ricard, Robert.
1933   *La "conquête spirituelle" du Mexique.* Paris.
Ruiz de Alarcón, Hernando.
1984   *Treatise on the Heathen Superstitions that today live among the
           Indians native to this New Spain, 1629.* J. Richard Andrews
           and Ross Hassig, trans. and eds. Norman: University of
           Oklahoma Press.
Sahagún, fray Bernardino de.
1950-82   *Florentine Codex: General History of the Things of New
           Spain.* Trans. by Arthur J. O. Anderson and Charles E. Dibble.
           Salt Lake City, Utah, and Santa Fe, New Mexico: University
           of Utah Press and School of American Research, Santa Fe.
Salinas, Miguel.
1965   *Datos para la historia de Toluca.* México: Jus.
Sánchez, Ricardo, Eric Van Young, and Gisela von Wobeser, eds.
1991   *Ciudad y campo en la historia de México.* 2 vols. México:
           Instituto de Investigaciones Históricas, Universidad Nacional
           Autónoma de México. (Contains several items of Nahuatl-
           based ethnohistory.)
Schroeder, Susan.
1984   "Chalco and Sociopolitical Concepts in Chimalpahin." UCLA
           doctoral dissertation.
1989   "Chimalpahin's View of Spanish Ecclesiastics in Colonial
           Mexico." In: *Indian-Religious Relations in Colonial Spanish
           America,* ed. by Susan E. Ramírez. Foreign and Comparative
           Studies / Latin American Series 9. Syracuse: Maxwell School
           of Citizenship and Public Affairs, Syracuse University.
1991   *Chimalpahin & the Kingdoms of Chalco.* Tucson: University
           of Arizona Press. (Revised and extended version of Schroeder

1984.)

Taylor, William B.

1972   *Landlord and Peasant in Colonial Oaxaca.* Stanford, Calif.: Stanford University Press.

1979   *Drinking, Homicide and Rebellion in Colonial Mexican Villages.* Stanford, Calif.: Stanford University Press.

Tezozomoc, don Hernando [Fernando] de Alvarado.

1949   *Crónica mexicayotl.* Trans. and ed. by Adrián León. Publicaciones del Instituto de Historia, ser. 1, no. 10. México: Imprenta Universitaria.

Tutino, John M.

1976   "Provincial Spaniards, Indian Towns, and Haciendas: Interrelated Agrarian Sectors in the Valleys of Mexico and Toluca, 1750-1810." In Ida Altman and James Lockhart, eds., *Provinces of Early Mexico.* Los Angeles: UCLA Latin American Center Publications.

Vetancurt, fray Agustín de.

1697   *Chronica de la provincia del Santo Evangelio de Mexico, quarta parte del Teatro mexicano.* México.

Wood, Stephanie G.

1984   "Corporate Adjustments in Colonial Mexican Indian Towns: Toluca Region." UCLA doctoral dissertation.

1989   "Don Diego García de Mendoza Moctezuma: A Techialoyan Mastermind?" *Estudios de Cultura Náhuatl,* 19: 245-68.

forthcoming 1: "Comparing Notes: Techialoyan Texts and Other Colonial Nahuatl Writings." To appear in a volume of papers edited by Monica Barnes from the Latin American Indian Literatures Association meeting at Cornell University, 1987.

forthcoming 2: "Accepting the Sword and Cross? Views of Spanish Conquest in Indian *Títulos* of Colonial Mexico." *Ethnohistory.*

forthcoming 3: "The False Techialoyan Resurrected." *Tlalocan.*

forthcoming 4: "Adopted Saints: Christian Images in Nahua Testaments of Late Colonial Toluca." *The Americas.*

Library of Congress Cataloging-in-Publication Data

Lockhart, James.
    Nahuas and Spaniards : postconquest central Mexican history and
philology / James Lockhart.
        p. cm. -- (Nahuatl studies series ; no. 3)
    Includes bibliographical references (p.   ).
    ISBN 0-8047-1953-5 (alk. paper) : ISBN 0-8047-1954-3
(pbk . : alk. paper) :
    1. Nahuas--Historiography. 2. Nahuas--Government relations.
3. Mexico--History--Spanish colony, 1540-1810. 4. Tlaxcala (Mexico
: State)--Historiography. 5. Tulancingo (Mexico) --Historiography.
6. Aztec language--Historiography. 7. Aztec language--Grammar,
Comparative. 8. Aztec language --Texts. I. Title. II. Series:
Nahuatl series ; no. 3.
F1219. 76. H57L63 1991
972' . 02--dc20

91-9895
CIP